Maps and Mirrors

Series Editor

Hugh Silverman

PHILOSOPHY, LITERATURE, AND CULTURE

Maps and Mirrors
Topologies of Art and Politics

Edited by
Steve Martinot

NORTHWESTERN
UNIVERSITY PRESS
EVANSTON
ILLINOIS

Northwestern University Press
Evanston, Illinois 60208-4210

Printed in the United States of America

10 9 8 7 6 5 4 3 2 1
ISBN 0-8101-1672-3 (cloth)
ISBN 0-8101-1673-1 (paper)

Library of Congress Cataloging-in-Publication Data

Maps and mirrors : topologies of art and politics / edited by Steve
Martinot.
    p. cm. — (Philosophy, literature, and culture)
    Includes bibliographical references.
    ISBN 0-8101-1672-3 (alk. paper) — ISBN 0-8101-1673-1 (pbk. : alk.
paper)
    1. Aesthetics—Political aspects—Congresses. I. Martinot, Steve. II.
Series.

BH301.P64 M37 2000
111'.85—dc21

00-010455

Contents

Acknowledgments

The papers in this volume were chosen from those presented at the Thirteenth Annual Conference of the International Association for Philosophy and Literature (IAPL), held in April 1988 at Notre Dame University. For having providing a welcoming and conducive atmosphere, many thanks are due to that university. The general theme of the conference was art and politics; its title was "Hermeneutics/Aesthetics/Politics." Although the essays in this volume were taken from that conference, this volume has been organized around certain philosophical considerations of the editor's choosing, which go beyond the thematics of that conference. These essays appear as autonomous works and at the same time as thinking that lends itself to the specific considerations of this volume. For the most part, final revisions on these essays were done in 1988, although some were revised at a later date. Some have been incorporated into other work by their authors.

During the last two decades, the IAPL has provided an important forum for critical investigations that have taken contemporary continental philosophy as their starting point. For this work, thanks are due to the many people who have helped make the association an ongoing endeavor, in particular to Hugh Silverman as executive director of the IAPL. But special thanks are also due to Hugh Silverman for his encouragement, support, and assistance in conceiving and realizing the present project. Finally, I would like to thank Stefan Mattesich and Jane Tomlinson for their invaluable ideational and technical assistance and inspiration.

Introduction

Historicity and Ideologization

Steve Martinot

There is a sense of confluence between art and politics that has often troubled philosophy, and to which philosophy has at times responded, from Plato's Republic to the present, by constraining, co-opting, or marginalizing art in the implicit name of the political. This confluence has found a more felicitous reception, however, in contemporary continental philosophy and the post-structuralist critique of language, for which aesthetics itself has become a mode of critique. Without centering the art activity as such, aesthetic critique reaches out to the means whereby meaning is made, beyond what is being said, through an attention to form (whether textual, discursive, or structural). When it addresses the political as an issue, it seeks to disclose the structures of presupposition, ideology, and reification that at once seem to empower and beset political thinking. Far from an aestheticization of the political in Benjamin's sense,[1] this approach opens political space beyond ideology and beyond the bunkers and barricades that constitute its alleged solidity.

The confluence of art and politics constitutes the overarching domain of the essays in this volume. Written in the mid-1980s, they project the buoyancy and momentum of the aesthetic critique, with a certain innocence toward its possibilities that reflects a time when many things were being rethought. A sense of innocence, if it needs explication, is not simply what is superseded by experience; for writing (which is admittedly never quite innocent), it is not an anticipation that the transformations one makes will be transparent but rather that what one does will be intelligible in a transformative manner.

But what complicates this innocence toward discourse is history. Where at first the post-structuralist critique made the political an issue, post-structuralism itself has now become an issue. Thus, it has been remapped on the historical terrain and given a certain historicity at the hands of real political processes that now configure it differently. In the process, these essays find themselves and their meanings recontextualized; confronting that history, they are made to bear issues that come from beyond them. Not only is their intelligibility transformed, but their manner of being transformative is as well. How they may have changed in meaning and perspective when reflected back through that history does not "re-author" them (though the thinking of their authors may indeed have changed), but they accrue an intangible dramatic energy that then wears the mask of history itself. We cannot now evade this history; its issues, which have been significant both politically and philosophically, have become part of the lens through which we now read.

Though this may be a fate foreseen for all textuality as such, it takes on a special character when it concerns a movement that has itself been made a political issue—and in that manner been given the aura of a historical actor. Not only do these essays become mirrors through which we may look back on what has transpired; they also provide a prior vantage point from which we may look forward at the intervening historical period that will have changed them and given them a historicity. Thus, in these essays, the motifs of art and politics, and the politics of aesthetic critique, engage the issue of the historicity of discourse itself. Grasping this issue in its specificity will mean apprehending not only the encroaching of history but its unfolding, which has evinced a certain turbulence.

These, then, are the issues that serve to organize this volume. How the dynamic of aesthetic critique, the dimensions of discursive historicity, and the contextualizing particularity of this history interrelate will be the subject of this introduction.

THE AESTHETIC DIMENSION

David Carroll argues that post-structuralism is not theoretical in itself but works critically at the limits of theory to give theory "a different form and critical function."[2] Part of that function entails "teasing out" (as Barthes would say) the activity of formal elements at the center of the textual endeavor. Though aesthetics as a discipline "implies the establishment of a theory of art and literature" (*P,* xiii), aesthetic critique concerns instead the "problems the aesthetic raises for theory." For the work of Derrida, Foucault, or Lyotard, in particular, Carroll claims, "there [is] no way to separate the questions of art and literature from the most important philosophical, historical, and political issues." The question is "not . . . what they say about art and literature, but rather . . . what they do with art and literature and what they make art and literature do for them" (*P,* 187). In the way that a parable mysteriously touches the core of a social sensibility, the post-structuralist critique is theoretical in being about theory.

There is a reason Carroll goes back and reviews the grounds of aesthetic critique. Writing in 1987, he says it is "extremely important at the present juncture, when the theoretical advances of the last two decades are more and more often distorted, blindly attacked, or simply dismissed, that such *work* be better understood." In part, he goes on to say, this dismissal involves the claim that certain "theoretical questions [are] illegitimate in themselves" (*P,* xi). Though his immediate project is to contest this claim, he is raising a more general problem. The very question of the admissibility or inadmissibility of certain modes of critique brings to the fore the source or framework from which the possible judgment of "illegitimacy" can be levied, let alone given importance. And the question of interpretive framework in general is the question of ideology.

To theorize ideology, it is not sufficient to be descriptive or interpretive; such approaches themselves rely upon the ideological as their source of perspective and coding. One must also look at the structure of ideological interpretation and the form it takes as that kind of interpretation. As a category, ideology appears primarily descriptive. But it reveals itself to be both insular and self-referential. Any description of the world is interpretive to the extent that it provides structured and coherent meaning in its description (whether political, religious, mythic, or even poetic). That is, as an interpretation, it already valorizes the description.

What characterizes ideology is the naturalization of its valorization by attributing "objective" referentiality to its interpretation. Each ideological structure describes the world, interprets it referentially, and valorizes that interpretation and its particular conceptual coherence as "objective." Contemporary philosophers from Heidegger to Foucault have pointed out, however, that coherence is already a filter through which one is led to notice what is to be described.[3] Interpreting "the facts" means to have already interpretively determined what constitutes a "fact." In effect, the interpretation itself becomes the ground for the descriptive. Descriptive coherence valorizes referentiality, and interpretive reference valorizes description. In effect, if ideology constitutes a lens through which the world is perceived, the referential relation thus established must be seen as self-formulating, through a prior and constitutive self-referentiality.[4] The central "fact" of ideology is not its definitude or descriptiveness but the structural operation through which its referential definitude about "things" produces itself. This should not be construed as rejecting definitude; it only argues for the importance of understanding where definitude comes from and to what it applies.

But if the definitude of interpretation is in part self-referential, as an unavoidable aspect of its discursive operation, then an insularity is given to ideological structures which necessitates that they derive their meaning from the differential space between them. While the content of different ideological structures may establish their existence, it is their confrontation and the form of interstice or interaction between them that provides their meaning—that is, the meaning of their existence in the way they give each other meaning. The interstices between different constructions of the world lie at the core of their reference to it. This holds for all politics. Insofar as politics addresses the world as what is to be changed or policed or toward which policy must be made, it necessarily renders itself ideological through a chosen mode of referentiality to that world. The ability to discern the form of such referentiality in the differences between ideological positions, on which the content of ideology and ideological confrontation depends, is at the heart of the aesthetic critique. As a number of essays in this collection will point out (see, in particular, Makkreel, Shepherdson, and Steele), this is part of the philosophical attraction for post-structuralism of Kant's *Critique of Judgment* (his analytic of interpretive judgment without prior principles or concepts).

To see how this reflects itself in the realm of philosophy, let us look at the question of "philosophical rigor."[5] The concept of logic and philosophical rigor is insisted upon by most Western philosophy. It traditionally refers to a tidy structure of reasoning, to logical procedures heedful that the truth values commanded, deployed, and produced remain within the bounds of logical validity. One follows logic as it leads through channels of truth, obeys its determination of what content or substance is permissible, and accepts its judgment on the permissibility of conclusions. But there are certain essential requirements for this procedure to work. The most important is that one's terms, propositions, and concepts must be as precise and well defined as possible; they must embody a univocality to which truth value can be attached. Logical rigor requires coherence, linearity, and definitude in its language. Under such conditions, formal logic presents itself as unconditional. But it also assumes that, at their foundations, philosophical questions are unequivocal and that equivocalities can be broken down to unequivocal cases and treated rigorously.

A different notion of rigor is suggested in Derrida's critique of language. For Derrida, a rigorous approach to a text means carrying the text's own inner logic—the implications of its different problematics of meaning, context, and language—to its own logical conclusions, undetoured and undeterred by the prior (exterior) requirements for coherence or logical unequivocality.[6] For instance, in discussing Saussure, Derrida points out that Saussure's account of language implies a logic of difference rather than a logic of positive entities. Saussure recognizes that a structure of signs produces meaning as a system of differences. But rather than pursue the logic of this insight, he remains committed to grounding his discussion of signs in their materiality.[7] In the logic of difference, however, that materiality and the very discernment of things (or signs) is produced through their relations to what differs from them. That is, the positivity of things, and the meaning and definitude that can be ascribed to them (and upon which traditional logic relies), are grounded and depend upon that other logic.

What is fundamental within a logic of difference is that what differs does not have to be there in order to function as difference; its absence and its elsewhereness to that from which it differs are always a necessary possibility. Two things follow from this in terms of language. Each signifier, in order to be a sign and as the condition for its signification, always has present to it the trace of other absent signifiers. It cannot be a sign all by itself. But if signification depends on what is not there, then meaning is deferred through the trace of what is not there to other differing signs, in an endless chain or structure. Meaning thus does not come from reference to the world but is generated by the structure of language itself.

Reference itself becomes an operation added to the generation of meaning, as itself an additional meaning. That is, reference is by nature a proto-ideological process. And second, the deferral of meaning to other differing signs implies that each sign already lends itself to a multiplicity of significations through its polyvalent relations in the overall structure of signs. Thus, in following the logic of Saussure's text, Derrida arrives at an understanding of language that makes highly problematic the very basic operations of logic itself, operations to which Saussure had returned in pursuing a metaphysics of the sign.

By following the logic of difference in Saussure's text, against Saussure's own faithfulness to the formal logic of metaphysical thinking, Derrida in effect remains faithful to Saussure's fundamental conception. If Derrida's critique disrupts Saussure's subsequent argument, it is because the two logics are incommensurable. In general, pursuit of a text's inherent logic tends to undo or unravel what argumentatively relies upon "exterior" formal logic. Conversely, attention only to the formal argument will leave the text's inherent logic unaddressed and lurking. To read the textual logic rigorously against (or in the face of) the formal logic of its conceptual discussion or analysis will not only reveal traditional logic to have been imposed, but produces a polyvocality for the text from within itself. The linearity of analytic or ideological reasoning remains readable, but it is no longer unconditional. And when confronted with this polyvocality, formal logic tends to find itself at sea.

The ramifications of this sense of double reading are enormous, not only for the philosophical but for the scientific, the political, the legal, and so on. In each domain, the language of specific discourses, upon which the domain's logic relies, escapes the confines or limits of decidability, truth value, reference, and so on, required by that logic. At best, it can only pretend to obey those limits by ignoring the import of its own textuality and discursivity. But that pretense to obedience to a formal (given) logic only reveals its logic to be "hegemonic" rather than "natural." A sense of what this control entails is given in William McBride's essay on Auerbach in this volume. McBride argues that Auerbach neglects part of the Augustinian text in order to find in that text the historicity that Auerbach desires.

By extension, for social or ideological structures that pretend to universal validity, the counterposition of an alternative reasoning from within them erodes and relativizes that universality as well as what depends on it. Such an operation may not produce a "politics" as such, but it changes and historicizes what it regards—and changes the way the political and the historical are understood or legitimized at the same time. This is, in part, what Marx accomplished with respect to the self-legitimized universality of the idea of capitalist property, upon which basis capitalism claimed its profit structure to be ahistorical; it was what he was not able to do with his own historical analytic or the configurations of social transformation that he projected as a politics as such.[8]

Ultimately, to pose an alternative to universality means to produce a language that renarrativizes it, steps beyond it, and renders it conditional. In this volume, Timothy Gould discusses the way in which feminist discourse poses an alternative to the traditional reading of philosophy. By critiquing the use of gender in late-eighteenth-century aesthetics, Gould discloses that alternative arguments reside in alternative genderings, suggesting there is a political project implicit in philosophy having chosen one of them. Similarly, Drucilla Cornell addresses a variety of alternative foundations for legal philosophy and argues that only through a language of alterity and dialogue will the totalitarian effects of relying on any one of them be avoided.

In the sense that the essays in this volume imply a change of language in the realms they address, they look forward to the history that we will shortly look back upon. In a profoundly political sense, our historical situation has already taken them (and the entire philosophical confluence and movement from which they emerged) into account, in opposition. For this reason, before situating the relation of aesthetic critique and politics within that history, let us look more directly at the inner dynamics of aesthetic critique. Four aspects of will be reviewed, each thematically relevant to one of the subsections into which this volume is divided.

THE AESTHETIC CRITIQUE

These essays belong to an epoch that was still flush with a certain joy and wonder at the possibilities wrought by the critique of language, of discursive structures and forms. One not only interpreted meaning but sought its dynamic and genesis, its contours and ecologies, within its textual landscape. Language was apprehended like the curved mirrors in an amusement park. One sees one's reflection distorted, appearing fat, thin, undulatory, or upside down in different mirrors. One transcends the sense of unfamiliarity by making a gesture and seeing it recognizably reflected. Though distortion be the content of the reflection, it is the curvature of the mirror itself that one's interaction with the reflection reveals. As such, the distortion doesn't exist in the mirror, nor does it exist in oneself. And similarly, what fascinates about language is the notion that meanings in their polyvocity do not exist in it but in its interactions with discursive surfaces. The four aspects of aesthetic critique to be reviewed here will, one hopes, show where some of that fascination and sense of wonder came from.

The first aspect, already touched on, is the recognition that language is polyvalent, that it resists being confined to the univocal, the monochromatic, the given. Part 1 of this volume ("Maps") presents a number of approaches to that polyvalence, each concerning a different discursive sign. There are two structural sources from which semiotic polyvocity arises. The internal source, described above, is inherent in the logic of difference; the second, external, source results from a necessary noninherence of context. Different readings of a text are possible because its language can be contextualized in different ways: that is, a necessary condition for its variable ideological or referential coherence is that an interpretive framework or context be overlaid upon it.[9] Though an ideational framework may be suggested by discursive content, that itself is already "a reading." One can read through a focus on certain connotations or tropes, or through the desire to see the text as primarily political, artistic, psychoanalytic, mythic, and so on. But, in general, the fact that we *can* overlay different interpretive frameworks implies that doing so is a necessity, as well as the impossibility that any one contextualization will establish an interpretive monopoly.

A further implication, however, is that there exists an uncontextualized state for the text, a state of pure textuality, of self-contextualization. Each sign that participates in constituting the text as a whole is in turn conditioned in its participation as a constituent sign by the whole. This is familiar as the hermeneutic circle: the parts constitute the whole as a whole, which then constitutes the parts as its parts. However a text may be coded, it interiorly recodes itself through self-contextualization at the level of formal configurations. Each component sign doubles itself as lexically given and structurally constituted. Ultimately, coded or ideological readings are possible only because of this doubling of the sign. The space between the lexical and the self-contextual instills a contingency that gives "different" interpretive structures a foothold in the text and allows each to claim a certain partial naturalness as a reading.

The second aspect extends the sign's unavoidable polyvalence to the interpretive operation itself. The structure of self-contextualization, as the mutual conditioning of a text and its constituent signs, produces a contour, a form (or shape) for the text's acts of meaning, for its reasoning and mode of argument. And this surface or contour underlying the text's statement constitutes the place where an inner textual logic can be discerned as a discursive form. Just as a person discerns the contour of a mirroring surface by generating an active reflection in it, so discursive form is discerned only interpretively, in a metatext. The elements of textual form—including the play of signs, circularities of meaning, and the geometrics of argumentation, style, and composition—present themselves as metatextual content. That is, they are discernible and articulable only as a critical operation.

Part 2 of this volume ("Mirrors") presents several ways in which this contour can be read from within the space between the text and its textuality. On this surface, one can follow (rigorously) the text's own inner logic. But that "inner logic" is itself not fixed in definitude; it depends on the perspective that one takes on those contours. As a case in point, two of the essays in part 2 address the form of Kant's third *Critique,* but from different points of view. They evaluate its philosophical project differently through different reflections on its contours.

Thus far, the issues have been that textual form conditions a polyvalence and opens the text to a multiplicity of interpretive operations (making possible different ideologized readings). In general, one could say that the great variety of critical interpretations to which literary or philosophical work lends itself is a reflection of the richness of textual form and its modes of resituating lexical significations. It is within this richness that a text evinces a sense of relation, a subtle but unavoidable reference to its own textuality, a mode of interior, self-generated metatext—which constitutes a third aspect of its inner dynamic. Like "self-awareness," both textual form and self-contextualization participate in opening a space within a text, an interstice between the laminations of its several constitutive languages. It is a space between what a text says and what it does in order to say it—between its meaning and its structure of meaning, between content and form, between statement and enactment. In part 3 of this volume ("Morphologies"), a number of political texts are addressed with respect to this space between content and form.

Beyond content or statement, this space is necessarily inarticulable, except through the form of its enactment. But also, beyond the formal concreteness of style, reasoning, genre, or voice (that is, as the vehicles upon which description and argument ride),[10] it is a space that opens on the existence of discursive forms that beget alternate significations. As reflections of the text in its own discursivity, these significations enhance, alter, or countermand the text's own discursive content. What enables form and its alternate significations to be discerned within a space of inarticulability is the construction of homological mappings of its repetitions. These mappings do not preexist the text; they are interpretive operations that constitute formal relations within it. Such homological relations are central to John O'Neill's description of the Montaignean exemplum, to Charles Shepherdson's bridge across the abyss between pure and practical reason in Kant, and to Don Bialostosky's explication of the different forms that the "sign of rhetoric" takes in the texts of Paul de Man. The essays in part 3 utilize variations of homological relation to reveal the alternate political implications of discursive form within the political texts they address.

For those who consider textual form to be only a vehicle for "authorial meaning," the notion of aesthetic, polyvocal interpretation of textual possibility is untenable. Many interpret it as a rejection of meaning, even a nihilism toward the ethos of concrete meaning. However, they rarely characterize their own denial of discursive multiplicity, or of the overflow of meaning beyond itself, in similar terms. In that denial, the wonder of textual heterogeneity, the beauty of the incommensurable, the shock of nonrecognition—all those common occurrences that keep making the universe bigger—are lost. The recuperation of these greater spaces, and their expansion of meaning beyond the merely literal, is the fourth aspect of this volume. Each essay in part 4 ("Movements") addresses the interplay of a text's reasoning with what emerges beyond it to deconstruct the continual recrudescence of constraint and definitude. R. Radhakrishnan, for instance, finds that a hegemonic linearity reconstitutes itself in Heidegger's discussion of art, even at the point where Heidegger himself critiques linear (metaphysical) approaches to art. Though each essay in part 4 preserves the plane of linearity or rationality that it discovers, it embeds it in a space of new possibility. And where the essays in part 3 by and large addressed political texts, in part 4 it is the critique instead that seeks to reveal an articulation of the political in its own critical activity.

What weaves the issues of this volume together is a set of images or motifs that thread their way through it. For instance, there is recurrent attention to a sense of the abyssal, of a hiatus in textuality, in response to which a leap across is often invoked. Seeking to traverse the space between ontology and historicity, art and history, exposition and narrative, the essays also invoke the notion of a bridge whose function is the transcendence of the inarticulable, of incommensurability, of the question of the abyss itself. In the spaces and heterogeneities of discourse reviewed here, the languages of philosophical discourse and aesthetic critique stand counterposed to each other. Donald Marshall, for instance, sets them in dialogue with each other, realizing in that interaction a terrain of the politics of art on which the political can discover itself as art. This double relation provides an opening to a political realm, beyond prior systems of judgment or metaphysical definitions, where social relations can be rearticulated.

Ultimately, the problem and promise of such a dialogue is its abandonment of the definitive in favor of a process (dialogue itself) that always faces the possibility of putting an end to itself through new definitiveness. In this light, Bernard Picard expands a Gramscian account of the predictive into a discourse of that subjectivity which will have already stepped into a space beyond the given, within the operation of the programmatic. But in that space "politics" as such must remain undefined, even as programmatic, in recognition of the need to examine the function of definition itself and its necessary linearity. Indeed, a glance at the etymological family of the political—which involves policy, police, polis, and the ways people and groups, whether politely or otherwise, make policy for themselves—discloses how unwise defining the political would be. What, then, is one to say, and how is one to construct a sense of historical being in the present, if the above cognate (and cognitive) list only problematizes its manifestations? Between the closed textuality of definitude with its history and the open textuality of dialogue in its historicity, there is a space in which a "politics" must endlessly occur. Conversely, consideration of the political heterogeneity of a space of dialogue reveals that definition serves to end a discussion rather than lay the basis for it. Definitude and the programmatic, against the ongoing sense of polis and policy, mark the end of the political, not the beginning.

THE HISTORICITY OF AESTHETIC CRITIQUE

We confront two dissimilar temporalities: the first is the historicity of a philosophical enterprise; the second is a history in real time. To approach the first is to approach, at the same time, its political dimension, which will always be recognizable, however nonprogrammatic or undefined it may appear, in the political attention it incurs in real time. It is through the debates and polemics that have engaged the post-structuralist critique, and indeed transformed it (into an issue), that a certain political weight must be granted it.

Barbara Johnson, in *A World of Difference.* published in 1987, put her finger on a central "issue" in this process:

> As soon as any radically innovative thought becomes an *ism,* its specific groundbreaking force diminishes, its historical notoriety increases, and its disciples tend to become more simplistic, more dogmatic, and ultimately more conservative, at which time its power becomes institutional rather than analytical. The fact that what is loosely called deconstructionism is now being widely institutionalized in the United States seems to me both intriguing and paradoxical.[11]

It is paradoxical for Johnson because the doctrinal formularity involved in "becom[ing] an *ism*" has been attached to thought that had called the formulaic as such into question. The interpretive choice to attach (or attribute) systematic content to an attitude of critique, to bestow definitude and method on what subverts the definite and the methodological, exemplifies a process that could be called "ideologization." It not only imposes an ideological structure or character upon what presents itself as nonideological in order to "discover" definitude and method, even in its absence, but in the process it suppresses the idea that the nonideological is possible — the nonideological being the recognition that definitude is never wholly coherent and interpretive conceptuality never adequate to the coherence it seeks. It transforms what questions into what answers, what opens into what defines, through another act of definition. In other words, ideologization is a resistance against the resurgence of form. But the difference between the nonideological and the ideological is not simply a difference between a decoding of the world and its interpretive recoding (all ideological structures do both). Rather, ideologization closes the space between text and metatext, between discourse and metadiscourse, by which a text enriches itself, in order to absorb that richness into prior meaning.

If, as Johnson notes, ideologization is a strange and unnatural fate to have befallen deconstruction, there is nevertheless a "foregone" or natural dimension to it. This "foregone" aspect, so easily reified, ironically emerges from the plane of dialogue that naturally ensues from critical activity, particularly with respect to political texts. The question arises, in the wake of a deconstructive critique: what are the possibilities of response? How is a dialogue to proceed? The deconstructive critique focuses on the language of a text; it addresses how that language necessarily fails to limit itself to what it states as its meaning (the possessive pronoun carrying full metaphysical weight here), while simultaneously failing to come up to that meaning adequately. In doing so, the critique does not refute the argument or "correct" its referentiality; it changes the language of the text by including the logic of its own textuality.[12] It reveals that the language of the text is not the language that the text conceptually claims for itself.

To respond to the deconstructive critique, one would have to resurrect the text's language, wrest it from recontextualization, and restore its unconditioned referentiality as the necessary medium and condition for a response. The alternative would be to accede to the critique, in which case there would be no need to respond. But to resurrect the text's language would be to reaffirm its claims for itself as appropriate, to repress the effects of its own textual form—in short, to ignore or simply erase the critique in order to engage in dialogue with it. In other words, the response must either do violence to the critique or put an end to itself.

The deconstructive discourse faces the same problem. In responding to a response, it must either return to and repeat its original critique (which had been disregarded), thereby ignoring or erasing the other's response (in the other's reappropriated language), or give up its critique of that language and thus have nothing to say—again, in order to engage in dialogue. In effect, dialogue becomes difficult or impossible in any direct way; the two languages appear homogeneous but are actually incommensurable. Though a common language may be possible in principle (indeed, the richness of incommensurability also creates new realms of possibility), it is achievable only by surpassing the inherent violence that attempts at direct dialogue engender, while depending on dialogue to surpass that violence. In this collection, Drucilla Cornell addresses a related problem in the realm of law through an appeal to the philosophy of Levinas.

For politically involved people, who often impatiently demand clear (linear) discussion of issues, these incommensurabilities can be annoying and frustrating, appearing as detours or changes of subject. Many would choose to dispense with the critique, or dominate it through the referential authority of their political positions. The effect of the latter is to impose a referentiality on the metadiscourse and, by thus reducing it to that literality and definitude, to ideologize it. Rather than refute the critique, this amounts to a silencing procedure, a mode of suppression. In the process, regardless of the collegiality of the original critique, certain hostilities are often kindled.

In sum, if post-structuralism has been ideologized as doctrinal or institutional, it has not just been the result of pernicious influences but a profound effect of the critical operation itself as well. Dialogue would seem to close the space between text and metatext because the incommensurability of that space would seem to close dialogue. Many of the essays here reveal this process in inverse; a suppressed heterogeneity is disclosed and recuperated by dislodging an overlaid ideologization, whose imposed coherence and definitude had served to suppress that heterogeneity (see McBride's critical discussion of Auerbach and Picard's appreciation of Adorno).

If incommensurability "plays" between the heterogenous richness of textuality and the ideologizing process (not of reading but of giving the text "a" reading), it bestows a temporality, constituting a possible foundation for a new form of dialogue, a non-narrative historicity, on the critical operation. This is what concerns Johnson when she asks, "[H]ow can the deconstructive impulse retain its *critical* energy in the face of its own *success* [having been turned into an *ism*]?" (*WD*, 11).

It is ironically against that historicity that established political positions (of the right and the left) have arrayed themselves. Reacting to deconstruction as too radical, the conservative tendency is to assume the position of "men [*sic*] of letters who attempt to defend their belief in the basic communicability of meanings and values against what is said to be the deconstructionists' relativism, nihilism, or self-indulgent love of meaninglessness" (*WD*, 11). The left ironically "mirrors" this by seeing post-structuralism as conservative and as "not living up to its own claims of radicality" (*WD*, 14).

Johnson addresses "the relation between deconstruction and the type of logic on which these opponents' accusations . . . are based" by examining particular charges they both make. One example she uses is the now famous enthymeme invented to describe the deconstructive approach, which reads: "If all readings are misreadings [as post-structuralism has been understood as saying], then all readings are equally valid" (*WD*, 12). This nugget of sagacity has all but become part of the folklore of the post-structuralist critique. The term "misreading" here makes reference to a metaphor the post-structuralist critique uses to signify the unavoidability of multiple meanings and of the coexistence of various coherent readings or codings of a text. Though any reading finds its foundation in the text, each reading will construct its coherence in different terms because a text is polysemic. On the authority of the validity of that coherence, it will view other readings as off the mark, less than valid—in a word, as misreadings. One would have to decline to grant any one reading a monopoly of validity insofar as it grounds itself upon its own coding of the text in the same way other readings do. In effect, all readings are on a par, each with its own validity. In the name of validity, each reading will be branded a misreading by another, in a mutuality of imputation which can be metaphorized as misreading in general. But, strictly speaking, one cannot say that all readings are misreadings (except metaphorically) because it is not clear what would constitute a "misreading" as such. In effect, the metaphor of "misreading" parodies the language of validity; it ironizes the very possibility of validity. To take this parody out of context and give it syllogistic form literalizes the metaphor. What gets concealed by the form of the enthymeme is this literal misreading of "misreading."

The assumption at the center of the "conservative" point of view is that a single valid interpretative reading is not only possible but discoverable, communicable, and of value in its "objectivity," over the opposition of other "subjective" stances (*WD*, 12). For the conservative point of view, the enthymeme's conclusion marks both a return to the language of validity, which is of central importance, and an absurdity—meaning it is to be read polemically. If the enthymeme's premise is made to state that non-misreadings are impossible, the literalization it accomplishes for the metaphor of "misreading" finds itself validated by the language of validity at work in the conclusion. In the language of validity, if misreadings are by definition invalid, then the absurdity of the conclusion suggests that non-misreadings are indeed possible. The premise is simultaneously given a doctrinal character (attributed to post-structuralism) and rendered meaningless. In one fell swoop, the language of validity has been resurrected, the metaphor literalized, and the critique of how validity constitutes itself in a reading ignored. Ultimately, by restoring (reassuming) a universal significance for the term "validity," the enthymeme (as a reading of post-structuralism) in content reduces post-structuralism to the level of doctrine (through its premise) and in form implies that a non-misreading exists.

There is, however, a hidden "irony" if we follow the discursive logic of the enthymeme to *its* conclusion. The concluding clause now has two meanings: the first is as an operator that reasserts the language of validity (or univocity); the second is as a trope that ironizes the metaphor of misreading in order to avoid (and silence) the critique it represents. Thus, a third meaning emerges in the concluding clause, namely, that, as irony, it does not follow logically from the first clause. In the service of univocal meaning, it equivocates; in the service of syllogistic logic, the proposition ceases to be syllogistic. But if the syllogistic connection is thereby broken, then the first clause escapes back to its original metaphoricity, free from the language of validity of the conclusion, and the idea that "all readings are equally valid" is left standing alone as the real premise the ideology of validity invented for the enthymeme. This, then, confirms the critique of ideology—that is, that the validity of a reading remains an operation brought to a reading from elsewhere. Ultimately, to question "validity" does not drive validity out of existence, but it calls into question the rigor (and "validity") of those modes of thought that depend upon it.

On the other hand, for left-wing critics, according to Johnson, deconstruction works "with too limited a notion of textuality, . . . applying its critical energy only within an institutional structure [of Western philosophical/academic discourse] that it does not question and therefore confirms" (*WD*, 14). Johnson agrees that a critique that questions boundaries must continually question its own to avoid institutionalizing itself; she adds that if the critique restricted itself to the literary text (as some critics tend to do), then it would indeed have been institutionalized and "conservative." What a deconstructive reading of a text (or of the "social text") should question "with rigor" is precisely the reading that that text assumes for itself, the logic and coherence that it advances for itself, as if in advance of itself (*WD*, 15).

What is at stake for the left-wing deployment of the enthymeme is not an assumption of meaning but a stance. The radical perspective is a desire to go actively beyond the text to the world, not merely to make "objective" reference to it. It seeks a reading (of text or world) that will at least point to or facilitate the contestation of institutional power or hierarchical domination—a contestation implicit in its charge against deconstruction.[13] Instead of universal validity, it seeks tactical strength from discourse, something to grasp and wield. The idea that all readings are misreadings obviates that possibility, and the idea that all readings are equally valid effectively erases access to the social hierarchies that structure oppression and domination. It lets those who dominate or oppress in real social relations off the hook. Where the conservative wants one reading to be objectively valid, the radical wants certain "readings" to be invalid (that is, without avoiding their existence or hegemony in the world, to foreclose their being "true" as such).

Hence, what concerns critics of the left is not the language of validity in the enthymeme's conclusion but its political implications with respect to hegemony. Validity isn't a language for radicals, but a program. In attacking the post-structuralist critique for interfering with program formation, they are reading the enthymeme as itself programmatic. They are thus also literalizing the metaphor of "misreading." As a result, the premise becomes oppositional (in programmatic language), an a priori statement on the (im)possibility of reading the "social text" or of "their" reading. They do not literalize the metaphor in the service of syllogistic logic but rather bestow upon that literality an ideological (programmatic) charge. Where the conservatives arrive at a meaningless ideologization of post-structuralism through a literalized logical formula, the left arrives at a meaningless formula through ideologizing a metaphor. Ironically, if the left ideologizes the post-structuralist critique as preserving hegemony, it does so by itself preserving a discourse of hegemony in the very logic of its programmatics.[14]

Drucilla Cornell, in her essay in part 4, offers a somewhat more historicized reading of these charges against deconstruction. In her discussion of different factions of the Critical Legal Studies movement, she points out that conservatives charge deconstruction with opening a meaningless future, while radicals accuse it of returning to a premodern past. In contradistinction, R. Radhakrishnan offers an insight into the power of the deconstructive critique to reveal the political, the social text within a text, where a programmatics or a syllogistic logic would remain at sea.

Ultimately, if left-wing critics were correct, the post-structuralist critique should have endeared itself to the right wing. But it hasn't because, rather than mask hegemony, it recognizes that hegemony is itself a discursive construct, an invention of hierarchy with no non-self-referential justification or authority beyond that. Indeed, the left and the right are able to talk to each other because both construct a logic of hegemonics (of programmatics and validity respectively) that sets both in opposition to discourses critical of hegemonic structure itself. The post-structuralist critique renders the self-proclaimed legitimacy of power invalid precisely by arguing that no reading or interpretation of a social situation has an inherent priority over another. The legitimacy of any institutional power rests upon an arbitrary and self-referential assumption internal to its own seizure of the situation, which it then claims legitimizes it.[15] To unveil that self-referentiality, to denaturalize (deuniversalize) power's claim to inherency, is already to pose an alternative to it. The effect is to renarrativize power, to pose its own contingency against it. Neither the power nor the hegemony to which one is subjected need be lived any longer as a destiny. An example is Marx's renarrativization of capitalism as historical rather than natural or universal, thereby providing the historical ground for an alternative working-class historical consciousness.

THE HISTORY OF A HISTORICITY

More is at stake in these textual dynamics, however, than mere ideological incommensurability or the difficulties of dialogue. In the historical unfolding of ideologization, a point is eventually reached beyond which discourse becomes empty; this is often the fate of a poem at the hands of a conceptualizing paraphrase. If that emptiness translates to an unintelligibility, it can nevertheless take on an iconicity that allows its continued use, sometimes even as a weapon. A case in point is the shadowy term "postmodern," which surfaces irregularly in these essays. It is a term that has been ideologized in contemporary discourse through an iconization of an unintelligibility.

Postmodernism is an older notion than post-structuralism, having been coined in various contexts by a spectrum of thinkers from Arnold Toynbee and Charles Olson to Ihab Hassan and William Spanos.[16] The term flaunts its inherent irony, that of a present subsequent to the contemporary, and it laughs at those who would, by literalizing it, bemoan, celebrate, or contest rendering the modern passé. It does not invoke a temporal subsequence, an "after" of modernism, but rather a response, an impatience, even a contestation of a modernity that can only succeed itself. Thus, it marks a resistance from within, an acceleration of the metabolism, so to speak, of a historical era. Does it therefore refer? To what? And can we answer that question without ideologizing it and ourselves in reflection?

Hassan understands the postmodern as a new style, a "paracritical" change in the characteristics of modernism. It is not simply that the subject or the world evinces a different texture; rather, referentiality itself becomes a felt break in connection. For instance, in Don DeLillo's novel *White Noise,* disaster, death, and history occur without anyone having real involvement with others. For Hassan, the social constructedness of ideation, agency, and subjectivity all point back to an attendant meaninglessness in a totally commodified socioeconomic domain—that is, commodification itself becomes the destructuring of social and cultural meaning.[17]

For Fredric Jameson as well, the postmodern marks the emergence of a social interpretation from within the consumerist economy. In a market that presents goods in massive arrays that glut meaning, the presentation of those arrays (of soup cans, aspirin bottles, suburban houses, or mutual-fund listings), of that glut itself, becomes the meaning of the market as such. Human life loses touch with its projects because it can articulate itself only in terms of a language of commodities whose meanings have been emptied and whose uses have been superseded by the market's monopolization of meaning, its own use of the glut. Commodification becomes the source of identity rather than its erasure.[18] What fascinates is the realization that this socioeconomic multilayering of the contingent, the unreal, and the meaningless has always been there since the dawn of commodification, though only emerging now through a self-deconstruction of social meanings. It is noninvolvement that materializes itself in the array, which ideologizes it in turn, and deploys the glut as its icon. In iconizing the meaningless, the array is both an interpretive schema and an iconoclastic opportunity. It performs a semiotic operation on modernism without giving it historicity. Agnes Heller describes Lukács's attempt to deal with just such a problem in his early (and abandoned) aesthetics.

Modernism, to which postmodernism reacts, can be understood in contrast to a still earlier -*ism:* realism. Realism assumed the possibility of referentiality (that is, a world of real events and objects that could be veridically represented), while modernism grasped the role that self-referentiality plays in representation. The act of representing took account of the fact of representation as an "aegis," a moment of "awareness," a point of view on the realm of "experience."[19] Modernist fiction, philosophy, art, and so on "understands" itself as reflecting and reflected in the very endeavor to be art, or philosophy, or fiction. Sartre, for instance (in *Being and Nothingness*), continually narrativizes his discourse in the first person as both a reasoning and an involvement; by employing narrative to preserve the radical singularity of subjectivity, of consciousness itself, the "I" of his "examples" becomes the self-referentiality of his ontological argument. In modernist fiction, the world in which the character acts is in some sense brought into existence for the character by that character's activity.

Postmodernism drops the pretense of a given reality (a given way by which existence represents itself), however interrelational it may be. If it understands the world as a language — and one's sense of the world as generated by that language — then meaning acquires a certain contingency, and language becomes what the world in turn refers to and represents.[20] It supplements the social establishment of the discursive with the discursive establishment of the social. Its turn to language is a return to the primordium by which there was a world in the first place. This is comparable to Heidegger's return to Being through his "de(con)struction" of metaphysical ontology, passing to the source of beings in Being at the limit of the metaphysics of entities. If Being must remain inarticulable in order to avoid falling into entityhood itself, that very inarticulability becomes its sign, an absence "coiled in the heart of" language (pace Sartre). Meili Steele asks: how does an ontological difference manifest itself through language in the light of its reversed referentiality? And what politics is created or opened by the process of decentering the cognitive in language? He returns to Lyotard for a means to articulate the transgression of the hegemonic represented by the inarticulable and the silenced.

Ultimately, one could contrast "postmodernism" with "post-structuralism" in the following manner. Post-structuralism is a critique of language and discourse, deploying approaches appropriated from phenomenology and structuralism, upon which a philosophical movement has constituted itself.[21] The postmodern, on the other hand, presents itself as marking a change of sensibility, a transformation of referentiality, subjectivity, textual coherence, and intuition, for which the questions asked by post-structuralism are exemplary. The meaning of "post" is different for post-structuralism and postmodernism. If post-structuralism temporally supersedes and carries structuralism along with it as a limit, postmodernism contests modernism in the space of the present and renders it archaic.

Between the social establishment of the discursive and the discursive establishment of the social, there is an aporia, beyond which two stances are possible. One can reject the reversal in the aporia as a nihilism, a pernicious emptying of given social values, or one can embrace the aporia itself as a new social logic that critiques the textuality of social endeavor and sets its meanings in motion at the same time.[22] The two stances are incommensurable. Where the first denies the critique from which the aporia springs, rendering the emptiness it perceives iconic, the second arrives at social values that in turn empty those values upon which the denial in the first case is made. What would get articulated between the two, in the name of communication, is incommensurability itself. But if incommensurability is already the site of a political battle of values, as Lyotard has pointed out[23]—a battle between history and historicity—then it already provides the site of transition toward a new language. It is appropriate that Nietzsche should enter this discussion here, through Stephen Barker's essay. If Nietzsche rejected the iconicity that philosophy itself foisted on the notion of truth, he counterposes a complex metaphorics that again sets the meanings of truth in motion.

Ultimately, the question "What is postmodernism?" not only invokes the feeling that a moment of transition has passed and that a cultural dethroning has already occurred, but it reenthrones a nostalgia in its stead. It is a political question because it begs for ideological reassurance, and at the same time it projects an ideologization as a mode of perception itself. It is also a desperate question. Already historicized and ironically historicizing, it is the final hope (in the face of postmodernism's inherent irony) that there is an "it," an object with properties to which one can refer. Yet this hopeful desire—whether one articulates postmodernism as a critique of values, a nihilist language of market glut, or an abyss—defers the very possibility of such an "it," making its question all the more desperate, unintelligible. For precisely these reasons, it opens itself not to the answer but to an artistic response. In its vast multiplicity of articulations of what cannot be thought in predefined language, art is the only possibility for transcending the desperation. It is for this reason that aesthetic critique has felt at home with postmodernism, while other critics and thinkers have only felt the angst of exile.

HISTORY IN REAL TIME

With this complex structure of political and historical moments in mind, let us turn to recent history itself. Real time has transpired since these essays were written; they have been given a historicity by worldly events (as is all writing) that was not written into them, but which must produce a difference of meaning and a concretization that is both theirs and imposed on them from elsewhere (this does not happen to all writing or to dialogue that historicizes itself, but it does happen to writing whose critique becomes an "issue"). Three seminal events have transpired in the political arena: (1) the Soviet Union has come apart, ending the balance of power and producing a certain political vacuum in which many historical signposts become unfamiliar; (2) the administration of the United States has changed in style and global outlook, producing a period of struggle for hegemony in which new policies attempt to unseat old entrenched structures, resulting in a certain ideological stalemate (the emptiness of that stalemate was reflected in the "bipartisanship" of Clinton's second campaign and second election); and (3) the social and cultural infrastructure of Iraq was technologically decimated (accompanied by unimaginable social misery) through the most intense bombing campaign in history (the equivalent of seven Hiroshima-size bombs were dropped in six weeks). As a result, our thinking in the United States about world politics, political administration, and the administration of war has been interrupted and transformed.

Each "event" was a disruption, a hiatus rather than an innovation. The demise of the Soviet Union deprived the United States of its Other, disrupting its identity as a pole in a polarized world and transforming it into an abstract global power. Questions of international administration (NAFTA, GATT, the Pacific Rim, etc.), which are not national issues, are presented as though they were, effacing the difference and creating abstract debate and concern (empty congressional rhetoric, ratification, etc.). In turning to war-making, the United Nations has similarly disrupted its identity as a peacekeeping body, rendering political spaces abstract in the process. Here discourse is supplanted by ideological rote: the war in Bosnia, as a spatialization of pure conflict (called "ethnic" by default and irresolvable as such), is an example. The gridlock in the Clinton administration's first Congress was an amplified jockeying for position, which the 1994 election of an ideologically oriented Republican Congress during the term of a Democratic executive only raises to a structural level, representing a power glut, an inflation of the currency of power, abstracted from political responsibility. Finally, the bombing of Iraq, though called a military action by default, was never a war; in its one-sidedness, it disrupted the concept of war by rendering raw social destructiveness an abstract act, devoid of national conflict or political program—a destructiveness whose "politics" remain unspoken even in 2000 as an embargo continues after almost a decade what the bombing began.

These events are relevant to this volume not because special explanatory powers or political insights are to be found in them. Rather, these "concrete" abstractions become the context in which we encounter discourse whose mode of operation is, inversely, to address form in order to return to the particular. In that sense, these essays become mirrors in which the self-referentiality of abstraction, as a cancellation of political meaning (at the levels of power, governance, or war), is discernible in reflection. That is, they become a terrain on which to invent a language that counteracts a real political cancellation of meaning (and our own obsolescence as people at its hands).

But there is a further relevance. This history has mapped itself onto the plane of the "political correctness" (PC) issue, which took post-structuralist thinking (and continental philosophy) as one of its targets.[24] The PC issue broke upon academia as a campaign to realign the universities politically. In one dimension, it produced a nondebate (a kind of discursive power vacuum) by dissolving one side of the debate through ideologization. In a second dimension, it produced a kind of gridlock of meaning through an abstraction of issues (by which "political correctness" was itself transformed into an issue). Though the issue pretended to be a debate and a critique of critique, it deployed a "technology" of derogation (for which "PC" itself became a derogatory term) as a mode of attack for its own sake. In the process, certain social critiques at issue (to which the word "correctness" ostensibly referred) were repressed, ignored, or divested of coherence; it became a one-sided war of secondary sources in which the primary sources (targets) too often simply remained unread.[25] One could say that the PC movement was as confusing and as productive of intellectual uncertainty as the demise of the Soviet Union has been for global politics. The attempt to roll back the post-structuralist critique has been as turbulent as the ideological deadlock that tied up political administration in the United States. And it has been as destructive of intellectual debate as a war that was not a war because only one side did any shooting.

An extended narrative on the PC debate would be out of place here.[26] But it was already on the horizon in 1987 when David Carroll wrote, "[A] battle is now raging on many fronts to impose or reimpose forms of previously challenged orthodoxies in order to cut short debate and experimentation and reestablish what is sometimes claimed to be more solid foundations for humanistic inquiry: namely, history, the real, man, subjectivity, etc." (*P*, xi). The term "orthodoxies" also refers to political structures such as racism, patriarchy, and heterosexism, which had come under attack by many social movements, often deploying post-structuralist modes of critique for political analysis. In particular, these chauvinisms, as "orthodoxies," were recognized as modes of dominating others in the name of concepts that had no social or biological reality; that is, they were contingent and gratuitous, without a non-self-referential basis. What remained unnarrativized in the PC issue was that the violence and injustice wrought in the name of those chauvinisms were infuriating—and not only to those subjected to them. Many people just "didn't want to hear it anymore." In the name of that anger and rejection, the critiques that decentered, deuniversalized, and disempowered those chauvinist discourses became a matter of serious attention, to be argued seriously, taken seriously, and projected toward serious alternatives.

The accompanying exasperation took the form of many demands: for awareness, sensitivity, inclusion, solidarity, an end to all derogatory language, and an opening of the canon to other literatures to end the exclusiveness of the hegemon, of white, male, Eurocentric thought. It is out of respect for the seriousness of these issues that they are included in the arguments of many of the essays here. However, opposition to the ongoing demands to take these issues seriously, whether in academic discussion, student activism, or day-to-day life, eventually labeled those demands "political correctness." Though referring to an insistence, this opposition read the demand as reverse domination (over the traditional), and in thereby charging it with reverse discrimination (that is, with a hegemony it never attained), it performed an act of abstraction that reduced the issue to one of free speech. In content the charge referred to a complex multiplicity of social contestations, while in form it invented a derogatory term to dispense with them.

In this context, the debate on the canon between traditionalism and its critics elucidates one of the subtexts of this volume: the necessity and possibility of thinking on two levels (text and metatext) at once. In that debate, the traditionalists contended that the canon's critics were attempting to impose a new standard; they insisted that the canon simply reflected a culture but was not actively involved in generating it or maintaining its dominion. The canon's critics held, in opposition, that the canon was politically involved in the cultural chauvinisms and exclusions on which the social movements focused. This skewing of the argument rendered the issue irresolvable. When the traditionalists claimed the canon was not politically involved in order to resist changing it, they reduced the political issues to the canon; when the critics demanded that the canon be changed, they thereby changed the canon into a political issue.

In addition, each side split into two camps. If the canon did not generate but only reflected a cultural matrix, as the traditionalists claimed, then their resistance to change amounted to an exclusion of difference, a rejection of diversity, and thus a chauvinism. As a result, some of the traditionalists opposed resistance to change because they opposed injustice. On the other hand, if the canon did essentially function to regenerate, and not merely to reflect, the white Western cultural hegemony and structure, then the critics' insistence on changing the canon would amount to an absorption of cultural difference into that tradition and, ultimately, a reduction of diversity. The result was that some of the canon's critics opposed changing it in order to avoid that absorption. In effect, each side split in a way that emptied the issue. If the traditionalists saw the canon as not politically involved in the cultural matrix, then why make an issue of it? And if the critics saw it as involved, then changing the canon would not change that involvement as a force for stasis, the co-optation of their own rebellion against chauvinism, whose dynamic they sought to preserve. Ultimately, however, on the abstract plane of free speech, traditionalism humiliated itself by relying on the power of tradition for its defense, which included a slight tinge of repression (as the canon's critics had charged). That is, the traditionalists (conservatives) enacted in form what they opposed in content.

If the deconstructive ironies woven through this affair appear irrepressible, this should not detract from its seriousness, as represented in the petulant words of John Silber, president of Boston University, to the trustees of that institution on April 15, 1993, and later reported in the *Boston Globe.*

> This University has remained unapologetically dedicated to the search for truth and highly resistant to political correctness and to ideological fads. . . . We have resisted relativism as an official intellectual dogma, believing that there is such a thing as truth, and if you can't achieve it, at least you can approach it. We have resisted the fad toward critical legal studies. In the English Department and the departments of literature, we have not allowed the structuralists or the deconstructionists to take over. We have refused to take on dance therapy because we don't understand the theory of it. In the Philosophy Department we have resisted the Frankfurt School of Critical Theory.
>
> Across the board we have refused to accept hiring quotas, either of females or of minorities, believing that we should recruit faculty on the basis of talent and accomplishment rather than any other consideration. We have resisted the official dogmas of radical feminism. We have done the same thing with regard to gay and lesbian liberation and animal liberation. . . . We have resisted the fad of Afro-centrism. We have not fallen into the clutches of the multiculturists. We recognize that Western culture, so-called, is in fact a universal culture.[27]

The animus (bordering on paranoia) of this statement should be obvious (its implicit location of feminism and Afrocentrism as opposed to accomplishment rather than *as* accomplishment, for instance). But also one notices immediately that if Western culture calls itself a "culture" and not something more general like "human nature," then it already suggests it is not universal in its own self-conceptualization. The question we confront, and Silber elides, is: who authorizes Western culture to speak for other cultures and claim universality beyond that self-conception? If this authority is self-arrogated, it both reflects and generates an impingement upon other cultures. The history of this domination is erased in Silber's refusal of affirmative action (so-called quotas), as if prior denigration of talent or accomplishment by chauvinist exclusion did not exist. Yet these factors (historicities, self-arrogations, etc.), which Silber includes by implication, are at the same time excluded in the name of a "search for truth." In thus authorizing his exclusions, Silber proclaims a truth to be already known, although the search for this truth has not yet culminated. In effect, no search for truth is going on that might question the parameters of that authority.

Allan Bloom suggests, in *The Closing of the American Mind*, that it is the post-structuralist critique of tradition and historicity that restricts and constrains thinking.[28] But in Silber's programmatic, thinking is already closed down. Silber later added, in a letter to the Faculty Council, that "Boston University has resisted the imposition of doctrines that would curtail intellectual and academic freedom,"[29] a statement that should have been the prelude to his own retirement for having imposed the doctrine of such resistance. But universal truth remains blind to its imposition of itself. The humanist simply wants to say that we are all just human, the same, and can get along as such. And one might remind the humanist that structures of inequality and domination construct differences within that sameness, which disrupt it. This is one of Cornell's central points in discussing the ideas of Levinas, as it is Radhakrishnan's in his deconstruction of Heidegger. Ultimately, just as the dominant and the dominated do not acquiesce in the same ways, so their respective rebellions are likewise different. Indeed, while individuality and social standing can be taken for granted by one side, they become the product of continual rebellion for the other.

What is at stake here is not a confrontation with the PC debate. To see it as such would only valorize the referentiality invented for it as an issue. But the deployment of the very notion of "PC" as a derogatory term (derogatory terms, by nature, invent their referent through generalization and thus have no other referent) effectively symbolizes the reduction of thinking represented by ideologization. And the ability to see past the brute existence of derogatory terms to their discursive form, to understand them as assault rather than discourse, would itself be an icon for the short-circuiting of critical thinking entailed in all ideologizing.

Against the Sturm und Drang of these political realities—and the shrillness of someone like Silber—the quietness and understated sharpness of these essays stand in contrast. It is a quietness that can do more than two things at once. Thus, it offers itself as an alternative to imposed literality, where the literal is often used as a disguise for repression or security. Though none of these essays raises the political issues of the PC debate, which had not yet erupted at the time they were written, those issues constitute a lens through which to look back upon this earlier élan. Because these essays reflect what post-structuralism attempts to do, they reflect what the PC "debate" attempted to do to it. And we may take that reflection as an accrued meaning that these essays could not have had at the time they were written.

In pursuit of that reflection, the first part of this volume will return to some fundamental semiotic notions through various investigations of the textual sign (as sign and as art analogue), mapping part of the theoretical terrain from which other aspects of the post-structuralist critique have emerged. The second part will then present some examples of what it is possible to understand in a text through the semiotics of the textual sign, and ways in which the text mirrors itself in form. It is at this level that the critique of textual form becomes interesting for analyzing political texts and their forms. In the third part, there are a number of investigations of political texts, focusing on the morphologies of interaction between ideologization and deideologization. And the fourth part will elucidate various political dimensions already contained in the textual movements evoked in the preceding parts.

Notes

1.   Walter Benjamin, "Art in the Age of Mechanical Reproduction," in *Illuminations,* trans. Harry Zohn (New York: Schocken, 1969), 217–51. The "aestheticization of politics" signifies, for Benjamin, the provision by political power of means of expression for subjugated people that gives them a sense of participation while leaving them powerless. For him, it was one of the characteristics of fascism.

2.   David Carroll, *Paraesthetics* (New York: Methuen, 1987), xi; hereafter abbreviated *P* and cited parenthetically in the text.

3.   Heidegger describes the problematics of and outlines his approach to this question in *Being and Time,* trans. John Macquarrie and Edward Rob-

inson (New York: Harper and Row, 1962); see in particular §§ 7, 9–11. It is precisely the structure of this problematic that Michel Foucault addresses through what he calls an archeology; see *The Archeology of Knowledge,* trans. A. M. Sheridan Smith (New York: Pantheon, 1972).

4.   This notion of ideology is consistent with the Marxist sense of the term "false consciousness," that is, a preconception overlaid upon the world and then referentially understood as reference. It would also include the non-Marxist notion of Marxism as ideology as well as the post-Marxist critique of ideology. In Marxism, the class analysis of capitalist exploitation constitutes a prior conceptuality whose referentiality becomes its claim to scientificity. For Louis Althusser, ideology is an imaginary relation to one's real relation to the world. His rendition first broaches the self-referential foundation for ideological referentiality, but still in terms of the attendant possibility of grasping that "real relation" in its "own" terms. See Althusser, "Ideology and Ideological State Apparatuses," in *Lenin and Philosophy and Other Essays,* trans. Ben Brewster (New York: Monthly Review Press, 1971), 121–73.

5.   This issue is also historically relevant to this volume. Robert Scholes delivered a paper at the IAPL conference from which these essays were drawn on precisely this issue. It later found its way into the pages of his book *Protocols of Reading* (New Haven, Conn.: Yale University Press, 1989). Other philosophers have taken issue with Derrida on this question. See Richard Rorty, "Is Derrida a Transcendental Philosopher?" *Yale Journal of Criticism* 2, no. 2 (1989): 207–17. Rorty divides philosophers into those who make sense within traditional frameworks and those who are creative and therefore don't; Derrida is in the latter category. Claude Evans, in *Strategies of Deconstruction* (Minneapolis: University of Minnesota Press, 1991), provides a more extensive argument on the issue of rigor and philosophical logic. While the issue is too far-reaching for these few pages, I am nevertheless picking up a piece of the argument here.

6.   See, for instance, Jacques Derrida, *Positions,* trans. Alan Bass (Chicago: University of Chicago Press, 1981), 6.

7.   Jacques Derrida, *Of Grammatology,* trans. Gayatri Chakravorty Spivak (Baltimore: Johns Hopkins University Press, 1976); see part 1, chapter 2.

8.   There is, Gayatri Spivak has argued, an ethnocentrism in Marx's historiography, in his insistence that non-European cultures or regions (for instance, India) traverse the same stages of development toward the same mode of liberation as Europe, as a kind of historical teleology. Gayatri Spivak, *The Post-Colonial Critic* (New York: Routledge, 1990), chapter 8.

9.   See Jacques Derrida, *Limited Inc,* ed. Gerald Graff (Evanston, Ill.: Northwestern University Press, 1988).

10.   Northrop Frye, for instance, looks at a number of vehicles for mythic meaning, such as imagery, dramatic type, and discursive genre, in *The*

Anatomy of Criticism (Princeton, N.J.: Princeton University Press, 1957). Fredric Jameson, in his discussion of Sartre, analyzes grammatical form and the way Sartre plays with it as the mode by which to articulate the inarticulable of the prereflective cogito: *Sartre: Origin of a Style* (New Haven, Conn.: Yale University Press, 1961).

11.   Barbara Johnson, *A World of Difference* (Baltimore: Johns Hopkins University Press, 1987), 11; hereafter abbreviated *WD* and cited parenthetically in the text.

12.   Derrida's *Of Grammatology* is, of course, the primary demonstration of this approach to textuality, under the rubric of a semiotic theorization of writing. See also Jacques Derrida and Christie MacDonald, "Choreographies," *Diacritics* 12 (1982): 66–76.

13.   bell hooks, in *Yearning* (Boston: South End Press, 1990), attempts to stand on both sides of this hiatus, representing the black activist and (black) cultural critique of the postmodern, while raising again some important questions for activism from the postmodernist perspective. See especially chapter 3, "Postmodern Blackness."

14.   One encounters this irony in the various simultaneous ideological calls to class unity made by different parties or radical groups. Each one gives the social text a different reading from a different strategic or theoretical perspective. And because each call for unity, as a "coherent reading" of the world, becomes the source of a programmatics, it "programmatically" separates itself from other such readings and calls. Each call to unity thus participates in producing disunity. What remains foreign to ideology is a vision of multiple positionalities that mutually contextualize (deinstitutionalize) each other and thus change each other's meanings.

15.   See, for instance, Derrida's deconstruction of the United States Constitution in "Declarations of Independence," *New Political Science* 15 (Summer 1986): 7–15.

16.   Michael Köhler, "Ein begriffsgeschlichter Uberblick," *Amerikastudien* 22 (1977): 8–18; translated into English as "'Postmodernism': A Survey of its History and Meaning" by Thomas Austenfeld, University of Virginia (1986).

17.   Ihab Hassan, *The Postmodern Turn: Essays in Postmodern Theory and Culture* (Columbus: Ohio State University Press, 1987). Hassan constructs a (now famous) chart that maps modernism (determinacy/metaphor) and postmodernism (indeterminacy/metonymy) onto orthogonal dimensions of the same space.

18.   Fredric Jameson, "Postmodernism, or the Cultural Logic of Late Capitalism," *New Left Review* 146 (July–August 1984): 53–92.

19.   It is this ideational accretion that Michel Foucault analyses in great specificity in *The Order of Things* (New York: Vintage, 1970).

20.   The following is my favorite allegory of the postmodern: a local

shopping mall, built on top of a disused dock, devotes its top floor to themed shopping; old film sets were used to replicate areas of New York, New Orleans, Mexico, and the Wild West, all within walking distance of each other. A visitor was heard to ask, "Are they real old film sets?" (Thanks to Andy Butler for this example.)

This is not a trivial example. Where the visitor had been asking for a pedigree as signifying "reality," that reality's pure discursivity is the nonreality of film sets and their mythified represented scenes. The involutions of meaning in this are by now commonplace ("real film sets" = "real fake realities" = real fake real mythologized social realities out of context = etc.). Meaning is undermined through the very language used to articulate it. The binaries real/fake, real/mythic, real/social are deconstructed, and the mutually contextualizing confluence of these binaries themselves, in which they produce and are produced by commodities, commodification, and the market arena of commodification, come to encompass all social realities, whether mythic or historical. For modernism, the illusion of a New York street scene would really represent a New York street scene; for the postmodern, an artificial scene represents a representation of a street scene in the sense that the streets of New York themselves are representations of something called a "scene." One has to suspend reality in order to accept the reality of such a place (something already quite familiar to New Yorkers anyway).

21.   That philosophical movement is known as "continental philosophy" in the United States. Though its roots lie in the structuralist theorization of the sign, it critiques the metaphysical presupposition of the sign (and of structuralism) and through that the modes of discursive production of the social at many levels: philosophy (Derrida), social structure (Foucault), history (Deleuze and Guattari), culture and ideology (Baudrillard), and so on.

22.   See Derrida and MacDonald, "Choreographies."

23.   Jean-François Lyotard, *The Différend: Phrases in Dispute,* trans. Geroges Van Den Abbeele (Minneapolis: University of Minnesota Press, 1988). See also Meili Steele's essay on Lyotard in this volume.

24.   There are two collections of essays on this controversy, both of which attempt to cover the different positions generated by the "issue" as well as the different arenas in which it was performed: academic disciplines, social institutions, and the political organizations (generally right-wing) that have been involved: *Beyond PC,* ed. Patricia Aufderheide (St. Paul: Graywolf Press, 1992), and *Debating PC,* ed. Paul Berman (New York: Laurel Press, 1992). Both have extensive bibliographies.

25.   See, for instance, Camille Paglia, "Junks Bonds and Corporate Raiders: Academe in the Hour of the Wolf," in *Sex, Art, and American Culture* (New York: Vintage, 1992), 170–248. Paglia singles out the trinity of Lacan, Derrida, and Foucault as the bad guys and spends some time attacking "the followers of" this trinity. Her argument is basically of the form "how could X

talk about Y and not mention Z" (fill in the blanks). When she gets to the trinity itself, there is no "Z" — it is the null set; she doesn't say anything about who it is. Thus, she becomes a sort of broken circle, doing what she claims others do and at the same time indicating that there is nothing to do it with anyway. Ultimately, her argument becomes a succession of forms of name-calling, whose pinnacle is that the followers of the trinity are "lily-livered, dead-ass, trash-talking foreign junk-bond dealers" (219). I love that line; it's right out of the TV cop shows, and Paglia is the sergeant who gets to stand guard at the crime scene.

26.   Alexander Cockburn provides a political narrative of the controversy in "Beat the Devil," *Nation,* 27 May 1991, 685ff. For him, the issues are: (1) the opening of American history and literature to critique from the point of view of other cultures and communities that have been integral to the United States and its development; (2) a certain historical amnesia toward the cultural (and educational) past in the United States; (3) the notion of "relativism" vs. the excellence of traditional truths; (4) a "politicization" of the university vs. its traditional disinterested (so-called nonideological) inquiry; (5) the question of restrictive speech codes concerning derogation as assault rather than speech or opinion; and (6) a fear of minority-group lawsuits and demonstrations by university administrations.

Such debates are raised to a different level when the political structure steps in. At a University of Michigan commencement speech on May 4, 1991, President Bush claimed that "the notion of political correctness . . . declares certain topics off-limits, certain expressions off-limits." He added that "although the movement arises from the laudable desire to sweep away the debris of racism and sexism and hatred," it had led to intolerance, and that "political extremists roam the land, abusing the privilege of free speech, setting citizens against one another on the basis of their class and race." Strange how the issue of racism always seems to invoke this image.

27.   "Silber Says New Theories Can Put Limits on Freedom," *Boston Globe,* 30 November 1993, 1.

28.   Allan Bloom, *The Closing of the American Mind* (New York: Simon and Schuster, 1987).

29.   "Silber Says New Theories Can Put Limits on Freedom," 1.

Part 1

Maps

All literary and philosophical criticism approaches a text as a sign, as that for which a signification can be discovered, constructed, or invented. A primary constraint in the variety of such endeavors is the possible conceptual overlay to which a text can be subjected. This involves the critical determination of a framework by which the text is to be rendered intelligible as well as what is to be excluded in the process. While the poststructuralist (aesthetic) critique would include itself in the category of these endeavors, it begins by embracing the text as a terrain of multiple intelligibility. It seeks to include meanings that emerge interiorly from discursive form and the operation of the text's own inner logic. To discern such "subterranean" machinery of meaning beneath a text's rhetorical veneer, a separation must be made, and a space discerned, between this internal technology and the predominant ideological overlays the text seems in different ways to reserve for itself, as they interweave on its terrain. Such a separation would not entail a contestation between formalism and ideological critique, for instance, or between ideologization and aesthetic critique. Instead, it constitutes a space between a reading and the way the text makes its meanings multiple, the forms and contours by which meaning constructs itself.

One could draw an analogy to art to the extent that artwork is always an experiential construction of given material elements of some kind. Though a text is the creation of a writer, it is also something constructed of given elements, a sign constructed of other signs (words, tropes, narratives, codes, or segments of exposition, argument, etc.). Both art and sign, it contains within itself the gap of the analogy between art and sign. As sign, it can be as-signed a meaning, while as art analogue, it preserves an inescapable concreteness and radical singularity. The semiotic interplay between these two modes of being is what an aesthetic critique seeks to apprehend. The first problematic of such a critique is to map the terrain of this space (of art analogue) both in its structural particularity and as instances of language(s). In this (plural) space, textuality itself mediates between the text as sign and the text as art, that is, between statement and enactment, between content and form.

The meaning of textuality as a mediation and a sign is the focus of part 1. Each of its four essays addresses a specific textual sign within a literary work and establishes both a commentary on it and a critical relationship to it. While the textual sign is given a critical reading as such, a third mediating metatext is invoked that also "views" the textual sign at a distance, setting it in a relationship analogous to a work of art. William McBride addresses figuration (*figura*), a tropic mode of "drawing" a distant (hi)story or idea into a contemporary conception or narrative. He reveals its operation in both the Bible and the writings of St. Augustine through the mediating text and eye of Erich Auerbach. Bruce Krajewski considers Paul Celan's poetry through the mediating text of Gadamer's singular essay on Celan in order to address the pronoun "you" as a sign in a dialogic relation to an "I" it both engenders and reflects. The sign John O'Neill discusses is the exemplum (a seminarrative tropic figure that functions in the mode of a philosophical "vignette") in Montaigne, for which the mediating critique is Montaigne's own self-deconstruction. And through the mediating text of Edmund Burke, and his rhetorical use of gender, Timothy Gould approaches the aesthetic itself as a sign, as it appears at a critical moment in the history of eighteenth-century philosophy. In each case, the textual sign (*figura,* pronoun, exemplum, and aesthetic) is both recontextualized by the mediating text and mapped onto a terrain of its own self-contextualization, where it engenders its own meaning.

McBride inquires into Auerbach's treatment of Augustine in terms of the trajectory of Christian figuration in the Old Testament. For Auerbach, figuration appropriates a textual "event or person," which it then uses to signify a certain "historical fulfillment" for a different ideational system. The figure both preserves its own identity and functions semiotically for another's. In its historical concreteness it differs from allegory or symbolism, while in its historicity it participates in the generation of an interpretive abstraction. Auerbach seeks to reconcile these with respect to Augustine. The problem for McBride is Auerbach's reconciliation of the figure's inherent multiplicity of meaning by declaring the figural to be unequivocal.

The issue is compounded by the political issue that absorbs Auerbach's attention, namely, the Christian attempt to integrate the Old Testament into its own project rather than jettison it altogether. By recasting the Old Testament as a series of figures of Christ, thereby assimilating it into the Christian text, the stories of the Old Testament are divested of their autonomy, their historicity, and their Jewishness. McBride asks how the Old Testament's historicity is preserved in the face of this figural appropriation and recontextualization. Either the historical act of appropriation is overlaid upon the figure's interpretive role, in which case the figural interpretation (the Christian Bible) literalizes itself and dissolves the historicity of the figure, or the historicity of the figure is preserved and the Old Testament's otherness remains unappropriated.

In effect, the figural, as a sign, must participate in two languages: that which bestows upon it a coded (ideologized) signification and that of its self-referential textuality. For Auerbach, this constitutes the Augustinian dilemma, which he seeks to resolve. But McBride argues that for Augustine meaning must be given the necessary possibility of being multiple. Thus, McBride plays Augustine against Auerbach's critique of Augustine and the content of Auerbach's text against its form. Ultimately, for McBride, Auerbach is repressing a dimension of the figural sign in order to arrive at a definitude about the sign as figural.

A question McBride leaves aside—not denied, but unaddressed—is the irreducible singularity of the text as artwork despite, or because of, its polyvalence. Krajewski asserts that one can apprehend that singularity only through a mediating critical text, even though it may be ideologized in the present. He begins with the unquestioned element of art and the art-sign, its eternal uniqueness in its own temporal present, and argues that its uniqueness can only be represented in dialogue. Thus, he demonstrates that at the point of singularity multiplicity of meaning is unavoidable. As in McBride's discussion of the figure, the sign is already polyvocal.

Krajewski addresses Gadamer's appreciative critique of Celan. In his essay, Gadamer focuses on the pronoun "I," which, in poetry, refers to a voice that is both the poet and not the poet. In Celan's poetry, the pronoun takes on the appearance of an existential sign, a sign that something happened, that life had occurred, and at the same time of something else, something remaining unsayable which nevertheless had left a public trace. For Gadamer, this opens a series of homologous diremptions in which Krajewski discerns two modes of supplementary logic: Gadamer's apprehension of the strange (the nonpoet) as an avenue to the beautiful and Celan's presentation of the unsayable as both the boundary and threshold of understanding (the poet himself). In so doing, Krajewski homologically extends the space of doubleness that the aesthetic object discloses for Gadamer to Gadamer's text itself. That is, the discourse that interprets the splitting of the sign also splits. If the poem must be understood as polyvalent, the act of understanding also becomes multiple.

But, in Gadamer's terms, this also reflects an ambiguity between the public and the private. In the division of public and private, the pronoun becomes a (mapped) relation between a "this" and an "over there," a relation that is played out undecidably between "I" and "you" as signifier and signified. Which signifies which becomes an unanswerable question, an abyss within a statement whose meaning in turn is ultimately given in the response that it elicits. In effect, Gadamer's hermeneutic structures itself as a dialogue. That is, dialogue, like art, is a singularity whose structure is given by an interaction of pronouns, each of which is empty except through the other.

While Krajewski unveils the dialogue of pronouns at work in a poem,

O'Neill looks at the structure of the dialogue that is always internal to any sign—the way the sign's existence is always double. He addresses Montaigne's essay "Of Idleness," in which Montaigne laminates a triple economy of images concerning agriculture, reproduction, and psycho-culture, and for which O'Neill develops schemata reflecting the differences in these economies. Though for Montaigne these economies are connected by analogy (of farm and woman or agriculture and writing), O'Neill shows them to be also structured homologously, constituting a system of exempla for each other. That is, across their three discursive planes, each economy produces homologic meaning in another by recontextualizing it. Thus, the exempla together remap the infrastructure of the entire triple economy.

But this mutual contextualization then produces a different dynamic within each economy. Each economy deploys a central binary (husband/wife, cultivation/wilderness, imitation/imagination). But in the form of exempla, these binaries are narrativized and lose their literal or nominative value. Thus, each economy is given a literary (semiotic) relation to another economy, whose form as an economy already contextually mediates its semiotic value with respect to the third. By depending on another for its meaning in two directions at once, in spite of the ostensive autonomy of the coded economies, each binary deconstructs. Its constituent signs divide against themselves and become dialogic. O'Neill argues that the structure of this deconstruction is already given in the presence of the writer (Montaigne) to himself as an "I" in the text. Montaigne himself is both an insubordinate and a subordinate being, reflecting the qualities of nature and farm, woman and husbandman, creative imagination and traditional essayist. The conflation of these categories within himself becomes the nature of writing and of himself as writer.

But Montaigne's image of woman (as exemplum) nevertheless represents a stereotype in the content of his discourse as much as it does a figural element in his system of exempla, and this is something that O'Neill's discussion does not address. Focusing on a particular moment in the history of philosophy, Gould addresses the issue of the stereotype of woman in its role as a "dis-figural" ideologized sign. He shows that the fissure or hiatus that renders the sign dialogic is also found in philosophical discourse itself as a sign. If Gould ultimately suggests a semiotic counterpolitics to the stereotype, and to stereotyping in general, it is through a counterdiscourse of gender itself.

The question that Gould examines is a shift in philosophical focus toward aesthetics at the end of the eighteenth century, marked most strongly by the appearance of Kant's *Critique of Judgment*. Against the background of Kant's text, he interrogates the use of gender in Edmund Burke's *Reflections on the Revolution in France*. Burke's deployment of the image of woman, within an aestheticized discourse on history, undergoes a shift of philosophical focus. Gould asks what historical values are at stake in this shift.

Reading Burke's stereotypic use of the image of woman as nature, in a man vs. nature antithesis, Gould argues that Burke has deployed the image to construct an aesthetic distinction between man and animal. Burke creates this distinction to articulate his view that the French Revolution dissolved the concept of "man" through its dissolution of the ancien régime. The figure of "woman" is doubly cast as an ancient ideal and as a contemporary animal dis-figuration, iconizing and "engendering" a differential valuation between politics and political upheaval. Burke thus empowers the aesthetic against political history. That is, the stereotype represents a form of reideologization. Gould argues that, in general, the deployment of stereotypes of women and the construction of aesthetics as a discipline represented an ideological crisis in late-eighteenth-century thinking. In effect, Burke's aesthetics reflected an anxiety toward history, an entry into the arena of history (and, at the extreme, a male hysteria toward male history) expressed philosophically. Ultimately, Gould discloses the sign of the aesthetic to have been a political operator aestheticizing gender discourses that the sign of the aesthetic had itself been deployed to "engender."

While these essays evince no common theme, they address a series of rhetorical forms, of approaches to textual form, within the space between semiotics and ideologization. In sequence, we have the tropic figure as anti-ideological for McBride, the nonfigural as dialogical for Krajewski, the configural as homological for O'Neill, and the dis-figural as ideological in Gould. They articulate a certain succession of approaches to the space between text and metatext: the semiotic separation of reference and self-reference grounded in an aesthetic critique; the aesthetic separation of the self-referential sign in the form of dialogue; the internal dialogue that a sign gives rise to within itself; and the referential separation of aesthetics from itself as a sign. These essays present a variety of approaches to the discernment of textual form, which will function critically throughout the rest of this volume.

Figura Preserves

History (in) Ajar

William Thomas McBride

Erich Auerbach explains the workings of figural interpretation as a system that posits "a connection between two events or persons, the first of which signifies not only itself but also the second, while the second encompasses or fulfills the first."[1] Readers of the 1944 essay "Figura" recognize this explanation as far as it goes; difficulty arises, however, when Auerbach introduces figural interpretation's sine qua non, maintaining that the figural system differs from allegoresis and symbolism in that "[b]oth [the *figura* and the fulfillment] remain historical events" ("F," 58), that is to say, there is a preservation of the "full historicity" ("F," 36) of the *figura* despite its seemingly secondary, merely prefatory status. How is this preservation possible and what are its implicit interpretative results?

Tertullian is offered as Auerbach's first paradigmatic figural reader, a "staunch realist" who "expressly denied that the literal and historical validity of the Old Testament [the *figura*] was diminished by figural interpretation" ("F," 30). Later we are presented with a brief genealogy of *figura* in the course of examining the interpretive practice of St. Paul, a practice conducted as a "bitter struggle on behalf of his mission among the Gentiles" ("F," 50). This polemical origin is important for an understanding of figural interpretation's ideological appropriation of meaning and will be taken up again later. Auerbach moves from these two figurists to Dante, whose creatures Cato, Virgil, and Beatrice are all capable of simultaneously signifying themselves and their fulfillment. For example, the earthly Beatrice is at once also "revelation incarnate" ("F," 72). The one interpreter selected for discussion who does not quite fit into Auerbach's three categories—that is, symbolist (Tertullian), allegorist (St. Paul), and figurist (Dante)—is Augustine.

While Augustine "on the whole . . . favored a living, figural interpretation, for his thinking was far too concrete and historical to content itself with pure abstract allegory" ("F," 37), he nevertheless had an "idealism which removes the concrete event, completely preserved as it is, from time and transposes it into a perspective of eternity" ("F," 42). Augustine plays, one might say by default, a "leading part in the compromise between the two doctrines" ("F," 37) of allegory and figural interpretation. It is, of course, incumbent upon Auerbach to show how his figural interpretation as practiced by the holy trinity of Paul, Tertullian, and Dante escapes allegory and Augustine's idealist transposition to the eternal. He seems to show something else as well.

Auerbach writes: "In the figural system the interpretation is always sought from above [from 'God's Providence, which knows no difference of time']; events are considered not in their unbroken relation to one another, but torn apart, individually, each in relation to something other that is promised and not yet present . . . the eternal thing is already figured in them" ("F," 59). How, in some significant way, is this not Augustine's *perspective of eternity?* On the one hand, Auerbach insists that figural understanding is a "spiritual act" which "deals with the concrete events whether past, present, or future, and not with concepts or abstractions" ("F," 53), while, on the other, he describes how in the initial event, person, text the *figura* is torn apart from its relation to contiguous events and is interpreted from up above. If these two movements are not abstract, that is, a drawing (*tractus*) away (*abs*), how is it that they are not? Auerbach answers that the collection of torn events or persons fly, or are flown, vertically, up above, to be interpreted in the "second coming," in God's kingdom which is "'not of this world'; yet it will be a real kingdom, not an immaterial abstraction" ("F," 53). In his discussion of Tertullian and how *figura* operates, Auerbach notes that, at times, in order to "find it [the *figura*], one had to be determined to interpret in a certain way" ("F," 29), to perform a spiritual act.

This *certain* requirement of a preestablished interpretive schema and the assurance that the second coming, the kingdom of God, "will be a real kingdom" should not surprise us; they are in keeping with Auerbach's project of gaining "an understanding of the mixture of spirituality and sense of reality which characterize the European Middle Ages" in order to "sharpen and deepen our understanding of the documents of late antiquity and the Middle Ages, and solve a good many puzzles," such as those posed by early Christian sarcophagi iconology ("F," 61). As a literary historian, he is attempting (he tells us in a note) to tap "different conceptions of reality" ("F," 236 n. 42), which will enable him to assert that *figura rerum*, or phenomenal prophecy, was the European/Gentile's "basic conception of history" until the Reformation ("F," 53).

Given the requisite pre-Reformation Christian cosmology within which figural interpretation functions, the question of the preserved historicity and equal status of the *figura* persists, as does the question of its alleged resistance to any idealist transposition to the eternal. How can figural interpretation avoid such a move while inhabiting its radically transcendent Christian epoch and eschatological worldview?

The system of figure and fulfillment is often described by Auerbach with a nominal insistence upon *figura*'s preserved historicity, but the *figura*'s implicit secondary, host/site status seeps through: *figura* wishes to "preserve the full historicity of the Scriptures along with the deeper meaning" ("F," 36). How can the fulfillment be understood as deeper than yet equal to the *figura?* If "in figural interpretation the fact [the *figura*] is subordinated to an interpretation which is fully secured to begin with" ("F," 59), if the *figura* "will pass away," and if in the "system of figural prophecy . . . the risen one both fulfills and annuls the work of the precursor" ("F," 51), then how is a subordinated, passed-away, annulled *figura* preserved? What is the nature of this preservation?

A clue to the beginnings of an answer lies in *figura*'s polemic origin. Auerbach writes: "Figural interpretation changed the Old Testament from a book of laws and a history of the people of Israel into a series of figures of Christ and the redemption. . . . Jewish history and national character had vanished" so that the "Celtic and Germanic peoples, for example, could accept the Old Testament" ("F," 52). So the Old Testament was cleansed of its Jewishness, purged of its national history, saved from the obliteration planned by the "new opposition . . . who wished . . . to exclude the Old Testament," and, as consolation, the Old Testament "gained in concrete dramatic actuality" ("F," 51). This reclamation of the Old Testament managed to secure for Christianity its conception of a providential history and its sense of intrinsic concreteness. To be more precise, then, the nature of this preservation, whereby the Old Testament is made palatable to the Celtic and Germanic Gentiles in order for them to "find pleasure and nourishment in it" ("F," 56), is rather like the process in which decomposition and fermentation of fruits, meats, and vegetables is prevented by boiling them down and quickly sealing them off. Maurice Blanchot writes in *The Space of Literature* that "[t]his demand for a premature dénouement is the principle of figuration: it engenders the *image,* or if you will, the idol, and the curse which attaches to it is that which attaches to idolatry. Man wants unity right away."[2]

Auerbach implies that the *figura* loses something in the figural interpretive process by contrasting that process with the "spiritual-ethical-allegorical method" which, like the figural, "transforms the Old Testament; in it too the law and history of Israel lose their national and popular character; but these are replaced by a mystical or ethical system, and the text loses far more of its concrete history than in the figural system" ("F," 55). With what, then, does the figural system replace the Old Testament's legal, historical, national, and popular character? Auerbach insists on something historical. As it turns out, it is the so-called charmed life of Christ via allegoresis. But these two historical poles (Old and New Testaments), pointing at each other, together must give way to their true fulfillment in the Redemption, their true salvation and preservation. How this result is not a replacement by a mystical or ethical system must seem, as Auerbach puts it, baffling to us as modern, nonphilological readers, but it is, in fact, quite simply the "medieval view of everyday reality" ("F," 61) of those who, thanks to the dominion of the figural system over other methods of interpretation, see "everything written for our sakes'" ("F," 51).

Two of Kierkegaard's main themes apply to the workings of Auerbach's figural system. Just as the timeless Providential Kingdom of God is a *real* kingdom and not an immaterial abstraction, so the "movement of faith must continually be made by virtue of the absurd, but yet in such a way, please note, that one does not lose the finite but gains it whole and intact."[3] Here we have the second parallel: neither the historicity nor the finitude are lost. It is the same paradoxical system and epoch Ernst Robert

Curtius depicts in which Clerval's Mary is "at once mother and Virgin" and the "creator [becomes] a creature," where, according to Walter of Chatillon, "nature falls silent" and "Logic is conquered," and for Alain of Lille "Rhetoric and Reason fail,"[4] all by virtue of the absurd.

The peculiar middle status afforded Augustine in Auerbach's history requires further study here. Augustine is ultimately restricted from club *figura* owing to his idealist transposition to the eternal (a move Auerbach is at pains to disown, but in the end fails to do so). More to the point, it is Augustine's adherence to the "doctrine of the different meanings of the Scripture" ("F," 36) that denies him membership, although Auerbach insists on Augustine's "leading part in the compromise between these two doctrines" ("F," 37). Witness that among the many works by Augustine cited in "Figura" (*Epistles, City of God, On the Trinity, Against Faustus,* etc.), his *Confessions* is notoriously absent. Book 12 of the *Confessions* presents an Augustine *committed* to the doctrine of many different meanings, and it is perhaps the linguistic insights contained in that book, insights inimical to figural doctrine, that Auerbach tries to suppress.

Augustine begins his manifesto of many meanings (whose liberal pluralism in itself would require interrogation) by opposing those "acclaimers" of the Bible who insist on their reading as the only right one.[5] To the practitioner of such a tyrannical interpretation he puts the question: "How can it harm me that it should be possible to interpret these words ["In the beginning God made heaven and earth"] in several ways, all of which may be true?" Particularly "since we believe that he [God, Moses, Paul] wrote the truth" (12.18)?

By a majestic, worthy-of-sainthood interpretation of God's injunction to increase and multiply, Augustine writes in the final book of the *Confessions:*

> We are meant to take them [the words "increase and multiply"] in a figurative sense. . . . It is only in the case of signs outwardly given that we find increase and multiplication in the sense that a single truth can be expressed by several different means . . . [and] that a single expression can be interpreted in several different ways. (13.29)

Augustine approaches here a more precise, if open, description of language's polysemy—an attribute arguably so central to the nature of language that it is difficult to see how it manages to escape Auerbach's philological ken.

Augustine playfully sums up his pluralistic interpretive position by projecting himself into a role which indeed describes his position as writer *and* interpreter:

> If I were called upon to write a book which was to be vested with the highest authority, I should prefer to write it in such a way that a reader could find reechoed in my words whatever truths he was able to apprehend. I would rather write in this way than impose a single true meaning so explicitly that it would exclude all others, even though they contained no falsehood that could give me offence. (12.31)

Unlike Augustine's system of interpretation, Auerbach's figural system suffers from oversystematization. The position from which one interprets is *fixed* in an *up above* that is nevertheless conditional, while the trajectory of that interpretation is rigidly bi-unidirectional; in this case, it moves from Old Testament event to the Second Coming, which will be a real kingdom, and back to the now-preserved Old Testament event in a process reminiscent of what Samuel Beckett has called "that glorious double-entry, with every credit in the said account a debit in the meant, and inversely."[6] Doesn't Auerbach's characterization of the Western medieval world's dominant mode of interpretation and its "basic conception of history" condescend by implicitly positing so limited an imagination for the European Gentile?

Perhaps it would be fruitful to project the figural gaze beyond the European Middle Ages in order to cast it into a modern/secular setting. Could Auerbach's figural interpretation be adapted for modern, secular texts read in a modern, secular epoch? One might seek to accommodate a language such as Paul de Man depicts in *Allegories of Reading* in which "the trope is not a derived, marginal, or aberrant form of language but the linguistic paradigm par excellence. The figurative structure is not one linguistic mode among others but what characterizes language as such."[7] That is to say, it is a language that is neither simply representational nor expressive, never purely denominating, but always allegorical, figural. It is such a linguistic insight that prompts Augustine to argue contra Auerbach for a certain irreducible, nonsynthetic plurality of meaning communicated in a language of "re-echoes." And if language, as de Man puts it in "Hegel on the Sublime," is the "*deictic* system of *predication* and determination,"[8] that is to say, if the function of words themselves is to *point* in this open and figurative way, then Auerbach's figural system all at once seems overcrowded by extra word relationships and haunted by unaccounted meanings.

As for the attempt to project a modern, secular version of the figural system, one could look to any number of disciplines, where a specifically rigid interpretive system would deny the validity of the rest of that interpretive community's readings. Or we could approach a perhaps more subtle version by focusing on Augustine's (and Plato's) *recognition* theory of truth, where, according to Augustine, facts "must have been in my mind even before I learned them" (10.10), facts "recognized by us in our minds" (10.11).[9] Here Augustine's disavowed training in rhetoric[10] stands him in good stead as he traces the *Confessions*' only etymology, positing the etymon *cogo* for *cogito* in order to show how "I assemble or I collect" my (already existing) thoughts (10.11). Such recognitions rhyme, but only nearly, with similar but limited provisions for Auerbach's *figura*. In our search for a secularized figural system, we might detect a strain of Augustinian recognition in Hans-Georg Gadamer's description of the interpretive process, where "what one experiences in a work of art and what one is directed towards is rather how true it is, i.e., to what extent one knows and recognizes something and oneself."[11] However, with Gadamer's and Augustine's projects, putting aside for the moment a necessary critique of their subjectivist aesthetic, we have certainly moved beyond Auerbach's bi-univocal *figura*, and find little to preserve.

Notes

1. Erich Auerbach, "Figura" (1944), in *Scenes from the Drama of European Literature* (1959), trans. Ralph Manheim (Minneapolis: University of Minnesota Press, 1984), 53; hereafter abbreviated "F" and cited parenthetically in the text.

2. Maurice Blanchot, *The Space of Literature,* trans. Ann Smock (Lincoln: University of Nebraska Press, 1982), 79.

3. Søren Kierkegaard, *Fear and Trembling/Repetition,* trans. and ed. Howard V. Hong and Edna H. Hong (Princeton, N.J.: Princeton University Press, 1983), 37.

4. Ernst Robert Curtius, *European Literature and the Latin Middle Ages* (1948), trans. Willard R. Trask (Princeton, N.J.: Princeton University Press, 1953), 42.

5. Augustine, *Confessions,* trans. R. S. Pine-Coffin (New York: Penguin, 1961), 12.14; hereafter cited parenthetically in the text.

6. Samuel Beckett, "An Imaginative Work!" review of *The Amaranth-*

ers by Jack B. Yeats, *Dublin Magazine* (July–September 1936); reprinted in *Disjecta: Miscellaneous Writings and a Dramatic Fragment by Samuel Beckett,* ed. Ruby Cohn (New York: Grove, 1984), 90.

7.　Paul de Man, *Allegories of Reading: Figural Language in Rousseau, Nietzsche, Rilke, and Proust* (New Haven, Conn.: Yale University Press, 1979), 105.

8.　Paul de Man, "Hegel on the Sublime," in *Displacement: Derrida and After,* ed. Mark Krupnick (Bloomington: Indiana University Press, 1983), 145.

9.　The temporal nature of this *"re"* is misleading. From the standpoint of Augustine's phenomenology of the soul's own con*figura*tion, i.e., absolute knowing, time is annulled. The "external" is somehow internalized; truth, that "hidden fruit," is always already "pre"-inscribed, no matter how dimly: "But they could not love it [truth] unless they had some knowledge of it in their memory. . . . their dim memory of truth" (10.23). Also: "In your word all is uttered at one and the same time, yet eternally. If it were not so, your Word would be subject to time and change, and therefore would be neither truly eternal nor truly immortal" (11.7). Augustine's claim of the timelessness of truth is based on his conception "that there was formless matter, in which there was no order because there was no form. . . . where there was no order there could be no successive movement of time. Yet this next-to-nothing, in so far as it was not utterly nil, must have had its being from him from whom everything that in any degree is derives its being" (12.15). While Augustine's interpretive "perspective of eternity" is akin to Auerbach's *figura,* which is rooted in "God's Providence, which knows no difference of time," and while both systems posit God as Guarantor of ultimate meaning, Augustine both allows for several "correct" human interpretations (their "breaking into song") and relinquishes dreams of securing anything like historicity, which in this case appears as Auerbach's inappropriate pasteurizing of spiritual and material modes.

10.　For example: "I read and understood by myself all the books that I could find on the so-called liberal arts, for in those days I was a good-for-nothing and a slave to sordid ambitions" (4.16); "I was a teacher of the art of public speaking" for the "love of money" and "was merely abetting their [students'] futile designs and their schemes of duplicity" (4.2); see also 1.19.

11.　Hans-Georg Gadamer, *Truth and Method* (1960), trans. and ed. Garrett Barden and John Cumming (New York: Crossroad, 1975), 102.

[I]t is more than likely that the "who," which appears so clearly and unmistakably to others, remains hidden from the person himself, like the *daimon* in Greek religion which accompanies each man throughout his life, always looking over his shoulder from behind and thus visible only to those he encounters.
　　　　—Hannah Arendt, *The Human Condition*

The poem becomes conversation—often desperate conversation. Only the space of this conversation can establish what is addressed, can gather it into a "you" around the naming and speaking I. But this "you," come about by dint of being named and addressed, brings its otherness into the present. Even in the here and now of the poem—and the poem has only this one, unique, momentary present—even in this immediacy and nearness, the otherness gives voice to what is most its own: its time.
　　　　—Paul Celan, *Meridian*

Gadamer's Aesthetics in Practice in *Wer bin Ich und wer bist Du?*

Bruce Krajewski

In one of Paul Celan's early prose pieces in Romanian, the last two sentences are: "It's up to you. Try to understand me."[1] Perhaps even Celan did not know how difficult that challenge would become, how imposing it remains. Celan's poems are songs sung on "the other side of mankind" (*jenseits der Menschen*), as Celan says in his poem "Fadensonnen." It seems significant that the philosopher of *Verstehen* should take up the challenge, especially since Gadamer's text on Celan is the only book-length example of Gadamer's readings of a single collection of poetry.

Gadamer is well aware of the ancient antagonism between philosophy and poetry. Still, he wants to say that there is no antagonism without kinship. As he says in his essay titled "Philosophy and Poetry," "Poetry and philosophy are both set off from the exchange of language as it takes place in practical activity and in science, but their proximity seems in the end to collapse into the extremes of the word that stands, and the word that fades into the unsayable."[2] Often Celan leads us to silence, into aporia that simulate the experience of falling into a well so deep that one knows it is useless to yell for help. Yet Gadamer is the one who insists that aporia will lead us to *euporia;* that is, being at a loss about something will lead you to insight, as long as you keep at it. If I understand Gadamer in the right spirit, listening can often be more important than speaking, so the uselessness of yelling from the bottom of the well might be a benefit in an odd sense, in that the well might be a fine place to practice listening. All beginnings lie in darkness, Gadamer says. Or think of the beginning of Celan's "Edgar Jené and the Dream about the Dream": "I am supposed to tell you some of the words I heard deep down in the sea where there is so much silence and so much happens."[3] Later, a friend of the "I" of this essay speaks of a "dark well" and then asks the "I," "But how can we ever succeed . . . if you and people like you never come out of the deep, never stop communing with the dark springs?" (*CP,* 5). The friend appears as the voice of Reason, a friend who finds nothing useful in dwelling in darkness, who seems not to understand about hearing in silence.

Remember that enigma and the Unsayable appeal to Gadamer. He knows that "the spark of the wonderful is born from the marriage of strange and most strange" (*CP,* 6). In the commentary to Celan's *Atemkristall,* Gadamer writes, "A poem that withholds itself and does not yield continual clarity always appears to me to be more meaning-full than any clarity."[4] Another hermeneuticist, Gerald Bruns, says something quite similar about ancient notions concerning figuration. For the ancients, Bruns says, "[t]hat which is easy to understand is not worth understanding except for those who can understand nothing else."[5] For us, living in an "information age," an age which wants language harnessed to the shortest leash possible, these statements by Gadamer and Bruns enter our ears at an odd angle. Some will miss the point here by dismissing their statements as mysticism or esotericism, even elitism.

If one version of aesthetics deals with the beautiful (*kalos*), then Gadamer's attraction to the opaque and the strange turns out to be something like the story of Beauty and the Beast, in which the Beast is Beauty too. Or you might think of it as the notion that pondering the beastly might tell us something about the beautiful that the beautiful by itself cannot. In the story of Beauty and the Beast, something other is taken as something beautiful, or at least the Beast is seen as a participant in the human condition. The story about two creatures relates to Gadamer's claim that art rests on an anthropological foundation. More about that later.

To speak about Gadamer's aesthetics in practice means to say something about Gadamer's aesthetics, a task which requires more space than I have. Here I can only touch on a few points. Two important texts to consult here are *Truth and Method,* particularly the first third, and *The Relevance of the Beautiful.* In these two texts, Gadamer stresses the didacticism of art—that art speaks to us because it has something to tell us about the past and about the present, and we listen and learn. However, this learning can be, and often is, unsettling, like the first encounter with a beast. Gadamer says in *The Relevance of the Beautiful* that "where no one else can understand, it seems that the philosopher is called for. . . . The poetry of our time has reached the limits of intelligible meaning and perhaps the greatest achievements of the greatest writers are themselves marked by a tragic speechlessness in the face of the unsayable" (*RB,* 9). In taking up the poems of Celan, Gadamer realizes that the Holocaust is part of the Unsayable for the poet. Further, reading Celan's poetry often leaves the reader speechless, bewildered, and this is when hermeneutics takes on greater importance. "The hermeneutic art," Gadamer says, "is in fact the art of understanding something that appears alien and unintelligible to us" (*RB,* 141). Gadamer does not run from the beast nor from the Unspeakable.

In an encounter with a beast or with the Unspeakable, it seems a natural inclination to ask a question like, What is it?—a question that reveals a desire to comprehend. Gadamer tells us that "[t]o understand something, I must be able to identify it" (*RB,* 25). Naturally, this statement conjures up all the talk about naming we are familiar with, but we need to remember that different sorts of naming exist, all contingent on presuppositions, predispositions, and contexts. For one, we can imagine a kind of naming that allows us to identify the beast or the Unsayable in order to relieve fear, the kind of name that leads to a cessation of curiosity. For instance, alone in the darkness of your room, you might hear strange noises, but once you feel secure that the noises emanate from a cranky heating system and not from a clumsy murderer, you can return to sleep and forget about it. It seems to me that this is not the kind of naming that Gadamer speaks of, that is, naming to forget, naming to categorize in order to shelve the now-named. In another sense, this is exactly the sort of naming Gadamer is speaking of, but without forgetting the forgetting. Again in *The Relevance of the Beautiful,* which we might rename temporarily as *The Relevance of the Beastly,* Gadamer discusses naming and identifying in connection with recognition, and this recognition implies acknowledgment in the same sense, I think, that Stanley Cavell uses the word. In his essay on *King Lear,* Cavell says, "[R]ecognizing a person depends upon allowing oneself to be recognized by him. . . . Why is it Gloucester whose recognition Lear is first able to bear? The obvious answer is: Because Gloucester is blind. Therefore one can be, can only be, recognized by him without being seen, without having to bear eyes upon oneself."[6] Gadamer says, "The recognition that the work of art procures for us is always an expansion of that infinite process of making ourselves at home in the world which is the human lot" (*RB,*151). Part of this making ourselves at home in the world involves acknowledging unpredictability, unpredictability that science cannot eliminate, like the capriciousness of the weather, and the possibility that the beast will remain other, will resist being identified.

In rethinking the story of Beauty and the Beast, we must at the same time place along side it the story of Dr. Jekyll and Mr. Hyde. Here, with this story, we learn that sometimes the beast can be myself, a disruption of self-identity. Now, with Dr. Jekyll and Mr. Hyde in mind, when I ask, What is it?, the uncomfortable response is: It is I. And then again, perhaps the response can turn strangely comfortable, as when Henry Jekyll sees Edward Hyde and says, "And yet when I looked upon that ugly idol in the glass, I was conscious of no repugnance, rather a leap of welcome. This, too, was myself."[7] Perhaps it pleases Jekyll that he is more than he thought. Naturally, at other times, one would deny one's divided self in the way that Spencer Brydon does in Henry James's "The Jolly Corner": "There's somebody—an awful beast; whom I brought, too horribly, to bay. But it's not me."[8] Note that the question has shifted from *What* is it? to *Who* is it? Hannah Arendt explains quite well the importance in the difference between the *who* and the *what:*

> The manifestation of who the speaker and doer unexchangeably is, though it is plainly visible, retains a curious intangibility that confounds all efforts toward unequivocal verbal expression. The moment we want to say *who* somebody is, our very vocabulary leads us astray into saying *what* he is; we get entangled in a description of qualities he necessarily shares with others like him; we begin to describe a type or a "character" in the old meaning of the word, with the result that his specific uniqueness escapes us.
>
> This frustration has the closest affinity with the well-known

philosophic impossibility to arrive at a definition of man, all definitions being determinations or interpretations of *what* man is, of qualities, therefore, which he could possibly share with other living beings, whereas his specific difference would be found in a determination of what kind of a "who" he is. Yet apart from this philosophic perplexity, the impossibility, as it were, to solidify in words the living essence of the person as it shows itself in the flux of action and speech, has great bearing upon the whole realm of human affairs, where we exist primarily as acting and speaking beings.[9]

This brings me back to Gadamer's book on Celan, for the very title focuses us on the perplexity of identity and the slipperiness of naming. Gadamer offers us a seemingly ridiculous question, "Who am I and who are you?"—a question that serves as a refrain throughout the commentary. The question that becomes the title for Gadamer's book is not rhetorical. Among other things, the question seeks to explore part of the indeterminacy about the "you" and the "I," which includes not only the speaker and the one spoken to but also the uncertainty of the poetic "I," "whether that 'I' is always to be read as Celan, or 'us', or something or someone else altogether" (*WBI*, 12). All of this calls our attention to the inconstancy of identity and the continual need for self-understanding; while this might be frightening, the way not knowing who you are would be, this acknowledgment of the unpredictability of identity wakens us, makes us more keen-eyed, the way I imagine some characters in Greek mythology were aware that a lightning bolt might be Zeus, or the stranger at the door might be a goddess or a god in mortal garb, or some farm animal might take on magical powers. In this semimythological context involving the always present possibility of metamorphosis, we can detect a willingness and an openness in the taking of things *as* something else. Moderns find this sort of instability and arbitrariness of identity unsettling, if not mad. "Schizophrenic" might be an example of a name we would attach to someone with more than one identity. "Impostor" is another name, a person who poses as another, who takes the position or place of another, making it clear that someone can take your place, so that you live with the threat of substitution. The more familiar, benign form of all of this comes through the expression: "You are not yourself today." If you are not yourself, who are you?

It is not so simple who you are and who I am, nor who Paul Antschel and Paul Celan are, for, as Gadamer notes, each one of us is divided. Gadamer emphasizes that though the "you" and the "I" in Celan's poetry are not fixed, "with that is not meant, for instance, that . . . the difference between the 'I' that speaks and the 'you' that has been addressed has been effaced" (*WBI*, 12). Gadamer writes:

> Whoever reads a lyrical poem always understands in a certain sense who "I" is here. Not in the trivial sense alone, that he always knows, that the poet speaks and not a person introduced by him. He knows much more beyond that about who the Poet-I actually is. Because the "I" spoken in a lyrical poem cannot be equated exclusively with the "I" of the poet, which would be an other "I" than the speaking-"I" of the reader. Even when the poet himself "carries assumed characters" and separates himself explicitly from the crowd, which "immediately jeers," it is as if he no longer meant himself, but the reader who slips into the poet's "I"-character, and knows himself that he too is divided. This is true even here with Celan, where in a completely unmediated, shadowy, indeterminate, and constantly changing manner "I," "You," and "we" are spoken. This "I" is not only the poet, but rather "each individual," as Kierkegaard had called it, who each one of us is. (*WBI*, 11)

Unlike proper names, each of us can read herself into an open "I" and see herself there in the place of the poet's "I." This looks like the reverse of the narcissism of the "I." Grammatically, pronouns are impostors, words that substitute for, or take the place of, nouns. (Can an impostor be a narcissist?) From Gadamer's discussion, these pronouns invite us to impose on them, to "slip into" them.

The "you" and the "I" in Celan's poems call out, as if we hear ourselves being called. Is this "you" you? This "I" in the poem about me? Note that you are not called by name. Yell "Hey, you!" on a crowded street, and many will turn around, for no one knows who is being called, but it could be you. Further, imagine turning and finding no one there—this is the kind of calling at hand. Who is calling? The title of Gadamer's text helps us to "listen away" to the "they," as Heidegger speaks of it in *Being and Time*,[10] since one characteristic of *Atemkristall* is the lack of a "they" and an emphasis on you and I.[11]

Who is calling? The caller remains indefinite, though Heidegger speaks of conscience as a call, perhaps in the way one's vocation is a calling. "And to what is one called when one is thus appealed to?" asks Heidegger. "To one's *own Self*" (*BT*, 317). This turns out to be disturbing, for while conscience is a mode of discourse according to Heidegger, it "discourses solely and constantly in the mode of keeping silent" (*BT,* 318). We are back in the bottom of the dark well, listening. But we cannot expect to get to the bottom of this calling, nor will we know who the caller is. To answer a phone and find no one there—this is the experience of uncanniness that Heidegger points to when he feigns to answer "Who is calling?" by saying, "The caller is Dasein in its uncanniness" (*BT,* 321). I mention the quotidian examples of "Hey, you!" being called out on a crowded street as well as the unnamed phone caller to hint at what Stanley Cavell calls "the uncanniness of the ordinary," something Heidegger also recognized: "Uncanniness is the basic kind of Being-in-the-world, even though in an everyday way it has been covered up" (*BT,* 322). However this cover-up goes on, Cavell pushes one to think that it might be that we have become so much at home with strangeness that the ordinary has become terrifying. In his splendid reading of the end of E. T. A. Hoffmann's "The Sandman," Cavell remarks on the ease with which Nathaniel falls in love with the beautiful automaton Olympia while ignoring the ordinary, human Clara, whose ordinariness Nathaniel cannot bear at the end of the story when Olympia is out of the picture. Cavell says, "[H]e could not bear . . . her flesh-and-bloodness, since it means bearing her separateness, her existence as other to him, exactly what his craving for the automaton permitted him escape, one way or the other (either by demanding no response to the human or by making him an automaton)."[12] Cavell's gloss on this story demonstrates that the "you" and the "I" in Hoffmann's tale are quite separate and discernible for Nathaniel, who views Clara as other. In other words, "Who am I and who are you?" is not a question for Nathaniel; the distinction seems oppressively plain.

I want to loop back to Gadamer's book and its plainness, its ordinariness. *Wer bin Ich und wer bist Du?* is a book without the usual scholarly apparatus of footnotes, bibliographies, and indexes. In fact, Gadamer shuns the role of scholar in his commentary, though he does, as we shall see, attend to other scholarly writings on Celan. From the beginning, Gadamer puts some distance between erudite readers and the sort of readers he has in mind. He writes, "He who would believe he 'has understood' Celan's poems already, I am not talking with him (I do not join in conversation with him—for him I do not write). He doesn't know what understanding is here" (*WBI,* 7). Understanding will take place as a result of an experience with the poems, and this is the experience "the patient reader devotes himself to. Certainly there cannot be a hurried reader who wants to understand and unlock hermetic lyrics. But it must by no means be a scholarly or especially learned reader—it must be a reader who keeps trying to listen" (*WBI,* 9). Furthermore, in the afterword to the second edition, Gadamer makes it a point to reveal that he came to understand these poems while lying in a sand pit in the dunes of Holland—not in a library—and that he had no dictionary with him (*WBI,* 138). Instead of leaving poetry to the academics armed with references, Gadamer posits a reader who can look at poetry on her own, not only outside the academy but simply outside, in an everyday setting, with only the poetry in hand. Gadamer seems to want to bring Celan's work out into the open, out of the sealed-off world of expert readers.

Gadamer is no ordinary reader, however, as we shall see from his commentary on the following poem from *Atemkristall:*

> Corroded by the undreamed,
> the sleeplessly traveled bread-land
> digs up the life-mountain.
>
> From its soil
> you knead anew our names,
> with an eye
>   like yours
> on each of my fingers.
>   I probe them for
> a place, through which I
> can wake onto you,
> the bright
> Hunger-candle in my mouth.[13]

In the first sentence of Gadamer's commentary on this poem, he startles the reader by identifying the absence in Celan's poem: the mole. The mole is never mentioned explicitly in Celan's poem; rather, we see the mole through the results of its actions—one might call it the mole's public character—so that a description of actions becomes a kind of naming. The life movement of the mole leaves traces, etchings, and we recognize these as the labor of a mole. From Gadamer's perspective, this activity of the mole is to be taken as a metaphor for life, as well as for an insight about identity and naming. Part of Gadamer's aesthetics leads one to self-questioning, to see oneself over and over again brought into the world of the work of art; and similarly he brings the work of art back into the world. In this case, you are asked to learn something about yourself by paying attention to the life of a mole. Gadamer pushes things out into the open, into the public sphere, and gives little attention to strictly private experiences with art. For Gadamer, the experience with art always implicates you. It is—to quote Levinas—"as if in going toward the other, I were reunited with myself . . . as if the distancing of the I drew me closer to myself, discharged of the full weight of my identity."[14]

To come at this from another angle, I think Gadamer would agree with Hans Blumenberg's reading of the Oedipus myth, a reading that runs counter to Freud's appropriation of the Oedipal story, and which at least opposes a notion of insight as private reflection about one's past. Blumenberg's reading of the Oedipus story reminds us that Oedipus learns who killed the king not by seeking solitude to contemplate the circumstances of his life, but rather by carrying out his public duties, by bringing people before him for questioning.[15] Who killed the king? It is I.

In a similar manner, Gadamer seeks to bring out the public side of Celan's poem, which is a way to get back to that anthropological foundation on which art rests, according to Gadamer. A good illustration of this comes through Gadamer's discussion of the hunger-candle. Through a conversation with a colleague, Gadamer learned that hunger-candles constitute part of a Lenten practice. "There is in the Balkans a custom of the hunger-candles," he says, "which makes the pious fast visible to all (at the church door)—an art of prayer. . . . It is an analogue of a fast that here accompanies the striving after light. But the specialness of the fast is public, in that the strivers after brightness hold the hunger-candles *in the mouth*" (*WBI*, 23). Another colleague told Gadamer that if someone was poor and had lost his earlier economic position and was forbidden to go begging, he laid himself disguised at the church door with the hunger-candles, in order to receive donations unseen and without having to look. Here is a playing out of Cavell's point about being recognized without being seen, "without having to bear eyes upon oneself."

From these accounts of the hunger-candles, we learn that the hunger-candles function as an identifying sign. Privation marks people. The sign indicates those who strive for something, penance or donations perhaps, but it is a kind of striving the mole does looking for light by casting up the mountain. Gadamer calls it the "I" that like a blind worm presses to the light; and then Gadamer quotes Jakob Burckhardt: "The spirit is a wriggler" (*WBI*, 24).

The poor knead their existence out of crumbs, but Gadamer wants to expand this in order to say that "all of us will have 'kneaded' names, since everyone's life-mountain will be continually cast up, and out of it one develops the sense and senselessness of each life" (*WBI*, 24). As each of us moves through life, each will leave etchings, tracings, like the mole, and from those etchings and tracings someone will be able to identify you, to recognize you, not you individually, by your name, not your ego, but the sort of "you" Gadamer sets in the title of his commentary. Someone will recognize you in a way similar to that of Gadamer's recognizing the mole in a poem where a mole isn't mentioned.

Another side of Gadamer's aesthetic reveals itself in his recognition of other interpreters, even of those who have objected to Gadamer's commentary. For instance, Otto Pöggeler, in his *Spur des Worts,* takes up Gadamer, so that Pöggeler can overtake Gadamer by showing the autobiographical connections in Celan's poetry to which Gadamer does not attend.[16] Pöggeler explains, in part, the pivotal poem "Schläfenzange" by referring to the fact that Celan's first child, François, was brought into the world with the help of forceps.[17] However, Gadamer's gloss on this is that "Schläfenzange" has to do with the graying temples of old age, for he works out his gloss within the poem, and with the poem's relation to the cycle, not from information about the poet's private life. Gadamer says that "who will understand a poem rightly must again, in each case, fully forget the private and occasional" (*WBI,* 138). In short, Gadamer deals with what is in front of him—the poem—not what lies behind the poem.

Gadamer admits that his understanding is limited, and instead of attempting to upstage Pöggeler in the new afterword, Gadamer exhibits Socratic humility by saying, "I wish I were so learned as Pöggeler, and Pöggeler certainly wishes he were as learned as Celan" (*WBI,* 153). Gadamer calls Celan a "*poeta doctus*" (*WBI,* 137), indicating his deference to Celan and his work, an attitude that, in this case, denies the role to the interpreter of master of the text. The Socratic humility reappears at the end of the commentary where Gadamer quotes from the *Phaedrus:* "for Gold, so much as only a temperate man might bear and carry with him." And here hear the echo of Celan's aphorism that returns us to well imagery: "The pitcher which went to the well once too often still gets by, but the well runs dry" (*CP,* 11). Perhaps there is a danger of trying to hear too much in this poetry, and Gadamer says that the reader needs to know only as much as his poetic ear can tolerate without going deaf (*WBI,* 155), as if this were a new gloss on the story of Odysseus and the Sirens.

Those looking to discover Gadamer's way of reading in *Wer bin Ich und wer bist Du?* will be frustrated. Gadamer states that there is no hermeneutical method (*WBI,* 150). Understanding is multiple, heterogeneous, always different. The task of hermeneutics is to understand this.

Notes

1.   Paul Celan, *Halo: Poems,* trans. Stavros Deligiorgis (Minneapolis: Coffee House Press, 1991).

2.   Hans-Georg Gadamer, *The Relevance of the Beautiful and Other Essays,* trans. Nicholas Walker, ed. Robert Bernasconi (Cambridge: Cambridge University Press, 1986), 133; hereafter abbreviated *RB* and cited parenthetically in the text.

3.   Paul Celan, *Collected Prose,* trans. Rosmarie Waldrop (Manchester: Carcanet Press, 1986), 3; hereafter abbreviated *CP* and cited parenthetically in the text.

4.   Hans-Georg Gadamer, *Wer bin Ich und wer bist Du?: Ein Kommentar zu Paul Celans Gedichtfolge "Atemkristall,"* 2d ed. (Frankfurt: Suhrkamp, 1986), 10; hereafter abbreviated *WBI* and cited parenthetically in the text. The first edition was published in 1973. All translations from the second edition result from the assistance Hilary Siebert gave me.

5.   Gerald L. Bruns, "Figuration in Antiquity" in *Hermeneutics: Questions and Prospects,* ed. Gary Shapiro and Alan Sica (Amherst: University of Massachusetts Press, 1984), 148.

6.   Stanley Cavell, "The Avoidance of Love: A Reading of *King Lear,*" in *Must We Mean What We Say?* (Cambridge: Cambridge University Press, 1976), 279. An important text to consult on this topic is Terence Cave's *Recognitions: A Study in Poetics* (Oxford: Clarendon Press, 1988).

7.   Robert Louis Stevenson, *Dr. Jekyll and Mr. Hyde and Other Stories* (Middlesex: Penguin Books, 1979), 84.

8.   Henry James, "The Jolly Corner," in *The Novels and Tales of Henry James,* New York ed., vol. 17 (New York: Charles Scribner's Sons, 1909), 482.

9.   Hannah Arendt, *The Human Condition* (Chicago: University of Chicago Press, 1958), 181.

10.   Martin Heidegger, *Being and Time,* trans. John Macquarrie and Edward Robinson (New York: Harper and Row, 1962), 316; hereafter abbreviated *BT* and cited parenthetically in the text. I thank Gerald Bruns for suggesting this connection between Gadamer's readings of *Atemkristall* and the sections in *Being and Time* on calling.

11.   For an analytical list of pronoun usage in Celan's work, see James K. Lyon, "Paul Celan and Martin Buber: Poetry as Dialogue" *PMLA* 86 (January 1971): 114.

12.   Stanley Cavell, *In Quest of the Ordinary: Lines of Skepticism and Romanticism* (Chicago: University of Chicago Press, 1988), 156.

13.   The German text is as follows:

> Von Ungeträumtem geätzt,
> wirft das schlaflos durchwanderte Brotland

den Lebensberg auf. Aus seiner Krume
knetest du neu unsre Namen,
die ich, ein deinem
gleichendes
Aug an jedem der Finger,
abtaste nach
einer Stelle, durch die ich
mich zu dir heranwachen kann,
die helle
Hungerkerze im Mund.

14.   Emmanuel Levinas, "Being and the Other: On Paul Celan," *Chicago Review* 29, no. 3 (Winter 1978): 20.

15.   Hans Blumenberg, *Work on Myth,* trans. Robert M. Wallace (Cambridge: MIT Press, 1985), 88–89. Blumenberg says, "Oedipus discovers his guilt, not in a process of self-examination and self-purification, but rather in pursuit of his official duty of complying with the oracle that assured the city of Thebes of freedom from the plague if the murderer of Laius was driven from the land. To search for this murderer and thus to get on the track of his own impurity is a political proceeding, not one of self-knowledge and self-liberation."

16.   Otto Pöggeler, *Spur des Worts: zur Lyrik Paul Celans* (Freiburg and Munich: Karl Alber, 1986). Pöggeler's comments about *Wer bin Ich und wer bist Du?* are on pp. 179–211.

17.   Ibid., 184.

Structure, Flow, and Balance in Montaigne's Essay "Of Idleness"

John O'Neill

The use of exemplum, an example in the general sense or by extension a fable varying from a few lines to a lengthy essay interspersed with several more exempla, as in Montaigne's *Essays,* has had a long history.[1] In the Middle Ages, the exemplum served to connect the world of the Bible to the daily context of European Christianity, as it still does in the ordinary Sunday homily. In Roman antiquity, exempla served like so many shining memorials to the greatness of the *Urbs Romana.* Similarly, in early and medieval Christianity, the exempla drawn from the lives of saints, philosophers, and, above all, the exemplary life of Christ (*exemplum exemplorum*) served to instruct and to guide Christians in their everyday lives as well as in the monastic orders. Gradually, the exemplum evolved from the use of starkly contrasted figures of good and evil, of the difference between man and woman, between saint and devil, to figures with a more differentiated psychology, wit and humor, reflecting the more practical values of the late medieval age.[2] By the time the exemplum reaches Montaigne, it is open to a further development imposed upon it due to the shifting ratio of *imitatio* and *inventio* reflected in the practice (*exercitio*) of the essay.[3]

In order to respect the economy of a short conference paper, and in view of other writing,[4] I shall select for analysis an extremely short essay, "Of Idleness," since it offers the convenience of full quotation for your scrutiny (see the appendix), even though its condensed form deprives us of the easier access offered by Montaigne's typically more "rambling" essays. By the same token, we shall see that, despite its title, "Of Idleness" is concerned with work. Moreover, despite its apparent simplicity as a continuous example, "Of Idleness" is in fact composed of a set of injunctions regarding the exemplarity of productive work in the triple economy of agriculture, reproduction, and psycho-culture (see figure 1). Within this triple structure, idleness is figured as wilderness, hysteria, and fantasy requiring the farmer, husband, and author to cultivate nature's unruliness. Thus an apparently simple example requires for its interpretation, that is to say, exemplifies in its own composition, an elaborate cosmology, which it condenses into a single short essay where the preeminent figure is that of the essayist as husband and wife to his own fantasies. Incidentally, the achieved complexity in such an early essay should be enough to set aside commonplaces about the evolution of Montaigne's *Essays,* since the phallocentric imagery[5] in "Of Idleness" is at once deconstructed in the overall figure of a gendered cosmology[6] in which nature, society, and the mind are rendered to our service.

The structures and figures that I have identified in figure 1 are offered in the interest of keeping our analysis within some reasonable bounds. However, I am quite aware of the artifactual troubles of such procedures, and I have tried to deal with them elsewhere.[7]

Although Montaigne is already at work in the essay "Of Idleness," he is still unsure of his enterprise. He is, after all, surrounded by examples of potentially more productive activities. He does not set himself above the farmer, the soldier, and the politician, whose work he sees around him. Nor does he set himself above his family or the work of his father managing his estate and the education of his children. Above all, he respects the life-giving birth and nurturance in woman and in nature, where each are husbanded according to their way. By the same token, he believes that nothing is productive, that is, creative and orderly, without

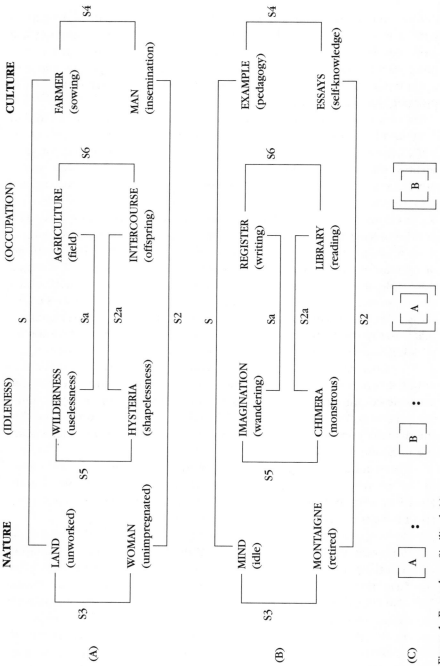

Figure 1. Example as Similitude(s)

human effort guided by the appropriate institutions of the family, farming, religion, and the state. He finds this wisdom in the great literature of the past, which, if itself properly used, also contributes to the fecundity and orderliness of civil life (see figure 2).

Montaigne, therefore, begins the *Essays* preoccupied with the task of setting them in the right furrow, so to speak. Yet he is simultaneously aware that, inasmuch as he has set to work upon himself, the example of the farmer is overdrawn; his imagination hardly lies before him and is not under his hand like a field of weeds beneath the farmer's plow. Similarly, the figure of the hysterical troubles believed to attend a woman's body until she conceives and gives birth (despite our differences with what it owes to Aristotle's view of reproduction) is applied by Montaigne to himself at the point where he finds himself struggling to conceive the essay form through which his labor as a writer will take hold of his otherwise wandering imagination. Thus no figure is any lower than the other; weeds, hysteria, and chimera all affect Montaigne as a writer in the early stages of his creative task. The writer, therefore, is not above the difference between nature and culture, nor that of man and woman. Rather, he is haunted by the figures of creation, order, and disorder; of procreation, waste, and monstrosity; and of the well-wrought, the felicitous and harmonious expression which composes our arts and crafts.

Montaigne's use of agricultural imagery in the formulation of his ideas on the work of the artist has been given considerable attention by Carol Clark, in particular, on the question of the respective contributions of nature and nurture to a good outcome.[8] She remarks that Montaigne does not adopt any fierce imagery of uprooting weeds or bad habits. Yet, while she sees the sexual pun carried over from the imagery of seeding the land to seeding women, she can make nothing of Montaigne's borrowing from Plutarch's *Conjugalia Praecepta* the strange idea that without intercourse women produce only shapeless lumps. She assigns it to "the kind of fascinated disgust inspired in the average uninformed male by the reproductive process."[9] But this will not do, partly because Montaigne is himself a prime commentator on the oddity of man's disparagement of all bodily functions and, for the rest, because what is involved is the historical availability of knowledge about conception, ovulation, and reproduction generally. Here Montaigne could not be ahead of the knowledge of his day, and this is the predicament of both men and women.[10]

At this point it may be useful to give the full context of the remark from Plutarch which Montaigne characteristically compresses, but thereby loses the gender balance on which the text turns:

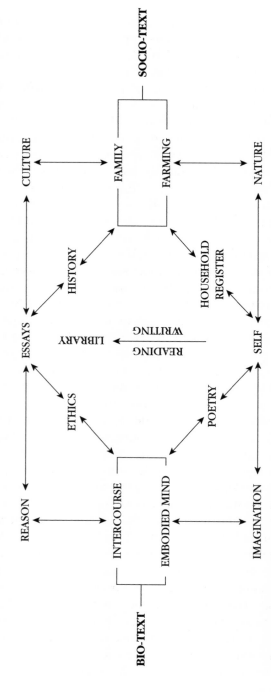

Figure 2. Example as Grammatology

> It is said that no woman ever produced a child without the co-operation of man, yet there are mis-shapen, fleshlike uterine growths originating in some infection, which develop of themselves and acquire firmness and solidity, and are commonly called "moles." Great care must be taken that this sort of thing does not take place in women's minds. For if they do not receive the seed of good doctrines and share with their husbands in intellectual advancement, they, left to themselves, conceive many untoward ideas and low designs and emotions.[11]

Plutarch is advising young husbands that a sexist attitude between men and women reduces the balance of their marriage, which is rather enhanced by the intellectual and moral cultivation of one another. And this is Montaigne's own view, as we know from the *Essays*.

I am trying to avoid—but who does not see that I shall fail?—an effect of tipping the complex structure of the example before us by reading it from any particular bias that can easily be given it, if we extract the writer from the structure to which he has in fact subordinated himself. To this end, I shall insist upon the *grammatological* structure, of the text and context, of the essay "Of Idleness." I am therefore defending it against a potentially anachronistic reading in terms of its perceived phallocentrism. The latter, I believe, would violate the engenderment of the essay by focusing upon its sexual imagery of impregnation, the reduction of woman to nature and of both to the rule of the plow and the phallus. The current fashionableness of such a reading requires, however, that it be unthought in its composition so that, as in the present example, Montaigne would have *unconsciously* assimilated himself, as though his imagination were seized by a chimera, to the figure of a "hysterical woman" in need of the pen as phallus to bring forth a culture child, namely, the essay "Of Idleness."

Montaigne is not biblical about weeds and women[12] any more than he is about hetero- or homosexuality. Rather, he considered sexuality, whether within or without marriage, to be better in friendship, more satisfied in its mirror of give-and-take than in the selfishness of either sex. Montaigne, then, is not the apostle of rigidity. Indeed, it is precisely the rigidity of the exemplary figure that repels him as, for example, with Cato. He rather prefers the chink in the armor—loving Socrates so much the more for the pleasure he took in scratching himself when released from his chains. At other times, Montaigne sets himself up as an antiexample of impotence and irresoluteness, a figure of self-indulgence unworthy of anyone's attention. Yet the *Essays* stand as a monumental resolution of such confessions of inconstancy.

Montaigne speaks of having begun the *Essays* as an act of infidelity, betraying his own otherwise changeable and melancholic nature. For this reason, the essay "Of Idleness" is particularly challenging. In it we see that Montaigne cannot separate idleness from work. Rather, he wants from the very beginning to bridle himself, to bring his imagination to order, to make his mind ashamed of itself for spawning nothing but shapes that violate their proper form. Yet he did not marry himself to the exemplum. The *Essays* do not record a secondhand morality. They far exceed any such pedagogy and are themselves misunderstood as an anthology to be picked from here and there by beautiful souls. The *Essays* are not a book of hours. They cannot be read idly but demand a productive reader (*un lecteur suffisant*), ready to respond to the intricacies of their composition. For such reasons, then, we think the essay "Of Idleness" subordinates the restricted economy of its sexual figures to the general economy of love, whose figures are family, marriage, and friendship. Thus, like his father who tended his estate and looked after his children, Montaigne sets about registering his thoughts, to produce a book whose pedagogy and politics are contributions to the reproduction of civil society and to the endurance of the body politic. Above all, he sets every relationship within a communicative ethic where nothing is enjoyed without restoration and reciprocity. Here, then, the figures of love, friendship, and the essay itself are inscriptions of the embodied self whose surrounding sociotext is inscribed within marriage, agriculture, politics, and the arts and sciences—in a general economy or grammatology,[13] as represented in figure 2.

I shall conclude with a further schematization of the essay "Of Idleness" (see figure 3) in order to reveal in it a characteristic movement of wandering and return, which, like the rest of his travels, always brought Montaigne back "with a fresh love for my family and . . . a sweeter enjoyment of my home."[14] "Of Idleness" opens with an eccentric movement surveying the wilderness, the cultivated farm, woman before and after childbirth, the unbridled imagination's monsters and chimeras, Montaigne's busy life and travels before his retirement, and the turmoil of his imagination when idle. As he moves through these spatial and temporal alternations, the quest for an exemplary fixed point becomes more urgent. Just as the land needs to be settled by the farmer and his family, so Montaigne needs to settle on his estate, within his own family and within the *Essays,* marrying himself to himself in the mirror of his own parental love, as well as in the mirror of his friendship with La Boetie (a topic we cannot develop here).[15] The movement from remote and exotic condi-

(A) Just as . . . fallow land . . . teems with . . . useless weeds, . . . and as we see that women, all alone, produce mere shapeless masses . . . so it is with minds

(B)   Virgil, *Aenid*, 8. 22-26

(A) And there is no mad or idle fancy that they do not bring forth . . .
                                                     Horace, *Ars Poetica*, 7

(B) He who dwells *everywhere*, Maximus, *nowhere* dwells

                                                     Martial, *Epigrams*, 7. 73

(A) . . . when I retired to my home . . . it seemed to me . . . my mind . . . in full idleness . . . [would] stay and settle in itself. . . . But I find—

                                                     Lucan, *Pharsalia*, 4. 704

that, on the contrary, like a running horse . . . (my mind) gives birth to so many chimeras . . . that . . . I have begun to put them in writing, hoping in time to make my mind ashamed of itself.

Figure 3. Example as Narrative and Deconstruction

tions to familiar and local arrangements, repeated in the mind's quest for self-identity, similarly shifting from errant places to the attachment of home, is nicely balanced in Montaigne's choice of Martial's epithet: "He who dwells everywhere, Maximus, nowhere dwells."

It turns out, then, that Montaigne's idleness is the product of a lively balance or a dance of thought in which reflection and imagination avoid overtipping the scale upon which Montaigne has set himself.

> We are great fools. "He has spent his life in idleness," we say; "I have done nothing today." What, have you not lived? This is not only the fundamental but the most illustrious of your occupations.[16]

The essayist's retirement is not to be spent hoarding his memories nor in squandering his days in idle fancies. He is resolved to test his own mettle. To do so, Montaigne discovers that he must become a writer, to cultivate a field in which he can manage the family of his thoughts and feelings, not as a figure outside of them, but as father, mother, child of himself in those last days of his life. The *Essays* are Montaigne's "home." In them, he is *chez lui*. He had learned as a journeyman never to be very far away from himself, and so, when the time came to compose himself, he needed no extraordinary system of faith nor any practice beyond the daily care of the *Essays*.

Appendix

The English version of Montaigne's "Of Idleness" is reproduced from The Complete Essays of Montaigne, *trans. Donald M. Frame (Stanford, Calif.: Stanford University Press, 1965), 20–21; the French version, "De l'oisiveté," is reproduced from Montaigne,* Oeuvres complètes, *ed. Albert Thibaudet and Maurice Rat (Paris: Gallimard, 1962), 33–34.*

OF IDLENESS

Just as we see that fallow land, if rich and fertile, teems with a hundred thousand kinds of wild and useless weeds, and that to set it to work we must subject it and sow it with certain seeds for our service; and as we see that women, all alone, produce mere shapeless masses and lumps of flesh, but that to create a good and natural offspring they must be made fertile with a different kind of seed; so it is with minds. Unless you keep them busy with some definite subject that will bridle and control them, they throw themselves in disorder hither and yon in the vague field of imagination.

> Thus, in a brazen urn, the water's light
> Trembling reflects the sun's and moon's bright rays,
> And, darting here and there in aimless flight,
> Rises aloft, and on the ceiling plays.
>
> VIRGIL

And there is no mad or idle fancy that they do not bring forth in this agitation:

> Like a sick man's dreams
> They form vain visions.
>
> HORACE

The soul that has no fixed goal loses itself; for as they say, to be everywhere is to be nowhere:

> He who dwells everywhere, Maximus, nowhere dwells.
>
> MARTIAL

Lately when I retired to my home, determined so far as possible to bother about nothing except spending the little life I have left in rest and seclusion, it seemed to me I could do my mind no greater favor than to let it entertain itself in full idleness and stay and settle in itself, which I hoped it might do more easily now, having become weightier and riper with time. But I find—

> Ever idle hours breed wandering thoughts
>
> LUCAN

that, on the contrary, like a runaway horse, it gives itself a hundred times more trouble than it took for others, and gives birth to so many chimeras and fantastic monsters, one after another, without order or purpose, that in order to contemplate their ineptitude and strangeness at my pleasure, I have begun to put them in writing, hoping in time to make my mind ashamed of itself.

DE L'OISIVETÉ

Comme nous voyons des terres oisives, si ellessont grasses et fertiles, foisonner en cent millesortes d'herbes sauvages et inutiles, et que pourles tenir en office, il les faut assujétir et employer àcertaines semences, pour notre service; et comme nousvoyons que les femmes produisent bien toutes seulesdes amas et pièces de chair informes, mais que pourfaire une génération bonne et naturelle, il les fautpourvoir d'une autre semence: ainsi est-il des esprits.Si on ne les occupe à certain sujet, qui les bride etcontraigne, ils se jettent sans règle par-ci par-là,dans le vague champ des imaginations . . .

. . . Et n'est folie ni reverie, qu'ils ne produisent encette agitation,

| "Comme des songes de malade, | VELUT AEGRI SOMNI, VANAE |
| ils se forgent de vaines chimères." | FINGUNTUR SPECIES. |

HORACE, *Art Poetique,* 7

L'ame qui n'a point de but établi, elle se perd; car,comme on dit, c'est n'être en aucun lieu, que d'êtrepartout . . .

. . . Dernièrement alors que je me retirais chez moi, ayant résolu que possible de ne me mêler d'autre chose que de passer en repos et à part ce peu qui me reste de vie, il me semblait de ne pouvoir faire plus grande faveur à mon esprit, que de le laisser en pleine oisiveté, s'entretenir soi-même, et s'arrêter et rasseoir en soi: ce que j'espérais qu'il pût désormais faire plus aisement, devenu avec le temps plus lourd et plus mûr. Mais je trouve,

| "L'oisiveté dissipe toujours l'esprit | VARIAM SEMPER DANT OTIA |
| en tout sens." | MENTEM. |

LUCAN, *Pharsale,* IV, 704.

que au rebours, faisant le cheval échappé, il se donne cent fois plus d'affaire à soi-meme, qu'il n'en prenait pour autrui; et m'enfante tant de chimères et monstres fantasques les uns sur les autres, sans ordre et sans propos que pour en contempler à mon aise l'ineptie et l'étrangeté, j'ai commencé de les inscrire sur un cahier, espérant avec le temps lui en faire honte à lui-même.

Notes

1. *The Exempla or Illustrative Stories from the Sermones Vulgares of Jacques de Vitry,* ed. T. F. Crane, Publications of the Folk-Lore Society, no. 26

(London: D. Nutt 1890); J. Th. Welter, *L'Exemplum dans la littérature religieuse et didactique du moyen âge* (Paris: E. H. Guittard, 1927); Caroline Walker Bynum, *Docere Verbo et Exemplo: An Aspect of Twelfth-Century Spirituality* (Missoula, Mont.: Scholars Press, 1979).

2. Frederic L. Tubach, "Exempla in the Decline," *Traditio* 18 (1962): 407-17.

3. John O'Neill, *Essaying Montaigne: A Study of the Renaissance Institution of Writing and Reading* (London: Routledge and Kegan Paul, 1982).

4. John O'Neill, "The Essay as a Moral Exercise: Montaigne," *Renaissance and Reformation* 21, no. 3 (1985): 210-18.

5. Robert D. Cottrell, *Sexuality/Textuality: A Study of the Fabric of Montaigne's* Essais (Columbus: Ohio State University Press, 1981), chapter 1, "Conception."

6. Ivan Illich, *Gender* (New York: Random House, 1982); John O'Neill, *Five Bodies: The Human Shape of Modern Society* (Ithaca, N.Y.: Cornell University Press, 1985).

7. John O'Neill, "The Literary Production of Natural and Social Science Inquiry," *Canadian Journal of Sociology* 6, no. 2 (Spring 1981): 105-20; "A Realist Model of Knowledge: With a Phenomenological Deconstruction of its Model of Man," *Philosophy of the Social Sciences* 16, no. 1 (March 1986): 1-19.

8. Carol Clark, *The Web of Metaphor: Studies in the Imagery of Montaigne:* Essais (Lexington, Ky.: French Forum, 1978). See pp. 58-62 and 123-29 for comments on "On Idleness."

9. Ibid., 126.

10. Thomas Lacqueur, "Orgasm, Generation, and the Politics of Reproductive Biology," *Representations* 14 (Spring 1986): 1-41.

11. Plutarch, *Conjugalia praecepta,* 145D-E, in *Plutarch Moralia,* 16 vols., with an English translation by Frank Cole Babbitt (London: Heinemann, 1928), 2:339-40.

12. Susan Suleiman, "Le recit exemplaire: Parabole, fable, roman et these," *Poetique* 32 (November 1977): 468-89.

13. I have in mind not so much Derridean grammatology, as in Gregory Ulmer, *Applied Grammatology: Post(e)-Pedagogy from Jacques Derrida to Joseph Beuys* (Baltimore: Johns Hopkins University Press, 1985), as that of Gilles Deleuze and Félix Guattari, *Anti-Oedipus: Capitalism and Schizophrenia,* trans. Robert Hurley, Mark Seem, and Helen R. Lane (New York: Viking, 1977).

14. Michel de Montaigne, "Of Vanity," in *The Complete Essays of Montaigne,* trans. Donald M. Frame (Stanford, Calif.: Stanford University Press, 1965), 745.

15. O'Neill, *Essaying Montaigne,* 154-62.

16. Montaigne, "Of Experience," in *The Complete Essays of Montaigne,* 850.

Engendering Aesthetics

Sublimity, Sublimation, and Misogyny in Burke and Kant

Timothy Gould

My title points in two directions: first, toward the problem of how and why aesthetics came to be generated, or engendered, around the middle of the eighteenth century; and second, toward the problem of gender or of becoming gendered.[1] My title also points to the persistent, often nearly obsessive, presence of ideas or fantasies of gender and, indeed, of sexuality in some of the principal texts of eighteenth-century aesthetics. I will be discussing some texts of Burke and Kant, but I do not think it is implausible to suggest that there are connections between these two problems in a far wider range of texts.[2] Since in some circles, punning has become a fashionable way to explore a topic, I should say immediately that I take the fact that the word "engendering" contains the word "gender" to be considerably more than a pun but considerably less than self-explanatory. We are inclined to forget, it seems to me, that our use of "gender" to mean "male" or "female" is quite recent. Indeed, for some people, the word has still not lost the sense of grammatical gender from which it was, presumably, borrowed. Moreover, until well into the nineteenth century, to say that something had been "gendered" was apparently a common way of saying that the thing had been *engendered*—that is, produced, created, or even begotten.[3]

One aim of this essay is to insist that both of these directions of engendering contain problems or puzzles worth investigating. We ought to see a problem about why and how aesthetics gets going. And we ought to see a problem in the fact that some of the crucial discourses of eighteenth-century aesthetics seem so especially disfigured by its stereotypes and fantasies of gender and sexuality. A second aim is to suggest that there are some connections between these two problems or at least between the two directions of investigation that the problems entail. I am far more tentative about this second aim, and I do not mean to suggest that the two investigations will finally coincide. Certainly, I do not think that the two investigations ought to coincide at their inception. For instance, I do not find it useful to suppose that some of the central aesthetic discourses of the eighteenth century came into existence simply *in order to* reinforce or to exacerbate the eighteenth-century system of gender classifications and stereotypes.[4] Yet I remain convinced that it is worth maintaining some contact and points of exchange between the two lines of investigation, even if the particular investigations themselves end up in quite separate places.[5] This essay should at least put the reader in a better position to assess the validity of this conviction.

I will begin by looking at some passages from Burke in the hopes of getting out in the open some of the more crudely ideological stakes in the issues of gender. I will then turn to Kant, who is certainly no less capable of crudity than Burke but whose critical and transcendental turns will force us to refine at least some of our formulations. In the middle sections of this essay, I will take a more extended look at a somewhat neglected article of Kant's, "Conjectural Beginnings of Human History." A central moment of this essay is an account of the origin of the taste for beauty in a "refusal" which is presented as a kind of sublimation. I will further suggest that Kant implicitly characterizes this moment of originary sublimation as a moment of sublimity.[6] In what I think of as a transcendental allegory, Kant shows us that there is no reason at the beginning of human culture for any difference between the sexes in the capacity either for the sublime or for sublimation. Here the very symmetry between the sexes in their initial engendering of a sense of beauty underscores all the more painfully the ultimate curtailing of this symmetry in Kant's remarks about the actual, empirical women in his society.

Throughout this essay, I am implicitly suggesting a contrast between the rising political or public confidence of eighteenth-century bourgeois thought and the more private—but no less political—crises of representation and philosophical methodology which I take the engendering of aesthetics to signal and to participate in.[7] Because of this contrast (and for other reasons less specific to the eighteenth century), I am inclined to insist that the problems of philosophical aesthetics be posed, at least initially, in philosophical terms. Even where the goal is to uncover certain mechanisms of philosophical defense or defensiveness, I have tried to suggest that these mechanisms cannot be understood apart from working through the philosophical methodologies that deploy and encompass these mechanisms.

I will begin by saying a word or two about the *kind* of problems posed by the "engendering" of aesthetics in the two senses just mentioned. Philosophers have been writing about art at least since Plato, and Plato himself was moved to characterize a "quarrel" between poetry and philosophy that was already "ancient" in his time.[8] It is becoming increasingly clear that Western philosophy has an equally inveterate tendency to repudiate passivity, or at least to strive for accounts in which the active and the passive powers of the mind are sharply distinguished from each other.[9] I take it that this repudiation of passivity is related to the philosophical and theoretical tendencies to shun the ordinary and the familiar and, at the same time, related to various masculine repudiations of the feminine and of women.

So a series of questions may emerge, which might seem to challenge the premises of this essay. What is so different about *these* philosophical discourses about beauty and the arts, beginning roughly with Shaftesbury and continuing throughout the eighteenth century? Do they really deserve to be thought of as constituting a new and to some extent independent field—with the name "aesthetics" as the seal of its newness and independence? And if we grant that there are indeed some important differences, however hard they are to characterize with any precision, then another question might emerge. Is the presence in this new field of aesthetics of gender stereotyping and fantasy really so distinct from the general level and the particular shapes of male ideology and fantasy in Western philosophy? And finally, even granted that we can make out the significant differences in these texts, why should we care? Or to puncture this rhetorical "we," however slightly: why should a woman or a feminist or a historical materialist or a historian of philosophy or a critic of the arts care about this odd proximity of gender fantasy to the engendering of eighteenth-century aesthetics?

There is not enough room in an essay to answer such questions. But at least I can say something about why the answers would, on my account, be worth having. We can note a couple of things about the first question. Independently of the terms proposed in this essay, we could characterize some of the key differences of eighteenth-century aesthetics as the rise to prominence of a new vocabulary of perception and a tendency to give priority to the questions of natural beauty over the questions of art.[10] Along with this vocabulary of perception, there went a concern—not to say an obsession—with the "ideas" that, following Locke and Descartes, were characterized as constituting perception and the experiences that could be analogized to actual perception. This concern or obsession is clearly linked with at least one other important critical concern of eighteenth-century aesthetics, namely, the concern with origins and with the "original" of our ideas. But there is no historical account that I know of that captures my sense of the tremendous rupturing of philosophy for which Kant's third *Critique* is at once the best sign and the most radical representative.

I regard the genesis of aesthetics in the eighteenth century as a radical shift not only in the ways in which philosophers address the arts and the experiences of natural beauty. I regard it equally as a shift in the way in which philosophers thought about philosophy and its unstable connections to history and culture. Indeed, I think it was potentially a shift in the ways philosophers *ought* to think about philosophy and its various cultural ties. But this casts the field of aesthetics as a sort of threat to philosophy's self-conceptions, a threat that had to be—and perhaps still has to be—contended with and, wherever possible, contained. I should also make it explicit that the various efforts to give the genealogy of aesthetics from which I have learned the most—Marxist, psychoanalytic, and Nietzschean—seem to me in general to pay too little attention to the radical destabilizing tendencies of aesthetics itself within the evolving economy of eighteenth-century philosophy.[11]

Having presented at least some of my sense of the dimensions of the problems concerning why and how aesthetics got going, or changed directions, in the course of the eighteenth century, I should make it clear that I am not going to say much in answer to the question of *why*. If I am granted the possibility that the flourishing of philosophical aesthetics has something to do with a crisis *within* philosophy, then I have no objection to the idea that both the flourishing and the crisis have something to do with the prevailing European social conditions and political upheavals. In a sense, I will be insisting on this connection of philosophical discourse to social conditions. But I am also insisting that we do not have adequate terms for depicting these connections, not at least in the kind of local detail that would be convincing to someone involved in trying to understand the philosophical texts of this period.

I take seriously the idea (which begins, I suppose, with Schiller and Hegel) that the shape of aesthetics in the eighteenth century is tied to a crisis in the representation of the human. I suggest, without trying to argue for it, that speaking of the so-called "universalist" aims of aesthetics is not an adequate way of characterizing this crisis. (This is not to deny that this characterization is invited by certain typical turns of aesthetic thought.) I suggest that the aspiration to "universality" must also be understood as containing the ambition for a human representation of human beings, one no longer sponsored by, or contrasted with, the representations of the divine.[12] That such issues of "representation" involve both the "political" and "aesthetic" senses of the word is by now almost a commonplace, if not an uncontroversial commonplace.[13] In turning now to Burke, I want to examine some moments in which interchanges between the "political" and the "aesthetic" get graphically expressed in terms of gender—or, more precisely, in terms of women.

Like other aestheticians loosely grouped together as "empiricist," Burke is interested in the "origin" of our "ideas," an interest which often translates into the questions of how we come to perceive what we perceive and how we come to represent what we represent. Burke criticizes earlier accounts of beauty that focused too exclusively on qualities of the object that can be "perceived"—either by the five senses or by some more intellectual or spiritual sense like Hutcheson's "sense of beauty" or the "sense of proportion." Burke characterizes "beauty" as the object of human love, but this characterization creates some tensions in his account. Other writers have noted his tendency to slip, both in his standpoint and in his pronouns, from a general account of the love of beauty to an account of a human (white, European) male's love of the beauty of women.[14] But this is only part of the story.

Let us look first at some passages in Burke's *Philosophical Enquiry into the Origin of Our Ideas of the Sublime and the Beautiful:*

> The passion which belongs to generation, merely as such is lust only; this is evident in brutes, whose passions are more unmixed, and which pursue their purposes more directly than ours. . . . But man, who is a creature adapted to a greater variety and intricacy of relation, connects with the general passion, the idea of some *social* qualities, which direct and heighten the appetite which he has in common with all other animals; and as he is not designed by them to live at large, it is fit that he should have something to create a preference and fix his choice; and this in general should be some sensible quality; as no other can so quickly, so powerfully, or so surely produce its effect. The object of this mixed passion which we call love, is the *beauty* of the sex. Men [!] are carried to the sex in general, as it is the sex and by the common law of nature; but they are attached to particulars by personal *beauty.* I call beauty a social quality; for where women and men, and not only they, but when other animals give us a sense of joy and pleasure in beholding them, . . . they inspire us with sentiments of tenderness and affection towards their persons.[15]

Burke characterizes beauty as the object of human love, but he is very unwilling to tolerate much connection (other than sheer concomitance) between sex and love. He is pretty clearly neither the first nor the last man to find such connections difficult to manage. But the point should not be construed as simply a matter of his personal "psychology"—at least not in the sense in which an individual's "psychology" is commonly still taken, namely, as an "inner stuff," which can be understood as independent of its social, political, and rhetorical tendencies to representation and to knowledge.

Burke, of course, is aware of the importance of beauty to sexual love: beauty "create[s] a preference," "fix[es] his choice," and "attach[es]" men to "particulars." Burke is all the more at pains to keep love and desire as sharply distinguished as he possibly can: "I likewise distinguish love, by which I mean the satisfaction which arises to the mind upon contemplating anything beautiful . . . from desire or lust; which is an energy of the mind, that hurries us on to the possession of certain objects, that do not affect us as they are beautiful, by means that are altogether different" (*PE,* 91). There is more than a little defensiveness, it seems to me, in this effort to keep love and desire so separate. And given the way in which this general account of human beauty slides over into a man's account of the beauty of women, we are not surprised to see this separation is also carried out from a male point of view.

We may, however, allow ourselves to be a bit startled, even at this late date, by the extremity of the denial that concludes his demonstration: "We shall have a strong desire for a woman of no remarkable beauty; whilst the greatest beauty in men, or in other animals, though it causes love, yet excites *nothing at all of desire.* Which shows that beauty, and the passion caused by beauty, which I call love, is different from desire, though desire may sometime operate along with it" (*PE*, 91; my emphasis). It seems to me fairly clear that this denial is the very stuff of the homoerotic panic that Eve Sedgwick has alerted us to in the infrastructures of eighteenth- and nineteenth-century English literature and society.[16] But, as in her book, the interesting questions come into focus only if we do not confine ourselves to inferring something about Burke's "psychology." Following Sedgwick, we are to look for the cognitive and politicized burden of Burke's characteristically masculine and aestheticized distress. And in this case, at least, we do not have far to look—no farther it seems to me than to some central moments in Burke's *Reflections on the Revolution in France.*[17] Compared to his earlier work on the beautiful and the sublime, the heightening and condensation of Burke's language is remarkable. In the space of a few pages, we find a masterful collage, including bits of a relatively intellectual analysis of the "barbarous philosophy" of the Rights of Man; the full-blown rhetoric of his political reaction against "the sophisters, economists, and calculators" who have helped to "extinguish . . . the glory of Europe forever," and a striking piece of chivalric romance, structured around his memory of seeing the Empress Marie Antoinette (the queen of Louis XVI) at Versailles (*RRF,* 86). It is worth trying to pick apart the peculiar combination of his measured prose and the dizzying trajectory of his intellectual and emotional flight. I single out two moments, separated only by a couple of paragraphs.

Here is Burke on his "delightful vision" of the queen of France ("then the dauphiness"), as she "lighted on this orb, which she hardly seemed to touch":

> I saw her just above the horizon, decorating and cheering the
> elevated sphere she just began to move in—glittering like the
> morning star, full of life and splendor and joy. . . . Little did I

dream . . . that she should ever be obliged to carry the sharp
antidote against disgrace concealed in that bosom, little did I
dream that I should have lived to see such disasters fallen upon
her in a nation of gallant men. . . . I thought ten thousand
swords must have leaped from their scabbards to avenge even
a look that threatened her with insult. But the age of chivalry
is gone. (*RRF,* 85–86)[18]

Burke recounts the queen's fate as a kind of tragedy, and he aestheticizes
the political tragedy as a spectacle for his own perceptions and feelings.
This process is neatly epitomized in a single, cadenced exclamation: "Oh!
what a revolution! and what a heart must I have to contemplate without
emotion that elevation and that fall!" (*RRF,* 85–86). The balance in what
is after all intended to record a kind of outburst embodies the balance he
is able to maintain among the different elements of the situation: astral
queen, terrestrial revolution, and himself as the spectator whose feelings,
at once both necessary and appropriate, serve to take the measure of
both spheres and consequently of the queen's fall from one to the other.[19]

But this cognitive and rhetorical control exacts a large price. I suppose that very few will nowadays be surprised to learn that women in
general pay the price for a man's chivalric overestimation of the woman
of his nostalgias.[20] But in Burke the payoff is very quick and very blunt.
He turns from Marie Antoinette to the general processes by which the
ideologists of the Rights of Man were undermining the "mixed system of
opinion and sentiment." Burke is quite clear that this system had its origin
in the "ancient chivalry," and he insists that it still works to "subdue . . .
the fierceness of pride and power," and that, furthermore, its "pleasing
illusions [make] power gentle and obedience liberal" (*RRF,* 86–87). Nowadays, Burke laments, the sophisters and economists and calculators have
"taken over":

All the super-added ideas, furnished from the wardrobe of a
moral imagination, which the heart owns and the understanding ratifies as necessary to cover the defects of our naked, shiv-
ering nature, and to raise it to dignity in our own estimation,
are to be exploded as a ridiculous, absurd and antiquated fashion. (*RRF,* 87)[21]

And then Burke gives us a look at one of his worst fears: "On this scheme
of things, a king is but a man, a queen is but a woman; a woman is but
an animal, and an animal not of the highest order. All homage paid to the

sex in general as such, and without distinct views, is to be regarded as romance and folly" (*RRF*, 87)[22]

That Burke omits the rhetorically and logically symmetrical thought that "a man is but an animal" testifies, it seems to me, to a good deal more than masculinist prejudice disguised by chivalry.[23] His ostensible aim throughout the book is to deprive ordinary, lower-class human beings of their natural title to the "rights of men." But now we see the double price his aesthetic chivalry is paying for its political entanglements: a momentary omission of the common animal nature of all "men" and a far from momentary inability to locate women as such within a merely human "scheme of things."

I connect these cognitive costs to both the political and the aesthetic passages we have been examining. The second sentence virtually declares that his "homage" to the "sex in general" was only rendered possible by his perceptions—his "vision"—of women in the aristocracy, women moving in an "elevated" and separate sphere. It seems as if only the existence of this sphere of women allows him the freedom—at once aesthetic, erotic, and political—to place their animality in the proper perspective. A queen, of course, provides good material for representing such celestial spheres, especially if she "hardly touches" (and presumably is hardly touched by) the earth. The message is clear enough: to acknowledge just any ordinary woman as a human being—without the representative sponsorship of his vision of the queen—is to reduce that woman to her animality.

There is another aspect to Burke's cognitive disarray at this moment, an aspect I can only touch on here. The passage seems connected to his earlier wish that aesthetics should be able to distinguish love from desire and beauty (which is the object of love) from the animal nature which is presumably the object of mere desire or lust. Burke's omission of the logically and rhetorically apt phrase that "a man is but an animal" certainly seems to be an additional piece of evidence of his resistance to the idea that male animal nature might become the object of male desire. But here again I am less interested in diagnosing Burke's particular brand of homoerotic panic than in exploring the cognitive and political burdens that he is passing along. The point is not that Burke is a reactionary because he is afraid that the success of the Rights of Man will mean that he has to marry his shoemaker. The point is rather that it requires a considerable amount of cognitive (perhaps even philosophical) labor to keep the categories "common human nature" and "human animal nature" from blurring into each other. And this labor can never be entirely distinct from the other effort of Burke's nostalgia, the effort to keep love and desire from contaminating each other. The brunt of both of these labors will be borne by women.

Politically, the burden will be borne by all women. Whether she is a queen or a commoner, every woman and her interests will be represented, politically and otherwise, by men. But the aesthetic/cognitive burden will be more specifically borne by aristocratic women and by Marie Antoinette in particular. Her animality is rendered invisible (or, at any rate, tolerable) by social distance, and her beauty (or rather her "splendor" and her "glittering") can therefore serve to guarantee the distinctness of the objects of love (which she epitomizes) from the objects of mere desire. But Burke's aesthetic-political economy is so structured that this distinctness serves in turn to demonstrate that love and desire can be kept distinct, at least in certain sorts of political representations or scenarios. I think it is not too much to conclude that in guaranteeing the difference between love and desire, such women, staged like Marie Antoinette in analogous scenarios, are at the same underwriting the difference between the appropriate and inappropriate objects of male desire. In Burke's scheme of things, the existence of women in those "elevated spheres" turns out to be a kind of cognitive security not only for the difference between men and their animal nature but finally, if circuitously, for the difference between men and women.

Admittedly, men of less political and aesthetic intensity find it relatively less complicated to saddle women with political and epistemological responsibility for our sexual differences. Male hysteria comes in more shapes than one, and likewise its correlated sublimations. But Burke's hysteria is potentially instructive exactly because of its explicit detours through the aesthetic/erotic problem of representing a human being as a human being. And Burke's aesthetics of nostalgia and uncontaminated representation is politically significant not primarily because it demonstrates the dangers of political reaction (to one's mental health as well as to the well-being of others). But in studying Burke's insistence that we acknowledge our inherently different and unequal human natures, we can learn something more of the threat contained in the opposite, more progressive assertion of a common human nature. For it is this nature that eighteenth-century philosophy—and Kant in particular—was learning to represent as possessing a common human dignity.

Burke was quite right, I think, in predicting that the practical politics of asserting a common human dignity (in particular, the politics of the French Revolution) would mean the end of the elevated spheres and orbit of human existence—at least the ones that were constituted and defended by the ancien régime. And we can see in the proximity of Burke's aesthetics of desire to his politics of gender that something more than privilege is being threatened by this "revolution." Within the political and the aesthetic efforts to represent the human as human, there is a cognitive threat to male desire, which is not clearly distinguishable from the political threat to male privilege. And if these crises in philosophical aesthetics and in traditional societies contained possibilities for a step forward in the histories of human beings, Burke's work makes clear that they contained more than one possibility of a step back. And as is often the case, women of all classes were far more likely to become the targets of the reaction then they were the beneficiaries of the progress.

In thinking about Burke, it is easy to feel both the inevitability of the category of sublimation and its inadequacy. I have mostly avoided the word in the hopes of keeping open the question of how much of the "subliming" is performed, so to speak, by the social structure itself and how much of the "subliming" is produced by the workings of Burke's text. In turning from Burke to Kant, I am more inclined to use the word "sublimation," but still suspicious of the way in which the use of the word seems to reduce our analytic options. In any event, my path to the topics of gender and sexuality is now routed explicitly through the sublime.[24] (I note in passing that we might have considered Burke's portrait of Marie Antoinette to be an example of the sublime of nostalgia. But Burke, so far as I know, never submitted his political writing to his own analysis of the beautiful and the sublime. I should make it clear that I regard this as a philosophical shortcoming.)

I think it is reasonable to suggest that the fullest flowering of eighteenth-century aesthetics comes about only when the idea of the sublime acquires a certain position in relation to the idea and the experience of beauty. Philosophers have tended to be interested in the sublime either as a second cousin to the beautiful or else in certain insights into the workings of literature, or else in the sexist use to which this category has been put. It is by now well known that some eighteenth-century writers—Kant is notorious among them—assign the attribute of the sublime to the male and the attribute of the beautiful to the female. It is also fairly common for male thinkers to severely attenuate—but not quite to eliminate—the feminine capacity to experience the sublime, or at least to get the full moral and cultural benefits from the experience.[25]

The power of such gender assignments is not to be underestimated, either in the way they helped (and go on helping) to restrict the possibility of women's roles in society or in the way they helped to organize perceptions of women, or, finally, in the way they help to organize texts as they are translated into perceptions and perceptions as they turn into texts. There is a great deal to be studied here. My guiding intuition is that we ought to study not just why the category of beauty was assigned to women in the restrictive way that it was; we ought also to study a slightly different question: why was the category of the sublime *withheld* from women?

The difference between these two questions—why beauty was assigned to women and why sublimity was withheld from them—may seem too slight to matter. But I think the formulations point to different sorts of investigations. In particular, if we take Kant seriously on the question of the sublime, then there are a number of features that warrant our attention in connection with these questions of gender. First, Kant says, for instance, that "true sublimity must be sought in the mind of the [subject] judging, not in the natural object the judgment upon which occasions this state" (*CJ*, 95). Second, he says further that "the sublime is that, the mere ability to think which shows a capacity [faculty] of the mind surpassing every standard of sense" (*CJ*, 89). So, on the one hand, I suggest that to withhold, or at least to severely curtail, the capacity to experience the sublime from women's subjectivity is akin to curtailing their power to confirm the superiority of their reason to sense.[26] This curtailing is of a piece with Kant's infamous declaration that the philosophy of women is "not to reason but to sense."[27] This does not quite withhold reason from women altogether, but it leaves their reason more subordinate to their senses. This depicts them as lacking the capacity to confirm in an experience the superiority of their reason, and so leaves them deeper in the state of immaturity (*unmundigkeit*) onto which he projected a feminine reluctance to take the step into maturity and autonomy.

Turning back from the question of women's capacity to experience the sublime to the denial that women are in general capable of "occasioning" feelings of sublimity in others, we might connect this denial to some other aspects of sublimity. I think here especially of Kant's understanding of the sublime as an alternation between repulsion and attraction, and Burke's understanding of the sublime as constituted by the right combination of fear and safety. We might well begin to wonder whether the male relation to—and fear of—the female is one of the repressed grounding topics of the entire field of the sublime. If this could be worked out, then we might see that the motives for denying female sublimity and also the female capacity for experiencing the sublime would be a kind of after-repression. On my account, this after-repression would have become necessary *within* philosophy because of the intensified threats of destabilization emanating from the placement of the experience of the sublime so close to the center of aesthetic discourse.

All this is admittedly speculative. Compared with my sense of what Burke is up to, I am far less certain that I know what to make of the peculiarity (and commonplaceness) of Kant's early reflections on the gender of the sublime and the beautiful. I do not know how far to push the possibility that the sublime and the aesthetics of the sublime were (and perhaps are?) structured as an experience of a denial—for instance, as a denial by reason of the adequacy of the senses to imagine certain totalities. One problem might be put like this: the structure of the sublime in a scene of denial is in some respects characteristically male. But in other respects the philosophers of the sublime are uncharacteristically tolerant—for men and for philosophers—of the confusions in our experience of the sublime between active and passive and between subject and object.[28] Rather than try to solve this problem, I want to take up a point at which Kant allegorically represents the genders as symmetrical with respect to the origin of the sense of beauty and, I believe, with respect to the capacity for the sublime. If, as I said at the beginning, this makes more acute our sense of Kant's shortcomings in his representations of actual women in society, it should also make more problematic the questions we might ask about the gender fantasies of aesthetics.

Let us take a brief look at Kant's essay "Conjectural Beginnings of Human History."[29] This short piece contains not only a discussion of Rousseau but an obvious effort to imitate Rousseau's *Discourse on the Origin of Inequality.* Moreover, Kant shapes his little story of human beginnings and the beginning of the human into a retelling of the most famous account of our beginnings—the book of Genesis. One might have expected that Kant's conjunction of Rousseau and Genesis, of culture and nature, and of the temptation and the expulsion from the Garden of Eden would be an invitation to a great deal of trouble about gender and sex. The funny thing is that while there are plenty of sexist pronouns, Kant never quite drops the other shoe.

Centrally, for instance, he eliminates the bit about Eve as the passive agent of temptation by the serpent—the moment, as the old poster put it, where Eve got framed. Kant's account differentiates the sexes explicitly only after the Fall. So, after the Fall, man sees the troubles and ever-increasing hardships of labor, while woman "foresaw the troubles to which nature had subjected her sex, and those additional ones to which man, a being stronger than she, would subject her" ("CB," 58) This is, of course, a secular rewriting of the moment in Genesis where female suffering in giving birth is ascribed to God's punishment for Eve's being tempted by the serpent, and where female subservience to men is characterized as God's command. In attributing female suffering and political subservience to nature and to natural weakness rather than to God and his peculiar sense of justice, Kant can be seen as taking a small step forward.

But my point is not to compensate for the sexism of Kant's *Observations* (which certainly persisted in other, later texts). Nor am I primarily concerned to paint a more balanced picture of Kant—sexist here, but maybe a little liberated at moments over there. My point is rather that Kant is committed to finding a symmetry in the sexes, at least with regard to the origin of the human power to choose as the human power to think. And Kant goes on to construe the power of denial as the power to think against instinct, past the surfaces of things. (These surfaces of desire are nicely allegorized by Kant as "perhaps the external appearance of fruit, which tempted him because of its similarity to tasty fruits of which he may have already partaken" ["CB," 56].)

> *Refusal* was the feat which brought about the passage from the merely sensual to spiritual attractions [*von bloss empfundenem zu idealischen Reizen*], from mere animal desire gradually to love, and . . . from the feeling of the merely agreeable to a taste for beauty, at first only the beauty in man but at length for beauty in nature as well. ("CB," 57)

You do not have to buy the whole Kantian story about reason in order to appreciate the force of this retelling of the myth by which human beings left their "first dwelling place" and embarked on the transition to the human estate. This is for Kant the estate of freedom and the first step toward a human history, as opposed to the history of God's dealings with his favored animals. And you do not have to think that the steps by which the human raised itself above its community with the animals were also the steps by which the human began to recognize other humans as ends in themselves. Much less does this recognition of equality with all rational creatures mean that women are in fact going to be getting their share, so to speak, of this equality.

And yet it seems to me worth paying attention to the fact that Kant's account of the development of reason over instinct is in principle symmetrical, exactly at a place in our culture (namely, the book of Genesis) where the asymmetry is about as glaring as it ever gets. And this circumstance encourages me to suggest that although the sublime is never actually mentioned by name, Kant is locating our capacity for the sublime exactly in this human power of refusal—the refusal of the immediacy of sense in favor of mediation of reason and imagination. Hence, in this account at least, the capacity for the sublime is also symmetrical in the two sexes. The sublime would be the capacity to receive from nature the impression that confirms our power to refuse. Kant also describes this power, with reasonable explicitness, as the power of "rendering inclination more inward" ("CB," 57). This locates the capacity for the sublime in a territory which faces equally toward repression and toward sublimation. And it is worth noting that this capacity for sublimity and inwardness and refusal is depicted by Kant as itself something sublime, worthy of our respect and awe.

The other particular symmetry I want to single out is the origin of the taste of beauty in the sexual attractiveness of the human being. It is this attractiveness which is the principal feature of the human animal that is rendered inward by our act of refusal. This symmetry is all but explicit. Kant is in fact presenting us with a genealogy of beauty, if not quite a genealogy of aesthetics. This is underscored by his use of the word *angenehm*—in the passage quoted above—as the contrast to the beautiful. This is the same contrast that structures the "Analytic of the Beautiful" in the *Critique of Judgment*.[30] At this stage of our investigations, we need to leave open the question of how far Kant's critical aesthetics can be taken to acknowledge this structure of sublimation/repression at the origin of our sense of beauty and how far it must be taken as a defense against the need for this acknowledgment.

Here is still another reason why eighteenth-century aesthetics might have insisted on keeping its gender fantasies intact, if not exactly under control. For no one should imagine that a male-engendered aesthetics even partially or covertly aware of its basis in sublimation or what Kant called "refusal" is likely to be tolerant of a women's capacities for sublimation—any more than it is likely to tolerate a woman's capacities for the sublime. If we require more testimony, we have the case of Nietzsche, who harped on aestheticians' bad faith about their sexuality but could scarcely even see the sublimity achieved by George Eliot, much less see its connection to his own projects.[31]

Instead of a conclusion, I wish to specify my sense of a limitation in this essay. I have omitted much of the philosophical work involved in posing the issues of aesthetics in what I think of as philosophically convincing terms. In particular, it seems to me that the issue of how to understand the eighteenth-century conception of the so-called universal and timeless aspects of aesthetic response remains philosophically unsettled — and potentially, at least, unsettling. My ultimate aim has been to undo at least a portion of philosophy's ignorance or its active shunning of its political and historical complicities. But we must first understand how the philosophers or the philosophical texts in question located themselves in relation to their context and their origins. We need to pay closer attention to the exact ways in which philosophers have characterized themselves, or fantasized themselves, as above history, beyond culture, and indifferent to sexual difference. A politically motivated criticism may well imagine, after Nietzsche, Marx, and Freud, that it knows more of philosophy's origins and complicities than philosophers do. But it would be unwise to conclude from this that we are in a position to know more of philosophy's complicities than philosophy has repressed or otherwise excluded from its domain of study. For those who are conscious only of what philosophy has repressed and who remain unaware of the mechanisms and methodologies by which philosophy has accomplished its repressions are likely to find themselves subjected to the very mechanisms they claim to be repudiating.

It has lately become fashionable to deny that either human beings or the products of their various arts possess the autonomy that was once, supposedly, claimed for them. No doubt the hugely defensive and ideological myths of autonomy deserve this demystifying response. But I would like to suggest that we do not require so total a demystification of autonomy nor so complete a reduction of the pretensions to universality. We are actually in a better position to understand the prevalence of gender fantasies in eighteenth-century aesthetics if we understand them as an unacceptably high price for what remains a step forward in the history of human thought.

One may, of course, still choose to deny that the human can ever be thought of, so to speak, as human, that there is anything there of value or held in common to be communicated or imparted — big words in Kant's aesthetics — or, for that matter, to be valued or evaluated. That position cannot, however, be supported solely by the history or the genealogy of aesthetics that it purports to tell. Those questions will not be decided by history or by the currently existing genealogies, at least not the ones I know of. In that sense, the engendering of aesthetics will require a reengendering of it. At the very least, it will require an elaboration of our perception of the beauties that we figure and disfigure, and of the impoverishment of our interest in the sublime and the meagerness of our sublimations.

Notes

1.   I want to thank Naomi Scheman for some early conversations about the impact of feminism on the formulation of philosophical issues and for my use of the word "engendering," which I borrow from the title of her essay "Engendering Skepticism." I do not know if the essay has been published. Thanks also to Carolyn Korsmayer for detailed comments on an earlier draft; to Nancy Kelly and Eve Sedgwick for some useful questions; and to Josh Wilner and Kathleen Whalen for each producing, among other encouragements, a set of notes and queries.

2.   Hutcheson would be a good test case for the earlier decades of the century, and Schiller, perhaps, for the later decades. Schiller's political drama and his overtly political *Letters on the Aesthetic Education of the Human* would make for an interesting comparison with Burke. Hume's own involvement with aesthetics—as opposed to "letters," literature, and history—is far less sustained than the ubiquity of his essay "Of the Standard of Taste" in contemporary Anglo-American aesthetics would lead one to believe. Locating the issues of this essay in Hume is correspondingly more difficult, though not less interesting.

3.   See the *Oxford English Dictionary,* s.v. "gender" and "engendering." The circumstance that the play on gender/engender is not sheerly or even primarily a pun I take to be evidence by the history of the words. They share a common root in "genus," and hence an even older root in the Greek "gen," as in "genesis" or becoming. This points to the usage I just mentioned, where to gender something is to produce it or to beget it. Indeed, by an interesting twist of history, the verb "gender" only lost its connotation of sexual intercourse sometime in the seventeenth century. And up until the last decade or so, the noun "gender" was used to refer to sex (i.e., to being male or female) only "jocularly," as the *OED* puts it. So under one set of pressures of politics and history, the verb lost its sexual ring and came to refer only to sexually indifferent manner of "begetting"—like the word "creativity" itself.

4.   This is the point at which my investigation touches closely on issues in current Marxism (and, I hope, in Marx). We must guard against assuming that an analysis which is appropriate to the aesthetic ideologies of the end of the nineteenth and in the early twentieth centuries is equally appropriate to the aesthetic methodologies and conclusions that were engendered in the eighteenth century.

5.   These points of contact between gender and aesthetics suggest lines of thought other than the ones I have explored. I have omitted almost entirely the significance of the connections between the topics of aesthetics and the line of thought which studies labor and productivity, especially the labor and productivity that goes into the production of the various arts. For instance, it is well known that the eighteenth century consolidated a ten-

dency to group the fine arts under a single head, which Kristeller characterized as "the system of the arts." But this suggests the possibility that various
forms of human labor—not just the ones called artistic—are being seen for
the first time as comparable, even if the comparison ends up as derogatory.
Ever on the alert for the most important trends to resist, Burke is as sharp on
the question of the incomparability of labor as he is on the questions of
gender: "The occupation of a hairdresser or of a working tallow-chandler
cannot be a matter of honor to anyone—to say nothing of a number of other
more servile employments" (Edmund Burke, *Reflections on the Revolution
in France,* ed. Thomas Mahoney [New York: Bobbs-Merrill, 1955], 56; hereafter abbreviated *RRF* and cited parenthetically in the text).

6. Kant can thus be seen as anticipating at least a portion of Nietzsche's criticism of aesthetics. See the third essay of the *Genealogy of Morals:*
"What Do Ascetic Ideals Signify?" Heidegger has already undermined the per-
tinence to Kant's text (as opposed, perhaps, to Kant's influence) of Nietzsche's criticism of Kant's insistence on the disinterestedness of our satisfaction in the beautiful. Cf. *Nietzsche,* vol. 1, trans. David Krell (San Francisco:
Harper and Row, 1979), § 15, pp. 107–14. But this is the topic of another
essay.

7. Choosing to study the reactions of a genuine conservative like
Burke is one way in which I reflect on the complexities of the relations
among philosophy, its class setting, and its ideological uses.

8. Plato, *Republic,* book 10. It is difficult to figure out to which philosophers and poets Plato was referring. Perhaps one should think more in
terms of the "archaic" quality of this quarrel, a quarrel bound up with the
very *arche* of philosophy and, consequently, with questions about the origins of philosophy. I addressed some of these questions in a lecture entitled
"Engendering Philosophy: On Passivity and Wise Passiveness in Parmenides's
Reception of the Word of the Goddess," delivered in the fall of 1987 at
Middlebury College, Amherst College, and at Kansas State University. Comments from Jim Hamilton, Stanley Bates, Andrew Parker, and Eve Sedgwick
helped precipitate the investigations contained in the present essay.

9. See my "Aftermaths of the Modern: The Exclusions of Philosophy
in Richard Rorty, Jacques Derrida, and Stanley Cavell," in *After the Future:
Postmodern Times and Places,* ed. Gary Shapiro (Albany: State University of
New York Press, 1990), 135–53. I discuss Derrida's provocative remark that
the "middle voice," in which the active and the passive are not wholly distinguishable, may be a way of characterizing the "prior" situation (or "chaos")
that philosophy had to repress in order to constitute itself as philosophy.
See Jacques Derrida, "Difference," in *Margins of Philosophy,* trans. Alan Bass
(Chicago: University of Chicago Press, 1982), 16–17.

10. These formulations do not work equally for all eighteenth-century
aestheticians and may not work at all for some authors. Hume, for instance,
borrows and criticizes some of Hutcheson's perception-related terms, but he

is far less interested in the taste for natural beauty than Kant or Burke. These comments should also not be taken to imply that the older concerns of philosophers writing about the arts somehow simply vanished with the advent of "aesthetics." Philosophers and other critics still wrote about the problems of the "imitation" of nature and of human action, about tragedy, and about the uses of poetry and painting for moral instruction.

11. A similar destabilizing role might be found for the "science" of political economy, as it rises through the hierarchy of philosophical concerns.

12. I mention, in this connection, Kant's depiction of the thought of beauty as, at the same time, an ordinary human invocation of the possibility of speaking with a "universal [*allgemeine*] voice," which cannot, however, demand agreement but can only promise it, on the condition that we learn how to separate the satisfaction in the beautiful from the blandishments of the pleasant and the lawful necessity of the good will. I would comment only that the question of "voice" demands at least as much study as the question of universality. I should add that the issues of voice need to be understood not only in the (anti-)metaphysical terms proposed by Derrida—wherein Kant is trapped in the phonocentric closure—but also in the practical-political terms, in which the human voice represents the "external" recovery of the human from its subjection to the dictates of others (whether theoretical or political). It is worth remembering that Kant introduces the idea of the "universal voice" with a discussion of the human wish to see for one's self, "to submit the object to one's own eyes" (Immanuel Kant, *Critique of Judgment*, trans. J. H. Bernard [New York: Hafner Press, 1966], 50; hereafter abbreviated *CJ* and cited parenthetically in the text). I do not know of any discussion of this passage which addresses either the political implications of this theme or the curious shift between the individual's "eyes" as the embodiment of the right to judge for one's self and the "universal voice" as the embodiment of the possibility of speaking for another.

13. Harry Redner made some useful suggestions in a talk at the University of Colorado, Boulder, in February 1988.

14. See Paul Mattick, "Gender Totemism and the Constitution of Art," a talk delivered at the 1988 meetings of the IAPL.

15. Edmund Burke, *Philosophical Enquiry into the Origin of Our Ideas of the Sublime and the Beautiful* (1759), ed. J. T. Boulton (Notre Dame, Ind.: University of Notre Dame Press, 1968), 42–43, Burke's emphasis; hereafter abbreviated *PE* and cited parenthetically in the text.

16. Eve Kosofsky Sedgwick, *Between Men: English Literature and Male Homosocial Desire* (New York: Columbia University Press, 1985). The reading that follows has equally benefited from Neil Hertz's analysis of male hysteria under political pressure. See *The End of the Line* (New York: Columbia University Press, 1985), chapter 10, passim. My debt to Hertz's book as a whole will be obvious, especially but not exclusively in my formulations of

philosophy's relation to the sublime. In fact, my debts to him go back too far in my education to be very easy to document.

17.   See note 5.

18.   I will not speculate on the imagery of the "ten thousand swords . . . leap[ing] from their scabbards," but compare Hertz, *The End of the Line,* 161–68.

19.   Burke's control extends to his quibble on the "revolution" of the spheres.

20.   Cf. Wallace Stevens, "Esthetique du Mal," stanza 10.

21.   As with some postmodern attacks on the Enlightenment, it is unclear whether Burke is attacking the thinkers of the eighteenth century for their intellectual pretensions or for their overwhelming successes in the transformation and "modernizing" of society. One should also note Burke's tendency to depict "human nature" as a woman defenseless against the ravages of the *philosophes.*

22.   A sentence later Burke writes: "The murder of a king, or a queen, or a bishop, or a father are only common homicide." If anyone doubts the hysteria (at least in the ordinary sense of the word) of this particular moment in Burke, he/she might ask why mothers are omitted from this list. I am not arguing for a yet deeper subtext of a repressed desire for matricide; I am merely suggesting that at this moment Burke is, at least rhetorically, out of control.

23.   That is, we need to think of Burke as more than a sort of Norman Podhoretz of the eighteenth century. Cf. Hertz, *The End of the Line,* 173 and 251 n. 13.

24.   Kant explicitly addresses his remarks on Burke in the sections on the sublime. I reserve a more systematic comparison for another occasion, but I note that Kant reserves his main criticism for Burke's conception of the "physiology" of our taste for both the beautiful and the sublime.

25.   Immanuel Kant, *Observations on the Feeling of the Beautiful and the Sublime,* trans. John T. Goldthwait (Berkeley: University of California Press, 1960), 78.

26.   Mary Wollstonecraft attacks the idea of the "fairness" of women on similar grounds in *A Vindication of the Rights of Women* (London: Dent and Son, 1992).

27.   Kant, *Observations,* 79.

28.   By confusion "between subject and object," I am referring most immediately to the way in which the sublime seems to be an experience of an object—or event—in nature but is actually an indirect experience and reaffirmation of the self's possession of reason.

29.   Immanuel Kant, "Conjectural Beginnings of Human History," in *On History,* trans. Lewis White Beck, Robert Anchor, and Emil Fackenheim (Indianapolis: Bobbs-Merrill, 1963), 53–68; hereafter abbreviated "CB" and cited

parenthetically in the text. The German version I consulted is in *Was ist Aufklärung* (Gottingen: Vandenhoeck and Ruprecht, 1967), 62–76.

30. Or, at any rate, the contrast between the "agreeable" and the "beautiful" is one of the two structuring contrasts, the other being the contrast between the "beautiful" and the "good." But notice that, unlike in Burke, the contrast between the beautiful and the agreeable is not said to be guaranteed by the nature of the two feelings. The relationship of the two feelings (or judgments) in a given experience is enormously difficult to characterize, as is the other relationship between the beautiful and the good. There is no formula that I know of for the relationship of the beautiful and the agreeable, corresponding to the formula that tells us that "beauty is the symbol of morality." Cf. Kant, *CJ,* 196.

31. See Nietzsche, *Genealogy of Morals,* third essay, especially §§ 1–8. It seems to me possible that the very idea of sublimation as the only alternative to repression and as the source of the higher aims of civilization is inflected toward male preoccupations. Then I hope my explorations will not be taken to close off the possible investigation of other routes to satisfaction and to accomplishment than are so far dreamed of.

Part 2

Mirrors

Where the essays in part 1, in looking at a variety of textual signs, addressed the space of difference between the sign's textual being as form and its signification as a sign, the essays in part 2 incorporate instances of how that space is to be read. Apprehending elements of textual form does not yet disclose them as signs, nor can one simply read them as if presented with a site of meaning. One faces the necessity of reading form as a hiatus, an absence, an interstice between a text and its own textuality. That is, one must read a self-reflective space as the difference and incommensurability between content and form, between what a text says and what it does by saying it. Furthermore, the self-reflective is in some sense metatextual to what it reflects on; it represents an interior metatext in which the text reflects its own form. Though the space in which form is discernible emerges from textual operations and its generation of meaning, the inclusion of form in a reading relies on those moments of textual operation that recognize that space. And this inclusion of the way the text means (at the level of logic, figure, or narrative rather than that of word, name, or syntactical construction, for instance) transforms its meaning by including more than the text says.

The essays in part 2 consider different modes of metatextual interstices. They do so within critiques of philosophical thinking that has participated in an important way in the growth and evolution of poststructuralism. Rudolf Makkreel addresses Kant's third *Critique* and discusses how reflective judgment, in the discovery of universals for particulars, already separates itself from the content of its judgment in a way that cannot avoid including the form of its procedure in the universal it discovers. Stephen Barker discusses the rift or "incision" in the understanding that Nietzsche in turn understands as characterizing art. If Barker metaphorizes this incision as both mirror and dagger, it is only to renarrativize the incision in Nietzsche's own text. Steve Martinot addresses a discursive incommensurability in one of Heidegger's later texts that opens between ontology and narrative as terrains that mirror each other homologically. Charles Shepherdson looks again at Kant's third *Critique,* at the interstice between aesthetics and history, and at Kant's effort to bridge the gap by reflecting each in the other. All consider an interior difference of discursive genre, a difference whose transformative nature will later reappear (in part 4) as political content.

It is immanently proper to begin a consideration of the semiotics of textual form, as contemporary as that idea is, with Kant's *Critique of Judgment.* At the core of an aesthetic critique of literary or philosophical, or indeed of ideological, structure is the realization that their discursive foundations are constituted by textuality and that even their claims to "objectivity" or reference to the world are a pretense that hide or disguise a self-referentiality. That is, the need for prior principles elides an assumed referentiality—a "mask" behind the mask, as Barker will say. The theorization of a mode of reason, after dispensing with prior principles, is the chief attraction of the Kantian critique for many contemporary thinkers.

Makkreel begins by dispensing with the notion that Kant's third *Critique* is a synthesis of the first two; rather, it extends the framework of the first two beyond them. What is at stake is the distinction between a systematic interpretation of the world through pure reason and a reflective interpretation that calls upon imagination to transcend the bounds of both prior principle and experience. Imagination carries reason beyond experience to meaning and to what commonly presents itself to judgment as feeling (pleasure, the beautiful, and the useful). As such, reflective judgment provides the possibility of a perspective on both pure and practical reason. It extends the framework of critique by recontextualizing it. It provides the possibility of differentiation between doctrinal and authentic ideas, where the latter involve a sensual relation to the world that is experiential, imaginative, and also interpretive within a common sense (*sensus communis*). Thus, aesthetic interpretation becomes a mode of thought anterior to reason, a mode that envelops reason.

Makkreel reviews the three concrete modes of reflective judgment: the normative, the aesthetic, and the teleological. Each mode of judgment concerns a different realm (pleasure, beauty, and the useful), and each is self-referential. Norms function as interpretations of natural archetypes or ideal objects adequate to reason, though they are hermeneutically (and thereby hermetically) conceived through the idea of a norm itself. Teleological ideas are those interpretive of the practical purposiveness of the world's objects—the reflective judgment of natural ends. Thus, both the normative and the teleological concern the natural in some objective sense. Aesthetic ideas, on the other hand, are interpretive of the rational (pure and practical); that is, the aesthetic bridges the gap between sense and reason.

Makkreel invokes the historical to contextualize these modes of judgment. For Kant, history realizes nature's purpose (not unlike Auerbach's account of figuration). And Makkreel argues that a judgment of history, which attempts to look forward to ends, encompasses all three modes; historical discourse is, in form, predictive (normative), prophetic (teleological), and divinatory (aesthetic). As such, it produces what Makkreel calls a perspective on itself, a way of apprehending its own operation, as the unfolding of history. The hiatus between norm and telos (the archetypal and the purposive) is apprehended through the divinatory (aesthetic). This concretely reflects the idea that aesthetic interpretation in general provides a perspective on reason and moral philosophy. A homology thus exists between Kant's critiques and the modes of aesthetic judgment. The issue for Makkreel is not how the third *Critique* relates to the first two but how the first two already constitute discursive modes within the sign of the aesthetic, as instances of the more general critique, though separated from it by an incisive incommensurability. Ultimately, this formal relation between history and the aesthetic echoes a structure encountered in the first section, namely, that of the third perspective, the viewer (as of an artwork), now extended to the realm of history, and to judgment in general.

Discussing Nietzsche, Barker performs a related reflection on the textual surface. Barker wonders if it is possible to see narrative from the point of view of a character in it. For Kant that question would be: can the historical participant see "his/her" event as history? Where Kant investigates the conditions for knowledge, Nietzsche regards art as that which breaks the hold of knowledge; it breaks the hegemony of knowing by being where knowledge is inadequate to the world. Though a differentiation is made between knowledge that is given directly and that which is given indirectly, they remain inseparable. For Nietzsche, this inseparability is where art mirrors the human, as the way the human mirrors itself in things. Thus, art is where the character in "history" as narrative would catch a glimpse of that narrative beyond knowing it.

On the other hand, Nietzsche understands that the inadequacy of knowledge constitutes an absence, a fissure in the world that only human activity can fill. For Barker, this raises the issue of how to elucidate this fissure in both its concreteness and its absence. For Nietzsche, art provides a means beyond representation insofar as it signifies the act of invention as such through the sign of its own creativity. As self-referential activity, art leads the content of knowledge back across the abyss to the form of knowing, to what is already a simulacrum. The meaning of the artistic endeavor as such is the necessity to give up understanding, to grasp the inarticulable as a sign. That is, for art, the form is the content; art is the mask that is in reality what is beneath the mask of reality.

Thus, for Nietzsche, there is danger in art. As a mirror, it reflects the separation between life and knowledge as an incision, a knife that slices through life. But for Barker, the mirror and the dagger are more than simply figures. He delves into this cut and shows its operation as mirroring the human return to life. In Zarathustra, one encounters a character who is the mirror image of his acts reflected in the inarticulable sign of this incision.

Where Barker finds Nietzsche's narratives embedded in his philosophical discourse, as a trope for the fissure that reflects, Martinot addresses a fissure between narrative and discursive philosophy itself in Heidegger. Heidegger's concern is how to approach the ontological difference—the inarticulability of the difference between thinking and world, Being and beings. In "Building Dwelling Thinking," he turns to narrative as a necessary recourse. But in the process, he engenders a separation within his text between these two genres of discourse. For Martinot, these mirror each other through a complex series of formal homological inversions.

Martinot looks at a moment when Heidegger appears to leap insouciantly over the abyss between genres and asks how that "leap" can be apprehended as a sign of the abyss itself, of the inarticulable. Heidegger facilitates this by presenting the image of a bridge along with his act of leaping between genres. The bridge is a thing from which Heidegger can distill the ontological difference and read in it the separation of discursive moments. The meaning of the bridge is not only the space it spans but the necessity of narrative to supplement ontology in order to reconstitute as meaning what ontology can only present as textual form. The bridge, as form (discursive "leap" and philosophical "thing"), becomes the sign of the inarticulable and the meaning of the inarticulable as a sign.

Martinot adds that Heidegger, by both including and theorizing the inarticulable in language as such, even while maintaining the incommensurability between the inarticulable and articulation, between the Being and being of language, produces a structure of language which is itself homologous to a mysticism (à la Meister Eckhart). Though Heidegger is not a mystic, and no mysticism as such appears in his argument, the form of Heidegger's argument nevertheless reproduces paradigmatically the articulatory elements that also characterize mysticism. This too, for Heidegger, is a way of arriving at a meaning for the absence, the hiatus, or incision for which the ontological difference is the articulation.

The final essay in this section returns to Kant's *Critique of Judgment.* Shepherdson argues that Kant himself conceived of the third *Critique* as bridging the abyss between the first two, not in the sense of a structure or region but of a movement of what is to be produced. Thus, while his reading of Kant differs from Makkreel's, he continues the investigation into how to approach the abyss of the inarticulable, of the incision between form and content. Like Makkreel, Shepherdson raises the "issue" of history and addresses the form of the third *Critique* through a homology with the form of history. Though both history and aesthetic feeling are empirical, neither obeys a priori rules or principles; that is, they are produced by human freedom but not within any pure moral legislation or with demonstrable telos. Neither belongs to either pure or practical reason, while each reaches into both (rather than beyond both, as Makkreel argues).

This approach to Kant is itself a reflection of Shepherdson's own historicization of the third *Critique.* He points out that there is no immediate necessity for Kant to address aesthetics, but that Kant simply needed a realm of judgment independent of reason and understanding. Thus, what most concerned Kant was the form of judgment rather than its operation or possible discursive content. By constructing a series of homologous relations in Kant's text, Shepherdson approaches the specifics of form as a structure. Each of these homologous relations—aesthetics and teleology, subjective and objective, beautiful and sublime—contains within itself an abyss of inarticulability. As Shepherdson concludes, Kant constitutes sensible experience as a bridge whose movement as the imagination occupies the abyss.

In effect, Shepherdson is arguing that Kant is making the abyss a general question for all philosophy, a question that resides at the core of all questions of nature and freedom. If this "general question" is mirrored in turn in the way aesthetics and history mirror each other, then it becomes, in Kant, the question of philosophical unity itself. Thus, the third *Critique* proposes an inverse historicity for itself, being in effect the "first" critique while existing as the last term of a series of critiques.

As in part 1, these essays evince no common theme, but they reflect a variety of approaches to the space and significance of textual form. In their disparate readings of philosophical texts, they seek different means of eliciting and disclosing a sense of the surface upon which form is to be discerned. Whether this surface opens on the hiatus between critique and self-reflection, discourse and its own artistry, ontology and its necessary narrativization, or aesthetics and its historicity, what is invoked progressively is the concreteness of a bridge already implicit in the disclosure of an interior interstice and surface of separation. In each, a sense of form is apprehended metatextually; it first transcends the metaphysics of the text it addresses and then points to a structural semiotic as its own meaning. Thus, it relates form to content, the internal conditions of signification to what is signified, enactment to statement. What this sequence of approaches reveals is how the bridge, whether as sign or mirror, metaphor or story, becomes an articulation for the inarticulable, for the location of inarticulability across the space of interior difference.

The Hermeneutical Relevance of Kant's *Critique of Judgment*

Rudolf A. Makkreel

Kant's *Critique of Judgment* can be regarded either as an attempt to synthesize the first two *Critiques* or as a way of providing a wider framework for them. According to the first approach, the foundations of Kant's system are fully established in the *Critique of Pure Reason* and the *Critique of Practical Reason.* The task of the third *Critique,* then, is merely to resolve tensions between theoretical and practical reason by showing not only that their respective domains of legislation are not incompatible, but also that the two types of reason can be felt to be in harmony in aesthetic judgments. Those who evaluate the role of the *Critique of Judgment* in this manner will concur with Hegel that it is a failed attempt at synthesis. The subjective, even contingent, manner in which we find aesthetic and teleological order in nature does not suffice to demonstrate the doctrinal coherence of Kant's philosophical system.

In proposing the second approach, I take seriously Kant's claim that the *Critique of Judgment* is not intended to make a contribution to doctrinal philosophy. The work neither adds to nor subtracts from the determinant judgments made in the first two *Critiques,* but opens up the further dimension of reflective judgment, through which a broader interpretive framework can be developed. Whereas determinant judgments are defined as judgments proceeding from given universals to particulars, reflective judgments attempt to find universals for given particulars. In the former case, judgment is legislated to by pure concepts of either the understanding or reason. The reflective judgment, however, is more free from external control and establishes its own principle for interpreting experience into a formally purposive system. The principle of reflective judgment does not impose an abstract formal order on experience but elicits concrete order from the content of experience.

Reflective judgment is interpretive rather than legislative and refrains from making doctrinal claims. Unlike the first two *Critiques,* which ground the doctrinal metaphysical systems of natural science and morals, the *Critique of Judgment* has no specific metaphysical application. Instead, it can be seen to establish something like a Weltanschauung that provides the reflective framework for interpreting all the functions of the human mind, whether they be cognitive, volitional, or affective. From this perspective, the *Critique of Judgment* is able to arrive at theoretical presuppositions that have not been uncovered in the *Critique of Pure Reason* without undermining any of the cognitive claims of that work.

Kant did not develop an explicit theory of interpretation in the *Critique of Judgment,* yet much in that work has a hermeneutical relevance. I will first review briefly what Kant says elsewhere about the understanding and interpretation of nature, and then develop some of the concepts in the *Critique of Judgment* that can contribute to the theory of interpretation in general.

DOCTRINAL AND AUTHENTIC INTERPRETATION

It is asserted in the *Critique of Pure Reason* and the *Prolegomena to Any Future Metaphysics* that the task of understanding is to give a reading of nature. Pure concepts of the understanding have no objective meaning if they are thought to go beyond natural appearances. To acquire such meaning, they must be applied to the manifold of sense. In Kant's words, concepts of the understanding "serve, as it were, only to spell out appearances, that we may be able to read them as experience."[1] By viewing nature as a text to be read, Kant suggests a way of exploring the relation between understanding and interpreting in ordinary and scientific experience.

We can elaborate his reading metaphor by distinguishing four operations involved in construing textual material, namely, spelling (*buchstabieren*), deciphering (*entziffern*), reading (*lesen*), and interpreting (*auslegen*). Normally, one reads a manifold of letters as words having meaning, but if there is a problem on the level of the letters such that they are illegible or scrambled, one must decipher them one by one. On the other hand, if there is a problem on the level of the meaning of words, then one must appeal to interpretation.

If the material to be construed is what Kant calls the book of nature, the task of deciphering is to discover the basic mathematical patterns (*Urbilder*) that run through the manifold of sense. Those patterns that recur can be derived from mathematical schemata. In an essay published in 1764, Kant specifically speaks of deciphering in relation to mathematics. It should be noted, too, that the German word for algebra used by Kant is *Buchstabenrechnung* (calculation by means of letters). Mathematical letters or ciphers become independent of their original reference and can then be manipulated without thinking of their object. Yet what is learned through the manipulation of the ciphers also applies to the objects.[2] The mathematical cipher becomes an intuitive replacement of the object (it is called a "sign *in concreto*"), whereas philosophical language is restricted to words that can at best represent their objects abstractly (*KGS*, 2:278–79).

To explicate what is involved in reading and interpreting nature as a text, we must first examine in some detail the section on "Ideas in General" in the "Transcendental Dialectic" of the *Critique of Pure Reason*. The opening discussion of ideas contains some interesting reflections on meaning and interpretation as Kant seeks to define his own use of the term "idea" through an interpretation of its past usage in the history of philosophy. After warning that "to coin new words is to advance a claim to legislation in language that seldom succeeds,"[3] he proposes a critical appropriation of Plato's theory of ideas. This is the context in which Kant makes the much-noted claim—subsequently associated with the hermeneutics of Schleiermacher and Dilthey—that it is possible to understand an author "better than he has understood himself" (*C1*, A314/B370).

Applying this hermeneutic maxim to his own understanding of past philosophers, Kant claims that Plato was wrong to conceive of ideas or forms as the archetypes (*Urbilder*) of things themselves. Yet Kant goes on to say that Plato "realised that our faculty of knowledge feels a much higher need than merely *to spell out* appearances according to a synthetic unity, in order to be able *to read* them as experience. He knew that our reason naturally exalts itself to modes of knowledge which . . . transcend the bounds of experience" (*C1*, A314/B370–71; emphases added). In this passage, Kant's language suggests a way to reformulate the differing goals of the understanding and reason as the difference between reading and interpreting. The goal of the understanding is to "read" as experience what is spelled out in the manifold of appearances. But reason seeks more. It seeks to interpret these experiences in terms of an idea of a whole. If concepts of the understanding provide the *rules for reading* the manifold of sense so as to produce knowledge of objects in nature, then ideas of reason can be said to provide the *rules for interpreting* these objects so as to form a coherent and complete system of nature.

The relation between the ideas of reason and our interpretation of nature is explicitly suggested in a *Reflexion zur Metaphysik,* where Kant warns that ideas of reason may not be used dogmatically to explain nature by means of causes that transcend nature. Such ideas of reason can only be used regulatively, "for nature is our task, the text of our interpretations" (*KGS*, 18:274). The notion of interpreting nature is more fully explored in the *Opus postumum,* where Kant discusses the systematization of fundamental forces and of the laws of nature. He distinguishes two kinds of "interpretation [*Auslegung*] of nature" (*KGS*, 22:173). The first kind is a "doctrinal" interpretation that he retrospectively attributes to the *Metaphysical Foundations of Natural Science* (*KGS*, 22:173); in that work Kant interpreted substance as matter that is movable in space and subject to motion in time (*KGS*, 22:189). The second kind of interpretation is called "authentic" and will be provided by the science of physics when it works out the actual laws of nature (*KGS*, 22:173).

Kant does not tell us explicitly what the distinction between doctrinal and authentic interpretations signifies. He calls the doctrinal interpretation of the *Metaphysical Foundations of Natural Science* "a scholastic system [*Lehrsystem*]" (*KGS*, 22:189), in contrast with the "experiential system [*Erfahrungssystem*]" of physics (*KGS*, 22:173). In the "Canon of Pure Reason" of the first *Critique,* Kant applies the term "doctrinal" to belief rather than interpretation. He places doctrinal beliefs between contingent pragmatic beliefs and absolute moral beliefs (*C1*, A825/B853–

A828/B851). A doctrinal belief is strongly held as "hypothetically necessary" (*C1,* A823/B851) for the attainment of some theoretical end. It falls short of a moral belief, which is absolutely necessary. This suggests that the doctrinal interpretation or scholastic system of the *Metaphysical Foundations of Natural Science* provides a systematization of nature that is still hypothetical or speculative. The authentic interpretation of nature aimed at by physics would provide a nonspeculative system in that it goes back to the original sources of experience and is purely law-derived.

The distinction between doctrinal and authentic interpretation was first used by Kant in the essay "On the Failure of All Attempted Philosophical Theodicies" (1791). The task of theodicy differs from that of interpreting nature as a scientific system. The problem is not just one of organizing our theoretical knowledge of nature but of finding a moral or practical meaning of the telos of nature. Kant writes, "All theodicy must be an interpretation [*Auslegung*] of nature and must show how God manifests the intention [*Absicht*] of his will through it."[4] In relation to the broader aims of a moral or teleological interpretation, nature also encompasses human history and is no longer considered the open book that it was for the theoretical point of view. According to Kant, nature is "a closed book when we want to read the *final* intention [*Endabsicht*] of God (which is always a moral one) from a world which is only an object of experience" ("F," 291; *KGS,* 8:264).

Traditional theodicies have been doctrinal in speculating about the final moral end that God intends nature to have. Whereas doctrinal interpretations of the theoretical system are hypothetical, doctrinal interpretations of the practical goal of nature can merely be "sophistical [*vernünftelnd*]" (*KGS,* 8:264). Their claim is not only to systematize the theoretical *meaning* of experience, but also to know what God *meant* nature to accomplish. They presume to be able to read God's intention into the course of human experience so that events seemingly "contrary to purpose [*zweckwidrig*]" ("F," 283; *KGS,* 8:255) are reinterpreted to disclose a deeper divine purpose. Such doctrinal interpretations are beyond our capacity.

Although traditional doctrinal theodicies must by their very nature fail, a more modest but authentic form of theodicy is possible for Kant. An authentic interpretation of the moral meaning of nature cannot appeal to experience and the laws of physics, but appeals to the laws of morality within us that precede all experience. Without speculating on how God acts in relation to nature, such an interpretation affirms the postulate of practical reason that He must somehow relate nature to the highest good for the sake of morality. Such an authentic, moral interpretation does not give a complete explanation of God's plan for nature, but by means of it at least "the letters [*Buchstaben*] of His creation can be given a sense [*einen Sinn*]" ("F," 291; *KGS*, 8:264).

Kant cites the story of Job as an allegorical model of an authentic theodicy. Job's friends give a doctrinal interpretation of his suffering in assuming that God has punished him for unknown past sins. Job, however, declares that his suffering is inscrutable to him and refuses their advice to plead for God's forgiveness. While recognizing his share of human frailty and the sovereignty of God's will, he relies on his own conscience, which did not condemn him. According to Kant, Job's rejection of doctrinal explanations is ultimately vindicated by God, who showed him "an ordering of the whole which manifests a wise Creator, although His ways remain inscrutable for us" ("F," 292–93). What counts is "only the uprightness of the heart, not the merit of one's insights, the sincere and undisguised confession of one's doubts, and the avoidance of feigned convictions which one does not really feel" ("F," 293). Thus an authentic theodicy makes no speculative theoretical claims. It is rooted in practical reason and appeals to genuine moral feeling as its guide.

Kant's later discussions of authentic interpretations of religious texts place less emphasis on the sincerity of feeling.[5] However, the reference to feeling is a factor in all interpretations that go beyond the objective meaning sought in a strictly scientific interpretation of nature. Insofar as interpretations of the world and of our place in it as human beings are evaluative, they require reflective judgments in which feeling plays an integral role. Here feeling is not understood in a mere private or emotive sense. In the *Critique of Judgment*, aesthetic pleasure is defined as a disinterested, formal feeling arising from a harmony of the cognitive faculties. This aesthetic pleasure is also conceived as the enhancement of a general feeling of life.[6] Kant uses this furtherance of life as an aesthetic criterion, but it can also be seen to accompany our reflections on the meaning of experience and to authenticate our interpretations of the world.

Although interpretations that are evaluative cannot be objectively demonstrated, they can approximate the intersubjectivity that Kant claims for aesthetic judgments. The intersubjective validity of aesthetic judgments is grounded in what Kant calls a *sensus communis*, or a sense common to all. A reflective judgment based on the *sensus communis* "takes account (a priori) of the mode of representation of all other men in thought, in order, as it were, to compare its judgment with the collective reason of humanity, and thus to escape the illusion arising from the private conditions that could be so easily taken for objective" (*C3*, 136; *KGS*, 5:293). This a priori sense shows how feeling can escape the narrowness so often associated with it. The aim of the *sensus communis* is most clearly formulated in Kant's maxim of enlarged thought, which requires us to compare our judgment "with the possible rather than the actual judgment of others" (*C3*, 136). This maxim is applicable to judgment in interpretation, where a text is to be regarded not so much for the actual meaning intended by the author as for the possible meanings that lie implicit in it as a human or cultural product. The author's intention can serve at best as a model for reflection on the common meaning of a text.

I have argued in a previous article that the feelings relating to life and to the judgments of common sense can assume an orienting function in interpretation.[7] Kant himself describes orientation in its most basic sense as a process whereby I proceed from one quadrant of my field of vision to the other three that make up my horizon. I relate what I see in front of me to the other quadrants by "a feeling of a distinction concerning my own subject, namely, that of my right and left hand" (*KGS*, 8:134). The distinction between right and left, which is an immediate aesthetic discrimination based on a subjective feeling, is indispensable in relating the quadrants of my spatial field into a coherent perspective on objective nature.

Similarly, the *sensus communis* and the feeling of life make aesthetic discriminations that can be used to orient the process of interpretation as it moves from what is directly given to what is only indirectly given. Thus the *sensus communis* whereby we distinguish between an actual and a possible judgment allows us to compare our own point of view with the norms of the community. The enhancement of life felt in pleasure and its diminution in displeasure provide points of reference that guide the formation of a coherent Weltanschauung. Just as a theodicy may be authenticated by a moral feeling of uprightness, so a Weltanschauung that evaluates man's place in the world can be authenticated by certain formal aesthetic feelings. An aesthetically rooted mode of orientation begins with what is directly given. But in interpretation we can equally well start with an idea of what is indirectly given. The interplay between the directly present and indirectly given is central to interpretation. It involves the part-whole relation of the subject or object to its context as formulated by the hermeneutic circle.

In applying his spatial metaphor to orientation in thinking, Kant says that to orient myself in thought is to allow myself to be guided by a subjective principle of reason when objective principles are not forthcoming. Accordingly, he relates the rational idea of God back to a subjectively felt need of reason (*KGS*, 8:139). In light of the *Critique of Judgment*, we can expand this claim about the use of reason to also include ideas of the imagination and subjective principles of reflective judgment in interpreting the world as a systematic whole.

SYSTEMATIC AND REFLECTIVE INTERPRETATION

On the basis of the *Critique of Pure Reason* we have spoken of the ideas of reason as establishing rules for a systematic interpretation of nature. In the *Critique of Judgment* Kant introduces a set of ideas that are produced by the imagination rather than reason. These ideas of the imagination provide rules for what I will call "reflective interpretation."

Because Kant's interpretation of nature in the first *Critique* was merely an extrapolation of reason from the reading of experience, it remained a one-directional abstract process not subject to the hermeneutic circle. The ideas of reason used to project the systematic unity of experience merely strove for the maximum integration of the rules of the understanding. Reason directed "the understanding to a certain goal upon which the routes marked out by all its rules converge, as upon their point of intersection. This point was indeed a mere idea, a *focus imaginarius* . . . quite outside the bounds of experience" (*C1*, A644/B672). In projecting the *focus imaginarius,* reason employed the imagination to extend the lines determined by the rules of the understanding rather than to mediate between it and sense.

In the *Critique of Judgment* nature is no longer regarded as an abstract system in which all events can be explained by one mechanical type of causality. Instead, reflective judgment approaches nature as a concrete order comprised of different natures with "different kinds of causality" (*C3*, 21). Here the interpretation of systematic order involves the articulation or specification of nature into subsystems. To grasp their interrelations requires the mutual adjustment of parts and wholes characteristic of the hermeneutic process. Thus interpretation is subject to revision through reflection on the imagination's efforts to link sense and intellect.

Whereas systematic interpretation proceeded architectonically by striving for ever more encompassing wholes that eventually transcend our understanding, reflective interpretation proceeds tectonically by allowing the parts of a given whole to enrich and revise our initial understanding of it. I will try to explicate this conception of reflective interpretation by examining three ideas that are not pregiven or rigidly prescribed by reason but are adaptive to the content of their subject matter. The normal, aesthetic, and teleological ideas discussed in the *Critique of Judgment* provide no determinant rules for interpretation; rather, they provide indeterminate guidelines. Whereas rational ideas were directed at the overall system of nature, these new ideas of the imagination can also be related to the more concrete level of the subsystems of nature.

The normal idea provides the rule for judging whether an empirical figure accords with the archetype used by nature in producing its species; it is interpretive since we cannot directly know the archetype of nature at the basis of an empirical form. Such an archetype is construed as an ideal that can be approximated by means of a model image intuited through the normal idea.

In the *Critique of Pure Reason* Kant had sharply separated archetypes and model images. An archetype was defined as an ideal individual object completely adequate to a rational idea. Thus the Stoic ideal of a wise man is in complete conformity with the ideas of virtue and wisdom. However, such a perfect individual can exist only in thought. Since the imagination cannot do justice to the completeness of ideas of reason, any attempt by poets "to depict the [character of the perfectly] wise man in a romance" is called "impracticable" (*C1*, A570/B598). Models that artists "profess to carry in their heads" are dismissed by Kant as "incommunicable shadowy images" (*C1*, A570/B598).

However, in the reflective context of the *Critique of Judgment* Kant gives a more positive account of the imagination's role in the presentation of ideals. Indeed, the ideal of beauty is identified as an "ideal of the imagination" (*C3*, 69) because it is based on an individual presentation rather than on concepts. Kant claims that the aesthetic normal idea, as one of the components of the ideal of beauty, "can be completely presented *in concreto* in a model image [*Musterbild*]" (*C3*, 70; *KGS*, 5:233).

Model and archetype are no longer sharply distinguished, as they were in the case of the ideal of reason. Thus Kant describes the archetype of taste as "the highest model" (*C3*, 68). This is in keeping with the judgment of taste, which relies not on a priori determinate rules but on given models that play an exemplary role. No such model can have more than a temporary guiding function, for ultimately everyone must produce the archetype of taste in himself.

Whereas the ideal of reason was a completely determinate archetype, the ideal of the imagination contains a model image that makes possible reflection about an archetype. The model image of the aesthetical normal idea represents a norm for judging what is typical and can give only a provisional estimate of nature's archetype. It serves as an interpretive rule for the typical presentation of the form of the species.

Just as normal ideas were interpretive in approximating the archetypes of natural species, so aesthetic ideas are interpretive in approximating rational ideas. The aesthetic idea mediates between sense and reason by indirectly supplying the intuitive content that is lacking in a rational idea. This capacity is best exemplified by the poetic imagination. The poet, Kant writes, "tries, by means of the imagination, which emulates the play of reason in its quest after a maximum, to go beyond the limits of experience and to present [rational ideas] to sense with a completeness of which there is no example in nature" (*C3*, 158). One example of an aesthetic idea is the representation of Jupiter as an eagle with lightning in its claws. Such imagery provides only "approximate representations" (*C3*, 158) that are not strictly subsumable under the rational idea of a god. They provide what Kant calls "aesthetical attributes of the object, which accompany the logical and stimulate the imagination" (*C3*, 159). Such aesthetic attributes of a god can only indirectly represent his power and majesty, but they help to enliven what would otherwise be mere abstract rational ideas.

Aesthetic ideas also allow us to integrate our experience in ways left contingent by the system of nature based on the discrete concepts of the understanding. By developing the intuitive content of experience "to which the understanding paid no regard in its concept" (*C3*, 160), the aesthetic idea occasions "much thought, without however any definite thought" (*C3*, 157). This thought inspired by an excess of intuition can be used to draw out "a concept's implications [*Folgen*] and its kinship with other concepts" (*C3*, 158; *KGS*, 5:315). Thereby aesthetic ideas can be said to contribute to the process of reflective interpretation that suggests meaningful affinities even where direct conceptual connections cannot be demonstrated. Although such ideas cannot enlarge concepts qua concepts, they broaden the ordinary reading of nature.

When we consider nature aesthetically, Kant asserts that its forms "have no meaning [*bedeuten nichts*], depend on no definite concept, and yet they please" (*C3*, 41; *KGS*, 5:207). Although beautiful forms in nature carry with them no determinate meaning, Kant calls them "ciphers [*Chiffreschrift*] through which nature speaks to us figuratively" and whose "true interpretation [*Auslegung*]" will show aesthetic feeling to be "akin to the moral feeling" (*C3*, 143; *KGS*, 5:301). To decipher the significance of beauty in nature is to read between the lines of the ordinary experiential reading of objects and to find a hint or "trace [*Spur*]" (*C3*, 143; *KGS*, 5:300) that nature is in general agreement with a principle of purposiveness. It is by conceiving beauty as the expression of an aesthetic idea that Kant interprets the beautiful forms of nature as indirectly or symbolically presenting the rational idea of a moral purpose.

So far I have been discussing the function of ideas in reflective interpretation by considering Kant's views on nature and aesthetics. In the final section, I will turn to the role of teleological ideas in the interpretation of culture and history.

THE TELEOLOGICAL IDEA OF HISTORICAL PROGRESS

In the "Critique of Teleological Judgment" Kant specifies the purposiveness of nature by showing that certain natural processes can be fully understood only if, in addition to being explained by mechanical causation, they are described in terms of purposes. Through the teleological idea of a natural purpose, determinant explanations of organisms on the basis of theoretical reason are supplemented with reflective judgments concerning their ends.

Man is a natural purpose like all organized beings, but he is also a moral purpose from the standpoint of practical reason. These two perspectives on man can be brought together through the idea of culture. According to Kant, the ultimate purpose of nature considered as a teleological system is culture, that is, the production of man's capacity to set his own purposes and make himself a moral being independent of nature. Kant also claims that for the maximum development of our human capacities, the ultimate purpose of nature requires the ordering of all civil states into a cosmopolitan whole wherein they will be unified in a morally grounded system.

This cosmopolitan ideal was first set forth in an earlier essay, "Idea for a Universal History from a Cosmopolitan Point of View" (1784), where human history was interpreted as a teleological extension of natural history. History was said to realize nature's plan to bring forth a cosmopolitan society in which all nations on earth will coexist in peaceful harmony. Kant admitted that this historical projection could strike critics as "only a romance,"[8] but defended it as philosophically pragmatic. In terms of our analysis of the third *Critique*, this idea of a cosmopolitan society functions as a teleological idea of the imagination. It serves as the counterpart in the historical realm of the abstract rational idea of a kingdom of ends. The hermeneutical implications of this cosmopolitan idea can be further specified by examining Kant's interpretation of the meaning of a particular historical event like the French Revolution.

Although Kant has been criticized for seeing history as an extension of nature, his analysis of different approaches to history shows him adopting an intermediate position between natural explanations and speculative theodicies. In the essay "An Old Question Raised Again: Is the Human Race Constantly Progressing?" (1798), Kant distinguishes among three kinds of history: predictive, prophetic, and divinatory. Predictive or *vorhersagende* history attempts to foresee the future on the basis of the known laws of nature. Prophetic or *weissagende* history attempts to supplement prediction by making a determinant use of supernatural signs, and is for that reason uncritical. Divinatory or *wahrsagende* history also goes beyond the known laws of nature, but it does so by using natural rather than supernatural signs. Its claims concerning moral progress in history must be based on some experience in the human race — an actual event that can be considered a "historical sign . . . demonstrating the tendency of the human race viewed in its entirety."[9]

It could be said that predictive history aims at a determinant explanation of the future. Were it possible to establish historical laws equivalent to the laws of physics, this kind of history would be authentic in the sense of the scientific interpretation of nature. Prophetic history using supernatural communication is a religious interpretation of history based on doctrinal speculations. Prophecies can at best be "theologically authentic" if they are based on an accepted Scripture. The divinatory or *wahrsagende*[10] history adopted by Kant looks for an intermediate position between supposed scientific explanations and religious interpretations of history. It can be shown to be both reflective in its use of teleology and philosophically authentic in its appeal to a principle in which "there must be something moral" (*CF,* 157).

Elsewhere Kant calls *wahrsagen* or divining the truth "a natural skill."[11] *Wahrsagende* history thus involves a reflective art of interpreting historical events rather than a determinant science of explaining them. Kant looks to the French Revolution as an actual event that could be interpreted as a sign of possible historical progress toward the idea of a republican state. But he focuses on neither its causal consequences nor the particular actions or interests of the direct participants. The reason for this is that some of the actual results of the French Revolution did not spell moral progress. For example, in the *Metaphysical Elements of Jus-*

tice (1797) he expressed a moral "horror"[12] at the perversion of justice involved in the formal execution of Louis XVI. Nevertheless, Kant finds a sign of historical progress in the experience of those like himself who had witnessed the French Revolution from a distance and sympathized with its republican ideals. Just as in the interpretation of a text the author's actual intention is not decisive, the actual intentions of historical agents are not central to *wahrsagende* history, which is concerned with the moral tendency of the human race as a whole. What is significant is the fact that even at a distance the French Revolution aroused in its spectators a "universal yet disinterested participation [*Teilnehmung*] of players on one side against those on the other, even at the risk that their partisanship could become very disadvantageous for them if discovered" (*CF,* 153; *KGS,* 7:85). The sympathetic response of disinterested spectators makes it possible to interpret the French Revolution as a hopeful sign of progress, for, as Kant writes, their "well-wishing participation . . . can have no other cause than a moral predisposition in the human race" (*CF,* 153; *KGS,* 7:85).

Kant's *wahrsagende* history thus uses a particular historical event as a sign that not only intimates a better future for mankind in general but also confirms a moral predisposition that can help bring it about. We can see here the movement of reflective judgment from particular to universal with the French Revolution serving as a historical intimation of the universal state projected by the teleological idea of a cosmopolitan society. Such a reflective interpretation is authenticated by a universal moral tendency disclosed in the historical experience of the disinterested participant.

For Kant practical reason must ultimately authenticate the interpretation of history, but, as we have seen, no simple determinant judgment based on reason alone can supply historical meaning. In the interpretation of historical meaning it is necessary to integrate determinant claims about moral purposes into the reflective framework defined by such teleological ideas as culture and a cosmopolitan society.

In closing I should mention that these explorations of the hermeneutical implications of the third *Critique* are part of a larger project showing that, contrary to the widespread assumption that hermeneutics must overcome its transcendental heritage, a Kantian approach can contribute to a critical hermeneutics. Although the Kantian understanding legislates the transcendental rules whereby nature is to be read, the formal character of these rules leaves the understanding severely limited in what it can know directly. The need to supplement what is directly given with what can only be indirectly given makes knowledge interpretive.

From the contemporary hermeneutic standpoint, the main shortcoming of Kant's transcendental philosophy is that it is foundational and appeals to a priori starting points that are not subject to reevaluation. However, unlike the fixed archetypes of the first *Critique,* the normal, aesthetic, and teleological ideas of the third *Critique* present types or models that provide indeterminate and revisable guidelines for interpretation. Moreover, the feeling of life and the *sensus communis* serve transcendental functions that are orientational rather than rigidly foundational. These functions allow us to modify our perspective on the world without losing our critical bearings. On the basis of transcendental reflection, hermeneutics can appropriate the traditional communal norms stressed by Gadamer or even engage in what Rorty calls the conversations of contemporary cultures, while maintaining a point of orientation that provides a critical perspective on them.

Notes

This paper is based on a keynote address given at the 1988 meeting of the International Association for Philosophy and Literature at the University of Notre Dame. A different version was published as "Kant and the Interpretation of Nature and History," *Philosophical Forum* 21, nos. 1–2 (1989–90): 169–81. Many ideas are also more elaborately treated in my *Imagination and Interpretation in Kant: The Hermeneutical Import of the Critique of Judgment* (Chicago: University of Chicago Press, 1990).

    1. Immanuel Kant, *Prolegomena to Any Future Metaphysics,* trans. G. Carus and L. W. Beck (Indianapolis: Library of Liberal Arts, 1950), 60. Here and throughout the essay, the German reference is given whenever I have revised the translation: *Kants gesammelte Schriften,* Publication of the Prussian Academy of Science of Berlin, 23 vols. (Berlin: de Gruyter, 1902–56), 4:312; hereafter abbreviated *KGS* and cited parenthetically in the text.

    2. See *Untersuchung uber die Deutlichkeit der Grundsatze der naturlichen Theologie und der Moral* (*KGS,* 2:278).

    3. Immanuel Kant, *Critique of Pure Reason,* trans. Norman Kemp Smith (New York: St. Martin's Press, 1965), A312/B369; hereafter abbreviated *C1* and cited parenthetically in the text.

    4. Immanuel Kant, "On the Failure of All Attempted Theodicies," trans. Michel Despland in his *Kant on History and Religion* (Montreal: McGill-

Queen's University Press, 1973), 291; hereafter abbreviated "F" and cited parenthetically in the text. See also *KGS,* 8:264.

5.   This idea has been expanded in my book on Kant's theory of the imagination: *Imagination and Interpretation in Kant.*

6.   Immanuel Kant, *Critique of Judgment,* trans. J. H. Bernard (New York: Hafner Press, 1974), 38; hereafter abbreviated *C3* and cited parenthetically in the text.

7.   Rudolf Makkreel, "Tradition and Orientation in Hermeneutics," *Research in Phenomenology* 16 (1986): 73–85.

8.   Immanuel Kant, "Idea for a Universal History from a Cosmopolitan Point of View," in *On History,* trans. and ed. L. W. Beck (Indianapolis: Library of Liberal Arts, 1963), 24.

9.   Immanuel Kant, *Conflict of the Faculties,* trans. Mary J. Gregor (New York: Abaris Books, 1979), 151; hereafter abbreviated *CF* and cited parenthetically in the text.

10.   Unfortunately, the English translation is not consistent in translating *wahrsagende.* The text begins by translating it as "divinatory" (see *CF,* 141) but at crucial points in Kant's later discussion renders it as "prophetic" (see *CF,* 151, 157).

11.   Immanuel Kant, *Anthropology from a Pragmatic Point of View,* trans. Mary J. Gregor (The Hague: Martinus Nijhoff, 1974), 61.

12.   Immanuel Kant, *Metaphysical Elements of Justice,* trans. John Ladd (Indianapolis: Library of Liberal Arts, 1965), 87n.

The Mirror and the Dagger

Nietzsche and the Danger of Art

Stephen Barker

In all the hyperbole and complexity of his writing, no part of Nietzsche's philosophy requires so much attention, and yields so much insight into the revolutionary nature of his view of the world, as his thoughts on art and aesthetics. The artistic impulse, for Nietzsche, lies at the very foundation of man; as the multiplicity of forces at work in us, it manifests our complexity and our aspirations. As Nietzsche points out in *The Will to Power,* "it has been the aesthetic taste that has hindered mankind most: it believed in the picturesque effect of truth, it demanded of the man of knowledge that he should produce a powerful effect on the imagination,"[1] a demand which Nietzsche claims it is impossible for the "man of knowledge" to accomplish. He states this dilemma succinctly later in *The Will to Power:* "One is an artist at the cost of regarding that which all non-artists call 'form' as content, as 'the matter itself.' To be sure, then, one belongs in a topsy-turvy world: for henceforth content becomes something merely formal—our life included" (*WP,* § 818).

In this topsy-turviness lies the problem and the value of art. Indeed, as Alexander Nehamas points out, "Nietzsche looks at the world in general as if it were a sort of artwork; in particular, he looks at it as if it were a literary text."[2] That is, for Nietzsche, art is always a sign, indeed the most important of signs. It is a sign of life, a sign for human life itself, as Richard Schacht and others have begun to suggest.[3] Though it is always in a dialogue with the nihilism Nietzsche sees as everywhere threatening human discourse, as he points out so extensively in *The Will to Power,* art provides the potential antidote for the nihilistic impulse.[4] Indeed, this fundamental signification of art is the very ground of Nietzsche's philosophy, the final ratification of the "ultimate self-referential application of the knowledge drive"; Nietzsche posits art as the sole agent for "the philosopher's chief function," namely, "to break the hegemony of pure knowing, not from without but from within."[5] Art attacks the panacea of knowing at its source, translating a false solution (however powerful) into a true one (which acknowledges, as we will see, its incompleteness—its desire). For Nietzsche, the rupture "of knowing" by art entails a transcendence of the state in which knowing is or seems to be sufficient; it entails what Nietzsche calls *becoming creative.* Since, in keeping with the centrality of art, for Nietzsche everything good and beautiful depends on (art's) self-professed signification, its illusion, art acts as the manifestation *and the imitation* of its own power to create. Indeed, art creates everything. In *The Will to Power,* Nietzsche establishes the framework for this transcendence: "[T]he world is a work of art that gives birth to itself" (*WP,* § 796). I want to analyze how and on what terms this typically hyperbolic and ostensibly extravagant claim is possible, and how, if at all, it can be defended.

ART AS AN INDEX OF HUMAN LIFE

Nietzsche's strategy is to posit that art is an *index* (an informer, a pointer) of human life. We may conceive of life by the art that results from our interaction with it.[6] "Nothing is beautiful," Nietzsche declares in *Twilight of the Idols,* "only man: on this piece of naivety rests all aesthetics—it is the first truth of aesthetics."[7] Human life, in other words, is distinguished from "life in general," and privileged. Strongly suggested in this "definition," and elsewhere in Nietzsche, is the suggestion that the distinction between human life and "life in general" is precisely the aesthetic faculty. In this respect, Nietzsche's comments on Kant in, for example, *Ecce Homo,* in which Nietzsche claims to go infinitely beyond Kant's rationality and teleology, and in *The Anti-Christ* ("The erring instinct in all and everything, *anti-naturalness* as instinct, German *décadence* as philosophy—*that is Kant!*")[8] are particularly indicative of the revolutionary nature of the power of the aesthetic in Nietzsche. It is no longer merely an adjunct to reason, or a confusion to the order of the mind, but a separate and fundamental power.

Nietzsche thus suggests that aesthetics—that art—is dialectical, which for him means oppositional, agonistic. Discussing Nietzsche's aesthetics, Theodor Adorno addresses this schismatic tendency directly: "art is beautiful," he says in *Aesthetic Theory,* "by virtue of its opposition to mere being."[9] This is Adorno's version of Nietzsche's claim that man vies with himself to make his aesthetic truth-claim. In *Beyond Good and Evil,* for example, Nietzsche says that "in man *creature* and *creator* are united: in man there is material, fragment, excess, clay, dirt, nonsense, chaos; but in man there is also creator, form-giver, hammer hardness, spectator divinity, and the seventh day."[10] This familiar bifurcation *in man* gives rise to art which "commands, wills" that one "become master of the chaos one is; to compel one's chaos to become form" (*WP,* § 842); thus, "truth" for Nietzsche is the will to master the multiplicity of sensations, of forces, at work in man. Art is that "form" which gives validity to the reflection of man's life.

Art, then, as an index of human life, acts in two ways. The first is as a mirror. But here Nietzsche does not infer the economy of mimesis held by Aristotle to be man's "natural state," the act of reproduction of an image of man's ideal state, which is to be taken as art. Aristotle's mimesis, like Plato's, is the impossibly and undesirably—falsely—pure world of Nietzsche's Apollonian, a dream of equivalences in which a work of art mirrors and re-presents either the universe (mimetic theory), the audience (pragmatic theory), the artist himself (expressive theory), or *itself as an artwork* (objective theory). These are the forms of art-as-mirror traditionally constructed around the logocentric serenity of order. But when Nietzsche declares in *Twilight of the Idols* that "man really mirrors himself in things, that which gives him back his own reflection he considers beautiful" (*TI,* 78), he reinitiates the question of the nature of the mirror and the artist's power and desire to reproduce himself.[11] Nietzsche's view of this reproductive faculty is that it is not *re*-production at all, but production. The "mask" of art is, actually is, what is seemingly "beneath" it. In one of his most prophetic aphorisms, Nietzsche declares that "without a mask one has no face to present"; appearance is (human) life. This is the dilemma of art: "if one has a talent, one is also its victim: one lies under the vampirism of one's talent." Nietzsche says in *The Will to Power:* "One does not get over a passion by representing it; rather, it is over *when* one is able to represent it" (*WP,* § 814). By this measure, the artist who can *truly* represent a passion causes it to cease to exist, which is inhuman. The human artist, then, goes on producing imperfectly, falsely. For Nietzsche, the seemingly ironic mimetic power of art is precisely its ability to reproduce falsehood, "only" appearance. As Gilles Deleuze states it:

> [I]t is art which invents the lies that raise falsehood to its highest affirmative power, that turns the will to deceive into something which is affirmed in the power of falsehood. For the artist, *appearance* no longer means the negation of the real in this world but this kind of selection, correction, redoubling and affirmation. Then truth perhaps takes on a new sense. Truth is appearance.[12]

For Nietzsche, the artist is *truthful,* as Paul de Man has put it, "in his recognition of illusion and lie for what they are";[13] thus he gains a strategic, affective freedom. Only the man/artist who can conceive of the entire world as appearance, who can see appearance as appearance, can make a truth-claim for art, and only this man is correct and accurate in so doing, since only art, of all human activities, can facilitate this truth-claim. Historically, it is the turning away from this notion of truth as appearance that led the most human of humans, the Greeks, into the error from which Nietzsche is attempting to awaken us. The Greeks' error began with the privileging of reason, the knowing subject, of course, which was the end of the extracognitive or intuitive aesthetic judgment employed before Socrates. Nietzsche asserts that the pre-Socratic Greeks engaged in just this play with appearance, before its consummate death in the advent of Aristotelian subordination of mimesis to the "real." Nietzsche's concept of the human is radically different and will not permit this subordination of the aesthetic to the rational. Nietzsche considers art and "nature" to be complementary mirror states in a quite different way. He states this most clearly in a seminal passage at the end of the preface to the second edition of *The Gay Science:*

> Oh, those Greeks! They knew how to live. What is required
> for that is to stop courageously at the surface, the fold, the
> skin, to adore appearance, to believe in forms, tones, words,
> in the whole Olympus of appearance. Those Greeks were su-
> perficial—*out of profundity.* And is not this precisely what we
> are coming back to, we daredevils of the spirit who have
> climbed the highest and most dangerous peak of present
> thought and looked around from up there. . . . Are we not, pre-
> cisely, in this respect, Greeks? Adorers of forms, of tones, of
> words? And therefore—*artists?*[14]

Freed from the constraints of referential truth, the artist is empowered
with the ability to pursue *life,* human life, which requires art for its existence.

The "fold" of Nietzschean aesthetics, however, creates an edge, an
incision. The second way in which art is an index of human life is, in
keeping with this fold, what I will call here a dagger, an incision, an
invasion. In "creating" human life, art is dangerous to it, since to be properly mimetic is to mirror the brittleness and danger associated with life,
its ephemerality and incompleteness. Nietzsche saw his life as being that
of the harbinger of such difficulty. It is in this spirit that Nietzsche's
school friends at Pforta called him a *Qualgeist*—a pain spirit, a thorn in
the flesh, or a pain in the ass. Thomas Mann and, even more clearly, James
Joyce in the character of Stephen Dedalus have faithfully followed up on
this aspect of man's learning about himself.

The "within-ness" of art, and of the aesthetic criteria for it, are very
problematic in Nietzsche. The incision of art, painful as it may be, requires a simultaneous objectification, a "point of view." This is one of the
most significant aspects of the *index* of art. In providing an index, a gauge
or measure of the difficulty of becoming human through creativity, art—
by virtue of its status as index—remains apart, aloof, reveals itself as an
incision into life. This is precisely the way in which Derrida refers to
writing in calling it a "dangerous supplement,"[15] and, from a different
perspective, it is what Adorno means, historically, when he says that
"works of art become what they are by negating their origin" (*AT,* 4): art
is *étrangeté,* a disjunctive principle. As such, for Nietzsche it is an index
of the life of the *Übermensch,* man's struggle to overcome himself. This,
according to Adorno, is for Nietzsche a posture of eternal (self-)cruelty
(*AT,* 74). Art mirrors the power of man to attempt to overcome himself;
great art signifies an approach to its achievement.

ART AS THE INDEX OF SUFFERING

This cruel posture of self-incision and self-overcoming is the positivity of suffering. As Deleuze points out, art "does not heal, calm, sublimate, or pay off, it does not 'suspend' desire, instinct, or will,"[16] but fosters them. In one of the most significant passages of *The Will to Power*, Nietzsche declares that art's affirmation is of a "being counted *holy enough* to justify even a monstrous amount of suffering" (*WP*, § 1052). Just in this way, the incision—the dagger—of art is an operation whose telos is the preservation of a certain type of man, the exceptional man or Overman.[17] This man, the highest artist, provides our index of the most fundamental value: preservation. "The beautiful and the ugly are recognized," Nietzsche claims, "relative to our most fundamental values of preservation" (*WP*, § 804). The issue of preservation is a fundamental one for Nietzsche, particularly in the crisis of the "modern," in which Nietzsche deeply believes. Indeed, one of Nietzsche's favorite and most-used puns is that on the word *moderne,* which in German means "up-to-date" as an adjective and " to putrify, decay, rot" as a verb. He uses this word devastatingly, for example, against Wagner in *The Case of Wagner* to describe "the modern artist par excellence."[18] Interestingly, Nietzsche describes "modernity" in *The Will to Power* as an "atrophy of types" in which "the overlordship of the instincts . . . has been weakened" (*WP*, § 74). This enigmatic declaration shows the way in which "the modern" confuses the issues of Apollo and Dionysus and vacillates between up-to-dateness and rottenness. This slippage within a word, and the indeterminateness of such a loaded word, is precisely the emblem, Nietzsche shows repeatedly, to capture the ambivalence of life-and-death-ness with which Nietzsche wants to invest "modernity." The *pharmakon* of art makes man "sick," to use Nietzsche's much-repeated word, in order to make him more than healthy. Nietzsche always uses this word to describe the enervation of the "last man," who can no longer will, can no longer aspire to the condition of the Overman. The most extensive use of the word occurs in *The Anti-Christ,* where "sick" is the continual designation for the priest.

In terms of art, Nietzsche is operating at another level of "sickness." Man is sick with regard to art because art always demonstrates, in its very existence, man's inability to achieve transcendence, his imprisonment within the dilemma of finite life and finite energy. Again, the word "sick" is caught in a double bind; indeed, in this adumbration of Derrida's double bind of the *pharmakon,*[19] this relationship of art to sickness and health results directly from the sharpness (*WP*, § 811) of the psychological state of the artist.[20] From his earliest writings, Nietzsche concretized this conundrum in the figures of Apollo and Dionysus. Artful as he is, Apollo represents deception, as the eternity of beautiful form. Apollo is the legislator of aristocratic stasis: *"thus shall it be forever!"* (*WP,* § 1049). The cruelty of Dionysus is in forcefully and forcibly reminding us of the transitoriness of life's forces, the *continual creation* in which we live. Thus the artist, like Nietzsche, is forever trapped between what Ronald Hayman calls "passive acceptance and violent rebellion, between *amor fati* and outrage."[21] This psychological state, along with the will to mimesis and intoxication, form the marriage of the Apollonian and Dionysian and give birth to artistic suffering:

> Life itself, its eternal fruitfulness and recurrence, creates torment, destruction, the will to annihilation. . . . One will see that the problem is that of the meaning of suffering. . . . The tragic man affirms even the harshest suffering: he is sufficiently strong, rich, and capable of deifying to do so. (*WP,* § 1052)

Nietzsche then says provocatively, "Dionysus cut to pieces is a *promise* of life: it will be eternally reborn and return again from destruction" (*WP,* § 1052). (I cite the entire passage in the supplement to show how Nietzsche juxtaposes Dionysus, the *pharmakon* and the *sparagmos,* with "the god on the cross.") The harshest suffering, art's dissection of life, in which the artwork is left behind as a memorial, a cryptographic sign, occurs when the extraordinary man "breaks his will to the terrible, multifarious, uncertain, frightful" upon a "will to measure." The actual work of art is an "'eternalization' of the will to overcome becoming" (*WP,* § 617); it is an index of suffering because the artist leaves it behind as a mark of a life-and-death struggle, a mark of difference, in a process of self-preservation in which "we possess art lest we perish of the truth" (*WP,* § 822). I have begun to suggest some of the complexities of this statement, centrally including the idea that "art" and "truth" are not in opposition either in life or in the statement itself; the opposition of art and truth gives way to the key word "perish" here. Nietzsche's concern is that the truth of art reveal itself in order to allow man not to perish of false truths, which we call "facts."

Although the nature of artistic—that is, *positive*—suffering changes over the course of Nietzsche's writing, it is always (as we have begun to see) a life-and-death dialogue. "Dionysus cut to pieces" is its emblem; intoxication is its strategy. The Dionysian force, which Nietzsche calls a "temporary identification with the principle of life (including the voluptuousness of the martyr)" (*WP*, § 417), is the "*aesthetic justification*" (*WP*, § 415) for juxtaposing the will to preservation and recuperation with the eternal-creative's compulsion to destroy: the will to pain, the state of animal vigor (*WP*, §§ 415, 801). Art is lost and life becomes *ugly* when we view them with a will to implant a singular interpretive meaning, which finally denies art. Thus do Apollo, the interpretive, and Dionysus, the eternal-creative, vie and merge in a perpetual state of agitation. One must remember that for Nietzsche art is neither Apollo nor Dionysus exclusively, that by his later writings "Dionysus" has become the marriage of *both* principles as articulated in *The Birth of Tragedy*. In this condition of desire and of latent meaning, art is born: "The man in this condition transforms things until they mirror his power—until they are reflections of his perfection. This *compulsion* to transform into the perfect is—art" (*TI*, 72). Thus art *is* exceptional man in a state of intoxication interpreting that state and leaving, *in his wake*, works of art. The artwork is for Nietzsche a remnant, a necessary memorial to the process of the eternal-creative. The parable at the opening of "On Truth and Lies in a Nonmoral Sense" captures just this sense of the wake, in its several meanings:

> Once upon a time, in some out of the way corner of that universe which is dispersed into numberless twinkling solar systems, there was a star upon which clever beasts invented knowing. That was the most arrogant and mendacious minute of "world history," but nevertheless, it was only a minute. After nature had drawn a few breaths, the star cooled and congealed, and the clever beasts had to die.[22]

Here Nietzsche captures and reflects the art and the artifice, the life-and-death-ness, of man's aesthetic dilemma. In this "fable," as Nietzsche calls it in the next sentence, art and the art of telling about art congeal in a parable of man's significance and insignificance: the story is that of significance itself, but it is about the insignificance of the teller. It is a "true story" about mendacity; that is, it is a story, a sign, a metaphor.

ART AS METAPHOR

Nietzsche thus resorts to a metaphor of the *arche*, the world-origin, to define man's aesthetic dilemma.[23] And it is precisely here, in metaphor, that Nietzsche sees the emblem of reflection and incision as constituting a transcendence. Nietzsche's own aphoristic and highly allusive poetic style attests to his privileging of metaphoricity, of the literary as a grounding of the sign; this is indeed Nietzsche's *philosophic* dilemma: "philosophy" for Nietzsche, as Paul de Man points out, turns out to be "an endless reflection on its own destruction at the hands of literature" (*AR*,115). Literature is the metaphoric collapsing together of the active-creative and the reactive-creative. Literature and even poetry and music all represent the "wake" of creativity, its sign, and therefore the sign of truly human being. Thus art catalyzes its own reactive impulse, which Gilles Deleuze has discussed so thoroughly. Nietzsche claims that "the essential thing remains the facility of the metamorphosis, the incapacity *not* to react" (*TI,* 73) both with the eye (that is, the Apollonian) and the "entire emotional system" (that is, the Dionysian). Metaphor is what is beyond good and evil, the framework for man. Nietzsche does not posit in his work a "self" being explicated by an artistic text, nor does he build a sense of self *through* a work; rather, he acknowledges the radical alterity and genealogical power of metaphor.

It is in this respect that Nietzsche redefines, for the twentieth century, the concept of the "aesthetic." In the face of this fundamental power of transference, aesthetics is no longer "about" beauty, because "in beauty opposites are tamed": art is the "power over opposites," not their cancellation but their subsumption into a system (art itself) of suspension in which "violence is no longer needed" (*WP,* § 803). Nietzsche's own art (his poetry and music), as well as the art of the latter nineteenth century and the beginning of the twentieth, art so deeply influenced by the aesthetic theory Nietzsche articulates, entails a new and different sort of violence that is still being defined and explored in the so-called postmodern art of the present day. In its "power over opposites," art transcends its more conventional specular role, mimesis of the "real," and becomes value itself. Art is not the balance to be found in Aristotelian mimesis, but transference, displacement, and slippage.

The great exemplum of Nietzsche's investment in the value of metaphor is the literary strategy of his poetic philosophy, to be found in its most distilled, subtle, and sustained form in the work he called "the greatest present" that has been given mankind so far: *Thus Spoke Zarathustra.*[24] In *Zarathustra*'s astonishing prologue, the mirror and the dagger of art coalesce in what Nietzsche lays out to be the secret of life: passage, transference, performance, change. *Zarathustra* begins with the act of exile: "When Zarathustra was thirty years old he left his home and the lake of his home and went into the mountains. Here he enjoyed his spirit and his solitude, and for ten years did not tire of it. But at last a change came over his heart."[25] This passage is fraught with transference, with leaving-behind. The unexplained changes that have caused Zarathustra's peregrinations are accepted ipso facto. When he changes, after ten years of stasis, at the point at which this very peripatetic story begins, he manifests his change in a series of layered, parabolic metaphors that begin with a declaration to the sun (above) about the need to *go under* (below). That is, from the beginning, Zarathustra is a manifestation of the caught-between-ness of man, his suspension in a state of flux, unable to rise or fall sufficiently to be what he is not. At the beginning of *Zarathustra,* Nietzsche achieves this (mimetic) effect through an unprecedented transference of form and content. Nietzsche's philosophy takes the form of parable, of mysticism, of irony, of trope—of anything *but* philosophy. The metaphoricity here is indeed literary, since for Nietzsche poetry is the highest art, the additive combination of music and language, but it only leaves its mark as *literature.* Having descended to the marketplace to inform man of his own nature, Zarathustra still sees himself as caught between—in this instance, between a high-wire performer and the crowd below, who must have the performance interpreted by a mystical seer in order to understand it; both Zarathustra and Nietzsche-as-philosopher must, in the prologue, share attention with the performance of the tightrope walker, and then with the jester who disrupts the performance; as the performer steps onto the rope, Zarathustra, watching from below, says:

> Man is a rope, tied between beast and overman—a rope over an abyss. A dangerous across, a dangerous on-the-way, a dangerous looking-back, a dangerous shuddering and stopping.
>
> What is great in man is that he is a bridge and not an end: what can be loved in man is that he is an *overture* and a *going under.* (*TSZ,* 4)

Man—aesthetic man—is *ein UBERGANG und ein UNTERGANG:* a tightrope walker and a prophet at once. More important, as Nietzsche shows in this passage, aesthetic expression is a function of metaphoric power. Man is a rope, tied between beast and overman—a rope over an abyss. Mimesis in the passage has become an act of poetic transference, at the level of both thought and action.

The levels at which the metaphoric incision of art, as a mirror and index of man's life, operates, are many. In "Zarathustra's Prologue," in the narrative of the tightrope walker, the figure of the jester appears as parable. Zarathustra stands below the high wire, "explicating" the meaning of the event above to the crowd below. His composure is shattered by the most unexpected of events. At the moment at which we think we understand the levels at which Nietzsche is working, we are surprised.

"Then something happened that made every mouth dumb and every eye rigid" (*TSZ*, 6). From the doorway behind the tightrope walker comes "a fellow in motley clothes, looking like a jester," whose movement is pure *tropos*, a constant turning and twisting. The "higher man"—the man on the tightrope—falls from it when he acknowledges the victory of his "rival"; he loses "his head and the rope," falling into the depths below, "a whirlpool of arms and legs" (*TSZ*, 6). Again and again Nietzsche impresses images of the confusion of order and of humanity, and of the threat to life itself. Zarathustra's decision to pick up the dead tightrope walker and carry him through the early part of the journey demonstrates—in an aesthetic image—his inability to deal sufficiently with the parabolic "lesson" of the death he has witnessed. *Zarathustra* becomes, in this earliest passage, about the art that redeems philosophy.

Zarathustra's confrontation with the jester and the tightrope walker is the first test of his transcendence, which he fails and goes on failing to the very end, as all artists must. As "the will to overcome becoming" (*WP*, § 617), to reject "stopping *here*," wherever it may be, art always aims at transcendence. Never seeing things as they are, but more fully and more simply—that is the intoxication of the artist (*WP*, § 800).[26] Thus, in his attempt at transcendence, the artist always accomplishes a transference instead, a substitution (such as that of intoxication for transcendence). The text is always a qualified failure, just as is Zarathustra's going under, which concludes at exactly the spot at which it began, before his cave, talking to the sun. In fact, Zarathustra has transmuted into a metaphor for the sun: "Thus spoke Zarathustra, and he left his cave, glowing and strong as a morning sun that comes out of dark mountains" (*TSZ*, part 4, "The Sign"). Zarathustra is himself, in Nietzsche's text, a sign for the transference with which the (human) artist must be (dis)contented.

THE DANGER OF ART

Art is, then, the danger to which one must always say *yes*. Aesthetics, insofar as it deals with art, its creative sources, its forms, and its effects, is always an analysis of distress. Nietzsche analyzed this relationship from his earliest writings.[27] "The greatest danger," Nietzsche declares in a section of *The Gay Science* by that name, "that always hovered over humanity and still hovers over it is the eruption of madness—which means the eruption of arbitrariness in feeling, seeing, and hearing, the enjoyment of the mind's lack of discipline, the joy in human unreason" (*GS*, 130). Remembering here the parable of the tightrope walker, Nietzsche is extraordinarily clear about how he intends madness (*Irrsinn*) to be taken, in the string of appositives he uses to define it: "the joy in human un-reason" (*die Freude am Menschen-Unverstande*) in the eruption (*Aus-brechen*) of arbitrariness (*Beliebens,* which could also be "choice" or "will") is the index of the exceptional man; indeed, he concludes the section with an underlined rallying call to "artists": "*We others are the exception and the danger*" (*GS,* 131). Thus unreason and art are meta-phorically conjoined, and the danger that links them is positive, a *yes-saying.*

This metaphorical relationship between distress and art, which Nietz-sche had treated directly in *The Birth of Tragedy* and to which he makes reference as early as 1872 in the already-quoted first paragraph of "On Truth and Lies in a Nonmoral Sense," finds its fruition in the "unreason" of his poetry. At the beginning of *The Gay Science,* in the section entitled "Joke, Cunning, and Revenge," a poem entitled "The Wanderer" appears; its parabolic depiction of the danger of transference distills Nietzsche's argument for it:

> "No more path! Abyss encircling and deadly still!" —
> You willed it! Left the path by your own will!
> Now, wanderer, you have it! Now look coldly and clearly!
> You are lost, if you believe — in danger. (*GS,* 50–51;
>   translation modified)

The narrativity of the poem captures in metaphor the nonposition, the *Unverstande,* from which Nietzsche approaches art. The path, like the tightrope for Zarathustra's tightrope walker, provides a link with the ra-tional world of man; but the wanderer has left the path in favor of the *abgrund* (abyss), just as the tightrope walker will fall from Zarathustra's rope. The danger of art entails both the wanderer/poet's fighting for his existence and his alienation from the world of men, his dagger coldness and clarity in examining and invading that world.

The appended last section of *The Gay Science,* a sequence of poems entitled "Songs of Prince Vogelfrei" ("Lieder des Prinzen Vogelfrei"), is further explication of Nietzsche's aesthetics, ostensibly *by* the poet, al-though this is suitably indeterminate in the title. The poet's name, *Vogel-frei,* which means "free-as-a-bird" and at the same time designates an un-apprehended capital criminal who may be shot on sight with impunity, and the metaphoric process of "unreason" by which this name is con-ferred, portray a life-and-death danger. This crossing-over echoes the motto Nietzsche declares in *The Will to Power:* "To spend one's life amid delicate and absurd things: a stranger to reality; half an artist, half a bird and metaphysician; with no care for reality, except now and then to acknowledge it in the manner of a good dancer with the tips of one's toes" (*WP,* § 1039).

But the metaphoric vertigo of the artist is only part of his danger. Another part is his dilemma with understanding—not with being misunderstood but with being understood. Clearly, here Nietzsche sees the role of the artist as that of the creator of parables (but *not* the Crucified). Parable, troping, the turning aside of meaning, is a vital metaphoric dialogue in Nietzsche's aesthetics. "The artist who began to understand himself," Nietzsche declares, "would misunderstand himself" (*WP,* § 811). "Art is not to be thought of as having to do with the revelation of fundamental truths about reality" ("NST," 242), and this is to its credit. This is its danger. We must read Nietzsche's aesthetics with attention to its rhetoricity; if we were to continue the investigation begun here, we would find, according to de Man, that "the general structure of his work resembles the endlessly repeated gesture of the artist" (*AR,* 118). And this endlessly repeated gesture is not one that privileges understanding but rather misunderstanding. His style is a gesture of transference toward *méconnaissance.* Art allows us to live at the highest levels by strategically allowing us a glimpse of the web of forces by which we turn aside from the death of reason. Within this web we are constrained and free simultaneously, metaphorized. Gary Shapiro has pointed out that after *Zarathustra,* that is, by early 1885, Nietzsche turned his attention to an increasingly select audience that *would* misunderstand.[28] In *The Gay Science,* this takes the form of a short, parabolic poem in the opening section:

Fastidious Taste

When man is left free to choose,
He would gladly choose a spot for himself
In the middle of Paradise:
Gladlier still—outside its gate! (*GS,* 64-65; translation
    modified)

To understand aesthetic life, one must give up understanding and live in its danger; one must come to see and value that danger for what it is.[29] To understand life, one must appeal to art, to understand the fluidity of transference, the nature of parable, the activity of metaphor. To come full circle myself, Richard Schacht points out that for Nietzsche art is *never* to be thought of as relative to "reality" ("NST," 241-47). It is "to its credit" that art, to use Mallarmé's words, *évite le récit.* Nietzsche's truth-claims are for an art that embodies and encompasses truth precisely in the danger of its never being what we want it to be.

Stephen Barker

The Danger Supplement

Some of the following pieces appear in the essay; others do not.

"The world as a work of art that gives birth to itself—." (*Will to Power,* 796)

"Nothing is beautiful—only man: on this piece of naivety rests all aesthetics—it is the first truth of aesthetics." (*Twilight of the Idols,* 20)

"In man creature and creator are united: in man there is material, fragment, excess, clay, dirt, nonsense, chaos; but in man there is also creator, form-giver, hammer hardness, spectator divinity, and seventh day." (*Beyond Good and Evil,* 225)

"It is art which invents the lies that raise falsehood to its highest affirmative power, that turns the will to deceive into something which is affirmed in the power of falsehood. For the artist, appearance no longer means the negation of the real in this world but this kind of selection, correction, redoubling and affirmation. Then truth perhaps takes on a new sense. Truth is appearance." (Gilles Deleuze, *Nietzsche as Philosopher,* 103)

"'Is it true that God is present everywhere?' a little girl asked her mother; 'I think that's indecent'—a hint for philosophers! One should have more respect for the bashfulness with which nature has hidden behind riddles and iridescent uncertainties. Perhaps truth is a woman who has reasons for not letting us see her reasons? Perhaps her name is—to speak Greek—Baubo?" (*The Gay Science,* preface, 4)

"Oh, those Greeks! They knew how to live. What is required for that is to stop courageously at the surface, the fold, the skin, to adore appearances, to believe in forms, tones, words, in the whole Olympus of appearance. Those Greeks were superficial—out of profundity. And is not this precisely what we are again coming back to, we daredevils of the spirit who have climbed the highest and most dangerous peak of present thought and looked around from up there—we who have looked down from there? Are we not, precisely in this respect, Greeks? Adorers of forms, of ones, of words? And therefore — artists?" (*The Gay Science*, preface, 4)

"Life itself, its eternal fruitfulness and recurrence, creates torment, destruction, the will to annihilation. In the other case, suffering — the 'Crucified as the innocent one' — counts as an obJection to this life, as a formula for its condemnation. — One will see that the problem is that of the meaning of suffering: whether a Christian meaning or a tragic meaning. In the former case, being is counted as holy enough to justify even a monstrous amount of suffering. The tragic man affirms even the harshest suffering: he is sufficiently strong, rich, and capable of deifying to do so. The Christian denies even the happiest lot on earth: he is sufficiently weak, poor, disinherited to suffer from life in whatever form he meets it. The god on the cross is a curse on life, a signpost to seek redemption from life; Dionysus cut to pieces is a promise of life: it will be eternally reborn and return again from destruction." (*The Will to Power*, § 1052)

"We possess art lest we perish of the truth." (*The Will to Power*, § 822)

"Once upon a time, in some out of the way corner of that universe which is dispersed into numberless twinkling solar systems, there was a star upon which clever beasts invented knowing. That was the most arrogant and mendacious minute of 'world history,' but nevertheless, it was only a minute. After nature had drawn a few breaths, the star cooled and congealed, and the clever beasts had to die. — One might invent such a fable, and yet he still would not have adequately illustrated how miserable, how shadowy and transient, how aimless and arbitrary the human intellect looks within nature." ("On Truth and Lies in a Nonmoral Sense," trans. Daniel Breazeale, 1)

"Philosophy turns out to be an endless reflection on its own destruction at the hands of literature." (Paul de Man, *Allegories of Reading*, 115)

"The essential thing remains the facility of the metamorphosis, the incapacity not to react." (*Twilight of the Idols*, 10)

"Man is a rope, tied between beast and overman — a rope over an abyss. A dangerous across, a dangerous on-the-way, a dangerous looking-back, a dangerous shuddering and stopping." (*Thus Spoke Zarathustra,* prologue, 4)

"What is great in man is that he is a bridge and not an end: what can be loved in man is that he is a overture and a going under." (*Thus Spoke Zarathustra,* prologue, 4)

"The greatest danger. — If the majority of men had not always considered the discipline of their minds—their 'rationality'—or embarrassed by all fantasies and debaucheries of thought because they saw themselves as friends of 'healthy common sense,' humanity would have perished long ago. The greatest danger that always hovered over humanity and still hovers over it is the eruption of madness—which means the eruption of arbitrariness in feeling, seeing, and hearing, the enjoyment of the mind's lack of discipline, the joy in human unreason." (*The Gay Science,* 130)

> Der Wanderer
> "Kein Pfad mehr! Abgrund rings und Totenstille!" —
> So wolltest du's! Vom Pfade wich dein Wille!
> Nun, Wanderer, gilt's! Nun blicke kalt und klar!
> Verloren bist du, glaubst du—an Gefahr.
>
> *The Wanderer*
> *"No more path! Abyss encircling and deadly still!" —*
> *You willed it! Left the path by your own will!*
> *Now, wanderer, you have it! Now look coldly and clearly!*
> *You are lost, if you believe—in danger.*
> (*The Gay Science,* 50-51; translation modified)

"To spend one's life amid delicate and absurd things: a stranger to reality; half an artist, half a bird and metaphysician; with no care for reality, except now and then to acknowledge it in the manner of a good dance with the tips of one's toes." (*The Will to Power,* § 1039)

"The artist who began to understand himself would misunderstand himself." (*The Will to Power,* § 811).

> Wahlerischer Geschmack
> Wenn mann frei mich wahlen liesse,
> Wahlt' ich gern ein Platzchen mir

Mitten drin im Paradiese;
Gerner noch—vor seiner Tur!

Fastidious Taste

When man is left free to choose,
He would gladly choose a spot for himself
In the middle of Paradise:
Gladlier still—outside its gate!

(*The Gay Science*, 64–65; translation modified)

Notes

1. Friedrich Nietzsche, *The Will to Power,* trans. Walter Kaufmann (New York: Vintage, 1968), § 469; hereafter abbreviated *WP* and cited parenthetically in the text.
2. Alexander Nehamas, *Nietzsche: Life as Literature* (Cambridge, Mass.: Harvard University Press, 1985), 3.
3. Richard Schacht, "Nietzsche's Second Thoughts about Art," *Monist* (2 April 1981); hereafter abbreviated "NST" and cited parenthetically in the text.
4. Nietzsche's preoccupation with the nihilism that results from the enervation of man's forces (particularly artistic forces) became more and more preoccupying for him. Indeed, it is in this view of nihilism that the heart of postmodernism, seen from a Nietzschean perspective, lies. For a most effervescent discussion of this issue, see Arthur Kroker and David Cook, *The Postmodern Scene* (New York: St. Martin's Press, 1986). As though in anticipation of the postmodern, Nietzsche's concern at the outset of *The Will to Power* is with the nihilistic impulse, centrally in its relation to art. Book 1 of the text, "European Nihilism," concludes with this precaution:

> The *multiple ambiguity* of the world is a question of strength that sees all things in the *perspective of its growth*. Moral-Christian value judgments as slaves' rebellion and slaves' mendaciousness (against the aristocratic values of the *ancient* world). How far does art reach down into the essence of strength? (*WP,* § 134)

The ambiguity of this statement, as Nietzsche is indicating, hinges on the issue of the strength of art; the multiple ambiguity of which the world consists is composed precisely of the levels of mirroring and incision that art *reveals*. In this light, Nietzsche's final question in the first book of *The Will to Power* is a central one for the responsibility of art and its willfulness. Art's power to "reach down" is the great endgame of human life.

5.   Daniel Breazeale, introduction to Nietzsche's "On Truth and Lies in a Nonmoral Sense," in *Philosophy and Truth: Selections from Nietzsche's Notebooks of the Early 1870s,* trans. Daniel Breazeale (Atlantic Highlands, N.J.: Humanities Press, 1979), xi.

6.   Here lies the beginning of the problem of nomenclature: to say that one may "know life" through art is already to have applied the Socratic/Platonic/Aristotelian principle of known subject to it and thus to utterly miss it. Language, in a tradition basing itself so fundamentally on such ideas of value, is constrained to recapitulate its own blindness and rigidity, as Nietzsche well knew. Hence his concentration on poetic, parabolic language and its inherent, desired warpage.

7.   Friedrich Nietzsche, *Twilight of the Idols,* in *Twilight of the Idols and The Anti-Christ,* trans. R. J. Hollingdale (Harmondsworth, Middlesex: Penguin, 1978), 78; hereafter abbreviated *TI* and cited parenthetically in the text.

8.   Friedrich Nietzsche, *The Anti-Christ,* in *Twilight of the Idols and The Anti-Christ,* 11.

9.   Theodor Adorno, *Aesthetic Theory,* trans. C. Lenhardt (New York: Routledge and Kegan Paul, 1984), 76; hereafter abbreviated *AT* and cited parenthetically in the text.

10.   Friedrich Nietzsche, *Beyond Good and Evil,* trans. Walter Kaufmann (New York: Vintage, 1966), 255.

11.   Nietzsche's mimesis is thus not Aristotle's at all, but rather something quite different. Gone for Nietzsche is the referent in the physical or metaphysical realm. Mimesis occurs in Nietzsche as the imitation of a state, or rather a state of flux, a condition of activity in which that set of forces of which life consists is eternally at work. Art mirrors this state-which-is-not-a-state. An understanding of the oxymoronic nature of the terms "state of flux" and "condition of activity" is necessary to a "proper" sense of Nietzsche's use of mimesis.

12.   Gilles Deleuze, *Nietzsche and Philosophy,* trans. Hugh Tomlinson (London: Athlone Press, 1983), 103.

13.   Paul de Man, *Allegories of Reading* (New Haven, Conn.: Yale University Press, 1979), 114; hereafter abbreviated *AR* and cited parenthetically in the text.

14.   Friedrich Nietzsche, *The Gay Science,* trans. Walter Kaufmann (New York: Vintage, 1974), 4; hereafter abbreviated *GS* and cited parenthetically in the text.

15.   Jacques Derrida, *Of Grammatology,* trans. Gayatri Chakravorty Spivak (Baltimore: Johns Hopkins University Press, 1976), 141.

16.   Deleuze, *Nietzsche and Philosophy,* 102.

17.   Recognition of the artist as an exceptional man occurs through the suffering of art. Nietzsche states in *The Will to Power:* "It is exceptional states that condition the artist—all of them profoundly related to and interlaced with morbid phenomena" (§ 811). The texture of this condition is formed by the irony of the text's next sentence: "So it seems impossible to be an artist and not to be sick." Discussion of this phenomenon of sickness in art follows.

18.   Friedrich Nietzsche, *The Case of Wagner,* in *Basic Writings of Nietz-sche,* trans. and ed. Walter Kaufmann (New York: Modern Library, 1992), 622.

19.   Jacques Derrida, *Dissemination,* trans. Barbara Johnson (Chicago: University of Chicago Press, 1981), 99.

20.   Sickness and ugliness have a particularly interesting relationship in Nietzsche. In terms of aesthetic judgment, Nietzsche completes his redefini-tion of the aim of aesthetics by declaring:

> How is the ugliness of the world possible?—I took the will to beauty, to persist in like forms, for a temporary means of preservation and recuperation: fundamentally, however, the eternally-creative appeared to me to be, as the eternal compulsion to destroy, associated with pain. The ugly is the form things assume when we view them with the will to implant a meaning, a new meaning, into what has be-come meaningless. (*WP,* § 416)

Though one must read the concluding statement of the above quotation many times and meditate on it to appreciate its disruptive, salutary, and mi-metic value, it describes the dialectical—even political—nature of Nietz-sche's revolution. In it one can perceive the bombshells of early-twentieth-century art and the confusion in contemporary art.

21.   Ronald Hayman, *Nietzsche* (Harmondsworth, Middlesex: Penguin, 1982), 353.

22.   Nietzsche, "On Truth and Lies in a Nonmoral Sense," 79.

23.   Paul de Man's characterization of Nietzsche's metaphoricity cap-tures beautifully what is at work in art:

> The idea of individuation of the human subject as a privi-leged viewpoint is a mere metaphor by means of which man protects himself from his insignificance by forcing his own interpretation of the world upon the entire universe, substituting a human-centered set of meanings that is reas-suring to his vanity for a set of meanings that reduces him to being a mere transitory accident in the cosmic order. The metaphorical substitution is aberrant but no human

> self could come into being without this error. Faced with
> truth of its nonexistence, the self would be consumed as
> an insect is consumed by the flame that attracts it. (*AR,*
> 111)

De Man here "resorts" to metaphor himself, imitating Nietzsche, in rewriting the parable at the beginning of "On Truth and Lies in a Nonmoral Sense." The point de Man is accentuating is that only through the strategic metaphorization of the world in art can man "come into being."

24.   Friedrich Nietzsche, *Ecce Homo,* in *On the Genealogy of Morals and Ecce Homo,* trans. Walter Kaufmann (New York: Vintage, 1969), 219.

25.   Friedrich Nietzsche, *Thus Spoke Zarathustra,* trans. Walter Kaufmann (New York: Viking, 1974), l; hereafter abbreviated *TSZ* and cited parenthetically in the text.

26.   Nietzsche, as always, encompasses multiple themes in his characterization of this impulse: "The thirst for enmity, cruelty, revenge, violence turns back, is redressed; in the desire for knowledge there is avarice and conquest; in the artist there reappears the repressed power to dissimulate and lie; the drives are transformed into demons whom one fights" (*WP,* § 376).

27.   *The Birth of Tragedy,* Nietzsche's first book, is about the relation of distress and art, as Nietzsche declares in *The Will to Power* (§ 463). In the early book, distress results from awareness of drives and of terror, from which tragedy is formulated.

28.   See Gary Shapiro, "Nietzschean Aphorism as Art and Act," *Man and World* 17 (1984): 399–429.

29.   Paul de Man characterizes this condition, and its difficulty, in *Allegories of Reading:* "If we read Nietzsche with the rhetorical awareness provided by his own theory of rhetoric, we find that the general structure of his work resembles the endlessly repeated gesture of the artist 'who does not learn from experience and always again falls in the same trap'" (*AR,* 118). De Man then concludes his chapter "Rhetoric of Tropes," which centers on Nietzsche, with the remark that "what seems to be most difficult to admit is that this allegory of errors is the very model of philosophical rigor" (*AR,* 118), which brings Nietzsche's thinking around to the beginning again.

Heidegger's Leap

Steve Martinot

At one point in his essay "Building Dwelling Thinking," Heidegger abruptly shifts his discourse from exposition to narrative.[1] Though the substitution of an aesthetic mode of writing for ordinary discourse to outflank metaphysics is a familiar Heideggerian maneuver, at the point in question, he seems to generate a non sequitur. The moment occurs when Heidegger is describing an ontological relation between building and dwelling, circling back and forth from one to the other in his familiar manner (Heidegger uses the noun form of the infinitive, *das Wohnen,* *das Bauen,* and so on, figuratively understood as gerunds);[2] dwelling unfolds as building and building unfolds as dwelling. "Human being consists in dwelling," he says, "dwelling in the sense of the stay of mortals on the earth." And then he leaps, abandoning the interplay of his gerunds:

> Human being consists in dwelling and, indeed, dwelling in the sense of the stay of mortals on the earth. . . . But "on the earth" already means "under the sky." Both of these *also* mean "remaining before the divinities" and include a "belonging to men's being with one another." By a *primal* oneness the four—earth and sky, divinities and mortals—belong together in one. (*PLT,* 149)[3]

For ontological discourse on dwelling, he substitutes landscapes (earth and sky) and launches into stories of mortals and divinities—that is, entities whose descriptions require narrative. His invocation of a "primal oneness" (*einer ur-sprünglichen Einheit*) of these narratives makes the shift conceptual as well as imagistic and engenders a sense of jumping from the circumference of a circle to its center. And this recalls his own call, in *Being and Time,* to leap from the circumference of the circle (of understanding) into its center.[4] Perhaps his shift in terminological style constitutes a narrativization of precisely this leap into the "abyss of Being."

But if a leap from philosophic language to a more poetic one is required in order to complete his project, to reveal a meaning undisclosable in the former style, the implication is that something would be left unfinished without it. The further implication is that the unfinished discourse he leaps from will achieve a different meaning or closure by making that crossing. His shift to the narrative arena is not one of continuing an argument, but suddenly recasting or revealing the meaning of his discourse in other terms.[5] In effect, the leap itself suggests that the discourse he has leaped from constitutes a signifier for which the narratives he leaps to are the signified, the meaning. In an untraditional philosophical inversion, narrative is no longer what means but what is meant. And this also implies that at the core of Heidegger's project there is a gap, a chasm of some sort, that requires overleaping. It is on the meaning of this metaphoric leap that I will focus.

The shift of style thus extended into a leap nevertheless has a contextual precedent in Heidegger's "turn," which names a change in Heidegger's interrogative direction between the publication of *Being and Time* and his postwar essays. It is less a change, it can be argued, in philosophical position or reasoning than it is a change in diction. It marks a period during which his understanding of language shifts from that which bespeaks interpretation and assertion (*BT,*188–210) to that which speaks itself ("language speaks") (*PLT,* 198ff.); and in the course of which he conscripts certain literary notions, such as Hölderlin's sentiment that "poetically man dwells . . . ," and gives them emphatic philosophical weight.

This is complemented by a shift from his earlier concern with the meaning of Being to a discourse on the "thinking of Being" and the "truth of Being." In general, his philosophical meanings become aestheticized in a way that implies we apprehend the world as if it were already literature.[6] In effect, he replaces his interrogation of the language of Being with one of the Being of language.

The concept of "dwelling" plays a special role in this. For Heidegger, as he puts it in "The Thing,"[7] Being calls from being, and to heed the call, to respond to the appeal of its presence behind beings, to release oneself toward the appeal, is to dwell authentically on the earth (*PLT,* 181–82). Rather than be conceptual, dwelling in the world as world is closer to thinking. To dwell poetically ("Poetically man dwells . . .") is one of the ways "man" does this in language. Language constitutes a connection, a way connections are constructed. The essay "Building Dwelling Thinking" dwells in the space of that construction, a thinking of the space provided by language.[8]

HEIDEGGER'S ROUND HOUSE

Between building and dwelling there is a triplet of relations: dwelling is the way mortals are on the earth; dwelling unfolds as building; and building is really dwelling (*PLT,* 148). Though man builds in order to dwell, he must already dwell if he chooses to build. Dwelling is the prerequisite for building. On the other hand, "the nature of building is letting dwell" (*PLT,* 160). Building is the condition for dwelling, while dwelling must already be the condition for building. We encounter the familiar aporia of the hermeneutic circle in which each is the condition for the other.

A similar condition is evident in what Heidegger calls a neighborhood ("Ger. *Nachbar,* from OE. *neahgebur,* meaning 'near-dweller'" [*PLT,* 146–47]). Building unfolds through the establishment of a location and a background or environment for that location. The neighborhood, the environment, was already there before any building was done in it; yet it was not there until there was a building, a location to environ, a building for which to be the background. Neighborhood establishes a location for building through building surrounding itself with a neighborhood. We can see that this interplay of neighborhood and location, through building, is similar to the interplay of dwelling and buildings, through building.

These are familiar circles. One encounters them in *Being and Time:* for example, in Heidegger's discussion of the ontological difference between Being and beings. How is one to question Being in its disclosure by beings without already having assumed Being to have been the condition of beings? Being and beings are the condition for each other. Furthermore, if to question Being is to confront the need to define an entity that in its Being is the basis on which the question of Being can be raised, a Being for whom Being is a question (*BT,* 27), then a similar circle has been generated: the question is the basis for the questioning being and the questioning being is the basis for the question. Finally, to raise the question of Being as Heidegger does, to consider it from the perspective of a discourse addressed to that question, is to reflect this same circle onto the plane of the text and its subject matter. If the first circle is the inescapable circularity of foundations, the second circle is the inescapable circularity of the self-referentiality of thinking, and the third is that of interior textual metatextuality, the ability and necessity of a text somehow to make essential reference to itself through the very thing it is about.

But in considering Heidegger's circle of dwelling and building metatextually, the term "building" can be seen to have two significations. Dwelling builds, and dwells in a building, in the sense that buildings are inhabited. There are two forms, viz., the activity and the functional thing, the act of building and the state of located residence in a building. Building is constituted by dwelling and building constitutes dwelling. Heidegger himself makes a terminological distinction: there is the "thingly structure of buildings [*der Bauten*]" and building (*bauen*) as the "making of such things . . . [as] a founding and joining of spaces . . . [as what] produces location [that] necessarily brings with it space" (*PLT,* 158). In effect, buildings are a way of being for the act of building. The form of building that enacts dwelling, and thus produces buildings, we can call Building with a capital B, to distinguish it from the functional structure (building with a lowercase b) constituted by that enactment. Building is the ontological condition for there to be buildings, as buildings are the ontic condition for the existence of Building, or what might be called the "presencing" of Building (in the same sense as Being and beings).

These three terms (dwelling, Building, and building) intertwine structurally in a manner that Heidegger does not speak about (he was perhaps more interested in how each notion relates to the fourfold). They can be seen to constitute a circle. It is a circle that can be considered an expansion of the earlier hermeneutic circle of dwelling and building, opened by the distinction between Building and building. People dwell as a way of being for buildings; people Build as their enactment of dwelling; and people inhabit as the state produced by Building. Dwelling is constituted by buildings; buildings are constituted by Building; and Building is constituted by dwelling. Or, to reverse the order: dwelling produces Building; Building produces buildings; buildings produce dwelling.

A similar circle can be constructed in terms of neighborhood, location, and building. Neighborhood is the context for location; location is the context for building; and building is the context for neighborhood, the way neighborhood establishes itself. In this case, rather than through forms of manifestation (or even levels of articulation), the discursive differential between moments on the circle is contextualization; each element of the circle provides a place for an entity to bring itself into being, and that entity in turn appropriates that background as a context for itself, around the circle. Thus, it is really a circle of hermeneutic circles. But this difference in mode of relation between each element and the one that succeeds it is enough to suggest that this circular structure is not homologous to that of dwelling and building. The "neighborhood circle" can be restated: neighborhood provides the space in which there can be location and for which location is the substance; location provides the space in which there can be buildings, and buildings provide the content; buildings provide the place at which there can be a neighborhood, and neighborhood constitutes a meaning for those buildings. The circle is Escher-like in that one goes down flights of stairs to finally end up at the top stair.

We can transform this description slightly. This structural interplay can be articulated in terms of form and content.[9] Thus, neighborhood provides the form for location as its content; location provides the form for buildings as its content; and buildings provide the form for neighborhood as their content.

The circle of dwelling, Building, and building can be similarly articulated in terms of form and content. Building is the form manifest by dwelling; buildings are the form manifest by (the act of) Building; and dwelling is the form manifest by buildings. Or, to rephrase this slightly, the form the inhabitation of buildings takes is dwelling itself; the form the act of Building takes is that of (constituted) buildings themselves; and the form of what dwelling does, what it constitutes, is Building itself. Thus, buildings give form to Building; Building gives form to dwelling; and dwelling gives form to buildings, not in terms of their inhabitability but in terms of their being inhabited—the filling of building, location, and neighborhood with each other. To consider this circle in a third perspective: the meaning or content of dwelling is that there are buildings it inhabits; the meaning of Building is that dwelling does it; and the meaning of buildings is that they are constituted by the act of Building.

Form and content interweave, as separate and inseparable, around the circle. And we might note that because this approach can be applied to two different (nonhomologous) circles, the notions (or labels) of form and content, though still descriptive of aspects of each of the circle's separate elements, also begin to take on the aura of paradigmatic descriptors. To describe the circle paradigmatically, one could say that each triadic element takes the next as its form while at the same time taking the preceding as its content. For each, the preceding moment on the circle becomes a source. Each is produced as a form by the prior element while at the same time producing the next as its form. In short, forms (signifiers) are at the same time meanings that generate other forms. That is, though form and content are never without each other, they find each other elsewhere, at different discursive levels, in what would be an incommensurability or aporetic relation without the circle to bring them "full circle."[10] This "elsewhereness" is not produced by the articulation of "form and content"; it is what is given, for which "form and content" articulate a semiotic relation.

These triadic circles are not foreign to Heidegger; the "as-structure" in his analytic of interpretation (as involvement, as signification, as ready-to-hand) is an example (*BT,* 191). But in the present case, he does not consider such circles. Here, he speaks of hermeneutic circles, which are dyadic: Being/beings or dwelling/building. And though he attempts to hold them apart through his etymological archaeologies, as we have seen, he only ends with a different interweaving of being and residence within the same aporia of dwelling and Building. But part of this dyad is its own form, the ontological difference (Being/beings:Building/buildings), which opens the dyad to itself and recontextualizes it from within. This mediation adds a third term to the circular form, engendering a triadic circle.[11] We can see that a similar opening occurs for the circle of Being and beings when mediated by the ontological difference, that is, by *Dasein,* the being for which the meaning of Being is a question (*BT,* 35). Being is the condition for the existence of beings; beings are the condition for the constitution of questioning; and questioning is the condition for the meaning of Being. This circle is a unitary structure that holds separate and inseparable the moments of form and content, while dispensing with the question of ontological foundation (which the hermeneutic circle poses) by finding its foundation endlessly in the circle itself. It is by invoking the endlessness of this circularity that Heidegger preserves the inarti-culability of Being and the question of Being.

The effect of the nonseparation of "form" and "content" (in/as a sign) is to endlessly connect and hold separate, that is, to endlessly relate and reengender by and for each other a lamination of different levels of dis-course: viz., text, metatext, and context. Each sign addressed (dwelling, Building, or buildings) takes the realm of one of the other signs as its arena of meaning and the realm of the third as its being. This is a relation of signifiers that is different from a system of differences. Here, a system of signs functions to "presence" its elements in interwoven terms—in the sense that Heidegger uses the notion of "presencing." When Heideg-ger says that "buildings give form to dwelling in its presencing and house this presence" (*PLT,* 158–59), he is speaking at three levels of discourse at once: dwelling is given the sense of what inhabits, of what Builds, and as the ontological difference. Rather than referentiality, it is possibility itself that each sign opens as presencing, precisely because its referent is always elsewhere, at a different discursive level.

Ultimately the triadic circle evinces the double aspect of being a form and using form as an inner relation. But further, the weaving of elements around the circle constitutes a "content" for the circle itself, where each element is already a textual content grasped metatextually as form. The triadic circle provides a formulation, in form, of the relations of form and content as a relation of separate and inseparable categories.

The idea that a hermeneutic circle can be opened up into a triadic circle reflects critically upon Heidegger's project. To develop the dyad of Being and beings, he moves from beings back to Being; beings raise the ques-tion of Being, and *Dasein* is the being for which this happens. But Being does not question beings, except through the mediation of *Dasein,* that is, through the mediation of the ontological difference. On the other hand, in the triadic circle, which now includes the fact and the meaning of questioning, where is the act of raising the question to be located? In fact, if the circle exists, its categoriality gives it a prior unity from which beings and Being have been separated out as elements, an analysand of the ontological difference (dissected, as it were, and rendered incom-mensurable by that dissection). The act of recompleting this circle, which is a possibility opened by Heidegger's hermeneutic circles them-selves, would then seem to obviate (again) the possibility of questioning. In the endless circle of mutual conditioning, there is no longer an incommensurability that requires questioning. One has moved to a different operation of language altogether.

In philosophy, circularity is a loaded question. Philosophers understandably tend to stay away from it. Its value as a critical weapon entails a fearfulness, and hence a social unsuitability as an argumentational structure. Without the common assumption of noncircular reasoning, questions of philosophical rectitude would become undecidable. Furthermore, circularity disrupts the calmness of logical process, of reason that is designed to move from one "place" to another, to traverse the map of ideas by "staying on the road." Unfortunately, in the philosophy of "mind," the circle is unavoidable. The general form it takes is: mind must be in order to define itself; it can only define itself for itself; it must define itself for itself before it can be. Philosophy addresses mind by dropping one of the terms of this circle. Phenomenology drops the second one; psychology keeps the second one but conflates the first and third; some contemporary analytic philosophers drop the first. Each procedure, however, only constitutes a third-person approach to mind. A first-person approach, and all discourse on the self-referential, must configure itself in such circularity. In *Being and Time,* this circularity appears as follows: Being is the basis for the meaning of Being; the meaning of Being is the basis for the unknowability of Being; and the unknowability of Being is the basis for Being. In general, it is the attempt to (dis)solve this circularity, or to straighten it out, that characterizes metaphysics.

As audacious a philosopher as he is, even Heidegger has an ambiguous, almost coy attitude toward circularity in *Being and Time.* Logical circularity is trivial for him, a child of mere "common sense." On the other hand, he recognizes descriptive circularity as unavoidable (*BT,* 27–28). And ultimately he proposes that we "endeavor to leap into the 'circle'" (*BT,* 363) as a metaphor for disclosing Being. However, he himself makes a different (substitute) leap to narrative, and therein lies his coyness. His ambiguity toward the circle becomes a romance with it—or rather, a love/hate relationship in which he is irresolute as a philosopher toward what he rushes moaning to embrace as a poet.

THE ONTOLOGIES OF THE FOURFOLD

Prefatory to discussing Heidegger's fourfold narratives, it should be noted that he relates each entity narrated (earth, sky, divinities, and mortals) to the circle of dwelling in a privative mode or as an injunction. (*PLT,* 150–51) With respect to earth, dwelling entails saving it, which means not despoiling, exploiting, or subjugating. Dwelling receives (*empfangen*) the sky, which means leaving it alone, not doing anything about it, not harassing it (*gehetzten Unrast*). Dwelling means waiting for the gods in expectation, who are therefore not present; it means not making substitutes, not taking active measures against misfortunes. Finally, dwelling means mortals, being mortal, initiate their own nature through "being capable of death as death" (*PLT,* 151); this means not making death itself a goal. Thus, the fourfold embraces nonsubjugation, noninterference, nonsubstitution, and nonconcern with the end or ultimate as a characterization of dwelling. (One might recognize this as at least the methodology, if not the analytic, of *a-letheia*—the disclosure of what must be let be, the disclosure of the hidden as hidden.)

If the activities already mentioned for the entities narrated—saving, receiving, waiting, or initiating—are defined by enumerating the narratives of what each is not, viz., narratives of despoliation, harassment, idol worship, or death wishes, then these unwonted activities surround dwelling. But they surround it in the negative with narrative possibilities that only make implicit reference to a distant and hidden human world, through the possibilities that the fourfold enjoins. If the injunctions and their categories of activity surround the fourfold as a narrative context, the alternative narrativized world lies hidden within what is surrounded, unseen and unheard in the center of the circle. The negations point to a world of hidden narratives they invert both topologically and categorially. The circumscribing narrative space brackets dwelling and building with a sort of negative epoche.

Each of Heidegger's fourfold narratives follows a common pattern. We shall consider them one by one. The earth is a "serving bearer (*die dienend Tragende:* 'the servingly bearing one'), blossoming and fruiting, spreading out," and always changing by "rising up" (*aufgehend*) to become plant and animal life (*PLT,* 149). This is more than just a use of metaphor. There is a feminine character given here, possibly (metaphorically) a woman, of whom four stories are told. She carries things, in a motherly sort of way, as a "bearer" of "servings" and a "bearer" who "blossoms," who yields things or gives them birth. She seems to change, to emerge through seasons or stages. She forms living spaces or surfaces. And she enkindles other life. There are, in effect, four forms of bearing. She serves; she brings herself forth or serves herself (up) in the sense that she herself blossoms; she forms the ground for things; and she brings forth new forms. In each, one becomes many. One could reformulate or represent these narratives of earth (service, fruitfulness, support, and emergence of the new) in a grammatical or semiotic schema of four components: bearing to others, bearing of self, bearing for others, and bearing others. And it is noteworthy that Heidegger's injunction for dwelling toward earth is nonsubjugation, where earth already serves.

The second narrative is of the sky (*PLT,* 149). Rather than be a character, the sky is given character (*gestaltwechselnde*). It is a roadway for what moves (sun, moon, stars), and it is motion itself: a turning of the seasons, an alternation of day and night, a changing of the weather, and a placid background of clouds and "blue depth." The linearity of the road with its traveling objects gives way first to cyclicity, then to two-phase oscillation, and finally to the continuously changing and the unchanging: a spiral from itinerancy down to stasis. Where the earth's labors were one to many, the sky's quiescences are many to one. Where earth bears to others ("serving bearer"), sky bears others. Things pass as pure occurrence, to be accepted and acceded to. Heidegger's injunction is noninterference, but interference is not possible with the given. Toward the earth, the injunction is not to do the unnecessary; toward the sky, it is not to do the impossible.

The third narrative, of the divinities, is more complex than the previous earth portrait or skyscape: "The divinities (*Gottlichen*) are the beckoning (*winkenden*) messengers of the godhead (*Gottheit*). Out of the holy sway [of divinity (*gottheit*)], the god appears in his presence or withdraws into his concealment" (*PLT,* 150). Four events are listed atemporally: a beckoning messenger, an emergence of god, an appearance of presence, and a withdrawal into concealment or disguise. There is a signal, a sign, and from the realm of that sign, what makes itself present also disappears into hiddenness. It is a poeticized version of the object, as presented in *Being and Time* (see *BT,* 49ff., 188ff.); there, things announce themselves, are pointed out, and thus present themselves as appearances while at the same time concealing themselves behind apprehension or conceptualization. An analogy is suggested, then, between beings (things) and gods, which would extend to an analogy between Being and divinity per se (*gottheit*).

But there is an ambiguity in this narrative; it is uncertain who the messengers are signaling to, the mortals or the god who appears. Thus it is uncertain who responds to the call. Heidegger's injunction is that mortals "await the divinities as divinities," and make no gods for themselves, no substitutes for the beckoning. "In the depth of misfortune, they [mortals] wait for the weal that has been withdrawn" (*PLT,* 150). If the divinities signal, as divinities, to mortals, to us, then it is as "weal" (health or deliverance). And as sky bears itself, the divinities bring forth, or bear for others. Godhead, divinities, signal, and well-being would all appear from the same quarter; Being emerges. If the messengers of the god-head beckon to god, then mortals become the godhead the messengers beckon for (Heidegger gives us no reason to assume an entity beyond the mortal/immortal binary). God, then, would emerge from mortals, meaning mortals are at once god, substitutes, and the withdrawal of their own well-being. (At the end of the Second World War in Germany, this was not a difficult idea.) Heidegger enjoins nonsubstitution, where substitution is either unfeasible or already the case (impossible or unnecessary). To the condition of non-necessity and impossibility is added the condition of undecidability. (One could understand these injunctions and conditions, as well as the grammatical schema of "bearing," as providing a system of indices for each of the fourfold, like "quantum numbers.")

In the fourth narrative, mortals initiate themselves by telling their death. Again, there are four parts. Mortals can die; they are capable of death as death; they are uniquely the only ones who die; and that latter is because they know death as death. It is not a narrative of death, because death cannot be narrated. It is a narrative of life, which can be known only through what it is not, through what delimits it. To be is to have death always a concern. Humans are the only ones who live, because they are the only ones for whom death is a concern. In this way, mortals "initiate their own nature"—they bear themselves. But as the delimiting, death's narrative inverts all four narratives. For mortals, death is first a possibility (the inverse of necessity), second a capability (the inverse of impossibility), third a uniqueness (the inverse of undecidability), and fourth the unceasing, the inescapable concern (the inverse of the delimitable). This progression, in which possibility is a precondition for capability, which is in turn the condition for uniqueness, with uniqueness determining inescapable awareness, is a progression toward greater concern, where Heidegger's injunction is precisely nonconcern.

Thus, the narrative structure of the fourfold entails a complex system of inversions: first, a constituting inversion between the character of death (the inverse of life) and the characteristics of life, of Being, as narrated by the fourfold's components (non-necessity, impossibility, etc.); second, an inversion between these characteristics and Heidegger's injunctions (the constituted characteristics: saving, receiving, etc.); and third, between the world abjured by the injunctions (the constituted referential world of subjugation, interference, etc.—the enjoined narratives) and the fourfold narratives (the nonreferentiality of Being) at its center. These inversions repeat the categories of the dwelling circle, which was an interweaving of the constituting, the constituted, and Being (Building, buildings, and dwelling). Thus, these inversions constitute a circle themselves. If we recall that dwelling is already related to the fourfold through its privative characteristics, triadic circle of dwelling becomes inverted in the realm of the fourfold; center and circumference change "places." Thus, not only is inversion the discursive operation, the paradigmatic motif of the triadic circle of the fourfold, but it characterizes the interrelation of circles.

Heidegger does not dwell on dwelling for its own sake. For him, "dwelling is the basic characteristic of Being in keeping with which mortals exist." And "thinking itself belongs to dwelling in the same sense as building" (*PLT*, 160). If, in his discourse of building and dwelling, he is really addressing Being and thinking, he is being at least metaphorical. If the circle of dwelling represents itself, at the other end of his leap, by the fourfold as a oneness, as the center of the other circle, his metaphor is metaphorized. It is the semiotics of this second-order metaphor that must be understood to grasp the meaning of Heidegger's leap to narrative.

Three aspects of Heidegger's so-called "Turning" are represented in this leap. The first is the change of diction. The second is an abandonment of traditional philosophical categories in order to address the notion of "thinking" as an undefinable. When he says, "We shall try to think about dwelling and building" (*PLT*, 145), he implies that the form of his discourse, rather than its content, will signify something about thinking. Indeed, his title itself ("Building Dwelling Thinking"), written without commas, with each term oscillating between noun (gerund) and verb (infinitive), could be construed to mean "On constituting a way of thinking called dwelling-thinking." And third, the chasm between discourse and image that Heidegger's leap signifies in general is here presented in iconic form symbolizing a coherence between the counterposed topologically separated structures and the substance itself of the chasm that separates them, the chasm to be bridged.

THE BRIDGE

Heidegger gives us a bridge. In his text, he writes of a bridge over a stream that, at the same time, is a "building" and a thing related to the narrative fourfold. It is at once an image, a structure, and a text. As an image of an actual worldly structure, it is textual, narrativized to be a part of a discursive landscape; and part of that narrative is that it has been built and functions to span the stream. As a structure, it is a "thing," a building in its landscape; it gathers its location and neighborhood into a site, a space.[12] That is, it contextualizes these notions, renders them images for itself in terms of its own ontological (discursive) presence. As a (philosophical) text, the bridge presents the stream as a stream to be bridged, the image of a building that creates an ontological space for which the fourfold becomes the structure: "[It] allows the simple onefold of earth and sky, of divinities and mortals, to enter into a site by arranging the site into spaces" (*PLT,* 158). Specifically, it creates the banks of the stream as separate by joining them (earth). It leads the stream under itself, allowing it to pass unhindered (sky). It awaits the stream and the stream's vicissitudes with equanimity (divinities). And it carries mortals to the other side (to the other bank, to their own "other side"). Thus, finally, the bridge is a (narrative) structure of texts.

In sum, as a text, it is an image of structure; as a structure, it is a text of images; as an image, it is a structure of texts. We recognize this "structure," of course, as a triadic circle (composed of image, structure, and text). But it is a circle that belongs to the bridge's narrative aspect, the realm of the fourfold narratives. The circle remains within the landscape of bridging, gathering, and presenting. That is, that aspect of the bridge that is narrative rests upon the discursive form of ontology, the circle of form and content, context and text.

At the same time, the bridge is an ontological structure. Insofar as it gathers the fourfold to it, in Heidegger's sense of a thing in its thingness, it both gives of itself and stays itself. In staying itself, it is a being that reveals Being through revealing itself in its being. In giving, the four elements of the fourfold dwell "all at once"; and in staying, the bridge, as a thing, "brings the four into the light of their mutual belonging" (*PLT,* 173). The ontological relation reveals itself revealing the operation of the fourfold narratives. That is, the aspect of the bridge that is ontological rests upon the narrative terrain.

In sum, Heidegger's bridge reveals a triadic circle when viewed narratively and a fourfold narrative when viewed ontologically. The aspect (the "end") of the bridge that is "told" through imagistic narratives is one that connects to ("rests" on the bank of) the structured interweaving of form and content, the circle of building and dwelling; and the aspect (the other "end") of the bridge that is explicated as ontological "rests" on the other bank, the realm of narrative, and the fourfold. The bridge that is a structure in and of narrative grounds itself upon the ontological, the circle of building and dwelling; and the bridge that structures itself onto-logically grounds itself on the oneness of the fourfold narratives. Narra-tive on the side of ontology and its circle, and ontological on the side of narrative and its four components, the bridge's narrativity takes ontology as its meaning and the bridge's ontology takes narrative as its meaning. The bridge does not traverse the gap, it simply inverts it; it joins ontology and narrative at each end and transposes the gap to a place internal to itself.

Thus, the bridge fails; it contains an infinite regress, since the gap within the bridge now needs to be bridged. Ultimately, the bridge be-comes the sign for the fact that the narratives of the fourfold don't derive from the ontology of dwelling, and those ontological propositions do not generalize the narratives. Each has its discursive source elsewhere; each emerges from a place that has become hidden behind the other one in Heidegger's account. The ontological resides behind plane of the fourfold figure, and narrativity resides within the elliptical (meta-metaphoric) cen-ter to the circle. Heidegger has placed the bridge at the place of his leap, in place of his leap, to displace the leap in his discourse, but the bridge itself now requires overleaping. The bridge is not a viaduct for new mean-ings; instead, it becomes a viaduct of new absences, a sign for what can-not traverse it. And its existence in Heidegger's textual landscape raises again the question of what the gap means for Heidegger's text.

I argued at the beginning of this essay that Heidegger's leap itself im-plied that the discourse leaped from became a signifier for the narrative leaped to; but now we can understand that move as a transformation of ontology to the hidden center it surrounds and an abandonment of the ontological signifier for a signified of oneness that remains ever at a dis-tance. The gap overleaped becomes a signifier for an effacement, for the production of an emptiness.

To approach this emptiness, let us first notice that there is a parallel between the two ends of the bridge. At the narrative end, the hidden is what lies behind Heidegger's list of privative characteristics: unseen signs named by the privatives, rendered both abstract and inexpressible by those names, and then particularized in narrative. In general, narrative escapes the limits of abstraction and answers the quest for content with specificity and concreteness. It bypasses nonarticulation or inarticulabil-ity through its presentation of the particular; it supersedes the general with the specific. That which cannot be presented in generality can be told as a story. The specific does not give meaning or content to the general; it substitutes itself for what is inarticulable. Not only does narrative represent hidden meaning, it is a metaphor for it, and part of its metaphoricity (of narrative as a special kind of metaphor) is precisely the inarticulability of its metaphoric meaning, preserved through narrativity's refusal to literalize the metaphoric relation, that is, through its refusal to relinquish its specificity to general statement. If the "oneness of the four-fold," as narrative, implies that there is a hidden text metaphorized by that narrative and whose title is "the oneness of the fourfold," then the content or meaning of that text is both the fourfold narrative itself and its own impossibility of articulation. The fourfold is then the signified of a hidden sign (text) that expresses itself metaphorically in turn through these superseding narratives; but as such, it is an impossible signified, because it emerges on the other side of a gap from the signifier. And that is precisely the implication of Heidegger's leap, his breaking off on one side, in "mid-stream," in order to resume on the other.

At the circular (dwelling) end of the bridge, we find a similar configuration; location and neighborhood emerge from the bridge as building, as a generalization of space. Space, in fact, is presented as a purely intentional notion.

> In dwelling [mortals] persist through spaces by virtue of their stay among things and locations. . . . We always go through spaces in such a way that we already experience them by staying constantly with near and remote locations and things. When I go toward the door of the lecture hall, I am already there, and could not go to it at all if I were not such that I am there. (*PLT,* 157)

This is a familiar picture from Husserl and Sartre; consciousness is always ahead of itself in being consciousness of something. The place to which one has "already" crossed is the content of one's intentionality toward that space.[13] But when we move through Heidegger's fourfold as it narrativizes the "there" of this intentional space, we encounter a chiasmus. The "there" toward which one walks is the foundation for walking toward it (it bears one toward it like the earth). One becomes absent in being elsewhere and becomes the other who is borne along by that "elsewhere" (like the sky that bears itself). One waits for oneself to arrive at the door toward which one walks (as though waiting for the divinities).[14] And the being of one walking is the foundation of a "there" toward which one walks (as self-initiated mortal). "Persisting through space" creates, receives, awaits, and is a means to an end. At the beginning, narrative is the foundation for walking, and for the being who walks toward; and at the end, the being who walks is the foundation for the "there" narrativized. One moves from where being is narrativized to where being narrativizes, from narrative as the foundation for intentional structure to intentional structure as the foundation for narrative. (And this implies that there is a centrality not of language in general but of the particular kind of language known as narrative to all thought, an idea to which we will return below.)

But Heidegger has narrativized a space, and in walking toward the door has positioned himself already at the ontological end of the bridge. To the extent that narrative and intentionality provide the being for the other, the object is put under erasure, ob-literated. Though the "there," as a "thing" toward which one walks, gathers the fourfold, its very gathering, like the bridge, is a location and neighborhood that renders the "there" a space, an ellipsis. To dwell in that elsewhere by walking toward it is to constitute a triadic circle of dwelling which abstracts it; it drops the "there" into the center of the circle because each component of the circle has already found its real content in the circle itself. Dwelling hides the object behind an interlacing of form and content that circumscribes it elliptically. The circle of dwelling, as the other end of the bridge, is a sign whose meaning is the superseded object, the hidden, the content that is no longer "there."

For Heidegger, intentionality, as "thereness," is not a subjectivity; it is a "letting-happen" (*PLT,* 64ff.). Rather than what structures or effects consciousness (as for Sartre), it is what effects or structures itself as consciousness. Consciousness, for Heidegger, is a metaphysical notion used to grasp hold of (and in the process denature) the "letting-happen." Letting-happen whelms up from an inarticulateness that finds its sign (its signifier) in the circle and its signification (its signified) in the fourfold narratives from elsewhere. It is the inarticulable center of the circle that grounds the narratives as well as the ellipsis into which those narratives fall as the inversions of the injunctions of ontological Being. The irony is that what whelms up affects itself nonarticulately as philosophy, but only as soon as it becomes articulately nonphilosophy (narrative). As philosophical discourse, it would be inarticulable if it were not couched in narrative, while as narrative it is already the meaning of a philosophical discourse about the preservation of inarticulability through that narrative. As the gap between ontology and narrative, intentionality is an impossible sign whose meaning is hidden.

In sum, the bridge traverses from ontology as an impossible sign whose hidden signified (object, "thereness") is metonymized by narrative to a formal textual structure as a hidden sign whose impossible signified (the outside, the enjoined narratives) is metaphorized by narrative. The bridge, as a narrative itself, spans (and does not span) the hiatus between narrative as an act of naming (the circle) and narrative as an act of meaning (the fourfold). It points out the fact that they are separate acts, differing in the nature of the hiddenness, yet themselves nothing less than the very upsurge, the manifestation, of the hidden.

What stands on both sides of the bridge, then, is the inarticulable (a hidden meaning on one side and a hidden text on the other) and the human being who is the subject matter of the discourse that engenders these hiddennesses (dweller/builder on one side and mortal on the other). Human being is "Man" in ontology and "mortal" in narrative. Human being as Man builds the bridge which allows the fourfold that narrates mortals, and human being as mortal initiates the bridge which allows "Man" to dwell.

Facing themselves across this bridge, humans are decentered in two ways. Man appears on the circumference of the circle on one side, and mortals appear as only one of four stories in the fourfold on the other. The mortals' side presents itself as a sort of sacred space, with an *axis mundi* and "four directions" (to use Eliade's paradigm),[15] and in that space Heidegger's chantlike telling, repeating "when we speak of [one], we are already thinking of the other three," is almost liturgical (*PLT*, 149–50); the other side, that of the circle of dwelling, the realm of "Man," presents itself as a secular, phenomenological site of "dwelling-thinking." Mortals, told in story, and "Man," an ontological idea, stand opposite and inverse to each other. But if mortals can die, then "Man" must be immortal. That is, mortality must be understood as what is mythic, residing in sacred space, and immortality only philosophical. This suggests that the divine messengers do indeed beckon to mortals who are mythic and that mortals are, without substitution, godhead.

Ultimately, the bridge seems to connect two religious propositions: an immortality (on a circle) whose text is hidden behind narrative as an act of naming and a mythic space (in an elliptical point) whose text is hidden behind narrative as an act of meaning. We have ended with two hidden texts whose content loses all its means of signification to the repetition of that hiddenness within itself. There is content, but it is forever rendering itself formless by finding that formlessness within itself as a gap, as absence. If the texts mirror themselves, it is in the way the world is reflected in a mirrored sphere. In the mirrored sphere, infinity appears at the center; the universe is inverted. The center, however, cannot be seen because the reflected head of the person looking is always in the way. And both are decentered, for if one were at the center, the other would be at infinity.

This returns us to the gap in the bridge, which is now between two inarticulables. In leaping to narrative to present the hidden and inarticulable, and in positing oneness as its signified (a formless content), Heidegger is presenting something that looks somewhat mystical. Let us look at this question of mysticism and the invocation of formless content in Heidegger for a moment. By understanding its relation to the notion of contentless form disclosed by Barthes, we shall have established the extremities of a space in which the discursive incommensurability between Sartre and Derrida can play.

HEIDEGGER'S MYSTICISM

The question of Heidegger's mysticism has attracted a certain amount of attention.[16] John Caputo, who presents a most extensive treatment, argues against the idea. To do so, he draws a parallel between Heidegger and Eckhart, a Christian mystic, and then, while pointing out significant differences, develops a definition of mysticism that fits Eckhart but not Heidegger. However, an affinity between Heidegger's concept of mysticism and his structure of nonsigns evades Caputo's gaze. It will be useful to look into this as an opportunity to enlarge on Heidegger's use of narrative (though taking sides in this issue would undoubtedly be an idle gesture).

Central to Heidegger's proximity to Eckhart is the notion of will-lessness (*Gelassenheit*). For Eckhart, will-lessness implies not lassitude but absence of telos. It also implies nonknowing in the sense of not obstructing god's will through conceptualization and self-conception. It connotes detachment, an escape from things, a release from self and passivity to divine will (*ME*, 119ff.). That is, the richest life is the poverty that "wills nothing and knows nothing and has nothing" ("PT," 210–13). Grounded in Eckhart's first principle, that "being is god," the import of will-lessness is that one has no independent existence but in god (*ME*, 103), a destiny one can only grasp experientially. The "fundamental experience" for Eckhart is constituted by this "realization," which he "tells" as "the birth of the Son in the soul," a oneness of individual and god (*ME*, 25). In general, mysticism posits a transcendence that subsumes beings and with respect to which beings have no real autonomy.

Heidegger uses *Gelassenheit* to signify "letting-be," allowing Being to be. In a manner similar to Eckhart, for Heidegger *Gelassenheit* means that man becomes a conduit for Being, that thinking "accomplishes" Being in the world and that it does so in response to Being rather than through mastery of things (*ME*, 27). Since "Being is the *transcendens* pure and simple,"[17] *Gelassenheit* becomes what allows Being's advent, its whelming up into the world as man and man's poetic language ("LH," 239–41). Heidegger's injunction is that man corral neither Being nor himself in the smallness of conceptualization.

In effect, both thinkers regard the ground of being as an undifferentiated and transcendent totality and pose the question of oneness in it. For Eckhart, oneness is the unification of individual and totality in "pristine simplicity and undividedness" (*ME*, 105); and for Heidegger, it is the fourfold within which the mythic mortal dwells (*ME*, 19). Both see man as the "work" of transcendence, of god or Being (*ME*, 174), and for both the essence of life is to be claimed by this transcendence, putting the world in epoche. Leon Rosenstein, arguing that Heidegger's thought is indeed mystical, points out that mysticism generally articulates itself in the negative, as what it is not and what should be abandoned, a notion common to Eckhart and Heidegger.[18] Both also posit an inarticulability as the ground of the world. Eckhart says, "The deepest ground and essence . . . lies in a nameless region from which all properties and attributes are excluded" (*ME*, 127). For Heidegger, Being is not determinate as "this or that," and its indeterminateness leaves it inarticulable. Man, he claims, must "learn to exist in the nameless" ("LH," 199). (To live in the nameless is to live in meanings for which there are only impossible signifiers.) For mysticism in general, oneness and direct experience of transcendence cannot be spoken. The nameless and the oneness are preconditions for each other; and rather than the specificity of a name, it is the fact of inarticulability that becomes the "name" for totality. Though a name may be given, it is a wistful act. The undifferentiable remains unarticulable. In "Building Dwelling Thinking," Heidegger leaps to narrative, not to represent but to present what remains (un)represented through preservation of the inarticulable. Both Eckhart and Heidegger bespeak the inarticulable behind narrative modes: sermons on the Bible for the one, the fourfold for the other.

Heidegger was attracted to mysticism first because it posited *Gelassenheit,* or nonwill, as a connection with transcendence, with Being—an openness to Being's nothingness (detachment and thinglessness) (*ME*, 21)—and also because mysticism went behind representations and thus participated in what Heidegger called thinking (*ME*, 142). Thinking is always already "divested of representations" ("PT," 211); it is conversely abandoned through representation. Herein lies the heart of Heidegger's attack on metaphysics. To "let Being be" means to free it from conceptualization. Caputo is careful to point out, however, that for Heidegger thinking is not a mysticism. In place of mysticism's "act of illumination," its irrationalism (*ME,* 223), Heidegger names an *ek-stasis,* a standing forth from Being in the world. But their formal purposes are the same; where telos, for Eckhart, takes one away from god, representation, for Heidegger, separates one from Being.

Caputo advances two types of arguments against Heidegger being considered mystical: one concerns God and the other language.[19] With respect to God, he points out that, for Eckhart, beings are formed from the ideal templates of God's mind; naturally, no such relation makes any sense for Heidegger. Being does not create beings; it is simply their ground, a question raised by the existence of beings and their changing forms. Eckhart speaks of union with God, for which no analogue exists in Heidegger's "thinking of Being." Ultimately, for Caputo, any mysticism must involve some notion of "cosmic mind," of which earthly mind is the reflection and conduit; in other words, it must involve a God, a "who" of transcendental subjectivity, in which to lose one's earthly selfhood.

One might respond to this argument in the following way. First, although Heidegger leaves the question of a God or "cosmic mind" unspecified, there is a suggestive ambiguity. In his "Letter on Humanism," he says that "thinking lets itself be claimed by Being so that it can say the truth of Being" ("LH," 194). "Thinking" becomes passive, to be appropriated or beset by what seems like an active agent that is not "thinking" per se. Being would seem to have subjectivity, bequeathing it a hidden (cosmic) aspect. Though a gratuitous point, this highlights the difficulty of leaving *Gelassenheit* unarticulated. Second, Caputo's conception of mysticism centers itself on the question of content. But how does one specify the content of mysticism when its core resides in the inarticulable? Because oneness and *Gelassenheit* take no object, the mystical point of view becomes purely formal and names precisely a noninvolvement in any particularity.

It is this aspect of the mystical experience, in fact, that differentiates it from the aesthetic experience, for instance. Like the mystical experience, the aesthetic experience is direct; but it engenders an aesthetic point of view as a mode of interpretation about the object of that experience. Because the mystical experience has no object, the mystical point of view can never be more than an intuition that the mystical experience is possible. In fact, no mystical experience or mysticism can be differentiated from another, if the essence of the mystical is the nonarticulate. The difference between names used for subsequent reference back to the mystical experience (God, Being, oneness, or Enlightenment) does not change the fact that one is naming unity or universality as such—by default, since nothing can be said. Any content given them is already not their content. The signified for all signs that name the mystical is the same, and is empty. Indeed, the mystical experience is precisely of the absence of particularity or differentiation. An invocation of "cosmic mind," whether by the mystic or the critic, is an empty gesture. Thus, the "object" that particularizes mysticism can only be the narrative used to bespeak the inarticulable. But that narrative becomes metaphoric of a signified, not a signifier. For the inarticulable, there can be no signifier, and "its" signified is empty until so metaphorized. The narrative must name, in some sense, the nonliteralizable meaning of a metaphor whose literal meaning is impossible, that is, a second-order metaphor. The content of mysticism is a literalized metaphor for the empty signified of an impossible signifier that in turn takes as its name, its form, that same literalized metaphor. And indeed, Heidegger's own philosophical use of narrative points this out by exemplifying it.

On the question of language, Caputo's view is again that Heidegger is too worldly to be mystical. He argues, first, that Heidegger seeks a renewal of language, one that will allow Being to appear, that will let Being be in language (*ME,* 224-25)—a renewal to provide an earthly arena for transcendence rather than lose the earthly in the inarticulable. Such a renewal of language would locate itself within the neighborhood of "living in the nameless," and thus position itself this side of the cosmic. Second, Heidegger addresses time rather than eternity—that is, he is concerned with the secular and historical (*ME,* 225-26). And finally, Heidegger's emphasis on poetry is both worldly and artistic rather than mystical. Poetry, Caputo says, "is the instituting of a world, the uncovering of the matrix of meaning in which an historical age lives and dwells" (*ME,* 235). Thus, for Caputo, the fact that Heidegger addresses language as he does renders his thinking nonmystical.

But again, this is an argument regarding the content of mysticism. It ignores the idea that the mystical experience, because it is necessarily what cannot be said, has to do precisely with language, but in form rather than content. It is in his formal address to language that Heidegger reveals a mystical bent. For instance, with respect to eternity: it is true that in writing Heidegger can speak only of time and the fictional; the eternal, as a mystical experience, cannot be represented. But Heidegger is clearly looking for something else. In his etymological derivations, he is asking what has been "let be" through all a word's transformations. He searches the history of words for the invariant, for what a word once meant and still conceals unlost in its present usage, even if only as a trace. Rather than embrace history, he collapses history to find the ahistorical, as an eternal, in language. If language is to speak ("language speaks"), its foundation must be more than mere presence.

Second, it is true that poetry is worldly and artistic and escapes the strictures of conceptualization. The poet is the one who has stepped out of the metaphysical dimension. The poem, as a text, is only a name (not to be confused with its title) for its own experiential being; the words of its text collectively (inseparably) do not name anything other than the poem. It fills its name as a poem, and it poetically circumscribes itself as a name. The poem, coextensive with its name, is hidden behind, or under the name as a text. In other words, as language, the text is a trope for the signified of the poem hidden behind the words that name and compose it (analogous to the relationship of the fourfold narratives to their inarticulable oneness). The poem's text is the conduit of the poem, in the same way that man is the conduit of transcendence. "Being's poem is man" (*PLT,* 4). Thus, self-referentially unconceptualized, the poem escapes metaphysical presence. For this reason, Heidegger, in his deconstruction of metaphysics, reaches into poetic language. The poem is a renewal of language because it dwells in the nameless by being *only* a name; the poem as name becomes a second-order metaphor for underlying namelessness that has manifest itself as newness. That a "historical age lives and dwells" in the poem does not save the poem from also being a second-order metaphor for the inarticulable. Again, if all inarticulables, as soon as they become objects of attention or focus, are indistinguishable, then Heidegger's use of poetic language to "live in the nameless" becomes indistinguishable in form from mysticism.

In sum, Heidegger does not embrace the content of mysticism, but he duplicates it in form (homologically) through the use of a tropic text to point to an unarticulable. Both mysticism and Heidegger's return to the Being of language through a leap to narrative reveal a structure of formless content. That is, formless content, which is one limit of the sign, is the limit of the text, the place where it must trope its own existence, the point at which the inarticulable affirms that its meaning has no signifier. The narratives, and the use of poetic language, which are metaphoric for unstatable signifieds (that is, impossible signifiers for which only second-order metaphors are possible), are texts which substitute particularity for an impossible generality. When Heidegger substitutes the narratives of the fourfold for the direct experience of Being, it is not they, the narratives, that acquire meaning, but rather the things they attach to (for example, the bridge), the things that "accomplish" them ("The thing is the intersection of the fourfold" [*ME,* 216]). These narratives, though they fulfill the project Caputo posits for Heidegger as worldly, finite, and temporal in content, simultaneously place Heidegger in the realm of the mystical in form. They substitute themselves in form for the content that has no form; they establish their own existence at the limit of textuality, and in that sense on the border of mysticism. In other words, Heidegger's text can be called mystical not because Heidegger was a mystic (an ultimately undecidable question), but because of what he attempts to do with language. And if the form of that project is homologous to the form of mysticism, then one can use the term "mysticism" to name the structure of that commonality, and thus to name the metadiscursive form Heidegger's text evinces in its attempt to do something else.

A THEORY OF NARRATIVE

All narratives are signifiers; they narratively point out components of their world while poetically naming themselves. Within the circular structure unavoidable in a text of mind or thinking, however, they dwell as signifieds of what remains elliptical because unarticulable behind that structure. As signifieds, the narratives' role is to metaphorize, and not engender, the unarticulated meaning. The role of narrative in philosophy, its substitution of the particular for the general, is to prevent literalization, to leave the inarticulable its "thereness." But when narrative metaphorizes an impossible sign or inexperiencible object it can only literalize itself and become the name the signifier it was originally designed not to become. It does what it is adopted not to do. This is what happens to Heidegger's "oneness." The formal mysticism of his text is constituted by a narrative oneness that metaphorizes both the possibility of the impossible experience of oneness and the impossibility of articulating the possible experience of oneness. If articulated or conceptualized, mysticism immediately fractures: it loses its hiddenness, and its oneness dissolves.

On the other hand, if we reflect back to the narrativization given intentionality by the fourfold, its structure points to an ellipsis circumscribed by an endless, oversignified generality, viz., the ontological circle. Intentionality, as ontological, is given as a sign system of the particular, of injunctions and of coming to awareness (the act of naming). In the chiasmus of narrativity and the ontological, it remains hidden behind a generalization, a continual recurrence of narrativity. Thus, it reveals a topology that is the inverse of mysticism, where the latter is an impossible sign system (the act of meaning) hidden behind the particularity of narratives.

Heidegger's use of narrative, as a second-order metaphor for dwelling-thinking, constitutes an escape from the necessity to define either Being or thinking, an escape from metaphysics. But the attempt draws Heidegger into a form of mysticism through the play of language in narrative (as direct experience) and etymology (as eternity) that he uses for his escape. That is, his deconstruction of metaphysics leads him to both the poetic and the mystical. All three, metaphysics, mysticism, and poetry—that is, the articulate, the nonarticulate, and the poetic, or reference, nonreference, and self-reference—stand in isomorphism to the dwelling-building circle of buildings, dwelling, and Building. Behind them, as an ellipsis in the circle of dwelling, lies the inarticulability of intentionality. Reference, nonreference, and self-reference are themselves the analytic products of this ellipsis, the forms taken by consciousness as their analysand. Essentially, consciousness (whose articulations or definitions we have already seen are circular) cannot be analyzed because the metaphysical, the mystical, and the poetic forms of doing so only testify to the fact that the analysis has already occurred. That is, thinking about consciousness has no origin, no point of departure, other than the narratives that are the modes of moving from one element to another around the circle.

Notes

1. Martin Heidegger, "Building Dwelling Thinking," in *Poetry, Language, Thought,* trans. Albert Hofstadter (New York: Harper and Row, 1971), 149. This volume hereafter abbreviated *PLT* and cited parenthetically in the text. The essay was originally published as "Bauen Wohnen Denken" in Martin Heidegger, *Vorträge und Aufsätze* (Tübingen: Gunther Neske Pfullingen, 1954), 145–62.

2. See Heidegger, *Vorträge,* 149.

3. For "belonging to men's being with one another," the German reads, "*das Miteinander der Menschen*" (Heidegger, *Vorträge,* 149). This could be translated literally as "a belonging or properness to the togetherness of men," since *Miteinander* is a conflation of adverb and noun.

4. Martin Heidegger, *Being and Time,* trans. John Macquarrie and Ed-

ward Robinson (New York: Harper and Row, 1962), 363; hereafter abbreviated *BT* and cited parenthetically in the text.

5.   It might be mentioned that the "fourfold" has a history of development in Heidegger. It first appears in the *Introduction to Metaphysics* as a fourfold path, still within a discourse of being and nonbeing. When it reappears in "The Thing," and in Heidegger's essay on Hölderlin ("Poetically Man Dwells . . ."), also in *PLT,* it is in its final narrativized form.

6.   See, for instance, Heidegger's treatment of the object in "The Origin of the Work of Art," in *Basic Writings,* ed. David Krell (New York: Harper and Row, 1977), 143–87. See also Robert Bernasconi, *The Question of Language in Heidegger's History of Being* (Atlantic Highlands, N.J.: Humanities Press, 1985).

7.   "The Thing" is an essay that ironically sets technological reduction of distance in the distance, as the science-fiction movie of the same name (which was an early national confrontation by the postwar United States with the homeless, those without dwelling) did for the interaction or intersubjectivity of beings.

8.   Heidegger gives the following etymology for these terms. *Bauen,* from Old German, means to build, but also to dwell. It is the Indo-European root from which the conjugations *Ich bin* and *du bist* derive, that is, from *buan* and *bhu,* respectively. Thus, *bauen* also means to be. To dwell is also a translation of *Wohnen,* from the early Saxon *wuon,* which also means to remain, to reside. See Vincent Vycinas, *Earth and Gods* (The Hague: M. Nijhoff, 1961).

Gerald Bruns points out that the fourfold constitutes the way Heidegger articulates being in the world in his later writing (*Heidegger's Estrangements: Language Truth, and Poetry in the Later Writings* [New Haven, Conn.: Yale University Press, 1989], 81). Bruns addresses Heidegger's argument, in "Language" (in *PLT*), that you can't tell poetry and thinking apart. They are what he calls "dif-ferent," which, Bruns argues, is a relation similar to Derrida's *différance* (ibid., 87).

9.   We should recognize that, for Heidegger, in general, the notions of form and content represent a false metaphysical separation between subject and object. But the rise of semiotics has provided a different framework in which to locate these terms. Heidegger uses "form" in the sense of shape or outward appearance and content in the sense of subject matter. "Form" can be recast as location or structure, and the meaning that structure gives to what it is "about," to what it concerns or to what concerns itself with it. This is especially germane here. If location provides the space for buildings, for instance, then those buildings are what that location is about, what gives that location its meaning. It is not an ontological but a semiotic relation between them.

10.   There are a number of different ways of articulating the same interrelation of form and content in a triadic circularity. Ultimately, they each

present a way of obviating foundations, or dispensing with the necessity of foundations, as a circularity, while providing themselves as foundations, as a circle. In general, we can say that something finds its form by manifesting a place to be and at the same time taking its source as its content. Or form can be understood as an articulation that in turn finds its content in what originally produced it as an articulation. Semiotically speaking, when something finds its form, it reveals itself as the signified of what it thus discloses as its signifier.

11.   A general account of this process can be given. A hermeneutic circle demonstrates that foundations themselves depend on precisely what they are presumed to ground. In any text, for instance, the text as a whole is constituted by its parts (its constituent signs); and in contextualizing them, it constitutes those signs as parts, as what participates in its textuality as a whole. The whole establishes its parts as parts, and the parts establish the whole as whole. To raise the question of ground for the hermeneutic circle is to raise it in the hermeneutic circle. And this generates another circle, a circle of contextualizations. If the meaning of a text depends on its own metatextual elements to disclose its contextualization, then the text grounds a metatext which grounds a context by which the text itself is grounded. To the extent that the text's metatextual elements are formal, or structural, then this triadic circle represents the simultaneous operation of three deconstructive moments: first, depriviliging a text's content with respect to its form, enabling form to function textually and contextually; second, depriviliging exterior context, deferring sociohistorical and ideological assumptions of how the text is to be read, enabling form to function contextually and metatextually; and third, depriviliging the text's "natural" or "literal" meaning with respect to second-order significations, enabling form to function metatextually and textually.

12.   Heidegger: "Gathering or assembly, by an ancient word in our language [German], is called 'thing'" (*PLT,* 153).

13.   The notion of "content" used here is not the same as that used earlier in the semiotic relation of "form and content"; in the structure of intentionality, it is the "something" toward which one gives attention, the "ofness" of consciousness. Sartre, by positing the structure in the negative, that what one intends is not the object and not the consciousness of the object, provides a less problematic formulation in not using the notion of "content" at all.

14.   This is a nonreligious use of divinities, we might add, that reveals an uncomfortable ethic. "The divinities are the beckoning messengers of godhead" (*PLT,* 150). To equate thought with godhead gives thought its head to become God, and renders one God. In being already at the door waiting for one to arrive, one is both the beckoning messenger and the God awaited, both presence and concealment. Intentionality, in Heidegger, becomes difficult to distinguish from divinity.

15.   See, for instance, Mircea Eliade, *Myth and Reality,* trans. Willard Trask (New York: Harper and Row, 1963).

16.   A number of articles have appeared in which various critics have explored the question of Heidegger's mysticism, taking sides for or against. See, in particular, Stephen Tynan, "Mysticism and Gnosticism in Heidegger," *Philosophy Today* 28, no. 4 (Winter 1984): 358–77; Leon Rosenstein, "Mysticism as Preontology: A Note on the Heideggerian Connection," *Philosophy and Phenomenological Research* 39, no. 1 (September 1978): 57–73; and Bernhard Welte, "God in Heidegger's Thought," *Philosophy Today* 26, no. 1 (Spring 1982): 85–100. There are two two-part articles in the *Journal of the History of Philosophy* by John D. Caputo (12, no. 4 [October 1974]: 479–94, and 13, no. 1 [January 1975]: 61–80) and Reiner Schurmann (12, no. 4 [October 1974]: 455–78, and 13, no. 1 [January 1975]: 43–60); both address a relation between Heidegger and Eckhart, to which Schurmann adds a consideration of Suzuki.

The most extensive treatment given the question is by John D. Caputo, *The Mystical Element in Heidegger's Thought* (Athens: Ohio University Press, 1978); hereafter abbreviated *ME* and cited parenthetically in the text. It is an extension of Caputo's articles in *Journal of the History of Philosophy.* Caputo also extends his treatment in a Heidegger Festschrift article called "The Poverty of Thought: Reflections on Heidegger and Eckhart," in *Heidegger: The Man and the Thinker,* ed. Thomas Sheehan (Chicago: Precedent, 1981), 209–16; hereafter abbreviated "PT" and cited parenthetically in the text. In his larger work, Caputo pays special attention to three other critics who have dealt with the question of Heidegger's mysticism: Paul Huhnerfeld, Karl Lowith, and Laszlo Versenyi (*ME,* chapter 1).

17.   From the introduction to *Being and Time* and reiterated in "Letter on Humanism," in *Basic Writings,* 216; hereafter abbreviated "LH" and cited parenthetically in the text.

18.   Rosenstein, "Mysticism as Preontology," 64.

19.   Caputo makes other arguments that concern Heidegger's context rather than his text. One is that mysticism lies within a tradition, and Heidegger's position is to rethink that tradition, not to find a place in or alongside it. Second, Caputo asserts that Eckhart's mysticism is both a step out of metaphysics and contains a residue of metaphysics. He places the same grid on Heidegger, leaving them both in the same camp. Caputo's main point is correct to the extent that metaphysics is present as soon as the mystic seeks to write or to speak his mysticism. Third, he argues that Heidegger is not mystical because his thought has been "thoroughly purged . . . of any ethical or moral dimension" (*ME,* 236). But the injunction to "let Being be" is already programmatic and calls for transcending representation, differentiation, and metaphysics. Program reflects morality in the same sense that beings reflect Being.

Why is it that all organic beings we know beget their kind only by the union of two sexes (which we then call male and female)? We cannot admit that the Creator, just as a whim and to establish an arrangement he liked on our planet, was merely playing, so to speak. It rather seems that, given the material nature of our world, it must be impossible to have organic creatures reproduce without two sexes established for that purpose.—In what darkness human reason loses itself when it tries to probe its lineage, or even merely guess what it is!

—Immanuel Kant, *Anthropology from a Pragmatic Point of View*[1]

This is also why we rejoice (actually we are relieved of a need) when, just as if it were a lucky chance favoring our aim, we do find such a systematic unity among merely empirical laws, even though we had to assume that there is such unity, even though we have no insight into this unity and cannot prove it.

—Immanuel Kant, *Critique of Judgment*[2]

Awakening Negativity

The Genesis of Aesthetics in the *Critique of Judgment*

Charles Shepherdson

The place of history in Kant's systematic philosophy would appear to be marginal at best. Works such as "Idea for a Universal History from a Cosmopolitan Point of View," "What Is Enlightenment?" "Towards a Perpetual Peace," and the *Anthropology* have been regarded for the most part as extrasystematic. There are reasons for this judgment: in these works, Kant is reaching for a broader audience, his style is more relaxed, his demonstrations less exacting; also, the material itself is more intractable, has a depth of impurity that is difficult to overcome.[3] Rooted in the empirical world, contaminated by human interests and desires, and prey to the extrinsic and irregular course of history, the field of inquiry in these texts would seem to lie irrevocably remote from the more rigorous construction of the critical edifice.

Now the *Critique of Judgment* has also been regarded as an after-thought, as if Kant, having finished the great projects of epistemology and ethics, could divert his attention to the remaining *region* of aesthetics. This view of the third *Critique* has a similar basis: as a treatise on feeling, on pleasure and pain, it concerns a region that is not governed by reason or understanding, that appears to be irremediably subjective and contingent, and that, even when it does yield a level of universality, still fails to provide cognitive or practical knowledge.

More recent commentaries have insisted, however, that the *Critique of Judgment* is not at all a marginal concern, that it does not in fact treat a particular region at all but rather undertakes to bridge the abyss that had been left gaping between the first two critiques: in aesthetic judgments, the imagination is not governed by reason or understanding but is nevertheless brought into a relation of harmony with these faculties. The third *Critique*, then, does not address an autonomous and marginal realm, a rigorously delimited region that one could call "the aesthetic"; rather, Kant shows that in aesthetic judgments the imagination is, as he puts it, "annexed" (*angeschlossen*) as needed to one or the other of the two separate branches of human thought. Recall section 2 of the intro-duction to the third *Critique*, entitled "On the Domain of Philosophy": "[A]n immense gulf is fixed between the domain of the concept of na-ture, the sensible, and the domain of the concept of freedom, the super-sensible, so that no transition from the sensible to the supersensible . . . is possible, just as if they were two different worlds" (*CJ*, 175–76). Gov-erned by neither, and as if relegated to a prephilosophical domain (feel-ing), aesthetic judgment nevertheless has *no proper region of its own* but mediates between the realm of nature and causal necessity, and the realm of morality and human freedom, thereby unifying what has hith-erto remained separate and fragmentary. In Kant's words, although "an immense gulf" separates the two domains of philosophy, "such that no *transition* [*Ubergang*] is possible" between them, nevertheless "there must after all be a basis uniting" them, which "does make possible the transition" (*CJ*, 176).

In the introduction Kant specifies this transition quite clearly in two ways. There is a "division of philosophy into theoretical and practical." The rift will be crossed, first, in connection with a family metaphor: phi-losophy is a divided house, "and yet the family also includes a mediating link. This is judgment" (*CJ*, 177).[4] In addition to the logical family (understanding, reason, and judgment) in which the third term has no domain but is the primordial possibility of transition between the others (homeless but originary), one also sees, second, the establishment—or rather the wager, since it is something yet to come—of pleasure, which Kant will now link to judgment. Thus, in addition to judgment, "there is also (judging by analogy) another basis . . . that seems even more important" than judgment's "kinship with the family" (*CJ*, 177). This is pleasure, which "lies between the cognitive power and the power of desire, just as judgment lies between understanding and reason" (*CJ*, 177–78). Thus, the judgment, in being linked to pleasure, "will bring about a transition [*Ubergang*]" from nature to freedom, "just as in its logical use it makes possible the transition from understanding to reason" (*CJ*, 179). Already one begins to see that the treatise on aesthetics will not be the investigation of a domain so much as the inquiry into a certain movement, and that this movement is not so much *there to be investigated* as it is something *to be produced*. The third *Critique* approaches this originary transition, this third term which is first, as a future:

> If a system of pure philosophy, under the general title metaphysics, is to be achieved some day (and to accomplish this quite completely is both possible and of the utmost importance for our use of reason in all contexts), the critique must already have explored the terrain supporting this edifice . . . so that no part of the edifice may give way, which would inevitably result in the collapse of the whole. (*CJ*, 168)

These two aspects of a question concerning time—first, that the aesthetic is (like history) not so much a region as a movement of displacement; second, that this movement is (like history) something to be accomplished, something futurally directed rather than something *given* (but then what would be the *mode of givenness* in the experience *that there is pleasure,* that experience from which the entire genesis derives its energy?)—will be the focus of our concern with the *genesis* in the third *Critique*.

Now the essays on history have precisely the same function. The Kantian horizon for the question of history is familiar, and it will be enough to recall its general features here. On one hand, *although* it is an empirical field, history does not exhibit the regular lawfulness of nature; instead of being governed by cause and effect, history is the product of human freedom. On the other hand, *because* it is an empirical field, it cannot simply be given over to legislation by the moral will; for the legislation that obtains when it is a question of whether to perform an action cannot be used to judge the sequence of historical events.[5] History, in other words, while indeed belonging to the realm of culture and freedom rather than to nature and necessity, at the same time falls outside the purity of the ethical law — as is clearly indicated, Kant says, by the degrading multitude of violent, superstitious, self-interested, and barbarous events to which not only the past but even the present bears humiliating witness. Like pleasure and pain, history belongs neither to reason nor to understanding.

Posed in this way outside the regularity of nature, and beneath, as it were, the pure self-determination of the moral will, history is at the same time — like feeling — to be transformed into a bridge between these realms: precisely by virtue of belonging to the abyss that lies between them, it will, Kant says, give evidence of their deepest unity. Thus, one finds, in Kant's "Idea for a Universal History" for example, not only the confession that history, like feeling, appears to be an unscientific field, chaotic and irregular, ruled only by passion and accident, but also an argument that redeems this field by seeking an underlying order for history in two different directions. Like the argument regarding the beautiful and the sublime, which annexes the imagination first into a harmonious relation with understanding and then into a relation, at first unpleasurable and finally pleasurable, of harmony with reason, the essay on history will argue in two directions — toward the regularity of nature and toward the lawfulness of the will. On the one hand, Kant says, whatever the intentions of men may be, whatever their desires and purposes, history is nevertheless ruled by a process of nature which supersedes all human intentions to produce a rigorously determined goal by exploiting human passion, conflict and antagonism for its own purpose ("IUH," prop. 4 and 8). That purpose is, of course, the complete fulfillment and realization of humanity's natural endowment, a goal expressed in the telos of the rational state and produced, Kant says ("IUH," prop. 8), by a blind and mechanical necessity that exploits human conflict for its own ends. This argument has been called Kant's "cunning of nature."[6] On the other hand, Kant will argue in the direction of the moral will: if nature had ordained that humanity should reach its highest goal through such a causal mechanism, it would have been both unnecessary and unreliable for the will to have been left free ("IUH," prop. 1 and 3).[7] And in fact, Kant goes on to argue, this natural purpose which governs history is not really demonstrable; it is not a matter of actual knowledge. To those of us who live in the debris of history and cannot actually see the ultimate purpose of nature that governs history when it is *regarded as a whole,* this underlying order cannot be mistaken for genuinely objective knowledge. Thus Kant writes, in the ninth and last proposition:

> It seems at first sight a strange and even an absurd proposal to suggest the composition of a history according to the idea of how the course must proceed, if it is to be conformable to rational laws. It may well appear that only a romance could be produced from such a point of view. However, if it be assumed that nature, even in the play of human freedom, does not proceed without plan and design, the idea may well be regarded as practicable; and although we are too short-sighted to see through the secret mechanism of her constitution, yet the idea may be serviceable, as a clue to help us penetrate the otherwise planless aggregate of human actions. ("IUH," prop. 9)

The discipline of history—what Kant calls its "composition" here—is therefore not a science, and universal history, which regards the *sequence,* as a *whole,* is, as Kant's title points out, only an idea. Such an idea may serve practical reason (being "serviceable" or "practicable"), but when it is a question of the discipline, Kant is obliged once again (resolutely) to anticipate the future:[8] the idea of a universal history may well be practical, he says, "but we shall *leave it to nature to produce* the man who is fit to compose it" ("IUH," introductory remark).

What nature produced, however, was Nietzsche, who replied that

> the human race is tough and persistent, and will not admit that the lapse of a thousand years, or a hundred thousand, entitles anyone to sum up its progress from the past to the future; that is, *it will not be observed as a whole.* . . . History, so far as it serves life, serves an unhistorical power, and thus will never become a pure science like mathematics.[9]

In short, just as Kant claims in the *Critique of Judgment* that beauty is not an attribute of the object but instead a subjective state of pleasure judged to be universal and necessary and therefore spoken of *as if* it were a quality of the object, so, too, Kant argues, in "Idea for a Universal History," that our apprehension of an orderliness in history, our sense of its purposiveness, is not to be attributed to the object as a matter of knowledge but is rather to be judged *as if* it belonged to the object, though in fact it concerns our (ethical) relation to history.[10] To judge history as a teleological unity rather than as an empirical series of accidents is to judge it not by reference to an actual concept but by reference to a regulative idea of reason—that is, an idea which is the illegitimate product of dialectical illusion, which therefore exceeds the limits established by the first *Critique,* but which, even without having genuinely cognitive status in regard to the object, can nevertheless by employed in the service of practical human striving (*CPR,* A508/B536–A515/B543). But what this shows is that the idea of history as a purposive unity has no proper employment in the hands of the historian, whose task, as Kant laments, is therefore "merely descriptive": the idea has not a cognitive but an ethical legitimacy; it serves not the speculative but the practical interest of reason. It is an idea that will serve our conduct, but insofar as Kant is addressing the domain of history as a field of inquiry, such an idea cannot be legitimately employed. The two directions of argument—toward nature and necessity, and toward freedom and the moral will—make it clear that this apparently extracritical, extrasystematic domain of history in fact poses for Kant the question of the unity of philosophy as such. In Kant's brief treatment of history it is not so much a question of establishing a domain (the field of history) and the principles obtaining to knowledge of that domain (the science of history) as it is a matter of *producing a shift* whereby one can make the leap from the sensible to the supersensible. It is the question of the abyss over which one leaps in thus crossing between nature and freedom that will be posed by interrogating the (possibly purer) field of pleasure; this will make up the task for the treatise on aesthetics.[11]

The connection between history and aesthetics is not just one of analogy, then, or of structural similarity within the critical project. To regard them as separate fields of inquiry, the one an *external* series of *empirical* events, the other an *internal* and *affective* experience, would be to misunderstand both fields completely, confirming their regional status and relegating them to a nonconceptual, prephilosophical domain. To regard history and aesthetics as separate regions of inquiry, drawing up a list of external parallels in order to establish their relation to one another, would be to ignore the deeper connection they share in belonging to the abyss that had been left gaping between the first two *Critiques.* Far from occupying separate but parallel regions of knowledge, history and aesthetics are not regional disciplines with rigorously demarcated boundaries; indeed, it could be argued that they possess their mediating function of uniting the first two *Critiques* precisely by virtue of belonging to no place, having no regional status, no clearly delimited content, either empirically or conceptually. It is only by a peculiar role of displacement that either region can serve as a third critique that also expresses the unity of the first and second; it is only by belonging to no place, no region, that either can serve in the construction of the edifice *as a part that also raises the question of the whole.*[12] In this sense, for Kant, history and aesthetics are not at all regional sciences, but belong more intimately together as the place, or the movement of displacement, in which philosophy itself is questioned as to its unity.

The third *Critique,* even apart from the essays on history, already sets forth such a movement. In fact, this genesis is the most fundamental movement of the book, and all the finer distinctions Kant is at pains to make could be shown to serve its demonstration. We cannot be concerned with the entirety of Kant's analysis, but we will isolate its operation briefly, at three separate levels. It will be a question, first, of the movement of genesis at work in the very general, but nevertheless quite precise, order of relations between the three *Critiques* (and here it will be a matter of the architectonic interest of reason) (*CPR,* A474–755/B502–3); second, of the movement of genesis as it appears within the general structure of the third *Critique* itself (and here it will be a matter of tracing the passage from aesthetics to teleology, and especially the transformation of the notion of finality or purpose or end); and finally, it will be a question of the movement of genesis that is at work or at play within the very narrow space from which this genesis takes its first steps (and here it will be a matter of the pure judgment of taste, the so-called experience *that there is beauty*).

1

Despite a large body of scholarship, the *Critique of Pure Reason* is not simply an essay in epistemology. The limiting of reason which it undertakes not only shows the conditions for the possibility of experience, establishing space and time as pure intuitions and laying out the categories of the understanding; it also exposes the dialectical and illusory nature of the ideas of reason—specifically those of the soul, the world, and God. The categories of the understanding, in other words, are rightly established as pure a priori syntheses giving us knowledge of nature, but the ideas of reason are shown to be unjustifiable inferences. This is why book 1, the transcendental aesthetic, is preparatory to book 2, the transcendental dialectic, Kant's critique of psychology, cosmology, and theology. In the course of this demonstration, the relation of the first *Critique* as a whole to the *Critique of Practical Reason* already begins to emerge.[13]

When, for example in the paralogisms, Kant shows how the transcendental unity of apperception is falsely objectified by reason and then converted into the idea of the soul, he does not pretend to banish this idea altogether. There is, he tells us, an inevitability of illusion, one that belongs to the very nature of human reason (*CPR,* A297/B363). Consequently, the idea of the soul persists, he says, "not as a *doctrine* furnishing an addition to our knowledge of the self, but only as a *discipline*" (*CPR,* B421). This discipline is precisely the continual limiting, the movement of constraining, by which reason's natural and irrevocable urge toward speculative illusion can be diverted in the direction of practical reason.[14] Thus Kant writes of the idea of the soul:

> [T]hough it furnishes no positive doctrine, it reminds us that we should regard this refusal of reason to give satisfactory response to our inquisitive probings into what is beyond the limits of this present life as reason's hint to divert our self-knowledge from fruitless and extravagant speculation to fruitful practical employment. (*CPR,* B421)

In the antinomies of pure reason one finds a similar deflection which directs rational cosmology into the service of practical reason. Like the idea of the soul, the cosmological ideas are the product of an inference, in this case, an inference in which the unity of appearances, a unity formed by the synthesis of understanding, is taken up by reason and converted into an absolute unity of the totality of appearances. The antinomies are thus worthy of greater attention here, since they concern the idea of *the world as a whole.* This is the specific idea to which Kant refers, both in "Idea for a Universal History," at the point where history is judged as an organized whole rather than as an endless series of disorganized events, and in the discussion of teleology in the *Critique of Judgment,* at the point where the analysis passes from particular objective wholes ("organic form") to the concept of nature as a whole. The transition in each case is accomplished by the employment which the faculty of reason gives to the categories of the understanding. The synthetic activity of understanding, in other words, which still remains bound to appearances and their *mode of givenness,* is extended by reason in order to satisfy a demand for absolute totality and completeness, a demand that is not fulfilled at the level of experience.[15] In Kant's words, "Reason does not really generate any concept. The most it can do is to *free* a concept of *understanding* from the unavoidable limitations of possible experience and so to endeavor to extend it beyond the limits of the empirical" (*CPR,*

A409/B435). Now what limits the understanding and leaves it incomplete is its relation to intuition, to the mode of givenness of appearances, to what Kant calls "the unavoidable limitations of possible experience." In transgressing these limits, reason takes the synthesis of appearances that is accomplished by the understanding and transforms it into the idea of the absolute unity of the totality of appearances. This yields the cosmological idea of the world as a whole. Like the idea of the soul, this idea has no genuinely cognitive status: there is no object of knowledge corresponding to the idea of the soul or the world as a whole. And the persistent though spurious emergence of these ideas, since they cannot be altogether suppressed, must, Kant says, be diverted from the speculative arena of pure reason into the service of practical reason.[16]

If, in the first *Critique,* the transcendental aesthetic was preparatory to the transcendental dialectic (which is the critique of reason proper), it is now clear that the *Critique of Pure Reason* as a whole will be completed, or find its fulfillment, only in the *Critique of Practical Reason.*[17] And yet, as we have already noted, the *Critique of Judgment* begins in turn by acknowledging the abyss that still remains between the first two *Critiques.* Thus, the movement of displacement or referral by which pure reason is directed toward practical employment has opened an abyss, one that the *Critique of Judgment* undertakes to explore, thereby overcoming the fragmentation, the disunity, that remains.

> If thus an abyss stretching out of sight (*unubersehbare Kluft*) is established between the domain of the concept of nature, that is, the sensible, and the domain of the concept of freedom, such that no passage (*Ubergang*) is possible from the one to the other, as between worlds so different that the first can have no influence on the second, the second *must* (*soll*) yet have an influence on the former. . . . Consequently, it must be (*muss es*) that there is a foundation of unity (*Grund der Einheit*). (*CJ,* introduction 5)[18]

Since the *Critique of Judgment* is thus the foundation for the critical edifice as a whole, let us turn to its internal structure.

2

The treatise as a whole is called the *Critique of Judgment* and claims to treat judgment as such, even though it is only concerned with reflective and not determinate judgment. Now as a treatise on reflection that is designed to link the realms of nature and freedom, the *Critique of Judgment* has no immediately obvious reason for becoming concerned with aesthetics. What it seeks is an a priori form for the faculty of judgment in its independence from reason and understanding. But at the start of the book Kant declares (as if by fiat, or from historical precedent?) that the basis for establishing an independent principle for judgment "is to be met with" (*findet sich*) "principally" (but not exclusively?) in the "judgments which are called aesthetic."

So the treatise on judgment as a whole will therefore treat one of the two parts of judgment. While determinate judgment already has concepts (pure and practical) at its disposal and uses them *to determine something as something,* it nevertheless cannot show the unity of these two kinds of concepts. It is this gap between the determinations of reason and the determinations of understanding that reflective judgment seeks to overcome, and this is why the treatise on reflective judgment claims to treat not one species (a part) of judgment but the ground which underlies judgment as a whole.[19]

The treatise is divided in two. The two parts of the treatise address the two forms of reflective judgment, aesthetic and teleological. The transition between these two parts, the movement from one to the other, is accomplished by the shift from subjective to objective purposiveness.[20] This is a shift from the subjective feeling, which nevertheless has universal necessity, to the teleological judgment, which has objective validity.[21] As Kant says in section 15, a judgment of taste is aesthetic, rests on a subjective basis, and is not determined by any concept. But, Kant writes, "objective purposiveness can only be cognized by referring the manifold to a determinate purpose, and hence through a concept" (*CJ,* 221). The subjective judgment is disinterested, while the objective and teleological serves the interests of reason. The passageway between these two parts of the whole treatise is thus a passing from disinterest to interest, from the universality of subjective feeling with no concept to an objective purposiveness given through a concept; and such a passing over to objective purposiveness is accomplished, Kant says, "by referring the manifold to a determinate purpose, . . . through a concept." The manifold here is the manifold of understanding, and it is referred to a determinate purpose through a concept of reason.

The major division of the text is therefore not at all a division of reflective judgment into two separate types or categories, set as it were side by side (esthetics and teleology); it is the mark of a transition, a passageway, between the subjective and objective, a passageway in which the manifold of understanding, bound to intuition, is unified by reference to a concept of reason, which surpasses intuition by providing a supersensible ground. The narrowness of this passageway is strongly marked. In the opening section of the book on teleology, at the point where he will have or should have passed (future perfect or future conditional?) from one half of the treatise to the other, Kant writes:

> Not only do we have no a priori basis for such a presumption, but even experience cannot prove that there actually are such purposes, unless we first do some subtle reasoning and merely slip the concept of a purpose into the nature of things [*es musste denn eine Vernunftelei vorhergegangen sein, die nur den Begriff des Zwecks in die Natur der Dinge hineinspielt*]. (*CJ*, 360)

This subtle reasoning, slipping us from understanding to reason (*hineinspielt*, playing us along), from the limits of experience to our supersensible destiny, is not a transposition from one category to another, but a genesis. Kant continues: "We would not so much cognize nature from objective bases as use the concept of a subjective basis on which we connect presentations within us . . . so that we can grasp nature by analogy with that subjective basis" (*CJ*, 360). Far from being a clear separation of parts, it is rather a hierarchical division in which aesthetic judgment *precedes* teleological judgment and makes it possible. The *Critique of Judgment*, that exploration of foundations to which we have been referred by the other two *Critiques*, is itself divided in two parts, and within this structure we are now referred to the first of these parts. By now the genesis, which Gilles Deleuze calls the "theme of preparation" (*KCP*, 66), has become explicit.

Now the first part of the third *Critique*, the "Critique of Aesthetic Judgment," is divided into two parts, which treat the beautiful and the sublime.[22] The transition between these two parts is explicitly marked in section 23, which opens the analytic of the sublime. Kant is explaining what distinguishes it from the beautiful. Whereas in the experience of the beautiful, the form of the object is presented as a unity, in the sublime, he writes, "*unlimitedness is presented,* and yet *totality is added in thought.* Thus, the beautiful appears to be taken as the presentation of an indefinite concept of understanding, the sublime as that of a like concept of reason."[23] The difference between the beautiful and the sublime is therefore a difference between the imagination's relation to understanding, in the one case, and to reason in the other; and this difference also entails a shift from form to formlessness, that is, from finite to infinite totality, and from the restful pleasure of the beautiful to the movement of pleasure and displeasure in the sublime.[24] Thus, once again, just as the two halves of the treatise were concerned not with two separate topics, two kinds of judgments, but rather with a generation of the second kind from the first, so also here the beautiful and the sublime do not constitute two separate categories but are both forms of reflective judgment, and it is the first which precedes and makes possible the second: the idea of totality that supervenes, even in the absence of our capacity to present a complete form at the level of imagination, is an idea taken from the experience of unity in the judgment of the beautiful. (Such an idea is, Lacan would say, precisely imaginary; and the notion of the sublime would move us, in keeping with our destiny, in the direction of the superego.) Put more accurately, it is the pure reflection of form given in the experience of the beautiful that prepares us to form a concept of reflection that we can put to work in determining objective purposiveness. With this text, one begins to appreciate the productive power of analogy, which may be nothing less than the common root, the bridge, that allows Kant to *encounter* and *overcome* the abyss between reason and understanding at one and the same time.[25] Before tracing our way back down from the totality given in the sublime to its source in the pure judgment of taste, let us consider the sublime somewhat more closely.

Two points are worth noting here, regarding an "awakening" and a "negativity." The idea of absolute totality is not a determinate concept; it is not simply an idea of reason, a spurious concept produced by dialectical illusion. Such ideas are, as we have seen, irrepressible and may be diverted toward practical reason; but in this text Kant is concerned not with the employment of such determinative concepts in their regulative capacity but rather with the more fundamental and archaic question of their genesis in the activity of reflective judgment. Consequently (this is the first point), Kant speaks here not of an "employment" but of an "awakening" in us, an emergence—not of a concept, however, but of a "feeling of a faculty." One can see this "awakening" precisely in the movement, the transition, from the beautiful to the sublime. In the opening section on the sublime Kant admits that "the feeling of the sublime may appear, as regards its form, to violate purpose with respect to our judgment [in contrast with the beautiful], to be unsuited to our presentative faculty and, as it were, to do violence to the imagination" (*CJ*, 245); in section 25, however, he explains that "because there is in our imagination a striving toward infinite progress, but in our reason a demand for absolute totality . . . this very inadequation . . . is itself the awakening of a feeling of a supersensible faculty" (*CJ*, 250). Second, and as a result, the *presentation* of this idea of totality is, Kant says, "purely negative":

> For though the imagination, no doubt, finds nothing beyond the sensible world to which it can lay hold, still this thrusting aside of the sensible barriers gives it a feeling of being unbounded; and that removal is thus a presentation of the infinite. As such it can never be anything more than a negative presentation—but still it expands the soul. (§ 29, general remark; *CJ*, 274)

Inadequacy presents: it is the inadequacy of the imagination and of our powers of sensibility that somehow presents the supersensible. Kant continues: "The *feeling of the unattainability* of the ideas by the imagination *is itself a presentation* of the subjective purposiveness of our mind . . . and forces us, subjectively, to think nature itself in its totality as a presentation of something supersensible" (*CJ*, 268). This negative presentation has been anticipated at the beginning of the analysis of the sublime, in section 23, where Kant puts the point in terms of "negative pleasure": "The satisfaction in the sublime does not so much involve a positive pleasure as admiration or respect, which deserves to be called negative pleasure" (*CJ*, 245). What is in fact "presented" in the sublime, then, is a discord, a fragmentation, a disproportion, and at two levels— between the mind and the world and also within the mind. It is a disproportion, first, between the excessive magnitude or power of nature and our inadequate mental powers of apprehension, and second, between our limited sensibility and the infinity of our reason. But from the presentation of this very discord, Kant says, a harmony is produced. As Deleuze puts it,

> [A]t the bottom of the dissention the accord emerges. . . . When imagination is confronted with its limit by something that goes beyond it, it goes beyond its own limit itself, admittedly in a negative fashion, by representing to itself the inaccessibility of the rational idea, and by making this very inaccessibility something which is present in sensible nature. (*KCP*, 51)

Thus, the twofold discord in the sublime distinguishes it from the formal restfulness of the beautiful. But again, the beautiful and the sublime do not constitute two separate categories, divided by such oppositions as rest and movement. Again it is a hierarchy in which the first precedes and makes possible the second; for in explaining the difference between the beautiful and the sublime, Kant makes it quite clear that, in the sublime, the idea of totality that supervenes in the absence of our capacity to present a complete form at the level of imagination, the idea of totality that is "negatively presented" or "awakened" or "aroused" at the moment when the imagination reaches its limit in the overwhelming excess of nature is an idea of totality that is taken from and based upon the experience of formal harmony that has been prepared by the reflective judgment of the beautiful. Such an idea is, as we have seen, not at all a regulative idea that would belong with the determinations of reason in its practical employment but a more abyssal, more primordial experience, and this is what it means for Kant to say that reflection will answer the question of the origin and unity of the determinations of reason in its pure and practical forms.

It turns out that the nonconceptual harmony of the faculties revealed by the pure judgment of taste is the condition for the possibility of any determinative use of concepts. We are therefore concerned with a transformation, a movement of genesis (this is the task of thinking), in which reflection changes its meaning: it is the experience, the pure pleasure of reflection in the face of the beautiful, which gives a pure form of finality without the representation of an end—what Kant calls "purposiveness without purpose"—that prepares us to form a concept of reflection that we can use to determine objects as purposive rather than exclusively mechanical; or, to put it somewhat differently, purely formal aesthetic finality is used as that by analogy with which we are able to apply a reflective principle of finality to nature. This is the genesis that allows the disinterested experience of the beautiful to contribute to the interests of reason and to objective finality. Since, therefore, this genesis takes its departure from the pure judgment of taste, let us consider this judgment more closely.

3

"The Analytic of the Beautiful" is divided into four "moments." We are now at a level that is distinguished in two ways. It is purely subjective in contrast to the objective judgments of teleology, and it is a level prior to the analysis of the sublime and therefore prior to the introduction of reason. The four moments are those of quality, quantity, relation, and modality, and Kant argues that, for the pure judgment of taste, in the case of the beautiful, the quality is disinterestedness, the quantity is universality, the relation is a relation to ends yet without the actual representation of an end, and the mode is necessity. By the time he has reached the fourth moment, he will write (in § 22), "subjective necessity, under the presupposition of common sense, is represented as objective" (*CJ*, 239). But in order to have been able to say this, we must first have taken our bearings from the first moment.

Let us consider this first moment more closely in regard to two preliminary points. First, as stated above, as a treatise on reflection that is designed to link the realms of nature and freedom, the *Critique of Judgment* has no immediately obvious reason for becoming concerned with aesthetics but seeks an a priori form of judgment independent of reason and understanding. Second, since aesthetic judgment is concerned at this stage not with the universality of logical judgment or with truth but with the particularity of the beautiful and the mere feeling of pleasure, it would require some explanation to show why the aesthetic analysis can proceed along these lines—quality, quantity, relation, modality—that have been imported from the table of logical judgments, as Kant admits, in the first note to the heading of the first page, and thus before the text proper even begins. Moreover, Kant admits in this note that the logical table has been altered, in that he will begin with "quality," the second category, justifying this beginning "because [again, as if by fiat] it is the one that the aesthetic judgment of the beautiful takes into consideration first" (*CJ*, 203).[26]

Several characteristics are essential to this first moment. It is, of course, not a matter of knowing, not a cognitive judgment but an aesthetic one. As such, it includes no reference to concepts. Aesthetic judgment is also pure in the sense of having no relation to appetite or desire. The first moment, in which the quality of this judgment is defined as disinterested, thus expresses a detachment from both conceptual and appetitive relations: it entails no interest in the attributes of the object, no interest in its existence or utility, no reference to need or desire. This purity in the pure judgment of taste is expressed in the fact that the judgment is concerned not with the object itself but only with what Kant calls the pure form of the object.

Disinterestedness would thus appear to be a kind of phenomenological reduction, a bracketing of questions of existence, psychology, personal taste, history, and so on. This bracketing of extrinsic matters would bring to light the field of what is intrinsic to aesthetic feeling in its pure form. And this aesthetic feeling is a certain sort of pleasure, given in the first moment. It is not the pleasure that we take in the thing, since it is not the thing that concerns us; disinterested pleasure is a pleasure detached from the object. But it is also not really a pleasure that is entirely subjective, completely internal, purely auto-affective, purely within the space of subjectivity; disinterested pleasure is thus an original relatedness, a being-toward, that is given, or gives itself, in taking in the pure form of the object. Thus, the pleasure that is given in the taking in of the pure form of the object is a subjective pleasure that amounts to a sort of hetero-affective self-giving (*TP,* 46–47).

The experience of pleasure, then, this disinterest, gives almost nothing, nothing that concerns the object itself, and no subjective content or representation; the judgment, Kant says, is not material but formal, and so the pleasure is never a content, like fear or desire, but only the disclosure of a more fundamental and purely formal harmony. The pleasure gives nothing, no object, no concept, and no affective content, but yet there is pleasure, at bottom. It is quite clear moreover that for Kant this is not a preexisting harmony, as theological dogmatism might wish, but rather a harmony that is *given,* one that is produced or *generated* in the experience of the beautiful, a generated, precognitive, pleasurable harmony that gives the unity upon which the various determinations or employments of reason are always based. This harmony is generated in the activity of reflection — or perhaps its passivity, since what is given in this experience is not the product of subjective agency; rather, it gives itself to be experienced. It is given, let us say, in the event of reflection.

The history of concepts in their rational use and in their empirical employment would therefore come to rest on the possibility of this other genesis. It would be premature to call this genesis a history; and yet Kant claims that within it one finds the unity that is not given at the conceptual level of understanding and reason, or in the empirical debris that Kant, in "Idea for a Universal History," calls "mere history."

How, then, are we to take this reflection? It moves from the particular toward a concept that is not already given. The movement toward the concept does not reach its end in a concept, as we have seen, because aesthetic judgment is essentially characterized as rigorously separate from concepts. Detached from the thing, moreover, the judgment in the pure judgment of taste has a peculiarly nonjudicial sense. The movement of reflection which comprises this judgment is a movement that, on one hand, frees the subject from being embedded in merely empirical awareness, since it is not the object but its pure form that is reflected. On the other hand, it is a movement that, according to Kant, establishes the free accord of the faculties — not actually giving the aesthetic judgment a grounding in any concept but only a subjective feeling of the harmony. This harmony is, at bottom, a movement of imagination, a peculiar movement in which the imagination takes up the object—not its content as an object of perception, but its pure form as an object of imagination. And this form is in turn referred in the direction, as it were, of the cognitive faculties—in this case, the understanding—yet without coming to rest on any concept. Instead, Kant says, the rest (though perhaps it is not rest but the movement of reflection itself) is established as a feeling of pleasure, a feeling, then, of a twofold harmony: in the subject, between sensibility and understanding, and outside the subject, between the subject and the world. This twofold harmony is one in which the imagination, in its freedom from empirical sensation, refers the form of the object to the faculty of understanding, thereby disclosing a noncognitive free play between the imagination and understanding. It is a movement that withdraws from the object as such, and withdraws without coming to rest in any concept, a movement of imagination that is given precisely by virtue of this withdrawal. The experience of pleasure would thus be given in this movement of imagination, a movement in which what is given is nothing but this movement, by virtue of which imagination occupies the abyss.

Notes

1.   Quote is a footnote to the analysis of "imagination as the 'common root'" of our two faculties of knowledge, following the phrase, "we cannot conceive how heterogeneous things could sprout from the same root" (Immanuel Kant, *Anthropology from a Pragmatic Point of View,* trans. Mary J. Gregor [The Hague: Martinus Nijhoff, 1974], part 1, book 1, paragraph 31, § C). Thanks to David Krell for some "peripheral" remarks on Schelling that sent me down toward this darkness.

2.   Immanuel Kant, *Critique of Judgment,* introduction 5. References to the *Critique of Judgment* will henceforth appear in the text according to the pagination of volume 5 of the German *Akademie* edition: *Kants gesammelte Schriften,* 23 vols. (Berlin: Koniglich Preussische Academie der Wissenschaft, 1908–). Translations are checked against J. H. Bernard (1892) and J. C. Meredith (1911) as well as Werner Pluhar's recent translation (Indianapolis: Hackett, 1987). The *Critique of Judgment* will hereafter be abbreviated *CJ,* while the *Critique of Pure Reason* will be abbreviated *CPR.*

3.   "Nor can one help feeling a certain repugnance in looking at the conduct of men as it is exhibited on the great stage of the world," Kant

writes, in the introduction to *Idee zu einer allgemeinen Geschichte in wel-tburgerlicher Absicht* (*Kants gesammelte Schriften*, 8:15–32).

English translation: "Idea for a Universal History from a Cosmopolitan Point of View," trans. Lewis White Beck, in *On History* (Indianapolis: Bobbs-Merrill, 1963), 11–26; hereafter abbreviated "IUH" and cited parenthetically by proposition number in the text.

4. Other metaphors play a role that is not innocent or merely descriptive here: judgment, Kant adds, may not have any domain, in the way reason and understanding do, but "even though such a principle would lack a realm of objects as its own domain, it might still have some territory" (*CJ*, 177). In section 2 he writes, "[T]here is a realm that is unbounded, but that is also inaccessible to our entire cognitive power: the realm of the supersensible. In this realm we cannot find for ourselves a territory on which to set up a domain. . . . It is a realm we must occupy with ideas" (*CJ*, 175). I would not be too quick to read this vocabulary of domain, territory, and region in a simple manner, but it needs to be considered.

5. Ernst Cassirer, *Kant's Life and Thought,* trans. James Hoden (New Haven, Conn.: Yale University Press, 1980), chapters 4 and 5.

6. Yirmiahu Yovel, *Kant and the Philosophy of History* (Princeton, N.J.: Princeton University Press, 1980), 125ff.

7. Gilles Deleuze, *Kant's Critical Philosophy: The Doctrine of the Faculties,* trans. Hugh Tomlinson and Barbara Habberjam (Minneapolis: University of Minnesota Press, 1984), 1–2; hereafter abbreviated *KCP* and cited parenthetically in the text. There are in fact three arguments here rather than one, but all concern the ends of reason, conceived as separate from the argument for the ends of nature and the mechanism we have called the "cunning of nature."

8. See Jacques Derrida, "My Chances/*Mes Chances:* A Rendezvous with Some Epicurean Stereophonies," in *Taking Chances: Derrida, Psychoanalysis, and Literature,* ed. Joseph H. Smith and William Kerrigan (Baltimore: Johns Hopkins University Press, 1984), 1–32. Cf. in this context Heidegger's words "Verfallenheit" and "Vorlaufen" in *Sein und Zeit,* especially §§ 38, 53, and 62. Martin Heidegger, *Being and Time,* trans. John MacQuarrie and Edward Robinson (New York: Harper and Row, 1962).

9. Friedrich Nietzsche, *The Use and Abuse of History,* trans. A. Collins (Indianapolis: Bobbs-Merrill, 1949), 12, 48.

10. In proposition 8 of "IUH," Kant explicitly presents three possible ways of viewing history: as a random series of accidents, as a continual decline, and as teleological. Elsewhere, these three views receive the respective names "Abderitism," "Moral Terrorism," and "Eudaemonism." The choice of the third is, Kant stresses, not a cognitive but a practical one. Nevertheless, it is a choice that, however useful it may be where actions are concerned, is not capable of producing a method for comprehending the domain of his-

tory—if there is such a domain. But this problem bears the entire burden of Kant's questioning. See Frank Manuel, *Shapes of Philosophical History* (Stanford, Calif.: Stanford University Press, 1965).

11.   One could follow Deleuze in bringing this parallel to bear on common sense. Aesthetic judgment, though subjective, lays claim to universality, but this universality, which will have been found (the future perfect is deliberate) in the harmony of all the faculties, is not at all the universality of practical ideas of reason. Rather, it is something to be produced in each of us, thus leading to the question: "Should aesthetic common sense not be the object of a genesis, a properly transcendental genesis?" (*KCP,* 46–50). Thanks to Arden Reed for insisting that I clarify this.

12.   "Since the *Mittelglied* also forms the articulation of the theoretical and the practical (in the Kantian sense), we are plunging into a place that is *neither* theoretical *nor* practical, or else *both* theoretical *and* practical. Art (in general), or rather the beautiful, if it takes place, is inscribed here. But this *here,* this place, is announced as a place deprived of place. It runs the risk, in taking place, of not having its own proper domain" (Jacques Derrida, *The Truth in Painting,* trans. Geoff Bennington and Ian McLeod [Chicago: University of Chicago Press, 1987], 38–39; hereafter abbreviated *TP* and cited parenthetically in the text).

13.   *CPR,* A319/B376–77. See also John Sallis, *The Gathering of Reason* (Athens: Ohio University Press, 1980), 41–64, 100–1, 130–31, 150.

14.   Thus, the architectonic interest is already manifest. As Deleuze writes, "[T]he Ideas of speculative reason itself have no other direct determination than the practical one." They express "the synthesis of the speculative interest and the practical interest at the same time as the subordination of the former to the latter" (*KCP,* 44).

15.   I would stress the transition here from the series-character or *seriality* that remains at the level of understanding to the *circularity* or wholeness that is introduced at the level of reason: the idea of totality, strangely enough, emerges only with the transition from the *finitude* of understanding (the limits established, against dogmatic metaphysics, by the first *Critique*) to the *infinity* of reason and our "supersensible destiny." Infinite seriality is finite; a closed totality is infinite. One would have to think this *production* of the infinite as closure, together with the idea of history that Kant conceives here—an idea of history not as an object of knowledge, but, in Husserl's phrase, as "an infinite task."

16.   Thus, as in the paralogisms, so also in the antinomies one finds a deflection, in this case one that directs rational cosmology into the service of practical reason. But this case is worthy of greater attention here, for two reasons: first, because (as in all dialectical illusion) reason claims to relate to understanding in such a way that what remains fragmentary at the level of understanding can be overcome and unified; and second, because the antino-

mies deal with the specific idea of the world as a whole—precisely the idea to which Kant refers both in "Idea for a Universal History" and in the *Critique of Judgment*. In the first text, the idea of wholeness is introduced in order that history may be judged (by reason) as an organized unity rather than (by understanding) as an endless series of disorganized events; in the second text, the idea of wholeness is introduced in two decisive places— first, at the moment of transition between the beautiful and the sublime, and second, at the moment of transition between that form of purposiveness which belongs to particular organized beings in nature and that form of purposiveness which is provided by the idea of organized nature as a whole. These moments, and especially the way in which one derives from another, would have to be followed closely in an adequate exegesis. For the present, let us only note that in the transition between the beautiful and the sublime, Kant points out that whereas in the case of the beautiful the form of the object is given as a whole, the case of the sublime entails an experience of formlessness. The opening gesture of the analytic of the sublime (§ 23) therefore reads: "*unlimitedness is represented* [in the sublime], and yet its *totality is added in thought*" (*CJ*, 244). The idea of the world as a totality, thus prepared, comes into play specifically in the very last section dealing with the mathematical sublime—in short, at the juncture between the mathematical and dynamic sublime. Here (§ 26), the passage from the form of the beautiful and its link with understanding to the formless but yet totalizable sublime and its link to the supersensible is established:

> [T]here is here a feeling of the inadequacy of [the] imagination for presenting the ideas of a whole, wherein imagination reaches its maximum, and, in striving to surpass it, sinks back into itself, but thereby is transposed into an emotional satisfaction. . . . Nature is therefore sublime in those of its appearances whose intuition brings with it the idea of its infinity. (*CJ*, 252, 255)

17.   See, inter alia, *KCP*, 44–45, 69–73.

18.   As Derrida points out, one could also, given time, explore the historical question opened here: "The reconciliation is only announced, represented in the third *Critique* in the form of a duty, a *Sollen* projected to infinity." Common sense, in its regulative capacity, is *to be produced* in us and yet is presupposed by the third *Critique;* and this difficulty, Derrida suggests, "ensures the complicity of a moral discourse and an empirical culturalism" (*TP*, 35).

19.   As Deleuze writes:

> [D]etermining judgment and reflective judgment are not like two species of the same genus. Reflective judgment

manifests and liberates a depth which remained hidden in the other. But the other was also judgment only by virtue of this living depth. If this were not so it would be incomprehensible that the *Critique of Judgment* should have such a title, even though it deals only with reflective judgment.

And also: "Reflective judgment expresses a free and indeterminate accord between all the faculties." "It does not legislate over objects, but only over itself; it does not express a determination of an object under a determining faculty, but a free accord of all the faculties" (*KCP,* 60–61).

20.   This distinction is first introduced in an anticipatory way in *CJ,* §15, inside the analytic of the beautiful, and specifically between the third and fourth moments of the pure judgment of taste. One already sees its transitional function—in this preliminary case, it forms a passageway between the third moment, the moment of relation, in which Kant introduces the subjective form of finality without the representation of an end, or "purposiveness without purpose" (*CJ,* 221), and the fourth moment, the moment of modality, in which Kant introduces the necessity that belongs to this subjective feeling, saying at precisely this point that "subjective necessity, under the presupposition of common sense, is represented as objective" (*CJ,* 239).

21.   Such a concept is not determinate but transcendental, as Kant writes in section 5 of the introduction: though it "is neither a concept of nature nor a concept of freedom" and though it "attributes nothing whatever to the object" (that is, is not a determinate judgment), nevertheless it is "a transcendental concept" providing "the one and only way in which we must proceed when reflecting on the objects of nature" (*CJ,* 184). This difficult section has been discussed by Rodolphe Gasché and the late Paul de Man. See, in the volume *The Textual Sublime: Deconstruction and Its Differences,* ed. H. Silverman and G. Aylesworth (Albany: State University of New York Press, 1990), the following: Paul de Man, "Phenomenality and Materiality in Kant," pp. 87–108, and Rodolphe Gasché, "On Mere Sight: A Response to Paul de Man," pp. 109–15.

22.   Strictly speaking, the "Critique of Aesthetic Judgment" is divided into an analytic and a dialectic. That the dialectic is a limiting which orients the critique back toward the pure judgment of taste (unlike the dialectic of the first critique, which can divert us forward toward practical reason) could be shown, especially by attention to "Comment 1" following § 57, and §71 of the book on teleology.

23.   To be precise here, let us note that Kant is not talking about concepts, strictly speaking, and especially not concepts such as are used in determinate judgments; he therefore uses the term "indefinite concept." What is an "indefinite concept"? As Deleuze writes, "The faculty of feeling in its higher form [that is, as a priori] can no more depend on the speculative

interest than on the practical. . . . We suppose that our pleasure is by rights communicable to or valid for everyone. . . . This assumption, this supposition, is not even a 'postulate,' since it excludes all determinate concepts" (*KCP,* 48). In reflective judgment, and in particular in the judgment of the beautiful, the object is reflected, taken up, by the imagination, with respect only to its form (hence imagination is not mere empirical perception); and in this movement of reflection the imagination, in its freedom from all conceptual or appetitive interest, is related not to a concept of the understanding but to the understanding itself—to the faculty of understanding. It is this relation to the faculty itself that Kant has in view when he speaks of an "indefinite concept of understanding." To pursue this, one would have to explore Kant's remarks about both "hypotyposis," which is perhaps the crucial mechanism here—as David Krell has suggested—and another peculiar term, "aesthetic ideas." These obscure terms, far from being technical details, come to bear the entire burden of the critical project. A start could be made from Deleuze's observation that "[a]t first sight an aesthetic idea is the opposite of a rational idea. The latter is a concept to which no intuition is adequate; the former an intuition to which no concept is adequate" (*KCP,* 56). But this is only "at first sight."

24.   The transition from the beautiful to the sublime can thus be read as a progressive *withdrawal* into the subject—from the form of the object (already detached from the object), to the subjective incapacity to measure (incapacity of sensibility), to the presentation of the supersensible in us, which emerges decisively in the dynamic sublime. The question would then be whether this movement of withdrawal into the subject itself comes to rest anywhere (as it does in the first two critiques), or whether the movement of withdrawal does not rather overtake and displace the subject without coming to rest at all. See John Sallis, *Spacings* (Chicago: University of Chicago Press, 1987), 84–86, 118–23, and passim.

25.   As Derrida says, "[E]conomize on the abyss . . . establish the laws of reappropriation, formalize the rules which constrain the logic of the abyss and which shuttle between the economic *and* the aneconomic . . . the abyssal operation which . . . regularly reproduces collapse" (*TP,* 37).

26.   The isolation of a purely aesthetic field is perhaps always undertaken from *within* the general territory of philosophy. To pursue this would be to suggest that the *line* of derivation we have been following down to its source turns out, at bottom, to have been, right from the beginning, not a line but a *circle,* one that begins where it ends. See *TP,* 74.

Part 3

Morphologies

The motif of part 2 was the sense and appearance of inarticulability as an abyss within textuality. The space of inarticulability is a space between meaning and the form meaning takes, between a text and its textuality, between representation and its self-presentation as representing. The inarticulable lies at the core of the sign, conditioning it as double; it also lies at the core of what we understand as art, the inescapable inner dynamic of articulation itself. One of the issues that surfaces in part 3 is how the inarticulable can be apprehended, rather than simply bridged, without violating its inarticulability.

The domain of this endeavor is inescapably political. What is at stake is referentiality itself, as well as a text's discursive participation in and disclosure of the world. The interior difference in textuality reveals referentiality (and its ideological determinations) to be an aporia between meaning and self-reference. The essays in part 3 address philosophical texts that are not only political (those of Lyotard, Adorno, Lukács, and Gramsci, respectively), but also represent attempts to open modes of discursive activity that resist and transcend ideologization. That is, each of these thinkers attempts to articulate how certain forms of discourse (narrative, communication, dialogue, programmatics) reveal themselves as political beyond the limits and limitations of ideological thinking. The problematic for each is the relation (or aporia) between resistance to ideologization and recourse to it in order to render discourse coherent, or dialogue intelligible, or "a politics" even discernible as such. Rather than resolve the aporia of referentiality, each produces an interface with a politics that articulates itself through textual form. At that interface, coherence emerges from the text's internal logic and construction, mapping a nonideological political intention onto its ideological topology. In effect, these essays perform a similar operation to those of part 1, but instead of a semiotic object being the focus of the subject text (as a viewer's eye on that object), it is a political form.

In principle, this is a project that can be accomplished only through a certain historicity, which takes the form of a dialogue. Since each dialogue provides an articulation of the morphologies of the text addressed, each essay becomes exemplary of a certain historical confrontation between what each subject text had projected and how it is seen in hindsight. While only the germ or ground of the implied incommensurability is discussed in the first essay by Meili Steele on Lyotard, the full future anteriority of its political operation is suggested in the last by Thomas Foster on Gramsci.

It is appropriate that the first paper in this part address Lyotard, who, more than most other post-structuralist thinkers, theorizes the space of discursive incommensurability and the necessity of a politics that can ground itself upon it (while respecting its essential irresolvability). Steele addresses the form of the space between dialogue, community, and politics, for which Lyotard's theory of the *différend,* and his critique of sentence and phrase regimens, provides a mode of articulation.

The *différend* marks a dispute of values that remain irresolvable because they are expressed in incommensurable languages. A *différend* occurs when a complaint is spoken in an injured party's language but remains unheard in the idiom of the injuring party. The effect is a silencing and a transformation of the injury into a wrong, the effective structure of which is oppression. Lyotard asks: what is the nature of discourse that makes this possible? He then asks: is it inevitable? To address this problem, Lyotard analyzes different categories of phrases and sentences (normatives, prescriptives, etc.) and investigates the process of linking them together. If the linking of phrases is never predetermined, then it is always a political act. If the manner of linking, of shifting category, creates incommensurabilities, then it entails an ethical dimension as well. Thus, the formulation of the political lies at the level at which incommensurabilities are created in discourse, particularly the discourse of community, gender, racializiation, class, hierarchy, and so on. Political confrontation contains not only differences of reference and interpretation, but differences in the way reference is constructed.

For Steele, Lyotard provides an account of the forms of reference that function at the core of political hierarchies, and thus at the heart of power. But he argues that Lyotard leaves insufficient room for the deconstruction of reference. That is, he feels Lyotard deploys the Kantian categories too uncritically. Citing Derrida, he points out that the arena for the critique of reference is already the text as a whole and not just the structure of its sentences. Eliding this difference, in the political realm, would translate into a neglect of subjectivity. That is, in understanding power as a structure of sentences, Lyotard leaves little space for agency. For Steele, Foucault offers a necessary alternative by moving beyond the constraints of the terrain of phrases to cultural practices. And to Foucault he in turn counterposes Nancy Fraser, for whom the questions of the need to struggle against domination remain central issues. In the final analysis, for Steele, Lyotard's discourse is not a politics but an intervention in the form of political discourse. Rather than a theory, it is a critical strategy that discloses the space of inarticulability and opens that which withholds itself from discernment to theoretical elaboration.

Where Steele addresses, through Lyotard, the danger and possibility of incommensurability in all discourse, Bernard Picard transposes similar considerations to the writings of Adorno, for whom the understanding of form and incommensurability in art guards against the dangers of ideology. For Adorno, the problem of referentiality and truth-content in art is its tendency to reflect preestablished (ideologizing) metadiscourses. Picard raises the following issue: if one seeks to explain reality through relations of forms, as Adorno proposes, rather than deriving it from axiomatic principles, then to whom or what must one turn for truth-content?

For Adorno, art is apprehended through recognition and resemblance rather than by pure subjectivity. It thus constitutes a dialectic between two languages, a sociolect (the terms of what is recognized) and an ideolect (the terms of recognition). Picard discusses the incommensurability of these languages. As a space or interstice between them, it decenters any ideological understanding of art and, at the same time, prevents a reduction of art to a purely formalist understanding. In the process, art (as a signifier) becomes double: a sign of individual creativity and a social fact. For Picard, this semiotics of art links it to Adorno's aesthetic theory. On the other hand, in the conjunction of its two languages, if art produces a truth-content, it is nevertheless existentially beyond being about something. In effect, art is political, but it is not about politics. It does not correlate with either a politics or an ideological structure. The logic of Adorno's aesthetics implies, then, that art is a social fact that already transcends ideologization, providing a social foundation for an ever-renewed language of the political.

What both Steele and Picard are investigating, through Lyotard and Adorno, are modes of articulation and renarrativization of the hiatus (or Nietzschean "incision") within meaning between semiotic structure and social construct. Both seek a way of articulating the political import of that hiatus. In the next essay, Agnes Heller offers a renarrativization of Lukács, a history of his philosophical thinking, through an early manuscript on aesthetics, in order to similarly discern the political import of the form of that story. The manuscript, which surfaced only at the time of Lukács's death, was written by the young Lukács, only to be abandoned and later disowned. For Heller, it represents the key to a philosophical crisis that beset Lukács concerning authenticity—a crisis that followed him throughout his career and that he resolved through Marxism. She reviews the manuscript and discusses the insight it provides into Lukács' movement between the poles of ontologization and historicization.

Lukács's question ("art exists; how is it possible?") reflects a double ontological problematic. On the one hand, each person is an isolated metaphysical subject, experiencing the world and others in the solitude of a subject-object relation. On the other, things, meanings, and ideas are socially and historically given, with a givenness that lies beyond one's participation. An abyss opens in social existence that represents noncommunication and incommunicability. Against these, expression must struggle without recourse to logic or ethics. What Lukács looks for—and Heller explicates—is the discernment of pure forms by which communication becomes possible, and through which the isolated (and solipsist) subject is transformed into a subjectivity for which a bridge to others is provided.

For Lukács, the artwork is apprehended as a double leap: a leap to form by the artist, who mirrors him/herself through the artwork in the world, and a leap to form by the "receiver" (viewer, reader), who mirrors the world in him/herself through the artwork. Lukács argues that art as form is the essence of the authentic. As such, it becomes normative, enabling the individual to establish a common experience with others and thus transcending his/her being as a solitary subject. The meaning of pure form does not become the mediation between individuals; it is the direct connection between them, the authenticity of a sociopolitical milieu. And the normative subject (whether creator or viewer) is one who existentially grasps meaning within the form of art. Thus, an existential hermeneutic, an authenticity of communication, and an aesthetics delineate the three dimensions of a structure of meaning by which art produces intersubjectivity. Through this structure, communication becomes apprehensible as the transcendence of historical givenness. It is in the authenticity of form that communication constitutes and traverses the incommensurability between real social subjectivities and from which it then looks back upon the metaphysical subject.

In the final essay in this section, Thomas Foster discusses Gramsci's analysis and positioning of prediction and predictability as a necessary form of political thought. For Gramsci, political thought and culture, and particularly alternate political thought, must be programmatic; and program entails a necessary subtext of prediction. Prediction, in turn, involves someone (a subjectivity) who predicts. As an involvement, program thus demands a cultural space in which a (new) involved subjectivity becomes both possible and necessary. For instance, a revolutionary who speaks programmatically "as if" from a "proletarian point of view" becomes, in that act, instrumental in bringing that envisioned and bespoken consciousness into existence. That is, prediction divides meaning by speaking from the given, the "already," in content while generating the "not yet" in form. It divides political consciousness between an historical existential and a process of narrativization, thus engendering an incommensurable divide between a materialist and a cultural dimension of historical process. For Gramsci, this reflected itself in both hegemonic and counterhegemonic politics, that is, in coercive force and an oppositional, alternative transformation of cultural values.

For Foster, the Gramscian fissure (and incommensurability) in prediction finds a rearticulation in Julia Kristeva's account of the future anterior. The future anterior historicizes itself between what one looks forward to and what one will be looking back upon. Gramsci would understand this in terms of a differential between conformism and struggle, as a programmatic reflection of the interstice between the historical subject and political thinking. For Foster, both delineate a space where a politics engages a subject culturally in the possibility of a nonhegemonic mode of struggle. In other words, a political program is a cultural production whose fractured being provides a discursive space in which conflict generates an alternative historical subject. This returns us to Lyotard's notion that the essence of totalitarianism, as political evil, lies in anything that disrupts dialogue as the most fundamental of all political moments. And this very notion is represented practically in part 3 by the dialogues these authors carry on with their historical subjects concerning the political import and potential of the semiotic space opened by the discernment of political form.

Lyotard's Politics of the Sentence

Meili Steele

Since its appearance in 1978, Jean-François Lyotard's *La Condition post-moderne* has been subjected to a number of attacks from many directions: it ignores nonlinguistic forces; it presents an irresponsible romantic aestheticism; it reinstates rather than deconstructs the logic of identity; it valorizes a naive liberal pluralism.[1] Lyotard's major work since then, *Le Différend* (1983), is at once a development of and retreat from the narrative pragmatics that he announces in his earlier work. First he retreats from the interdisciplinary scope of his earlier work to the texts of philosophy and thus minimizes his sketchy speculations about social and economic conditions. Then he shifts his focus from narrative to the delineation of types of sentences and discourses so as to mark out the moves by which one type can silence or oppress the idiom of another. Lyotard wants to flush out the conflicts between sentences and reveal their *différ-ends:* "A *différend* takes place between two parties when the 'settlement' of the conflict that opposes them is made in the idiom of one while the injury from which the other suffers does not signify in that idiom."[2] These conflicts emerge not simply at the level of the word (for example, the meaning of proper names) but at the level of the sentence or, more precisely, in the relationship between two sentences. Thus, politics is not a genre of discourse itself but "the question of linkage [between sentences]" (*D*, 200). Lyotard's analysis of the *différend* is an important philosophical intervention in the study of language and politics. If his previous recommendation that we "wage a war on totality" and "be witnesses to the unpresentable" (*PC*, 82) seemed like an appeal to neoromantic idealism, his new work does indeed offer an incisive critique of the pragmatics of oppression. The first part of this essay will give an exposition of Lyotard's argument, while the second part will address some limits and strengths of his work.

Before jumping into Lyotard's text, we need to recall his argument with Jürgen Habermas about the "unity of culture," since Habermas still lies in the background of his new book. In "Answering the Question: What Is Postmodernism?" Lyotard characterizes Habermas's project: "What Habermas requires from the arts and the experiences they provide is, in short, to bridge the gap between cognitive, ethical, and political discourses, thus opening the way to a unity of experience" (*PC*, 72). Lyotard associates this project with Hegel and "the notion of a dialectically totalizing experience" (*PC*, 73). For Hegel and Habermas, one kind of sentence is granted dominance over the others—the speculative sentence. The stakes of this *différend* are not simply error but terror. "We have paid a high enough price for the nostalgia of the whole and the one, for the reconciliation of the concept and the sensible, of the transparent and the communicable experience. Under the general demand for slackening and for appeasement, we can hear the mutterings of the desire for a return of terror" (*PC*, 81–82).

In *Le Différend,* Lyotard suggests his reasons for his return to the texts of philosophy. In a section called "context," he cites familiar notions such as "the linguistic turn," a "decline of universalizing metanarratives," and a "laziness with regard to 'theory' and the lack of rigor that accompanies it"; in impatience, he protests, "new this, new that, post-this, post-that. It is time to philosophize" (*D*, 11). Indeed, Lyotard wants to "defend and illustrate philosophy in its *différend* with its two adversaries: from the outside, the economic genre of discourse . . . ; from the inside, the academic genre of discourse" (*D*, 11).

Le Différend is divided into numbered paragraphs—like Wittgenstein's *Philosophical Investigations,* a text that continues to inform Lyotard's work—into which are inserted readings of various philosophers: Plato, Hegel, Levinas, and especially Kant. These readings, which are done in terms of Lyotard's philosophy of the sentence, do not carry out a hermeneutic dialogue with the other text, nor do they work out the rhetorical potential of the text à la Derrida; rather, they emerge in the present in response to a request: "[O]ne writes because one hears a request [*demande*] and in order to answer it; I read Kant or Adorno or Aristotle not in order to detect the request they themselves tried to answer by writing but in order to hear what they are requesting from me while I write or so that I may write."[3]

The notion of *demande* comes from Levinas, and it is woven throughout *Le Différend.* In Levinas's discussion of obligation, the Other cannot be constituted as Other, even though the self is tempted to do so. "The violence of the revelation [of otherness] is the expulsion of the self out of the instance of speaker" (*D*, 163). The universe of the ethical sentence is "an I stripped of the illusion of being a speaker of sentences and gripped incomprehensibly by the instance of receiver" (*D*, 164). The self as speaker can issue a subsequent sentence that tries to master the ethical sentence but that can never deny the event or "forget the transcendence of the other" (*D*, 164). In such a move "the passage between the ethical sentence and the cognitive sentence can be made only by forgetting the first of these" (*D*, 165). The cogito and Husserl's constitution of intersubjectivity are displaced by the request.

The ethical or prescriptive sentence is not to be confused with a normative sentence: "The norm makes a law of the prescription. 'You must perform such an action' says the prescription. The normative sentence adds: 'It's a norm decreed by X or Y'" (*D*, 206). Obligation is thus independent of any normative legitimation. The aporias that all attempts to legitimate authority are drawn into—the vicious circle ("I have authority over you because you authorize me to have it"), an infinite regress ("X is authorized by Y who is authorized by Z"), and so on—illustrate the normative sentence's incommensurability with other sentences (*D*, 206). Since norms require "communities of listeners for prescriptive statements" (*D*, 207), moving from prescriptive sentences to normative sentences marks the shift from ethics to politics for Lyotard.

For example, authorization in a republic is formulated this way: "We decree [*édictons*] as a norm that we are obliged to perform action x," where the roles of speaker and receiver are commutable. However, this statement includes two different sentence types, normative and prescriptive. The "we" of the normative is a speaker; the "we" of the prescriptive is a receiver. Thus, there is always skepticism about the identity of the "we." Another difference between the two types is that normative sentences are like performatives. In order to have a norm, all that has to be done is to formulate it. Prescriptives, on the other hand, require a succeeding sentence that tells whether the sentence was obeyed or not. This liberty of obligation marks the division between ethics and politics (*D*, 147–48).

Furthermore, politics involves a notion of community. Lyotard articulates this using a Kantian vocabulary that distinguishes between concepts and Ideas. "Community," like all totalities, is an Idea for which there is no ostensible referent or, in Kant's terms, no intuitions, as there are for concepts. Speculative and dialectical sentences present *analoga*. "The dialectical sentence acts as if it referred to phenomena" (*D*, 191). Hence, there is no ethical community that can be formed from such an Idea (*D*, 188).

Plato and Marx, on the other hand, violate the incommensurability between cognitive and ethical sentences, for they have "the conviction that there is a true being of society and that society will be just when it conforms to this true being. One can thus draw just prescriptions from true descriptions."[4] In other words, for Lyotard, "revolutionary politics rests on a transcendental illusion in the political domain; it confuses what is presentable as an object for a cognitive sentence with what is presentable as an object for a speculative and/or ethical sentence—that is, schemas or examples with *analoga*" (*D*, 233). Thus, notions of community whether they participate in *petits récits* or *grands récits,* are Kantian Ideas. Lyotard does not denounce such sentences but articulates their relationship to other sentences.

Marx, for example, makes two mistaken moves. The first is that he goes from the "sign of enthusiasm [in Kant's sense][5] to the ideal of a revolutionary subject, the proletariat"; the second is that he goes "from this ideal to the real political organization of the real working class" (*D*, 247–48). The (revolutionary) party confuses an ideal object, the proletariat, "with real working classes, the multiple referents of cognitive sentences" (*D*, 248); and it masks this *différend* by monopolizing the procedures that establish historical reality. However, Lyotard points out, "the repressed *différend* returns inside the workers' movement" (*D*, 248). In the same gesture, Lyotard affirms and rewrites Marx's critique of capitalism. Before the capitalist tribunal, the worker is forced to use "the language of capital"—that is, he can complain in terms of his wage earning but cannot put into question the very category of wage earner ("JD," 61).

Lyotard's discussion of community raises several questions. A notion of community is a necessary presupposition of the sentence that permits disagreements to emerge. But this does not mean, as David Ingram concludes (in his fine essay), that "the reflective judgment encompasses and even incorporates the differential structure of language encapsulated in the notion of *différend*."[6] By making community an Idea and not a concept, Ingram argues, Lyotard exposes the *différend* to arguments that use presupposition to reinstate logocentrism. But Lyotard, like Derrida in a different way, explodes those arguments that use a notion of shared assumption to assert a common ground and to reduce the logic of difference to the ontology of the same.[7] If my utterance presupposes a community, the sentence in which I do so does not commit me to the same ontology as my interlocutor. Ontological *différends* emerge not just between radically different cultures—the usual field for speculation in Quine and Davidson—but in living rooms, where referential dramas displace the known and the unknown.[8] The spatial metaphor "of common ground" that underwrites "sharing" collapses since heterogeneity is not simply between but within communities. Lyotard reminds us that "being is not being but 'there is'" (*D*, 200), that the fissures in the language of being open within sentences. He does not propose "a neo-liberal pluralism" or Richard Rorty's "contextual pragmatism," as Seyla Benhabib claims.[9] This liberal hermeneutics presumes a "free" dialogue that ignores ontological and social positions. Unlike Rorty's notion of conversation, where dialogical possibilities are divided between those who are within a community and those who are outside it, Lyotard's theory of the sentence discloses the heterogeneities not only within communities but in the ways the concept of community is phrased. His work thus has a potential for ideology critique that Rorty's does not.[10]

Lyotard dismisses Gadamerian hermeneutics with the cavalier comment that it "guarantees that there is a meaning to know and thus confers legitimacy on history" (*PC*, 35). That is, Lyotard, like Habermas, rejects Gadamer's presupposition that agreement subtends disagreement. Gadamer says, "Is it not, in fact, the case that every misunderstanding presupposes a 'deep common accord'?" "No assertion is possible that cannot be understood as an answer to a question, and assertions can only be understood in this way."[11] For Lyotard and Habermas, on the other hand, the effects of ideology rupture the dialogical situation. However, Lyotard does not construct an ideal speech situation, or a theory of spheres, in order to "rectify" the situation; nor does he privilege cognitive sentences. Rather, he remains within a critical pragmatics, informed by the values of justice and freedom, that discloses the linkages of sentences bearing such Kantian Ideas. Lyotard does not rule out mediation—indeed, his notion of linkage shows how ubiquitous mediating ideas are in discourse; rather, he exposes the cost of mediation.

At this point, we need to clarify the relationship between sentences and narratives. In Lyotard's taxonomy, narrative is part of the category called genres of discourse, a higher level of abstraction than the sentence. Genres resituate *différends* from the level of the sentence to the question of ends (*D*, 52). Thus, genres orient sentences of various types toward a finality by providing rules for their linkage. Linkage is both necessary and contingent. One cannot not link one sentence to another. Yet there are no necessary connections between any two sentences. For example, the sentence "The door is closed" can be followed by: (1) "Yes, of course. What do you think doors are for?"; (2) "I know. They're trying to lock me up"; or (3) "Good, I want to talk to you" (*D*, 123). But this should not be confused with a mere emphasis on language. "Politics consists in the fact that language [*le langage*] is not language [*un langage*] but sentences" (*D*, 200). And here, Lyotard opens a space for critique that shows the obfuscatory powers of narratives: "the multitude of types of sentences and genres of discourse find a way to . . . neutralize the *différends* in narratives" (*D*, 228). He thus corrects a confusion created by *The Postmodern Condition*, namely, that the absence of metanarratives of legitimation collapse the space for critique; in actuality, first-order *petits récits* are an irreducible category, the guarantors of heterogeneity against totalizing metanarratives.[12]

However, if the sentence is the irreducible category, a number of problems emerge. What is the site of critique where critical philosophy marks out pure sentence families and prescribes that we respect the integrity of each type? As Samuel Weber asks in his afterword to the English translation of *Au juste*, "Does not the concept of absolute, intact singularity remain tributary to the same logic of identity that sustains any and all ideas of totality?" That is, "by prescribing that no game, especially not that of prescription should dominate the others, one is doing what it is simultaneously claimed is being avoided: one is dominating the other games in order to protect them from domination."[13] Weber is raising what could be called a Derridean objection. In *Positions,* for example, Derrida says, "[S]pacing is the impossibility for an identity to be closed on itself, on the inside of its proper interiority, or in its coincidence with itself." [14]

To ignore this would be to offer a familiar Wittgensteinian account. I don't think Lyotard is doing this. Instead of working the borders of the concept or the name, like Derrida, Lyotard intervenes and offers a double writing at the level of the sentence (rather than at the level of the word). We can see this through his reading of Kant, first with regard to the faculty of judgment and then with regard to the autonomy of the other faculties (*regimes de phrases*).

Lyotard finds in Kant's faculty of judgment a means of "passage" among different language games. "Each of the genres of discourse is like an island; the faculty of judgment, at least in part, is like a ship owner or an admiral who sends expeditions from one island to another, expeditions that are intended to present to one what they have found . . . in the other and that could serve for a first as an 'as-if intuition' in order to validate it" (*D,* 190). The *als ob, comme si,* "as if," neither accentuates nor obliterates the gap between sentences; rather, the phrase takes the gap into consideration; it is an "*Übergang* that is the model for all *Übergänge*" (*D,* 181). "The 'as if' comes from the transcendental imagination for the invention of the comparison, but from the faculty of judgment for its regulation" (*D,* 181). There is no totalization of faculties. If analogies are part of a faculty (family of sentences), then the faculty is always open, undetermined. The critic or judge "who examines the validity of the claims [*prétentions*] of various families of sentences . . . judges without a rule of judgment" (*E,* 11). Thus, critical philosophy "does not come from a faculty but from a quasi-faculty or 'as if' faculty (the faculty of judgment, sentiment) in as much as its rule of determination of pertinent universes is indeterminate" (*E,* 12). Lyotard insists that we do not mistake his "passages" for "bridges," for such a reading would put us right back with Habermas. There are no rules for crossing from one domain to another, but it is through these passages that "one sentence family finds in another the basis for presenting the case that would validate it in the form of the sign, the example, the symbol, the type, the monogram" (*E,* 111). Moreover, the notion of the "sea" in Lyotard's metaphor suggests his sense of linkage—linkage that is at once necessary and contingent. The sea figures the space of indeterminate passage rather than a community that embraces these various sentence families.

Lyotard does occasionally move outside the Kantian vocabulary and thematize his own writing, which falls into the genre of philosophical discourse. "The rule for philosophical discourse is to discover its rule. It's a priori is its stake [*enjeu*]" (*D*, 95). But philosophical discourse is not a genre that is all encompassing: "the examination of sentences is a genre that cannot take the place of politics. . . . The philosophical genre, which has the appearance of a metalanguage, remains in this genre only if it knows that there is no metalanguage. Thus, it remains popular and humourous" (*D*, 227).[15] Lyotard insists on the positionality of all discourse—that is, the positions within the pragmatic scheme of the sentence (sender, receiver, referent, and sense)—and the position of a given sentence type within larger structures of discourse.

What emerges from Lyotard's dislodging of the cognitive sentence is the dynamic energy of the request that ruptures mapping and calls for new idioms. We can see this in his reading of Kant's discussion of the French Revolution. For Kant, the enthusiasm of the spectators of the revolution is a "sign of progress." Following Kant, Lyotard maintains that political judgments, like aesthetic ones, do not present determinate objects of knowledge. The revolution is a "sign" because the spectators, as opposed to the participants, witness the event as they would undergo the experience of the sublime. However, if in Kant we can make the easy accusation of an aestheticism, in Lyotard's reading we cannot. Lyotard wants "to break the monopoly granted to the cognitive regime of sentences about history and risk lending an ear to what is not presentable under the rules of knowledge. Any reality includes this demand [*exigence*] in as much as it includes unknown possible meanings" (*D*, 92). Thus, the spectator's enthusiasm "is an aesthetic analogue of a pure republican fervor" (*D*, 241). Lyotard is not suggesting we replace engagement with spectatorship, referential statements with aesthetic ones; rather, his gesture has a double meaning in that he defines the integrity of each sentence and makes a demand on the receiver to generate passages to other domains. In Kant's terms, the spectator's "enthusiasm," which is "a modality of sublime feeling," asks the imagination "to furnish a direct, sensual presentation of an Idea of reason . . . but it does not succeed and thus experiences its impotence" (*D*, 233).[16]

However, the appeal of the sign and the problematic of positionality do not answer arguments against a different Kantian dimension of his project, the historical status of the categories. On the one hand, Lyotard explicitly distances himself from Kant's anthropology and his notion of reason: "[W]e feel today, and that is part of the *Begebenheit* of our time, that the fission that is unleashed in this [*Begebenheit*] reaches this [i.e., Kant's] subject and this reason" (*E*, 113). On the other hand, he can hardly be said to defend either his taxonomy as a project or the definitions within each category. His work leaves problems in three areas: reference, subjectivity, and the status of his reading of Kant.

Lyotard defines the problem of reference as follows: "[T]he question of the reality of the referent is . . . always resolved by the play, the free play of three phrases: one carrying the meaning, one carrying the name, and the third carrying what Kant calls the presentation" ("JD," 55). In his narrow definition of cognitive sentences, which is Kantian, and his discussion of reference, which is woven from Kripke and others in the analytic tradition, he ignores not only the deconstruction of reference from Heidegger to Derrida and de Man but also Rorty's sustained attack on the analytic tradition in *Philosophy and the Mirror of Nature*. In particular, Lyotard resolves too easily such problems as the inside and the outside of language, or the concept and its Other. He gives no place to critical genealogies of vocabularies and their relationship to the text. One needs to recall Derrida's remarks on reference and textuality here: "What is produced in the current trembling is a reevaluation of the relationship between the general text and what was believed to be, in the form of reality (history, politics, economics, sexuality, etc.), the simple, referable exterior of language or writing."[17] If Lyotard would remind Derrida that his writing does not escape the contingency of linking sentences, Derrida would remind Lyotard that we need to reverse and reinscribe the vocabularies of Kant and Wittgenstein and that the space of critique is the general text and not simply the refiguration of the sentence. If, for example, Lyotard discloses the *différend* that emerges in sentences containing the word "proletariat," he ignores the rhetorical deconstruction of Marx's concepts that we find, for example, in Derrida's complex reading of value through the exchange of linguistics and economics in "White Mythology."[18]

Another difficulty emerges from Lyotard's failure to lay out the stakes of his reading of Kant. To borrow a distinction from Rorty, he does not distinguish a "rational reconstruction" of Kant, which reads a philosopher's work in light of modern problems and shows "that the answers he gave to these questions, though plausible and exciting, need restatement or purification," and the metaphilosophical reading of *Geistesgeschicte,* which "works at the level of problematics rather than problems."[19] In his rational reconstruction, Lyotard valorizes the theory of heterogeneity Kant employs in his distinctions between concepts and Ideas, determinate and indeterminate judgments. And Lyotard fails to do the metaphilosophical work necessary to make his appropriation of Kant's distinctions have bite in contemporary philosophical vocabulary—that is, by articulating further his problematic with regard to those of other philosophers and the relevance of the Kantian problematic. For example, if cognitive and ethical judgments are both considered to be cultural practices, does the distinction between them remain so clearcut? Is there interaction between them? By merely maintaining that ethical and aesthetic judgments are indeterminate, Lyotard avoids addressing the question of what informs such judgments. Moreover, by reading Kant against Hegel in order to keep the ethical independent of the dialectic, Lyotard continues to give cognitive sentences center stage and thus reinstates as much as he subverts of the tradition. That is, he continues to separate epistemology and ontology from ethical or aesthetic value.

This brings us to a paradoxical moment in Lyotard's text: against the dynamic energy invoked by his notions of the "request," the "passage," and the call to judgment, we find a refusal to open a space for subjectivity. The subject is simply a discursive position: "our 'intentions' are tensions to link a certain way that genres of discourse exercise on the senders, receivers, referents, and meanings" (*D,* 157). He often sets up the unified individual or agent as a straw man. Thus, in the beginning of *Le Différend* he makes one of his objectives "to refute the [reader's] prejudice, reinforced by centuries of humanism and 'human sciences,' that there is 'man,' that there is language, and that man uses language for his ends" (*D,* 11). But this "dead" argument provides no space in his pragmatics for the agency that his text urges. Agency can be separated from the humanism that he wants to avoid. One can talk about acting from a subject position without reinstating the self-present actor.[20]

The issue of agency brings us to the most famous and troubling of Lyotard's Kantian phrases, "presenting the unpresentable," which appears in almost all of his recent work. In *Le Différend,* he says, "Our destination . . . is to have to furnish a presentation for the unpresentable and thus, when Ideas are at issue, to exceed everything that can be presented" (*D,* 238–39). This formula has drawn the charge of "pluralism for its own sake." Lyotard's defense against such an accusation involves not only his deconstruction of accepted notions of pluralism, as we have seen, but the power of what he calls alternately *le genre economique* and *le tribunal du capitalism* to nullify *différends.* I will give several formulations to illustrate this in which Lyotard uses a language of agency. He says: "[T]he only insurmountable obstacle that the hegemony of the economic genre encounters is the heterogeneity of *régimes* of sentences and of genres of discourse. . . . The obstacle does not depend on human will but the *différend*" (*D,* 260). "Capital grants hegemony to the economic genre" (*D*, 205). "The tribunal of capitalism makes the *différend* between *régimes* of sentences or genres of discourse insignificant" (*D*, 255). "Capital is that which wants a single language and a single network, and it never stops trying to present them" ("JD," 64). The power of economic discourse is clearly not a discursive property—as the power of, for example, the Christian narrative to absorb events (*D*, 229–30); rather, it alludes to the social force of this genre, a force that is made more explicit in the third sentence with the phrase "le tribunal du capitalism." In the last formulation, "capital," a Kantian Idea, has agency, desire, and power over language and subjects bound up with it. Even if we leave aside this dubious characterization of capitalism,[21] we could still ask why Lyotard does not thematize what is omitted by his approach but remains within the horizon of the *différend*, which talks about power only in terms of sentences. For example, in pragmatic terms, all one need do to have a norm is to formulate it. However, this leaves out social and economic practices that are also at work; to articulate the positionality of the subject requires a richer vocabulary than the one provided by pragmatics. As Benhabib points out, "[T]he difficulty of political liberalism, old and new, is the neglect of the *structural* sources of inequality, influence, resource and power among competing groups."[22] Moreover, Lyotard offers no account of change in language games. How do linkages change over time? What is the relationship of discursive to prediscursive practices?

One way of recuperating Lyotard here, of reading for the request he makes on me (us) is to supplement his work with that of the late Foucault, who moves outside the terrain of the sentence to address the issues of discourse, power, and subjectivity. For example, consideration of what Foucault calls "moral practices" would help address values other than justice and freedom as well as move outside the narrow opposition between obligation and norm that informs Lyotard's discussion of ethics and politics.[23] What makes their work compatible, however, is also what makes it controversial: their commitment to a critical freedom that offers no ends. In his essay "What Is Enlightenment?"—which is a discussion of Kant's famous essay of the same title—Foucault reopens Kant's notion of critique. "The point, in brief, is to transform the critique conducted in the form of necessary limitation into a practical critique that takes the form of a possible transgression." Through archaeological and genealogical investigation we "separate out, from the contingency that has made us what we are, the possibility of no longer being, doing, or thinking what we are, do or think. . . . it [this kind of critique] is seeking to give new impetus, as far and wide as possible, to the undefined work of freedom."[24] This "undefined work of freedom" lends itself to a reactionary charge because it proposes no revolutionary utopia or political ideal. In his defense of Foucault, John Rajchman argues that postrevolutionary critique does not exclude the possibility of revolt: "[F]reedom does not . . . lie in discovering or being able to determine who we are, but in rebelling against those ways in which we are already defined, categorized, and classified." "Our real freedom is found in dissolving or changing the polities that embody our nature, and as such it is asocial and anarchical. No society or polity *could* be based on it."[25]

However, Rajchman's formulation does not answer Nancy Fraser's questions about Foucault's project: "Why is struggle preferable to submission? Why ought domination to be resisted? Only with the introduction of normative notions could he [Foucault] begin to tell us what is wrong with the modern power/knowledge regime and why we ought to oppose it."[26] A similar charge could be made against Lyotard, since he also offers no justification or development of the abstract call to present the unpresentable. The unpresentable, the beyond, is the counterpart to the *différend,* the suppressed, since they both are defined only negatively against existing discursive structures. Lyotard offers no discussion of how competing *différends* are to be adjudicated. Thus, we find statements such as: "Politics cannot have for its stake the good but must have the least bad" (*D,* 203). The "bad" is defined as the "interdiction of possible sentences at every moment" (*D,* 204). These citations raise numerous questions about *différends* and value for which Lyotard has no satisfactory response. Are all *différends* equivalent? Does minimizing the bad mean simply reducing the number of *différends?*

Even though these problems are serious, I do not think that they undermine the project so much as limit its horizon. The analysis of *différends* can be an important critical moment in normative political projects. Moreover, by keeping their critiques free of normative baggage, Lyotard and Foucault maximize the capacity to intervene in complex local discourses. If neither offers us paths to revolt or virtues to practice, both offer analyses that disclose hidden adversaries in the practices of contemporary culture. However, their two approaches are not merely complementary, for the spaces of their critique are not entirely commensurate and homogeneous but heterogeneous. If Foucault would unfold the lines of power that subtend Lyotard's rather traditional taxonomy of sentences, Lyotard would expose the way Foucault's language of practices functions in sentences and the *différends* produced by his formulations.

Thus, we can say that Lyotard offers a dynamic critical philosophy of freedom. First, his philosophy of the sentence is strategic rather than foundational or merely critical. His text is an intervention in the current reflection on language and politics, not a theory. Second, Lyotard's taxonomy is not a static set of categorical identities (Weber's objection) but a dynamic call to theorize and to face the impossibility of theoretical totality. Thus, Lyotard not only maps but spaces the refiguration of the map. Politics and literature, which do not fit one of his generic categories, have as their stakes the discovery of their stakes. "When Cézanne takes his brush, the stakes of painting are questioned; when Schönberg sits at the piano, the stakes of music; when Joyce grabs his pen, those of literature" (*D,* 201). Art and politics are undetermined discourses that bring together heterogeneous sentences and challenge the singular autonomy of sentence types. The rules for these "quasi"-genres do not preexist. The power of the text or the painting is not what it says or what it is but what it asks of the receiver: "Painting will be good (will have achieved its end, will have approached it) if it demands [*oblige*] the receiver to ask himself what it is" (*D,* 201). Thus, "the stakes of a certain literature, philosophy, and perhaps politics are to bear witness [*temoigner*] to *différends* by finding them idioms" (*D,* 30).

Hence, Lyotard's recent work employs categories not in order to proscribe but to disclose what is suppressed by following rules and by not following them. *Le Différend* develops the sketch announced in the last line of *The Postmodern Condition* for "a politics that would respect both the desire for justice and the desire for the unknown" (*PC,* 67). The quest for the unknown thus does not deny the desire for justice but contributes to the uncovering of silenced *différends,* the sentential means of oppression. This is not to say that there are not other means of oppression or other means of searching for injustice. Lyotard's affirmation of "heterogeneity" is not a shallow, irresponsible aesthetic claim in which the "paralogical" method of science joins that of the arts. The notion of *différend* situates the two desires that inform Lyotard's politics in social/textual conflict. However, the *différend* is not a mark on the map of social discourse but an exiled, uncharted space that not only challenges the procedures of referential sentences but makes demands on us. "In the *différend,* something cries out in respect to a name. Something demands to be put into phrases, and suffers from the wrong of this impossibility" ("JD," 65). The philosophy of the *différend* does not naively maintain the value of heterogeneity in the face of a political and economic system that thrives on apparent diversity but offers an analysis of the pragmatics that makes such absorption possible. Lyotard's philosophy of the sentence opens a new critical space not simply for articulating politics but for politicizing articulation.

Notes

1. Fredric Jameson, "Foreword," in Jean-François Lyotard, *The Postmodern Condition,* trans. Geoff Bennington and Brian Massumi (Minneapolis: University of Minnesota Press, 1984). See also Seyla Benhabib, "Epistemologies of Postmodernism: A Rejoinder to Jean-François Lyotard," *New German Critique* 33 (1984): 103–26; Richard Rorty, "Habermas and Lyotard on Postmodernity," in *Habermas and Modernity,* ed. Richard Bernstein (Cambridge, Mass.: MIT Press, 1985), 161–75; David Ingram, "Legitimacy and the Postmodern Condition: The Political Thought of Jean-François Lyotard," *Praxis International* 7 (1987–88): 284–303; and David Ingram, "The Postmodern Kantianism of Arendt and Lyotard," *Review of Metaphysics* 42 (September 1988): 76. For a sympathetic reading of Lyotard, see Geoff Bennington, *Lyotard: Writing the Event* (Manchester: University of Manchester Press, 1988).

2. Jean-François Lyotard, *Le Différend* (Paris: Minuit, 1983), 24–25; hereafter abbreviated *D* and cited parenthetically in the text. All translations are my own unless otherwise indicated. Other works by Lyotard referred to in this essay are: *L'Enthousiasme: La critique kantienne de l'histoire* (Paris: Galilée, 1986) (hereafter abbreviated *E*); *The Postmodern Condition,* trans. Geoff Bennington and Brian Massumi (Minneapolis: University of Minnesota Press, 1984) (hereafter abbreviated *PC*); "Judiciousness in Dispute, or Kant after Marx," trans. Cecile Lindsay, in *The Aims of Representation: Subject/Text/History,* ed. Murray Krieger (New York: Columbia University Press, 1987), 23–67 (hereafter abbreviated "JD"); "Interview," *Diacritics* 14 (1984): 16–23; *Au juste* (Paris: Christian Bourgeois, 1979); and "Histoire universelle et differences culturelles," *Critique* 456 (1985): 559–68. The term *différend* means dispute, difference, disagreement.

3. Lyotard, "Interview," 19.

4. Lyotard, *Au juste,* 48.

5. I discuss the importance of Kant's notion of signs later in the essay.

6. Ingram, "Postmodern Kantianism," 30.

7. See Donald Davidson, "On the Very Idea of a Conceptual Scheme," *Proceedings of the American Philosophical Association* 47 (1973–74): 5–20. Davidson maintains that the idea of various conceptual schemes that organize the world differently is unintelligible since no language radically different from our own would be translatable. As Hilary Putnam says in his update of Davidson's argument, "However different our images of knowledge and

conceptions of rationality, we share a huge fund of assumptions and beliefs about what is reasonable with even the most bizarre culture we can succeed in interpreting at all" (*Reason, Truth, and History* [Cambridge: Cambridge University Press, 1981], 119). Lyotard (and I) would also reject the scheme/world distinction and accept the necessity of some shared concepts; however, I would not accept the conclusion that sharing some concepts is sufficient to mediate any "significant" incommensurability.

8.　See chapter 6 of my book *Realism and the Drama of Reference* (University Park: Pennsylvania State University Press, 1988) for an analysis of how such differences emerge.

9.　Benhabib, "Epistemologies of Postmodernism," 123, 124.

10.　See the interesting exchange between Rorty and Lyotard in *Critique* 456 (1985): 559–84, where Lyotard says in response to Rorty: "There is a *différend* between Richard Rorty and me. . . . My genre of discourse is tragic. His is conversational" (580). For instance, Rorty says, "To be ethnocentric is to divide the human race into the people to whom one must justify one's beliefs and the others" ("Solidarity or Objectivity," in *Post-Analytic Philosophy,* ed. John Rajchman and Cornel West [New York: Columbia University Press, 1985], 18).

11.　Hans-Georg Gadamer, *Philosophical Hermeneutics,* trans. David E. Linge (Berkeley: University of California Press, 1976), 7, 11.

12.　See Christopher Norris, *The Contest of Faculties* (New York: Methuen, 1984). The confusion results from Lyotard's discussion of the Cashinahua. My reading is that the narrative knowledge of this culture is the other of his discursive analysis; see Benhabib's lucid comments in "Epistemologies of Postmodernism," 118–20. Lyotard criticizes his earlier discussion of narrative in *Le Postmoderne expliqué aux enfants* (Paris: Galilée, 1986): "It is not right to give the narrative genre an absolute privilege over other genres of discourse in the analysis of human or in particular 'language' (ideological) phenomena, and even less in a philosophical approach. Certain of my previous reflections perhaps succumbed to this 'transcendental spectre' (*Presentations, Instructions païennes,* even *La Condition postmoderne*)" (45).

13.　Samuel Weber, "Afterword: Literature—Just Making It," in Jean-François Lyotard with Jean-Loup Thébaud, *Just Gaming,* trans. Wlad Godzich (Minneapolis: University of Minnesota Press, 1985), 103, 105.

14.　Jacques Derrida, *Positions,* trans. Alan Bass (Chicago: University of Chicago Press, 1981), 94. See Derrida's essay "Parergon," in *La Vérité en peinture* (Paris: Flammarion, 1978), where he discusses Kant's attempt to frame aesthetics.

15.　Several pages before, Lyotard says that "the law must always be respected with humor because it cannot be completely respected without making it the mode of linkage of heterogeneities" (*D,* 208).

16.　In Derrida's work, we see a similar emphasis on the energetic as well as the semantic dimensions of textuality, particularly in his discussion of certain key terms, such as *différance,* dissemination, spacing, and the unreadable: "[S]pacing is a concept which also, but not exclusively, carries the meaning of a productive, positive, generative force. Like *dissemination,* like *différance,* it carries along with it a *genetic* motif" (*Positions,*106). "The unreadable is not the opposite of the readable but rather the ridge [*arête*] that gives it momentum, movement, sets it in motion" (Jacques Derrida, "Living On/Border Lines," in *Deconstruction and Criticism,* trans. James Hulbert [New York: Seabury Press, 1979], 116).

17.   Derrida, *Positions,* 91. Benhabib points out with regard to *The Postmodern Condition:* "The privileging of developments of mathematical and natural science is problematical and does not break with the tradition of modern sciences which simply ignores the knowledge claims and problems of the human and social sciences" ("Epistemologies of Postmodernism," 117). In his subsequent works, Lyotard's recurrent use of Kantian vocabulary continues this effect.

18.   Jacques Derrida, "White Mythology: Metaphor in the Text of Philosophy," in *The Margins of Philosophy,* trans. Alan Bass (Chicago: University of Chicago Press, 1982), 207–71. See Gregory S. Jay's fascinating reading of this essay and his general discussion of the textuality of value in "Values and Deconstructions: Derrida, Saussure, Marx," *Cultural Critique* 8 (1987–88): 153–96.

19.   See Richard Rorty's "The Historiography of Philosophy: Four Genres," in *Philosophy in History,* ed. Richard Rorty et al. (Cambridge: Cambridge University Press, 1984), 57.

20.   For recent discussions, see Calvin Schrag's *Communicative Praxis and the Space of Subjectivity* (Bloomington: Indiana University Press, 1986); Paul Smith, *Discerning the Subject* (Minneapolis: University of Minnesota Press, 1988); and my "Value and Subjectivity: The Dynamics of the Sentence in James' *The Ambassadors,*" *Comparative Literature* 43 (Spring 1991): 113–33.

21.   For Stephen Greenblatt, it is a reduction of the complexities of capitalism. Greenblatt contrasts Lyotard to Jameson. If for Lyotard capitalism reduces *différends,* for Jameson it is "the perpetrator of separate discursive domains, the agent of privacy, psychology, and the individual." Hence, "[h]istory functions in both cases as a convenient anecdotal ornament upon a theoretical structure, and capitalism appears not as a complex social and economic development in the West but as a malign philosophical principle" ("Capitalist Culture and the Circulatory System," in *The Aims of Representation,* 262).

22.   Benhabib, "Epistemologies of Postmodernism," 124.

23.   See Arnold I. Davidson's fine discussion of Foucault's enrichment of the traditional field of ethics: "Archaeology, Genealogy, Ethics," in *Foucault:*

A Critical Reader, ed. David Couzens Hoy (Oxford: Basil Blackwell, 1986), 221–33.

24.   Michel Foucault, "What Is Enlightenment?" in *The Foucault Reader,* ed. Paul Rabinow (New York: Pantheon, 1984), 45–46.

25.   John Rajchman, *Michel Foucault: The Freedom of Philosophy* (New York: Columbia University Press, 1985), 62, 123. Barry Smart makes a similar case for Foucault in "The Politics of Truth and the Problem of Hegemony," in *Foucault: A Critical Reader,* 157–73.

26.   Nancy Fraser, "Foucault on Modern Power: Empirical Insights and Normative Confusions," *Praxis International* 1 (1981): 238. See also her "Michel Foucault: A Young Conservative?" *Ethics* 96 (1985): 165–84. Lyotard could respond to Fraser: "[W]hatever the claims or forms of normative legitimation (myth, revelation, deliberation), a genre takes hold of heterogeneous sentences and subordinates them to the same stake" (*D,* 208).

The Problem of Truth-Content (*Wahrheitsgehalt*) in Adorno's *Aesthetic Theory*

Bernard Picard

Among Adorno's works, his *Aesthetic Theory*[1] offers the most elaborate example of the author's views on the shortcomings and danger of theory. In *Negative Dialectics,* Adorno had explained the appeal of rigid systems of explanation through our need for cohesion and "the bureaucrats desires to stuff all things into their categories." He had already tried to prove that "theory and mental experience need to interact. Theory does not contain answers to everything; it reacts to the world which is faulty to the core."[2] Adorno's further views on the inadequacy of theory may well be seen as veering toward postmodernism in its two related senses. Postmodernism is both a state of mind, defined by Lyotard as "a skepticism [*incrédulité*] toward metadiscourses,"[3] that is, discourses that philosophers produce to justify and legitimize their own views; and an explanation of reality through several coexistent forces rather than through one dominant principle (for example, means of production, sexuality, the positivist's belief in the "voice" of facts, etc.).[4]

On the other hand, truth-content still appears to be a very modern notion since it implies, according to Gottlob Frege's distinction, sense and reference. In other words, meaning or a complex of meanings (sense) must relate to a certain reality. This assertion applies also to modern art, even if it has consisted, with some notable exceptions, in a long and varied breaking away from mimesis. Thus, abstract paintings or an atonal piece of music should tell a truth about some objective aspect of the world. For example, suffering, cruelty, and despair are the truth-content of abstract works when one "reads" scenes of crucifixion in them, as Rosalind E. Krauss does in a series of 1951 untitled works by Jackson Pollock.[5] Understanding such a relation is not easy, and Adorno was the first to recognize that in art, whether abstract or not, the truth-content of a work is hard to grasp: "What has irritated the theory of art no end is the fact that all art works are riddles; indeed art as a whole is a riddle" (*AT,*176).

Following Paul Valéry's distinction between prose and poetry, Adorno explains art's enigma by the fact that, in art, the referential function of the sign is drastically altered. "Concepts in art are not what they are outside. The word 'sonata,' for instance, has an absolutely unique ring in poems by Georg Trakl, giving rise to diffuse associations none of which suggests any reference to an actually existing sonata, much less to the sonata form in general" (*AT,*179). Signs, as what stand for something else,[6] are no more mere significants pointing to signifieds that, once understood thanks to a common code, as Valéry says, are "to be dissolved, irremediably destroyed, entirely replaced by the image or the impulsion it [prose] signifies according to the convention of language."[7] In art, signs exist for themselves, and "diffuse associations" result in great part from sensory impressions created by the material aspect of the signs and their combination within a given work.

There is no doubt that works of art will produce impressions—even a Rorschach test does—but where is its truth-content? And Adorno, a Marxist philosopher of the Frankfurt School, never says that understanding art is purely subjective because words and other signs have lost their accepted meanings. Shape does exist; and, as we all know, meaningful impressions in poetry do not so much result from concepts as from sounds, length of lines, rhythm, repetition, rhymes, ungrammaticalities, and tropes. In other words, the choice, nature, and handling of the significants create significations different from those assigned to them by existing codes. But if a sonata is no more a certain genre of musical composition or a pipe is not a pipe (as Magritte wrote under a famous realistic picture of a pipe entitled *The Betrayal of Images*), who is going to be the authorized interpreter of signs—signs which have lost their accepted meanings?

The first people to turn to should be the artists, those who may know what they are doing; but can we rely on creators' declarations of intent to grasp the meaning of their works? In keeping with Valéry, Adorno also answers negatively: "[A]rtists who think that the content of their works is what they consciously put into them are naive and rationalistic in the worst sense of the term" (*AT,* 33). Yet Adorno, who shared some of Valéry's premises on the distance between creator and creation, never concluded, as the French propounder of an aesthetic of reception did, that

> [o]ne shall never insist enough on this point: *there is not a true meaning of a text.* No authorial authority. Whatever the author meant to say, he wrote what he wrote. Once published, a text is like a device that every one may use as one wishes . . . it is not certain that the constructor will use it better than anyone else.[8]

To save the notion of truth-content, defined as "the objective answer or solution to the riddle posed by any particular work of art" (*AT,* 186), Adorno must first save the independence of the artistic object. Against the proponents of subjectivism, the aesthetic experience is not solely what is happening inside a viewer, "a device every one may use as one wishes," but becomes a reaction oriented toward the object: "True aesthetic feeling is oriented to the object, not some reflex in the viewer" (*AT,* 236). And here Giacometti would concur: "What interests me in all paintings is the resemblance, that is, what is for me the resemblance: what makes me discover a little bit of the outside world."[9] Resemblance does not mean here copy, replica, or icon, but a small fragment of what seems to be the essence of the world. Art's ability to represent truth is also an extremely important notion for Adorno, who shares the romantic conception in which, from Kant and Hegel to Heidegger, art is considered as that which reveals the essence or unveils the being of things.

In a nondogmatic manner, Adorno, trying to account for this difficulty, suggests first that art may lead to the intimation of the in-itself, as Kant believed; but in so doing, it uses "phenomenal" means to pursue "noumenal" ends. "According to Kant's theory, human beings are cut off from the in-itself by a kind of block. Now, it is this block that shapes the in-itself into enigmatic figures" (*AT*, 184). And this duality is one reason why "art works talk like fairies in tales" who bring the absolute, "but only in disguise." Adorno's second hypothesis is the existence of a realistic relation between representation and model. Art is enigmatic because "it may even be the repository of the enigmatic quality of real life" (*AT*, 184). Its unveiling may reveal illogical representations that our logical frame of mind may not easily understand. This suggestion, adopted for different reasons by Bergson and the Surrealists, considers real life as a flow whose reality defies the logic of our mental habits. In order to understand phenomena, intelligence must first immobilize them, classify them, dissect them; in short, in order to understand life, intelligence has to mutilate it. Faithful here to a long-established romantic tradition that prefers intuition to discursive intelligence, Adorno deplores the fact that "man has spun a conceptual network around everything outside his subjective spirit" so that "he has lost the sense of wonder in the presence of the other" (*AT*, 184). In these impoverished conditions, art will rescue our vision by saving the rainbow from being a mere measurable instance of light refraction, and it will let us see again the strangeness and power of matter in a common fruit when painted by Cézanne. Yet, when art has restored the wonder of real life, we may not easily understand it, because we grew up in a world where real life "has been consigned to ossification and oblivion" (*AT*, 184). This type of alienation not only includes the social notion of estrangement in a bad society but also involves a metaphysical assertion about man's reifying intelligence.

On the other hand, it is also in man's nature to have created, through art, a means to unveil truth. In spite of all the semiotic, metaphysical, and sociological difficulties, art, like science, leads to knowledge. But, as Adorno points out, "the essential distinction between artistic and scientific knowledge . . . is that in art, nothing empirical survives unchanged; the empirical facts only acquire objective meaning when they are completely fused with a subjective intention."[10] The subject of art is not so much the artist as language,[11] another mediation between the collective—the sociolect or language of a group or a period—and the idiolect, the personal use of the language. Even the most individualistic works of art "speak the language of the 'We'": for instance, nonconformism, in order to exist, needs as the object of its negation the larger sociolect called conformism (*AT*, 240). Truth-content is ultimately the result of deciphering the relation existing between object (as meaning and purpose), the *intentio recta* of the work, and a subject who, in turn, requires the understanding of the existing relation between idiolect and sociolect. All of these terms are linked in a dialectical manner, since the modification of one will alter the others.

Finally, in spite of all the difficulties, art's nature makes the knowledge of truth-content possible. Two ideologically divergent reasons explain this process. First, Adorno stresses the importance of form (*Gestalt*). An artwork has a form that should be studied with great care because it will lead to the comprehension of the work. Specialists in stylistics and poetics would certainly agree with Adorno's remark that "cognition of art works is possible because their makeup is susceptible of cognition" (*AT,* 476). And more contemporary semioticians, in the course of their analyses of meaningful deviations or concordances between idiolect and sociolect, would develop the concept advanced by Adorno that the double nature of language is already the subject of art.

Yet, a too-attentive focus on form as key to understanding might trigger the once lethal reproach of "formalism," the charge (à la Lukács and his more intolerant masters) of ignoring the social realities of the superstructure. Contrary to the semioticians, Adorno does not limit himself to explaining how style, the individual practice of a collective language, generates meaning. By its double nature, art is an individual creation and also a social fact. This characteristic, which is eminently "susceptible of cognition" (as we have known since Durkheim), will affect the truth-content. As social fact, art depends on society for its existence, and publishing houses, theaters, art galleries, museums, and concert organizers may influence the production and distribution of art. Society, through a culture industry which knows the value and necessity of entertainment, may make demands detrimental to art's health.

Adorno leaves himself open to criticism when, moving from conditions of production to content, he generalizes about "social conflicts and class relations" that "leave an imprint on the structure of works of art" (*AT,* 329). "Leaving an imprint" is a statement with an extremely discrete deterministic value; few people would deny that art and other human creations bear the mark of history, especially social history. That is, it is not the veracity of this statement but its generality that is questionable. For instance, Baudelaire speaks about poor people, brothels, and hospitals; but explaining Baudelaire's satanism as a reaction to the social conditions of his time (which Adorno does) constitutes the same sort of reductionist reproach as Adorno (to a postmodernist's delight) launched against psychoanalysis. For instance, Laforgue's remark crediting Baudelaire with a mother complex might have been true, but it was also meaningless in the sense that all people suffering from a mother complex are not necessarily great French poets. The poor glazier in Baudelaire's *Le Mauvais vitrier,* while an example of oppressive social conditions, is refused by Baudelaire in a sadistic act of destruction. One might ask: is it a sadistic tendency that motivates a negative social act or the negative social conditions that create a sadistic behavior? Postmodernists would simply recognize the presence of forces in the text without trying to assert an order of causality between them.[12] Furthermore, certain artworks are not easily explained in terms of social conditions; the relationship between Debussy's *La Mer* and the state of the French bourgeoisie in the late nineteenth century has yet to be proven. Though class differences and poverty are as present in Baudelaire as they are, for example, in Zola, their treatment is so different that too broad a concept of them, however real, is of little explanatory value.

On the other hand, Adorno's interest in social research never led him to define the truth-content of a work of art as "the representation of socioeconomic conditions." On the contrary, Adorno points an accusing finger at "socialist realism" as a reactionary throwback to nineteenth-century bourgeois realism, which was unaware that art and literature are compelled to observe the difference between fiction and reality. He insisted that social conditions are always mediated by a subject, reminding Walter Benjamin, in a letter written a long time before *Aesthetic Theory,* that relating elements from the superstructure "immediately and perhaps causally to corresponding features of the infrastructure"[13] was the wrong methodological approach to art, whose elements are mediated, as we have seen, through the much more complex subject-object relation. To think, as Benjamin did, that "Baudelaire's wine poems may have been motivated by the wine duty and the town gates"[14] was to practice a form of criticism which Tzvetan Todorov would call in jest "evhemerist": "Evhemerus, an author of antiquity, read Homer as a source of information on the people and places described in the epic, as if it were a true narrative (and not imaginary)."[15]

Adorno, who rejected such an approach, thus calls our attention to the limits imposed on the notion of truth-content. Art, through the right fusion of form and subject matter, is able truly to express a major part of the human experience. Adorno especially liked Beckett's contribution to the matter because Beckett's props, settings, and style (clownish clothes, pants on the verge of falling, characters speaking from garbage cans, trivial and erratic figures of speech) were best fit to express messages of loneliness, absurdity, and anxiety. Yet absurdity and pain in Beckett's writings are never equal to the real pain we experience in the world. Three centuries ago, Boileau remarked that "there is no serpent or odious monster / which, once imitated by art, cannot please the eye."[16] And Richard Rubenstein, in *After Auschwitz* notes that art, by its structure, is linked to an aesthetic pleasure, however tenuous the links may be.[17] Art cannot always represent truth. Adorno, for instance, explained his great discomfort when hearing Schönberg's *Survivor of Warsaw:* "The esthetic principle of stylization, and even the solemn prayer of the chorus, make an unthinkable fate appear to have some meaning; it is transfigured, something of its horror is removed."[18]

If art transfigures and removes horror, truth-content and the concept of mimesis, which is essential to sociocriticism, are under constraints. The remaining and unsolved riddle of art is to know why suffering and death, such as in scenes of crucifixion, passion cantatas, Goya's *Dos de Mayo,* or Delacroix's *Death of Sardanapalus* and *Massacre at Chios,* become beautiful and give us pleasure. But, even if Adorno's *Aesthetic Theory,* a work of philosophical reflection and not of art exegesis, offers few demonstrative examples of solving art's riddle,[19] it leaves the viewer better equipped to understand truth-content. We know now, when looking at the *Death of Sardanapalus,* that we should forget the title, having been warned against referentiality, and we should also forget what history or the play by Byron tells about this Assyrian king in order not to interpose "a conceptual network" between what we see and what we feel. Then, the massive figure of the king with his statuesque beard represented at the rear, and the muscle of the soldier in the foreground, frame a painting not about death but about life and its dreams of power, riches, and lust. Any ideological resemblance between the 1826 painting of a king acting as wanton god toward his creatures and Charles X, the reigning monarch who, at the time, showed a bent toward absolutism, would be, according to Adorno's warning, gratuitous and methodologically unsound.

Adorno's reflection shows a deep mistrust toward reducing the truth-content of art to a meaning assigned by a philosophical system. His break with rigid systems was a result of his own historical experience. As we all know, he had to face two major failures: the failure of civilization at Auschwitz and the failure of the Marxist state in Stalinism. In a world he judged "faulty to the core," there was no place for the perfection of theory. In *Aesthetic Theory,* Kant has a place alongside Marx with respect to "the riddle of art." Because he wished to save art's autonomy, Adorno rejected pure subjectivism as well as the strict Marxist sociocriticism practiced by Lukács. On the other hand, art for him was still a social fact. Trying to resolve this antinomy, he formulated a conception of the truth-content of artworks in which Valéry's influence and his own reflection on the nature and handling of the artistic sign opened the way to a more contemporary theory of semiotics.

Notes

1. Theodor Adorno, *Aesthetic Theory,* trans. C. Lenhardt (London and New York: Routledge and Kegan Paul); hereafter abbreviated *AT* and cited parenthetically in the text.

2. Theodor Adorno, *Negative Dialectics,* trans. E. B. Ashton (New York: Seabury Press, 1973), 24, 31.

3. Jean-François Lyotard, *La Condition postmoderne* (Paris: Editions de Minuit, 1979), 7.

4. Richard Rorty, "Habermas, Lyotard et la post-modernité," *Critique* 244 (March 1984). Rorty notes that Habermas, refusing such a meaning, taxes Lyotard and Foucault in his inaugural lesson at the Collège de France with being neoconservatives because "they have replaced the model repression/emancipation developed by Marx and Freud by a plurality of discursive formations and power formations" (182).

5. Rosalind E. Krauss, "Reading Jackson Pollock, Abstractly," in *The Originality of the Avant-Garde and Other Modernist Myths* (Cambridge, Mass.: MIT Press, 1986), 221–42.

6. Saint Augustine's definition still best defines the transitory nature of the sign: "Signum est res, quod preater speciem quam ingerit sensibus, aliud ex se faciens in cogitationem venire" (a sign is something which, beyond the impression it creates on the senses, makes something else come into thought) (*De doctrina christiana* 2.1.1).

7. Paul Valéry, "Au sujet du 'Cimetière Marin,'" *Variétés III* (Paris: Gallimard, 1936), 61: "L'essence de la prose est de périr, — c'est à dire d'être 'comprise' — c'est à dire d'être dissouté, détruite sans retour, entièrement remplacée par l'image ou par l'impulsion qu elle signifie, selon la convention du langage." In *Prisms,* Adorno shows himself to be an attentive and informed reader of Valéry.

8. Ibid., 68.

9. Alberto Giacometti, quoted in Georges Charbonnier, *Le Monologue du peintre* (Paris: Julliard, 1959), 172.

10. Theodor Adorno, "Reconciliation under Duress," trans. Rodney Livingstone, in *Aesthetics and Politics,* ed. Ronald Taylor (London: Verso, 1977), 163.

11. Adorno uses the term "linguisticality" to distinguish art from the other systems of signs that acquire meaning through natural or artificial codes.

12. Paul Veyne, "Foucault Revolutionizes History," *Comment on écrit l'histoire* (Paris: Editions du Seuil, 1978), 211: "[T]he method consists in describing, very positively, what a paternal emperor does, what a leader does, and in supposing nothing else; one should not presuppose the existence of a target, an object, a material cause (the governed, the relations of production, the eternal State), one type of behavior (politics, depolitization)."

13. Theodor Adorno to Walter Benjamin, 10 November 1938, in *Aesthetics and Politics,* 129.

14. Ibid.

15. Tzvetan Todorov, *La Notion de littérature et autre essais* (Paris: Editions du Seuil, 1987), 139.

16. Nicolas Boileau-Despréaux, *Art poetique* (Paris: Diderot, 1946), III, l:

> Il n'est point de serpent ou de monstre odieux
> Qui par l'art imité ne puisse plaire aux yeux:
> D'un pinceau délicat l'artifice agréable
> Du plus affreux objet fait un objet aimable.

17. Richard Rubenstein, *After Auschwitz* (New York: Macmillan, 1966).

18. Theodor Adorno, "Commitment," trans. Francis McDonagh, in *The Essential Frankfurt School Reader,* ed. Andrew Arato and Eike Gebhardt (New York: Urizen Books, 1978), 313.

19. In addition, truth-content is often asserted without demonstration. Thus, one is not necessarily convinced, for example, that the truth-content of "Clair de lune," a poem by Verlaine, is "sensuality divorced from sense" (*AT,* 218). A literary critic would analyze how a recurrent element in the romantic sociolect, such as the moon, combined with the trope of the mask (with the connotations of truth versus appearance and the pathetic fallacy) of the third stanza, gives way to a very personal treatment of another romantic idea, that of an impossible happiness in a transient world. Finally, the water fountains in the last line intimate a simile between the flow of water and the passing of life.

The Unknown Masterpiece

Agnes Heller

Habent sua fata libelli. The dictum holds true in general, but Georg Lukács had a singular talent to author books of extraordinary fate. The vicissitudes of *History and Class Consciousness* are well known. The story
of the *Heidelberg Aesthetics* has yet to be written.

Lukács occasionally made mention of his early attempt at writing a
systematic aesthetics. In his recollection, this had been a disastrous undertaking which had never come to fruition. (The plan had been abandoned; so had the basic ideas, as well as the vision of his still immature,
"not-yet-Marxist" self.) Lukács was apparently oblivious to the fact that a
part of that old manuscript had been well preserved and that the copy
could actually be found in his apartment, among the papers of his wife.
He never reread it. Yet it happened that in the very year of his death, the

remaining, and bulkier, parts of the manuscript reemerged. The author had descended into his grave, his work ascended thence: actual life has, after all, a sense of the symbolic. It seemed as if the work had a flair for proper timing. The author, whose unconscious had protested against its resurrection, had died. Yet the students for whom everything Lukács ever wrote was dear, who were familiar with his way of thinking—and writing—were still around. Under the extreme and delicate care of György Márkus, the manuscript has revealed its secrets. Deciphering them was a long, insightful, and meticulous labor; yet Márkus succeeded in reading, dating, and ordering the somewhat chaotic manuscripts. The work is now here, and it lends itself to our scrutiny and interpretation.

Reading the so-called *Heidelberg Aesthetics* came as a minor shock to all students of Lukács: the book rewrote the story of the man who had just recently vanished. It will have a similar effect on anyone who cares to participate in a journey of reinterpretation; for all the great and deep insights, all the lofty ideas of the late Lukács, insights and ideas which surface once the straitjacket of "dialectical materialism" has been removed, are transfigured into traces of the newly found work.[1] The *Aesthetics* of the old Lukács, a remarkable work despite its weaknesses, is but the privileged shadow of the idea, of the real and the original, of the *Ur-Aesthetik*. There are no final gestures in life, Lukács wrote in his early essay on Kierkegaard. While the general validity of the statement can be questioned, it is a painfully correct self-description. For Lukács's own philosophy was so intrinsically interwoven with his life that the philosopher's blessing of devising his own final gesture was simply not granted to him. His gesture was ambiguous. Why the lapse of memory? Quite obviously, the form in this case failed to perform what the form, according to Lukács, was supposed to do. It failed to communicate to the soul in a manner so as to annul our interest in the soul itself. The gesture seems awkward and thus it will always remain.

1

The *Ur-Aesthetik* consists of two different works, or, more precisely, of a completed work and a lengthy fragment. The first, titled *Philosophy of Art*, is in fact not a fragment at all, although it is sometimes discussed as such. For the author's dissatisfaction with his own work does not transform the work into a fragment. *Philosophy of Art* is completely rounded off. The problem addressed at the outset has been exhausted to the degree it could be exhausted within the framework set by the writer himself. It would be impossible to continue the work; nothing could be added to its conclusion. The book is certainly a first draft and, although not a fragment, is sloppily written and full of repetitions. Certain lacunae could even be detected in it.[2] Under "normal conditions," which I will later specify, an author will return to a draft, make abbreviations and additions, and set the balance straight. This never happened to the manuscript in question.

The second manuscript, titled *Heidelberg Aesthetics,* can indeed be termed a "fragment," but only with qualifications, for it is not a fragment of a particular work. Its first two chapters *seem* to be clarifications of certain categories that had remained undefined or unreflected in *Philosophy of Art.* But in fact the concepts in question were as clear in the first (accomplished) version as they ever needed to be. The demand for clarifications which we view in the *Heidelberg Aesthetics* in fact signals a change in the author's philosophical conceptions.

The "normal condition" for writing a book stands for the author's relatively steady viewpoint where fluctuations of philosophical interpretation are not excessively vehement and do not disrupt its general framework. Without occupying such a relatively steady viewpoint, a book on philosophy cannot be written. Yet the four years that elapsed between the drafting of *Philosophy of Art* and the attempt at rewriting it were those between 1913 and 1917, at once the first momentous years of our century (if we date the twentieth century from 1914) and years of crisis in Lukács's personal life. As a result of these, and perhaps other, factors, certain basic concepts of the first work appear in the "fragment" in the framework of a new philosophical approach; certain analyses overlap with previous ones, certain others do not. In addition, the second manuscript contains a lengthy, predominantly historical, dissertation on the transcendental dialectics of the idea of the beautiful.

The shifts and changes of the conception include and signify a general change of the author's attitude. In fact, it is precisely this change of attitude that offers the broadest horizon for understanding what has happened there. The work titled *Philosophy of Art* is the crystallization of the ideas of *Soul and Form* as well as the very avenue leading to *The Theory of the Novel.* The main bipolarity of human existence remains authenticity/inauthenticity, and the artwork appears as *the* form of utmost authenticity: as Truth, the Sense of senselessness. In being Truth and Sense, artworks can either reveal the complete or ultimate senselessness of world and life (the latter appear as what they are: senseless, precisely because Sense only exists in the form of artworks); or they are nothing but traces of a hidden and unknown Sense.

All of the early work of Lukács, *The Theory of the Novel* included, lend themselves to both a tragic-pessimistic and a mystical "reading." However, in the studies titled *Heidelberg Aesthetics,* neither tragic pessimism nor mysticism are present. Artworks appear in the final reading as mere forms of existence, void of meaning, unfit for communication, and, as such, Luciferian (diabolical). Despite the substantial shift in Lukács's position, his old themes remain unaffected; some are rethought and reformulated, but this happens in a manner which is sometimes at variance with the sarcastic-ironical conclusion (if there is a conclusion at all, which again remains an open question). At any rate, it is the crisis of a worldview that the reader witnesses here, despite the philosophically elaborate character of the second manuscript as compared to the sloppiness of the first. Lukács plummeted into a deep theoretical crisis, and he made various attempts (in different directions) to get out of it with healthy spirit and mind. His jumping into Marxism, which had been a constant possibility on his philosophical horizon since his first work, can also be understood as a rescue operation aimed at finally regaining a foothold, a standpoint to create a cosmos out of chaos. The writings of 1916–18 cry out, like Hölderlin's *Alabanda,* with their textual body: give me a banner to live and to die for and, above all, under which I can write philosophy again.

There is thus a historical as well as a personal gap between the two manuscripts. Yet as they now stand, both in their unity and discrepancy, they are in fact the very centerpoint of Lukács's whole creative activity. The completed work and the fragment together constitute the bridge between *Soul and Form* and *History and Class Consciousness.* One could even indulge in the dangerously unhermeneutical idea that there is no understanding of Lukács without having been immersed in reading the *Heidelberg Aesthetics.* The *Heidelberg Aesthetics* can be invented without even having the text, given a sufficient amount of sensitivity to its author. One such "inventor" was Lucien Goldman in his well-known treatise on Lukács and Heidegger. In a way, Goldman invented the deeply Heideggerian passages and trains of thought of a text he had no opportunity to know.

The main factor of Lukács's theoretical crisis, the trigger to his search for a banner in the "times of ultimate sinfulness" (*vollendete Sündhaftigkeit*), was constantly accompanied and reinforced by secondary ones.

His wish to habilitate at the University of Heidelberg, a decision strongly supported by his friend Max Weber, was constantly frustrated by Heinrich Rickert and to a lesser extent by Emil Lask. Rickert and Lask, who were familiar with parts of Lukács's manuscript (and perhaps with the whole of *Philosophy of Art*), persisted in their opinion that Lukács's talent as well as his work were "essayist" in character. They expressed doubts as to whether Lukács was able to accomplish a "systematic" philosophical inquiry, which they regarded as the entry ticket into the sanctuary of the German academy. Those who met Lukács know perfectly well that the rejection by such a rigid and vain personality as Rickert could not have had the slightest impact on him. If the whole issue had revolved around Rickert, he would have made certain formal concessions to the academy while firmly standing by his own philosophy. There is little doubt that thus he could at the end have achieved habilitation. Yet Lask, whom Lukács highly esteemed and who, in contradistinction to Rickert, appreciated the philosophical essay as a legitimate genre, not less precious than the "systems" of philosophy, equally subscribed to Rickert's objection. So did, with failing heart, Max Weber. He, the most sensitive man of his generation, felt for Lukács as the "younger brother in spirit," for Lukács's struggle was a mirror image of his own. But he had also subjected the existentialist dimensions of his own vision to the solid and morally grounded pursuit of science, and he simply had to have an ambiguous attitude toward the younger man. Of course, Weber believed that what he had done was the right thing to do, and he urged Lukács to do the same. The utterly subjective tone of a letter he addressed to Lukács, after having read the first version of *The Theory of the Novel,* a letter in which Weber expressed his hatred for the work that made Lukács interrupt the systematic rewriting of this *Aesthetic,* discloses this ambiguity. On the one hand, Weber remained committed to systematic work; on the other hand, he was prepared to turn to Rickert with Hamlet's words to Horatio. The very dimension of life and fate that Rickert's cold philosophy could not even fathom was presented and represented in Lukács's essays.

However, not even Lask's and Weber's objections would have brought Lukács to the point of conforming to the postulate of devising a system. At this point, one of the organic weaknesses of Lukács's philosophical character can be detected. Lukács saw and explicitly formulated that every soul needs to find its *own* form, and he was also familiar with the fundamental fact that certain times are more hospitable to certain forms than others. Yet, always the absolutist, the holist, Lukács did not see much value in anything short of the supreme form. So why then the seemingly unsystematic, seemingly derivative form of the essay? It was this medium that made his spirit fly high. His enormous talent was indeed that of the philosophical essayist. His theoretical personality could not find its home in the disciplined systematic pursuit. *Philosophy of Art* is indeed an essay of approximately 250 typewritten pages, the maximum proper size an essay can cope with. Naturally, *History and Class Consciousness,* too, is an essay. All the so-called great systematic works by Lukács, with the sole exception of the early masterpiece *Modern Drama-history,* are nothing but essays blown out of all proportion, stuffed with empirical, quasi-empirical, and historical "matter" which invariably remains unformed and inorganic.

As long as Lukács believed that his times called for fragmentation, there was no discrepancy between his absolutistic taste and his own talent. For him, the constellation seemed to be straightforward. Since our time calls for fragmentation, it is in the essay, the fragment, that the spirit of the time can come to full fruition. The fragment is thus the highest, the modern philosophy par excellence. In his old age, Lukács frequently mentioned how his early encounter with Ernst Bloch resulted in his (first) conversion. It was Bloch, or rather his "example," that proved for Lukács that the classic format of philosophy was still possible, that one could still write philosophy in the manner of ancient times. In itself, a recognition like this should not necessarily have led to a crisis. However, it did lead Lukács to a crisis, whereby we have returned to the weakness of his philosophical character. The conclusion he drew from the "example" of Bloch would read as follows: if the traditional manner of writing philosophy is still possible, if the Absolute is not crushed at the barriers of the Times, then we *should* philosophize like the ancients did, we *should* aim at and achieve the supreme system itself. I stressed "should" twice. For Lukács every sphere was normative; so was the sphere of philosophy. It was a validity sphere; you *should* live up to it. An understanding of the task of philosophy such as this does not offer any rational defense line against Rickert, much less against the urgings of a Lask or a Max Weber. Insofar as their call was to devise a system, they were expressing the norms intrinsic to philosophy. Lukács simply had no cognitive recipes with which to resist the postulate addressed to him, and yet he was unable to write under the guidance of that postulate. He felt that he failed to live up to the exigencies of the protocol for writing a worthy work, of remaining what he was and of "being systematic" at the same time. As a result, he struggled. He wrote a brilliant essay (*Philosophy of Art*) but remained dissatisfied with it and unable to proceed. He sought refuge in writing yet another essay, this time on Dostoevsky. The brilliant first part of the latter, a jewel put together from two precious stones (two essayistic chapters) was to become *The Theory of the Novel*. Lukács was organically incapable of saying: I have talent for philosophical essays, therefore this is what I am going to do; whatever others do is not my concern. His haughtiness and pride could not bear the failure of not living up to the norm, or rather what he believed to be the norm. At the same time, he was neither vain nor narcissistic enough to celebrate his own talent as the very norm of which others have fallen short.

It is essential to have an insight into the problematic aspects of Lukács's philosophical character; one must dig under the crude explanations in order to understand this subtle human being. The monocausal explanation of Lukács's philosophical decline after *History and Class Consciousness* loses it plausibility if the problem is illuminated from another angle. *History and Class Consciousness* is not the first swallow of a philosophical system which was never written for political reasons. Nor was *Philosophy of Art* the first swallow of an aesthetics which, for momentous historical reasons, has not been accomplished. In an essay, the beginning and the end coincide. *The whole is a fragment.*

2

Philosophy of Art is a classic statement on general hermeneutics. More precisely, it represents a unique combination of the existentialist and the hermeneutical traditions.

Philosophy of Art is exactly what the title states: a philosophy of art, since its narrative is about art. Yet "philosophy of art" also stands for philosophy as such, for philosophy in general. Given that the task of philosophy is discussing meaning, truth, and sense, and given that truth, sense, and meaning are embedded in, and are disclosed by, the artwork and nothing else, universal philosophy only exists as a philosophy of art. Lukács had been toying with this idea already in the Kassner essay (*Soul and Form*), and he had been taking it up in almost all of his writings with greater or lesser emphasis ever since. At some point, the old idea had returned and become what Lukács used to term the "viewpoint," the all-embracing and all-illuminating, the all-synthesizing and all-organizing idea that makes the work what it is.

The book starts with a brief introduction to the fundamental question: "Works of art exist; how are they possible?" This fundamental question will remain the same in the *Heidelberg Aesthetics* despite all modifications in its elaboration. This strikingly original reversal of Kant was hailed by Weber, probably the only one who understood the full implication of turning the Copernican question upside down, seemingly as a return to the pre-Kantian status of aesthetic inquiry, though in fact a gesture of "second naivety."

This reversal can be considered as an indication of and an attempt to reach back to the "natural attitude" as the foundation of our knowledge, our aesthetic judgment, and our moral norms. Certain elements of Lukács's own discussion indeed point in this direction, for example, his emphasis on the circumstance that the fact asserted in the statement "works of art exist" is not analogical but a *factum brutum.* Since in his later aesthetics Lukács did regard everyday thinking as the foundation of both scientific thought and aesthetic imagination, we might, as I believe, be wrongly inclined to attach great significance to the signs of this approach in the early manuscript. The main argument against such a position is not rooted in the young Lukács's morphology of everyday life and communication; rather, it lies in the other circumstance that Lukács did not reverse the Kantian questions in the spheres of theory (science) and ethics but only and exclusively in the aesthetic sphere. Restricting the reversal of the Kantian question to the aesthetic sphere alone would have been impossible had Lukács believed that everyday life or the natural attitude could in any decisive manner be regarded as the foundation of knowledge, judgment, and action. But indeed, in ethics, the possibility of reversing the question had been discussed by Kant himself in *The Foundation of the Metaphysics of Morals.* In this work, the very existence of good persons serves as a starting point from which the critique of practical reason can be derived.

Lukács, however, never explored the possibility of proceeding toward a general theory of intersubjectivity. He accepted the first two Kantian *Critiques* without much ado in order to be free to concentrate on the reversal of the third. Even later, in his *Heidelberg Aesthetics,* when he spent more time arguing on behalf of the "logical" and "ethical" validity spheres and when he polemicized against the neo-Kantian deviation from Kantian orthodoxy, Lukács never tried to remove the two basic pillars of the architectonic edifice laid out by the master. The reversal of the Kantian question in the new formula ("Works of art exist; how are they possible?") was meant as the foundation of the autonomy of the aesthetic validity sphere alone; at least, this is what Lukács emphasized and what seemed to be his intention. The concept or idea of beauty, the experience of the beautiful, Lukács argued with references to Fiedler, could never lay foundations for an autonomous aesthetic sphere. If beauty is objectively given, the aesthetic sphere cannot but be the handmaiden of metaphysics (or theology), an "emanation" of the supreme, but not the supreme in itself or any form of it. If the beautiful is posited by the subjective-reflexive judgment, as is the case in the Kantian system, the very existence of the aesthetic sphere presupposes the previous existence of the logical for the simple reason that things must already be there (must already be posited theoretically) before their beauty can be posited in reflexive judgment.

Whilst establishing the autonomy of the aesthetic sphere, Lukács also placed this sphere into a privileged position as against the logico-theoretical and the ethical. The aesthetic sphere is grounded in an aesthetic fact, in the very fact which also embodies the norms of the sphere (this fact being, of course, the artwork). Thus fact and norm coincide. The fact is a "thing" like other things, yet it is unlike others insofar as it is normative. This discussion, together with so much else to come, reminds us of Heidegger's famous essay "The Origin of the Work of Art." The artwork, as a thing, is an object that exists independently of human subjects. The aesthetic fact (the work of art) is a thing created by men, yet it is not only a thing as human creation but also as the embodiment of norms, by virtue of which it is a thing belonging in the validity sphere of the aesthetic. While it is a living experiencing subject who creates the work of art, the artwork is what elicits direct effects, as does every other thing. The specificity of such effects consists in their being normative.

If the artwork *is* what Lukács asserts it is, namely, a normative thing created by a living and feeling-experiencing subject which as such elicits normative experiences in other living subjects, then the very existence of the artwork warrants intersubjectivity. For once one has assumed that a subject, a contingent existence, brings a normative some*thing* into the world which can be appropriated as such (as a normative some*thing*) by another subject—or rather, by any and every other contingent subject—then the work of art is the bearer of intersubjective meaning. It does not bear one or another intersubjective meaning, but Meaning as such, the meaning of all meanings.

Once this is borne in mind, the other two validity spheres, theory and ethics, come to occupy a fairly inferior position in the realm of human understanding and experience. Ultimately, Lukács brushes them aside unneeded. He discusses the one and the whole; a subject which is not the one (the transcendental subject) and a universal which is not the whole (the categorical imperative) have no place in his vision. Lukács's work is the manifestation of a vision, not the layout of a system.

Works of art exist; how are they possible? Assume that works of art are what Lukács asserts they are. Their possibility is to be *illustrated* on the relation (sequence) subject-object-subject. The subject in question should be a subject proper (an "existence" in Kierkegaard's sense and not, therefore, an example of a certain abstraction or generality), and the object should be a world of Meaning (not the encapsulation of one meaning or another). This "world" would be a thing which, as such, is the vehicle of communication, insofar as it is the vehicle of mediating Meaning without mediating any concrete meaning. It is this philosophical framework that I call "existentialist hermeneutics." It is an existentialist philosophy insofar as the human subject appears in it as a contingent existence thrown into a contingent history of inauthentic communication, and having to cope with the task of becoming authentic.

And it is also a hermeneutics, moreover, a general hermeneutics, on two counts. Lukács's message in this work widens the horizon of his attempts at hermeneutics far beyond the scope to be found in *Soul and Form.* There, to give one example, he remarked, "It is simply not true that . . . the truth of Grimm's, Dilthey's, or Schlegel's Goethe can be tested against the 'real' Goethe. It is not true because many Goethe's, different from one another and each profoundly different from *our* Goethe, may convince us of their life."[3] This meant to say, in the wake of the Diltheyan tradition, that the meaning of the artwork can be read (interpreted) in several different ways, that there is no one exclusive true interpretation but several, and that certain historical epochs give priority to certain kinds of interpretation. However, in *Philosophy of Art,* Lukács makes highly different statements. His major message is that artworks do not embody any concrete meaning whatsoever that could be read, interpreted, deciphered as such. Reading a work of art thus is not tantamount to interpreting but to creating a meaning in communication with the Meaning it embodies.

I am going to return to this issue later in some detail. It is only the obvious conclusion that needs to be added at this point: if artworks carry Meaning (not any particular meaning), hermeneutics is not a particular way of communication; it is the only possible way of communication. The question then becomes, do subjects understand each other while experiencing a particular meaning in their (our) communication with Meaning? Is this the road from soul to soul? By raising the problem as such, hermeneutics becomes the centerpoint of the question concerning the authenticity of human existence.

3

The first chapter of *Philosophy of Art* has the title "Art as 'Expression' and the Forms of Communication of the Reality of Lived Experience." "Reality of lived experience" is the inevitably awkward English rendering of the German term *Erlebniswirklichkeit*. The complexity of this rendering can be accounted for by the circumstance that the original German term carries the meanings of its genesis, as does the usage of the term. *Erlebniswirklichkeit* is not identical with "living" (*das Leben*), nor with common life, un-real life, as juxtaposed to real life (in the manner that those terms had been explicated in Lukács's works prior to *Philosophy of Art*). *Erlebniswirklichkeit* also signifies "living" as well as common (unreal) life, since the term is also in those shades of meaning. In certain circumstances, the term refers to mere subjectivity, to subjective experience, both deep and shallow; and in other frames of reference can be understood as Husserl's "natural attitude." Shades of meaning invariably depend on the context. Yet in the last instance, *Erlebniswirklichkeit* is synonymous with everyday life, with the sphere of everyday action, thinking, and experiencing. In terms of *Soul and Form,* this sphere is the realm of necessity (of mere living), where a person, insofar as s/he dwells in it, is by definition inauthentic. But in terms of *Philosophy of Art, Erlebniswirklichkeit* is a primary sphere, not derived. It is not yet the wastebasket of higher-validity spheres that it will became under Husserl's influence in one of the fragments of the *Heidelberg Aesthetics.*[4] *Erlebniswirklichkeit* is thus everyday life experience, the primeval experience (*Urerlebnis*) of our world and subjectivity, of our constant yearning for self-expression and communication, and of the frustration of the selfsame yearning.

Lukács's treatment of *Erlebniswirklichkeit* alternates between radical ontologization and radical historicization. At the beginning of the chapter (and in some later places as well), his use of *Erlebniswirklichkeit* resembles a description of the modern condition (in the spirit of *Soul and Form*), and the rendering of the subject of *Erlebniswirklichkeit* becomes a description of the modern problematic individual. Yet the more we proceed, the more the term becomes radically ontologized: *Erlebniswirklichkeit* becomes ultimately identical with the human condition in general. Later, in the fragments of the *Heidelberg Aesthetics,* its historical and concrete elements are melted into the ontological "deep-text." Every subject, ancient or modern, is seen alike as contingent, and the vision of social utopia fades. Lukács certainly understood himself as a critic of romanticism rather than a romantic. Still, the juxtaposition of "community" and society, of a homogeneous world populated by noncontingent individuals with a modern world populated by contingent ones, was not alien to Lukács's special brand of historicism as it appeared in *Modern Dramahistory*.[5] And yet, the ontological turn did not come out of the blue either. Indeed, it would explain the alternation between two conceptions of utopia in *Philosophy of Art*. Certainly, "art" is the sole utopia Lukács recognized: art had always been utopian, it still is, and so it will remain. Yet, as we shall see, "art" is *misunderstanding;* thus its utopian character does not indicate the presence of a utopian state rather the absence thereof.[6]

In what follows I will discuss the concept of *Erlebniswirklichkeit*, while temporarily departing from *Philosophy of Art* and incorporating elements from the *Heidelberg Aesthetics*. The task here is to reconstruct a major conception and not simply to meticulously document the last word.

Erlebniswirklichkeit is the state of "living" and experiencing, the "human fate" into which we are born. Living as experiencing is the complete and unbridgeable abyss between the person who experiences and things (objects) to be experienced. What we experience is completely transcendent, beyond positing (*Setzung*). This transcendent apparatus orders things according to their effects but not according to their meaning. It is "beings," complexes of things, which confront the experiencing subject who wrestles with the apparatus or circles around it. The apparatus is a scheme of the most abstract conceptualizations. The subject as subject experiences his/her subjectivity while all forms of expression come from without (the transcendent apparatus). The subject must fill these alien things with his/her feeling qualities. Since we experience ourselves as subjects insofar as we experience our own experiencing, the need to be (to become) what we are (subjects), and the need to communicate what we are (subjectively, in experiencing), is so deeply entrenched in our soul that a complete "unification" with the apparatus cannot come about. (Lukács's conviction that alienation can never be complete should be traced back to this train of thought.) Yet true subjectivity cannot constitute itself either; and even if it could, subjectivity would remain uncommunicated. The subject is and remains solipsistic; she is closed into the prison house of her own experiencing. Intuition and the high intensity of experiencing destroy communication rather than creating it. Lukács quotes the third thesis of Gorgias as the true rendering of *Erlebniswirklichkeit:* even if something existed and could be known, it still could certainly remain uncommunicable. "Living" (everyday life) is thus the tension between "the given," "the necessarily existing" unposited world of objects on the one hand, and the lonely, isolated, solipsistic subject on the other. Neither the logical sphere nor the ethical sphere offers remedies for the human condition. Although both are value spheres, spheres of pure forms, and as such are realms of true communication, whoever enters these spheres has to leave far behind her experience, her living subjectivity. Logical forms and ethical form(s) are not forms of expression (self-expression). They lift the person out of *Erlebniswirklichkeit,* but without quenching her thirst for communication within life, without supporting her in the efforts to open the doors of her solitude.

Let me briefly summarize the problem that had been haunting Lukács already in *Soul and Form* (in particular in "Metaphysics of Tragedy"). Forms are vehicles of communication, but only true forms are the vehicles of authentic communication. In everyday life communication is inauthentic because the experiencing (self-experiencing) person is guided by schemas and apparatuses. Yet the need to bridge the gap that isolates the soul from another soul, the subject from another subject, is rooted in our very existence. This need can elicit a drive for meaning in us, for it is meaning that opens our prison house of solitude (as well as the prison house of the present). This "meaning" is not simply the meaning of categories but the meaning of life itself, the meaning of Being, as an experiencing subject should be disclosed, that is, communicated. Only pure forms are then the vehicles of authentic communication. The meaning-of-being-as-an-experiencing-subject can be disclosed (communicated) if there are pure forms that express, disclose, and mediate this meaning. Since such forms are supposed to disclose the meaning of Life, they should be open to subjective experience (*Erlebnis*), and *they should be experienced as if they were Life*.

Needless to say, the validity sphere in question is the aesthetic sphere and the pure forms in question are artworks. Works of art embody the normativity of the aesthetic sphere. Like all value spheres, the aesthetic sphere also requires a normative attitude. Thus, the persons who create and who enjoy (appropriate) the artwork need to be normative subjects. The normative subject should be a complete, sensual, living, feeling, and experiencing subject. This normative subject cannot be identical with the solipsistic subject of *Erlebniswirklichkeit* (which is a non-normative, inauthentic subject), yet at the same time it must be identical with this subject (it should be the same person, for otherwise meaning would not be disclosed to her by her own experience). This identity of identity and nonidentity in the normative and the empirical subject is a problem, with wide connotations to which I shall return shortly.

What is interesting at this point is that the *understanding of meaning* (alias the interpretation of meaning) takes off from the *subjective* (albeit normative) *experience;* and furthermore that the Lukácsian recipient never attains to the understanding of meaning alias the interpretation of the meaning (of life, being, subject), whether by means of theoretical reflection or cognitive interpretation. Of course, cognitive interpretation is not excluded from normative reception, but it should remain secondary. It is the experience of Meaning and Truth that remains irreplaceable. (Here Lukács left out of consideration the circumstance that interpretation can guide experiencing itself.) The "Platonist" or the "essayist" (*Soul and Form*), the person who speculates about the artwork, the philosopher par excellence of modernity, must also experience the artwork prior to interpreting it. In a more radical formulation, interpretation takes place in the process of experiencing, whereas reflection makes this "lived interpretation" merely explicit and discursive, thereby shaping experience into another, analogous, but not identical, form. The priority of the lived interpretation of the direct aesthetic experience, as against the secondary (the discursive) interpretations, was not meant to be a concession to Schelling or to romanticism in general. Even if the privileged position of the aesthetic sphere as against other spheres has a touch of romanticism, Lukács never failed to make a sharp distinction between aesthetic and mystical experience.[7] Mystical experience is the experience of the transcendental whereas works of art embody the metaphysics of all (subjective and meaningful) life experiences where the "what" of experience is invariably immanent. This issue is of major importance for the work of Lukács: misunderstanding and understanding are tantamount to *living*. Interpretation is an aspect of living itself and not an addendum to it.

Whoever experiences (normatively) a work of art has already opened the prison house of his/her subjectivity, for s/he partakes of intersubjective (and timeless) meaning. But is such a lived reception really a form of communication of *Erlebniswirklichkeit?* Lukács's answer to the question is highly ambiguous. For nothing but *Erlebniswirklichkeit* is communicated in and by works of art, yet the same *Erlebniswirklichkeit* is not at all communicated by the same works of art. Lukács discusses the paradox on two levels.

The first level of the paradox comes into relief when we return to the subject of *Erlebniswirklichkeit* whose experiencing is confined within, and guided by, what has been termed "apparatus." The prime longing for meaning has been described as the subject's longing for self-expression and as the desire to find a direct avenue from soul to soul. This longing is constantly thwarted in everyday life. When the empirical subject is transformed into the normative subject, in preserving its identity as non-identity, a form has been given to *Erlebniswirklichkeit;* or the other way around, it is exactly *Erlebniswirklichkeit* that is thereby formed. Nevertheless, the empirical subject remains mute. No work of art opens up the avenue of direct communication between two subjects in daily life. The isolation, the solipsism, the inauthenticity of the subject-object relationship can be overcome, and thus lifted, but only through the mediation of the work of art. As far as the empirical subject is concerned, *Erlebniswirklichkeit* cannot be formed authentically. Lukács sometimes formulates this ambiguity by reversing the signs. It is only the emergence of normative subjects that enables subjects to become aware of their empirical isolation, of the senselessness of everyday living, of the unbridgeability of the abyss that divides them from their fellow creatures. At any rate, as subjects of *Erlebniswirklichkeit,* we are condemned to solipsism. However, the same *Erlebniswirklichkeit* attains to the form of perfect communicability by the grace of art.

Already this first level of the paradox offers a host of fecund possibilities for theoretical elaboration. The discourse provides us with a cue to understand the cult and deification of art in modern times. Modern men and women feel themselves encapsulated in their own subjectivity; they perceive themselves as merely contingent beings. Since the traditional modes of understanding and self-understanding, as well as the traditional norms for action and judgment, are constantly queried and tested, the vision of the world becomes fragmented, and personal communication (self-expression and the understanding of the other) is problematized. The more one chooses oneself as a unique subject, the greater the difficulties one will encounter in personal communication. Among cultivated and oversensitive persons, artwork serves as a vehicle of communication. Lukács himself portrayed this constellation in his "Dialogue on Sterne" in *Soul and Form.* The young men are unable to discuss their own feelings (love, jealously, desire for intimacy, despair); therefore, they articulate them by discussing the novels of Sterne and Goethe. In reflecting upon their own respective experiences of artworks, and in appealing to a girl's experience of the same artworks, they do communicate with one another and with the girl *indirectly* everything they were unable to communicate or perhaps even feel directly. The latter qualification is important for certain feelings, the existence, intensity, or depth of which are in fact evoked by works of art. Thus, works of art that replace traditional vehicles of communication, which have to some extent only elicited feelings adequate to them.

However, the paradox inherent in the relationship of *Erlebniswirklichkeit* and art can also be espoused on a much broader basis. Actually, Lukács himself hinted in this direction. He mentioned culture, or rather the "forms of culture" in general, and added that there is a similarity between forms of culture and works of art. Lukács had to make a distinction between art and culture for obvious reasons. Artwork is the thing that embodies the norms of the aesthetic sphere. Of course, not everyone articulates perfectly within forms of logic, nor does everyone live up to the categorical imperative. But the validity sphere, as the sphere of norms, only takes into consideration these norms and not their inferior fulfillment or the deviation from them. If artworks are the embodiments of aesthetic norms, then one seeks to discuss those works of art that embody the norm in its purest form (the perfect work of art), just as one would only discuss forms of creation and reception that were to be *imputed* to the normative artwork; that is, one discusses normative creation and normative reception.

Although Lukács did explore the typical deviations from the norm, sometimes in far greater detail than was warranted (as in the case of naturalism), he still tried to narrow the discussion to the realm of pure aesthetic forms. His self-limitation, however, is not binding for us. The forms of culture in general may be understood as the symbolic forms of communication, as the vehicles that embody, mediate, and guide interpersonal understanding and self-expression. In a Bible-reading community a quotation from the Book illuminates a constellation we could not make understood in the language of everyday life. I express myself with the quotation and someone at the other end catches the signal and understands. The problem of communication through symbolic-cultural forms is identical with communication via art. It is I who express my feelings, my intentions, my subjectivity in a quotation from the Bible; I feel "uplifted" while quoting, I send the message. If the other catches it, s/he will feel that s/he understood it, s/he too will be uplifted and touched. But do I indeed express my special feeling, the feeling of an empirical subject via this quotation from the Bible? Is quoting from the Bible not like throwing a bottle into the sea, where my sole message is contained in the gesture of throwing and in the emotion that has triggered me to throw precisely this particular bottle into the sea? Is the meaning of everyone who had ever illuminated the experience of his/her soul with this particular quotation from the Bible in fact contained in this quotation? Who communicates what?

Perhaps on this first level of the Lukácsian paradox there is no qualitative difference between the forms of culture and aesthetic forms. Aesthetic forms (artworks) are, after all, also forms of culture. Yet Lukács's strong emphasis on the pure form, on the paradigmatic-normative artwork, is already important at this level, and important not only with regard to the system Lukács was pursuing with such great zeal. The more paradigmatic a form of culture, the deeper the paradox it incorporates; and the paradox is the puzzle philosophy must decipher. Paradigmatic artworks lend themselves as vehicles of communication to all human beings, past, present, and future. They serve as the vehicle of communication for everyone. They are revelatory insofar as they reveal Truth for men and women, for denizens of all possible cultures and traditions. But it is exactly this propensity of the paradigmatic artwork that deepens the paradox. For the paradigmatic artwork is not only open to many different, sometimes contradictory, interpretations. The infinite possibility of experiencing them, or rather, of experiencing a sense guided by the Sense they embody, is exactly what makes an artwork paradigmatic. Infinitude of interpretability, infinitude of experienceability—this is the very essential, constitutive quality of the normative work of art. Works which only permit a few divergent interpretations cannot by definition be great or paradigmatic artworks. Of course, they can become vehicles of aesthetic communication, but only in a given time, space, community, and circle.

Let me thus sum up the first level of the paradox. The great (normative) artwork is the paradigmatic, absolute vehicle of authentic communication precisely because as the vehicle of infinite experience-communication it does not encapsulate any particular experience but stamps the mark of veracity on the experiences of the normative recipient. The veracity of the personal experience, but not its communicability, is warranted (communicability can never be warranted). However, when we communicate via an artwork, when we feel deeply moved by the artwork, those at the two poles of communication mutually recognize a Meaning, Sense, and Truth, but they recognize it only as the meaning, the sense, and the truth of their own respective experiences. "My" experience is never like "yours"; moreover, one cannot experience the same work of art twice in the same way. The lived interpretation will always be new and never repeatable.

If this is what happens in normative reception, the artwork is by no means expressive. More precisely, the aesthetic sphere is incorrectly understood as expressive. If it were expressive, the recipient would be bound to understand the experiences of the artist embodied in that work. However, it is not this kind of understanding that normative reception is all about. Indeed, Lukács insists that the relationship between creator and work is no less inadequate than the relationship between recipient and artwork. Lukács invokes Fiedler's and Riegl's theories of misunderstanding only in order to radicalize them in elaborating his own theory. The gist of the matter is that although the artist's life experience pours into the created artwork (similarly to the process in which the recipient's life experience pours into his/her normative reception), this experience is by no means embodied in the artwork. In Riegl's and Fiedler's conception, misunderstanding is due to the inadequate communication of the artist's life experiences. In Lukács's understanding, the artist's life experience, which is one of the driving forces in artistic creation, is not at all expressed in the thing that had been created. Misunderstanding is due to the circumstance that artworks appear as if they were forms of expression, the form of communication of a lived experience. In fact, they are nothing of the sort. Normative artworks embody meaning, truth, sense. They constitute the a priori of all possible authentic life experiences, artistic genres being the a priori of all subjective life experiences of a specific kind. The conclusion is obvious: misunderstanding is the only direct mode of communication.

Erlebniswirklichkeit is life, it is living; there is no other kind of life. The artwork is the a priori of all authentic life experiences, although it is not the expression of any subjective life experience. As an a priori of all authentic life experiences, it must be like life. Yet since it is not the expression of any concrete *Erlebniswirklichkeit,* it must be unlike life. The more an artwork is "like life," the more it is indeed "unlike life." Closest to *Erlebniswirklichkeit* are those works which are quite lifeless (a case in point is naturalism). Misunderstanding manifests itself once again. *Erlebniswirklichkeit* is meaningless, senseless, void of truth; the subject of *Erlebniswirklichkeit* is inauthentic, solipsistic, unfit for direct communication. Yet there is direct communication; it is through the work of art, the only medium of a communication that elevates the subject to normativity-authenticity. Thus, the artwork is utterly unlike life. Normative perfect artworks are utopias; they are the utopian reality. They do not anticipate a future (a better, a more authentic) reality, nor are they recollections of a bygone (perfect, authentic) reality. The aesthetic sphere is by definition the utopia of *Erlebniswirklichkeit,* the utopia of Life itself. As such, it is a semblance of life and at the same time the opposite of life. The golden age is not in the past nor is it in the future. It is always here, for artworks exist here. The artwork, itself a misunderstanding, is conducive to misunderstanding the artwork itself. The most banal of our misunderstandings is our longing for bygone ages when the artwork, our bliss, our salvation, had been created. We mistake our longing for the utopia of the artwork, a longing for the life-world this artwork allegedly expressed. Yet the *Erlebniswirklichkeit* of all epochs is senseless and meaningless and void of truth. The epochs of Sophocles, Shakespeare, Rembrandt, and Mozart are no less inauthentic than ours. Only the artworks created by Sophocles, Shakespeare, Rembrandt, and Mozart are authentic.

This theoretical edifice, which I have termed "existentialist hermeneutics," results in the demystification and deromanticization of genius. The genius is one of the protagonists of Lukács's *Philosophy of Art.* The creator of the perfect, normative artwork is a genius par excellence — and it is exactly the perfect artwork that Lukács has in mind. Yet the genius is of interest for him as the vessel of creation, not as a person, that is, the subject of *Erlebniswirklichkeit.* As a subject, the genius is like any other perceptive and sensitive person, no more authentic and no less contingent than anyone else. There is basically no difference between the genius and the recipient. The particular person who happens to be a genius is worshipped for something he achieves and not for something that he is. Becoming a genius from among millions of sensitive and receptive persons is a matter of sheer luck, for it is the accidental coincidence of heterogeneous skills and abilities as well as the equally accidental coincidence between this coincidence and the epoch into which the person happened to be born. If every human being is contingent, the genius is the coincidence of many contingencies.

In the first two chapters of *Philosophy of Art,* as well as in the fragments of the *Heidelberg Aesthetics,* Lukács repeatedly discusses several factors which have to coincide for the genius to appear. Irrespective of the number of listed factors, the bottom line remains the same: the genius embodies the *praestabilita harmonia* between forms of lived experience (*Erlebnisformen*) and forms of technique. With some simplification, this formula amounts to the following. There is nothing unheard-of or unique in the empirical life experiences of the genius. His person qua person is yet another experiencing subject of everyday life. Unique, however, is the circumstance that the genius experiences (lives) in the perfect medium of a technical form. For a genius there are no lived experiences (*Erlebnisse*) on the one hand and technical forms on the other hand. He does not experience (live) first and translate his experiences (joys, sorrows, shocks, elevations, and the like) into the language of a technical medium afterward. He experiences in this very medium (colors, forms, sounds, and their perfect patterns). That is, a genius emerges if the perfect technical medium in and through which he experiences is by accident adequate to his experience. Different experiences can be the driving forces of artistic creation. Yet one particular experience is the adequate driving force in one medium and in one genre, whereas another is the adequate driving force in another medium and in another genre.

We can understand what an old philosophical problem we face here by remembering that Plato himself had pondered whether the same person could write tragedies and comedies. Lukács makes the obvious point that if X lives in the medium of sound but his life experiences are inadequate for becoming the driving force for perfection in the medium of music, he will not become a genius. In addition, the life experiences of a person should be such as to permit finding the standpoint (viewpoint, worldview) of creation. For the standpoint is the organizing center of the world of an artwork. One is lucky if one is born in times when the "standpoint" is offered, as it were, on a silver platter by the ethos of the given era. And if one is not lucky enough, additional coincidences are needed to get the standpoint straight, if it is possible at all. Moreover, it should be noted that not all historically given forms of a technical medium (painting, music, drama) coincide with the lived experiences they require as their driving force to the same degree of perfection.

Lukács also mentions the frequently addressed dialectic in the life of the creative genius: while enriching the world with his creations, the genius becomes increasingly empty. This, however, is a minor point in his argument, and he allows for the existence of a particular type of genius who has been enriched rather than emptied out in the process (as in the case of Goethe, for instance). Men of genius can be seen as those "favored by nature," as Kant wanted to have it; yet there is no genius in *Erlebniswirklichkeit*. A person, a subject, is after all the necessary condition of the artwork. What matters is the artwork because it exists, "it is given" (*es gibt*). The genius creates the work insofar as it is "given by him." Yet the genius is nothing but the miraculous coincidence of divergent "blessings"; ultimately, he cannot even grasp the "something" he gives us. Insofar as this is the case, artworks are not given by the artist. Yet, they are given, for they exist. *Es gibt Kunstwerke.* How are they possible?

4

The second chapter of *Philosophy of Art* is the phenomenological sketch of the creative and the receptive attitude. Here Lukács made the (usual) distinction between phenomenology and postconstruction. Yet he emphasized, in particular in the *Heidelberg Aesthetics,* that his phenomenology is closer to Hegel's than to Husserl's. Hegel, in Lukács's understanding, describes the non-normative (nonethical) transformation of the subject of *Erlebniswirklichkeit* into a metaphysical subject. It is a movement toward the unconcealment of metaphysics. All stages of transformation are conceived of in their relation to the final unconcealment. What is decisive in and for metaphysics is not *Erlebnis* itself but the "what" of *Erlebnis.* In the *Heidelberg Aesthetics,* Lukács makes it clear that the "what" of unconcealment is the subject-object identity. Yet he adds that, in phenomenology, this unity of subject and object remains a mere idea. Although this refers to certain aspects of the *shift* in Lukács's position from the *Philosophy of Art* to the *Heidelberg Aesthetics,* I include it in what follows. Similarly, I include all arguments from the later fragments insofar as they do not disrupt the composition of the earlier work.

The condition of the possibility of the artwork is creation and reception; both are of equal importance. However, in this thesis, Lukács does not associate himself with the currently widespread idea that artworks cease to be artworks if and when they are not appropriated ("received") as such and can only become artworks when new recipients emerge. On the contrary, Lukács insisted (for example, in his Dilthey obituary or in his remarks on Croce) that the grave blunder of mixing up "objective spirit" with "absolute spirit" must be avoided. A mere object of culture (a cultural form) ceases to be a form of culture when there are no recipients, but an artwork (as a distinguished and unique form of culture) never ceases to be an artwork, especially if it is truly perfect. With some exaggeration, it could even be stated that, according to Lukács, a lost artwork (that is, a work of art of which no one can be the recipient) does not cease to be an artwork. We bemoan the loss of masterpieces about which we only know from hearsay, yet they remain masterpieces for all eternity. What Lukács meant by his emphasis on the equal status of reception was the consideration that without the normative attitude of reception in general, artworks would not be possible at all.

In answering the question of how artworks are possible, one first needs to answer another question: how is the *normative* subject (of both creation and reception) possible? According to Lukács, a phenomenology of the creative and the receptive attitude demonstrates this possibility. Lukács proceeded according to his own interpretation of the Hegelian phenomenology. In so doing, he made it evident that the subject of *Erlebniswirklichkeit* transforms itself into the normative subject of aesthetic reaction and aesthetic reception. He also demonstrates how such a transformation occurs. Further, he insists that the same subject never transforms itself into a metaphysical subject, creative or receptive. The metaphysical subject is the artwork. Neither the creator nor the recipient can ever be united-merged with the object. The metaphysical object as such *is* at the same time the subject, and this is the genuine subject-object identity-unity.

A proper phenomenological procedure begins with the subject of *Erlebniswirklichkeit,* and it proceeds with its transformation into a normative subject as if artwork did not exist. It is postconstruction that the existence of the artwork is already posited, and the transformation of subject is reconstructed from an aspect of the "given," the artwork itself. As mentioned, Lukács strongly emphasized this distinction, yet in practice he constantly confused the two approaches. The confusion is not the result of methodological neglect or inconsiderateness; it is rather due to the circumstance that once phenomenology is practiced in a Hegelian sense, the opposition of phenomenology to postconstruction must be nominal rather than real. Lukács, we may recall, described phenomenology as the philosophical procedure wherein all steps in the transformation of the empirical subject into the metaphysical are discussed in relation to the metaphysical (idea). Thus, the philosopher must have this metaphysical idea in mind before the process gets off the ground. Phenomenology will become postconstruction if it reconstructs the transformation of the artist and the recipient into normative subjects from the position of the idea of the "world" of the artwork. In the most charitable interpretation, this can be understood in the following manner: either phenomenology or postconstruction will be paramount, but neither of them will be the opposite of the other.

Lukács emphasized that the empirical subject of creation and reception is transformed but not according to ethical normativity. Though it had been understood in *Philosophy of Art,* it remained unmentioned because Lukács had not yet attributed the significance to the issue that he did later in the *Heidelberg Aesthetics* (dealing with the subject-object relation in aesthetics). Lukács radically eliminated ethical normativity from phenomenology in general at the very moment that he imputed the idea of the metaphysical subject to the subject of aesthetic normativity. And this aspect of his conception sheds light on a matter of extreme importance, namely, that Lukács's intuition about aesthetics and artwork would remain basically the same throughout his life, while his intuition of ethics was constantly changing. In *Soul and Form,* and particularly in "Metaphysics of Tragedy," it is precisely ethical normativity that positions the subject where it can catapult itself beyond everyday formlessness into the (peak) experience of the final tragic gesture. In *Philosophy of Art,* Lukács discards this possibility, probably due to his dissatisfaction with the kind of ethics to which he had committed himself earlier. At that stage he conceived ethics in Kantian terms rather than in the language of a Kierkegaard or a Nietzsche, though he would return to the latter at the very moment when the plan of his aesthetics was finally abandoned. Lukács never had problems with the notion of the "beautiful"; he simply never treated it as the central category of his own aesthetics. However, he could never make a similarly firm decision about the notion of the "good" qua morally good. This important issue cannot be pursued further here. Suffice it to say that in *Philosophy of Art* and the *Heidelberg Aesthetics,* there is but one way to authenticity—that is, by adopting the position of aesthetic essentiality, the position of readiness for artistic creation and reception. What a readiness of this kind is concretely all about might be difficult to summarize. It would include readiness to self-abandon, to live (*erleben*) another world as if it were ours; it includes the readiness to enter the realm of an active passivity; the readiness to let our own experiences be homogenized by a medium; and finally, the readiness for experience through a single standpoint. As far as the normative creator is concerned, the position of subject-essentiality also includes the readiness for so-called "constitutive ignoring"—that is, for a kind of process of selection in which several of our subjective experiences must simply be abandoned and forgotten. It further includes the readiness for homogenizing the artistic material around a single center; the readiness for uncoupling facts and values; the readiness for bringing facts which are, in relation to values, constitutive for the artwork; that is, the readiness for living in the world where all signs carry their own significations. Last but not least, it includes the readiness to put an end to the act of creation.

Lukács describes the transformation and transposition of the everyday subject into the normative subject of creation (artwork) and reception (vision) through process of "readiness." There are two poles to its "stages." At one pole, there is the subject or *Erlebniswirklichkeit,* termed "human person as a whole" (*Der ganze Mensch*) by Lukács. At the other pole, there is the normative person termed the "whole human" (*das Menschenganz*). The terminology (which he kept intact through his later life) is right on target, for it implies a host of categorical determinations. A person is a whole, both as the subject of everyday experience and as normative subject; but in the first case "whole" means the sum total of heterogeneous experiencing, and in the second case "whole" means totality, that is, the completeness of the form of experiencing. Although the form (the meaning) of experience is not beyond experiencing (if it were, we would be dealing with *Bewusstsein Uberhaupt* of a kind), still the purer the experience becomes, the less the subject is ego-like (*ich-haft*). Whereas "the human person as a whole" is an ego who experiences objects such as are given by "apparatuses," "human wholeness" lives her experience as the meaning of her experiencing, so that the two poles (ego-object) become volatile. When "the human person as a whole" homogenizes itself into a "whole human," it liberates itself to an ever greater extent from its ego determination (*Ichgebundenheit*) without ceasing to be an experiencing-living "whole" human being. The human person as a whole is thus transformed into an intersubjective subject without ceasing to be an ipseity, a concrete subject. Intersubjective subjectivity is imputed to the subject by the artwork where the term "imputed" is tantamount both to "adequate" and "ought." The first step needs no further elaboration; the second, however, I will elaborate upon. It indicates that the total "transformation" of the human person as a whole into "the whole human" is the total liberation of the subject from its own *Ichgebundenheit* and that the unity of the object and the experiencing subject is counterfactual, for it is the work, the thing itself, which embodies the "what" of experiencing. It is the thing (the work) which is the unity of subject and object. *It* is the thing that *is;* it is this thing (the only normative thing that *is*) that authentically exists, or that exists completely authentically. The work (the normative thing) is the universe, the microcosm, the truth, and the meaning. The norm is truth, not the subject to which the norm is given as the pure form of its own lived experience.

When Heidegger discusses the *Ur-Sprung des Kunstwerks,* he, too, is right on target, for *Ur-Sprung* means "beginning" and "primeval leap" at the same time. In *Philosophy of Art,* Lukács mentions the "absolute abyss" that separates creator and creation to the same degree as work and recipient. Between creator and creation, work and recipient, there is the leap.

Both the process of creation and the process of reception are "being-towards-the-leap." The artwork, in that it exists, is something else and more than the creation of the artist. It is something that can never be completely understood by its creator. The perfect artwork appears to the artist as a gift from heaven, although it is only to the complete normative readiness that a gift like this can be granted. Thomas Mann once remarked: "Alles hangt vom Segen ab," everything depends on grace. If the leap takes place, grace has been there; if it does not, there has been no grace. Every time the artwork is simply the execution of the will (the plan) of the author, one can surmise that the work remains unblessed, imperfect, merely subjective, particularistic, or temporal.

In the case of the genius, that most contingent subject of us all, the decisive leap is preceded by smaller ones, the most typical of which have already been discussed: that is, Lukács's distinction between the leap of "good luck" and the leap of grace. The decisive leap, the leap of grace may happen to the artist when he decides to put an end to the process of creation. The artist hesitates: as long as he is creating the work, it is still his; it is still the vessel that carries his sorrows and his joys, his malice and his enthusiasms. Feelings, emotions, meanings, sufferings, elevations, and self-humiliations have already been transformed, selected, and homogenized. The creator is thus no longer himself, yet he is still himself also. But the moment he lets the work go, everything is lost for him. He opens his palm and the work slowly drifts away. The moment the work has been set free, it rounds itself up, it becomes itself: a microcosm, a world of its own, a world as alien from its creator as it is from anyone else. For a little while the work continues to follow the direction of the hand of its creator, but then it takes its own path. This metaphor reminds me of Michelangelo's fresco of Creation. God's finger and Adam's outstretched hand have just been separated; they are still moving across the same path, the same line. Yet Adam's hand, we know, will soon be dropped. The creature, "the creation," will start its earthly journey on its own.

The leap of grace is not granted to the dilettante nor to the virtuoso. They fail earlier than the stage of grace, namely, on the level of the first leap: the leap of mere good luck. Lukács occasionally attempts to explain why certain works of art remain without blessing although their authors' leap of "good luck" was faultlessly performed. But these efforts are the least interesting and the least persuasive parts of *Philosophy of Art* (and of the *Heidelberg Aesthetics*). His personal taste and value standards are too heavily superimposed on the matter of inquiry. Furthermore, if grace cannot be explained (if it could be, there would be no "grace"), then pondering the concrete (even the stylistic) conditions of grace, or declaring ex cathedra that certain types of creative styles are excluded from grace, weakens rather then strengthens the main argument. At one point in the *Heidelberg Aesthetics*, Lukács concedes that his aesthetic judgment is faulty because his sense of the value of the individual, the unique, is far inferior to his sense of the speculative-universal. This self-description is undoubtedly correct.

Lukács was more charitable toward the recipient. The complete homogenization of the subject, the total self-abandon to the work, are obviously necessary preconditions for a normative reception. However, Lukács does not construct a typology of the recipients in the same fashion that Adorno would do later. Adorno excluded, as is well known, almost all recipients (and certainly every untutored recipient) from the grace of the leap. Lukács, for his part, had such awe for the perfect artwork, for the meaning of meanings, for the a priori of all lived experiences, that he could not help believing that whoever turned normatively to a work like this, naive or sophisticated, would leap. The recipient's leap of grace means something radically different from that of the creator, although it also means exactly the same. The state of grace is there whenever a person gives meaning to her own life experiences, to her own life and her own world within the framework of an alien world. And that second aspect is decisive; one can only impart meaning to one's own life experiences insofar as one really lives those experiences within the framework of an alien world, that is, the world of the artwork. For if this were not the case, "experience" would be like the mood of everyday life, circling around the work yet not formed by it. The grace of the leap happens *wherever* "the alien" is ours. It is thus that the recipient jumps the abyss. Yet the abyss remains there. As mentioned, the only authentic direct communication is the communication with the artwork (and also within the artwork). This communication is intersubjective, the unity of subject and object, a unity that no living subject can ever achieve.

Having thus followed Lukács in his circling around the artwork for the second time, we have arrived back at misunderstanding. At the end of the first circle we came to understand that the artwork seems as if it were like life but was not. The more it looks like life, the less it is life. The artwork is the utopia of meaningful life, the life of Sense, of Truth, of everything actual life is not. We now can add that it is not the feelings, desires, and wants of the creator that we can grasp in our experience as understanding, for the creator has disappeared whereas the work has been set free. It is a misunderstanding to assume that we communicate with the author of the work in communicating with the work itself. It is a similar misunderstanding to assume that we communicate with any human being who has ever lived, or will live, on our planet when we communicate with the artwork.

But at the end of the second journey, the focus has been shifted to another aspect of misunderstanding. The artwork, this embodiment of authentic subjectivity qua living intersubjectivity, this exclusive vehicle of direct communication, will never be understood. The work itself, this training ground of endless amounts of experienced understandings, remains closed. It remains the alien microcosm frozen into eternity. In the earthly heaven of the aesthetic sphere, each and every artwork lives in perfect isolation. Artworks are neither connected with any other artwork nor can they conduct a discussion with any other. Cold stars bringing warmth into living souls for brief moments, they remain unaffected and closed. Here is the most important root of all kinds of misunderstanding in reverse; artworks are the mirror images of living subjects because they are unfading, eternal symbols of our existential solitude.

5

In the third chapter of *Philosophy of Art*, we circle for the third time around the artwork. Once phenomenology and postconstruction have been left behind,[8] the metaphorical puppets ("subjectivity as such," "artwork as such") are replaced by historical subjects, artists and works. The title of the third chapter, "Historicity and Timelessness of the Work of Art," indicates that this time our journey will cut across the traditional fields of the history of philosophy of art and hermeneutics. The paradox that serves as the starting point of the discussion was a constant focus of attention at the time *Philosophy of Art* was written. The artwork embodies timeless value; thus, every perfect work of art is eternally valid (it is valid *sub specie aeternitatis*), yet the artwork does not represent a timeless idea. Moreover, its genesis, its very existence, its effects are all timebound. The roots of Lukács's special way of interrogating artworks seem to be Hegelian, although in fact they are rather Kierkegaardian. For Hegel, the contrast delineated above did not constitute a paradox. But Kierkegaard never ceased pondering the issue, in his own life, of the historical emergence of eternal and absolute validity—of "Christianity," which had indeed emerged historically.[9] In Kierkegaard, this paradox of all paradoxes is tantamount to the absurd. Lukács came near this idea without sharing it completely.

It is not the accidental temporality of artworks that is in question in the paradox nor the ephemeral appearance of an eternal essence in every unique and temporal artwork. The puzzle is deeper than that; the paradox is real, not apparent. Every perfect artwork must be new; only the new can be eternal. Yet everything (every thing) understood in terms of "new–no longer new" is by definition historical. Artworks are historical in a twofold sense. They are new in relation to the former works of the same creator, and they are new insofar as they are conceived in a historical moment or period different from all earlier (no longer new) ones. It is precisely the novelty of the historical moment that provides the material for subjective experience; it is this moment and its novelty that the normative subject grasps and seeks. The genius never tries to form the eternal; rather he forms the temporal, the new. Eternity is achieved by the genius *malgre lui*. The more he dives into the novelty of his own historical experience, the greater the chance his work has of living eternally. In this way, Lukács thoroughly protected his notion from Hegelianism. The "new" he had in mind was not conceived of as progressive, higher, more sublime. It was simply and exactly new.

At this point, *Erlebniswirklichkeit,* which had been ontologized in the first two chapters, reenters history on a plane different from what has been examined before. In the earlier works of Lukács, everyday life, inauthentic life, and modern life had coincided on both the descriptive and the analytical planes. As we might recall, in the opening section of *Philosophy of Art,* Lukács vacillates between the historical concreteness of his vision on the one hand and the ontologization of his vision on the other, deciding finally in favor of ontological universalization. For Lukács, the rehistoricization of the theory leaves this basically ontological structure unchanged. The norms of the aesthetic sphere have an eternal validity; and between the ordinary life and the value sphere there is a leap, both in creation and reception, irrespective of the historical *hic et nunc* of creation and reception. Life is by definition ontologically inauthentic, and direct communication between subjects is by definition impossible. The subject of everyday life is ontologically solipsistic, and the apparatuses can never be posited; they are and will remain transcendent within all possible human worlds. The rehistoricization of the ontological constant is performed within the framework of this basic structure.

Yet, at this point, Lukács runs into difficulties with which he cannot conclusively deal. As soon as the novelty (the "newness") of the perfect artwork becomes the basic constitutive element of the normativity of the artwork, as soon as the perfect artwork is identified as the timelessness of historicity, certain variable moments of everyday life emerge that must be accounted for. It is odd to stick to the vision of a totally inauthentic daily life and to emphasize *in uno actu* the historical aspect which is termed "novelty." In Lukács's model, the normative subject is both the negation and the fulfillment of the empirical subject of everyday life. Without an experiencing, living subject there is no normative subject. If "newness" is the basic constitutive element of the normative artwork, that same "newness" is imputed to the normative subject. But the "newness" within the readiness of the normative subject must be rooted in the "newness" of the empirical life experience of the same subject.

Empirical life experience is historical. If, however, everyday life is totally reified and alienated, how can "newness" emerge in life at all? How can history, any history, exist at all? How can empirical subjects experience what others do not? How can an empirical subject experience the historically new? The new that pours into the creation and reception of the artwork is not the contingent element of our solipsistic experiencing; it is not tantamount to changing moods or changing perceptions. As experience, it is the constitutive new, the new as formed experience. If it were not like this, artworks could not exist, at least not as the "timelessness of historicity." Moreover, it is difficult to maintain that the same level and experience of contingency and inauthenticity can allow for all kinds and types of experience in whatever medium they may be homogenized, in whatever genre they might find their final home.

Lukács should have been more charitable to "everyday life" and its experiencing subject to make the rehistoricization of his ontology more plausible. Instead of making this gesture, he returns to his model (creation-artwork-reception) in order to insert "the historically concrete" into the scheme. He makes efforts, not always successfully, to keep phenomenology and postconstruction apart. Historicity is introduced in the process of creation in terms of motivations, such as the "idea," which is the a priori of the lived experience appearing as the "image" of the work or the "sketch" (a combination of sense and life). The importance of the "aesthetic matter" can be perceived at this stage. In contradistinction to merely technical matter, the former is to be understood as a complex of the "contents of experiencing" as they result from the motives that had already been transformed into a vision. Lukács also introduces the notion of spiritual disposition (*Gesinnung*), which bridges the distance between the means of expression and the thing that is to be expressed. These postconstructivist categories (which could have also been understood as phenomenological ones) are there to bear witness to the mode in which our historicity is preserved (although sublated as well) in the normative subject.

Despite inconsistencies, there are a few remarkable observations in this section: in particular, the discussion of the "spiritual disposition." Spiritual disposition is the mind in its state of saturation with formed contents. As such, it is already the unity of historicity and timelessness. The experiences of a particular historical period are adequate to certain kinds of spiritual dispositions and not to others. This explains why it is only from the insight into works of art that "intellectual dispositions" can be postconstructed, and why it is only via this postconstruction that we can have access to the actual historical experience of an epoch. Lukács wisely adds to this that "coupling" intellectual dispositions with types of historical experiencing is legitimate (for example, as it is practiced in the sociology of arts), while no causal relationship between the two can and should be established.

The philosophy of art does not turn directly to life experiences, as does sociology, but only indirectly. It is not interested in the distance between life and utopia; rather, it is concerned with the forms of objective "distancelessness" (*Distanzlosigkeit*) as achieved in the artwork. Artistic style becomes the organizing principle of a philosophical undertaking of this kind. In offering a list of the fundamental styles (classic, primitive, classicist, romantic, baroque, heroic, and the like), Lukács gives a foretaste of this enterprise. The fundamental styles in his view encompass all the possible ways of "undistancing distance" within an artwork, which explains why all of them constantly recur. Lukács believed that his typology could be refined but that new items could not be added to the list of fundamental styles. The latter, he believed, exhaust all possibilities of a perfect artwork. Whether or not one accepts Lukács's typology, he made a substantial point. The more art objects we collect from remote times and places, the more we perceive the finitude of the fundamental forms of artistic-creative imagination.

In the third (and broadest) circle around the artwork, the recipient once again appears, this time qua historical recipient. This particular type of recipient is infinitely interested in the *content* of the artwork. Therefore s/he divides content and form in a gesture of misunderstanding. This is indeed misunderstanding, for the artwork "has" no content. What seems to be content is form. Yet the recipient readily receives an artwork that satisfies the postulate of "having" a particular content. Every historically concrete individual has his/her own image of "perfection" (his/her own utopia), and only the artwork that fits the model of such perfection will be pleasing. At this point, it becomes obvious why Lukács so adamantly rejected Kant's opening gambit in the *Critique of Judgment*. Taste is one of the most historical aspects of aesthetics. Although without taste there is neither creation nor reception (there is no artwork, nor is there an aesthetic sphere), taste remains an aesthetically contradictory phenomenon. It divides the indivisible (form and content) in order to reinforce misunderstanding, and it is the "readiness" that raises the living creature into the sphere of a utopian universe.

Every perfect artwork is new. A work of art is perfect if it presents itself as new for every "readiness." "The work of art is eternal if it is able to evoke the normative effect by the subject of aesthetic reception." [10] Both statements included in this brief formula are of equal importance. The work of art should lend itself to normative reception, but the artwork has no say concerning the "what" of reception. Whatever this "what" will be depends solely on the historical individual. If readiness is there, normative effect must also be there. Here, one approaches misunderstanding from yet another angle as the central category of this book. The aesthetic recipient does not appropriate the "real content of the work; he never grasps its intrinsic structure. Only the elements of his own experience, which are heterogeneous in quality and at the same time incommunicable, are rounded into a closed world in his soul, such that he will live and experience this world as if it were the work, something independent of his existence." As a consequence, "the more timeless the artwork, the more the experience of that artwork and its intellectual interpretation is going to be subjected to the change of times" (*GLW*, 203–4). The normative recipient thus once again becomes the mirror image of the normative creator. The deeper the creator dives into the unique and new experience of his own time, the greater the chances that his work will attain eternal validity. The more timeless an artwork, the more historical and eternally changing its never-accomplished reception will be. The interpretation in lived experience is followed by the intellectual interpretation of the work. The timelessness of the artwork thus presupposes a dual historicity. The historical moment is eternalized, and eternity is historicized.

It is here that misunderstanding is given a dialectical twist. We now know that the artwork is misunderstanding incarnate. We have already discussed one major constituent of misunderstanding, namely, the artwork as a utopia (which, in its capacity as a priori of all meaningful human experience, of the world of authenticity, is to be contrasted to the inauthenticity of real existence). However, the work of art is not a social utopia. Its eternal forms do not recall or recollect a once-meaningful world, nor do they anticipate a meaningful world which is to come. And Lukács does not intend for us to conclude on such a gloomy note, which can be seen in his own personal approach to the question. After all, not only works of art but also works of philosophy become cachets of "the spiritual disposition" of their authors. Existential solitude was Lukács's own personal experience. He did not find the medium of true communication and self-expression in life. In his reminiscences on his childhood, Lukács actually said that he had perceived his parental house as an "unreal" world, whereas he had discovered the world of true reality in the novels of James Fenimore Cooper.[11] His *Aesthetics* is thus his own distilled normative experience. However, a trait of Lukács's character, perhaps inherited from his rabbinical ancestors, did not allow him to permanently indulge in existential isolation. There is no better term for this attitude than "readiness for redemption," a messianic yearning with an anticipation of eventual fulfillment. Lukács could never finish a book without touching the chord of redemption, even if only faintly. This also happens here and not without preparation.

Although the work of art is not the recollection of a once-existing golden age, it is still a kind of recollection. Every great artwork carries the birthmark of the age of its conception; every history eternalizes itself in its works of art. Human suffering and joy, the multitude of the forms of human experiencing, are not devoured by the darkness of oblivion. For the artworks are there, they are eternal, they are moments of once-existing persons, of their never-fading memory. And the recipient, who can never communicate with the author, who lives in the present and through the present alone, s/he too sheds the straitjacket of isolation which is the straitjacket of the *hic et nunc.* The world of bygone ages, encapsulated in the forms of the artwork, liberates the recipient from the *hic et nunc,* lifts her up in the moment of eternity, and (herein lies the paradox) provides her with insight into real historicity. It is thus that the world of artworks, the mirror image of our existential solitude, becomes the Olympus of our mythology. Interpretations of artworks are ever changing, but they remain interpretations of a common artistic pantheon. The mirror images of our existential solitude are what connect us with our past and present.

Although the artwork is not the anticipation of a utopian future world, it is still anticipation. "Every artistic form is theodicea," Lukács writes, "for it relates in a way to salvation." Furthermore, "all the things that make their appearance in its homogeneous world attain to a Being adequate to their Idea." That is, these things, as identities of idea and being, "are just placed into a universe which seems as if it were preordained for them in order to attain perfection and thus themselves" (*GLW,* 213). Artworks, we know, are mirror images of our existential solitude. Are they also mirror images of our expectations and anticipations? Do they promise without a promise that what had happened to them can also happen to us? Can we hope that we, like them, will attain to a Being adequate to our Idea, and that we, too, can be placed into a universe preordained for us, to attain perfection and thus ourselves?[12]

On a more subdued yet stubborn note, Lukács returns to the same theme at the end of *Philosophy of Art.* The work concludes with a discussion of the possibility and impossibility of a history of the philosophy of art. Lukács does not mean to pose the problem in terms of genre; he is concerned with the question of the disappearance of the paradox. If one could understand the unity of the historicity and the eternity of the artwork instead of merely pinpointing it (as Lukács himself had been doing), then the paradox would be transformed into a merely apparent paradox and wither away. As long as one cannot understand this unity, the paradox remains with us, an absurd and all-encompassing paradox of all paradoxes (concerning the normativity of the artwork). As long as we do not understand what should be (normatively) understood, we can merely state, "works of art exist," without ever being able to answer the question, "how are they possible?" To the extent that we never know the answer, the artwork remains absurd.

If we adopt the viewpoint of history, Lukács ruminates, the artwork, the aesthetic sphere as such, remains irrational. For how can Truth emerge out of Untruth, Meaning out of Meaninglessness, Eternity out of History? The artwork must somehow be seen as the messenger of Truth, as the objectification of a Meaning, which is at work in history yet not produced by history. If we could only find a unifying Reason in the historical process itself, then we could grasp artworks as the objectifications of that Reason. Thus, coming as close as he can to Hegelianism, Lukács immediately turns in another direction. The philosophy of the history of art must become metaphysics in order to recognize, in the notions of aesthetics, "the traces and signs of the ultimate, metaphysical meaning of the course of the world, and to try . . . to decipher the hieroglyphs" (*GLW,* 231–32).

Works of art exist; how are they possible? This is the question of aesthetics. The reversal of the sign proves fruitful. Lukács makes a case for the autonomy of art, yet not in the manner in which the "autonomy of art" is nowadays understood. The autonomy of the aesthetic sphere is established against the logical-theoretical and the ethical value spheres, that is, against the arrogant truth-claim of rationalized and intellectualized "bodies of knowledge." If Truth, Meaning, and Sense leave traces on the body of artworks, the claims of modern science are false and fraudulent; their true knowledge is not the Truth, because it is unrelated to the meaning of human existence. When Lukács repeats the Kierkegaardian dictum that Truth is subjective, he means exactly that; no true knowledge, which remains unrelated to our subjective existence as such, can be Truth. If art is completely autonomous in relation to logic (theory) or ethics, it nonetheless is not completely autonomous in relation to life. That is, it is autonomous and nonautonomous at the same time.

Insofar as art contrasts Meaning to the meaninglessness of life, art is autonomous vis-à-vis life. But insofar as art emerges out of life, insofar as the normative subject (the very precondition of art) is nothing but the (normative) transformation of the empirical subject, of the "human person as a whole," art can never become autonomous in relation to life. Created by subjects, enjoyed by subjects, (theoretically) interpreted as something that had been experienced by subjects, the Truth of artworks is Truth-for-the-subject. It is Truth for us, Truth for you and me, for every "you" and every "me." Only the utopia of life can be Truth; it is the only hieroglyph worth being deciphered.

However, the closing sentences of *Philosophy of Art* are ambiguous on several counts. It remains uncertain whether the metaphysics of art (in this case, the question concerning Being that manifests itself in history and in the artwork) was conceived as a real enterprise, a project Lukács had wanted to address, or as the limit to human theoretic reasoning—that is, a kind of thing-in-itself, or a metaphysical Ultimate no one grasps theoretically except through personal mystical experience (by reading the hieroglyphs). Though Lukács's theoretical biography in the war years does not exclude any of these speculations, speculations they remain.

The autonomous sphere of aesthetics is discussed as a validity sphere. Lukács treats aesthetics as if it were logic or ethics in a neo-Kantian understanding. In a normative sphere, one discusses norms and norm fulfillment. The possibilities of nonfulfillment of the categorical imperative are infinite, yet Kant is simply not interested in them. In a similar vein, in aesthetics, as a validity sphere, only perfect artworks, perfect modes of normative creation and reception, can be accounted for. Yet, as Lukács pointed out, the aesthetic sphere is one in which validity and valorization coincide. This circumstance can cause some embarrassment. Norm fulfillment is individual, not universal-formal; thus it must be exemplified in single artworks and, at the very best, in single ways of creation and reception or single styles. The latter is certainly already a compromise. Lukács never would have asserted that imperfect artworks, which do not represent a completely closed microcosm, are not artworks at all, nor would he have stated that reception falling short of an absolute readiness is no reception at all. He was simply not interested in the "deviations" from the norm unless they were representative deviations (in ethics, we can certainly find representative motivations for the infringement of norms). Lukács occasionally dwells at great lengths on "deviations" that are, to his mind, typical. This is an approach that may be appropriate in ethics but that seems to be completely out of touch with our own aesthetic intuitions—all the more so since Lukács remained silent about the circumstance in which artworks are not adequate to his norms but can be strictly normative in certain other senses, even in certain ways that he himself pointed out.

Personally, unlike several postmodernists, I would not object to Lukács's fundamental conception of the aesthetic sphere as the normative sphere of the artwork. I do oppose the rigidity of Lukács's ways of positing norms as well as his sometimes royal gestures of inclusion and exclusion. Royal gestures of this kind can border on the ridiculous. For example, Lukács states that there is only one paradigmatic creator of a particular epoch in each and every artistic medium. He mentions Mozart as the paradigmatic modern composer. Yet in the manuscript he first committed to paper the name of Bach appears—later deleted in order to insert Mozart's name instead. He was convinced that there could be no more than one paradigmatic creator; he was only unsure which was the one. And yet, such absurdities cannot blur vision. What Lukács fought against was the absolutist claim of logocentrism. His extremist plea for the uniqueness of normative artworks should not be misunderstood in the ephemeral context of contemporary debates.

The reversal of the Kantian question proved tremendously fruitful, even if the question has remained unanswered. More precisely, it has been answered, and yet it has remained, to us, without an answer. Between creation and the work, between the reception and the work, there is the leap. The possibility of the artwork has been proven, presented, illuminated, argued for, portrayed. Yet the leap has remained a leap not only for the creator and the recipient but also for the philosopher of art—and how could it be otherwise? The leap would cease being a leap only if it could be explained. We do not know how artworks are possible, yet we know that there is the leap. And finally, we do understand how artwork is possible. It is possible due to everything we understand and something we do not understand: namely the leap (*Ur-Sprung des Kunstwerks*). Our problem has shifted. We know that works of art are possible because there is the leap. And what we do not understand can now be formulated as follows: the leap exists; how is it possible? This is what Lukács's shift toward metaphysics means. The shift opens up the way to speculation. And speculation is never ending.

Notes

1. I can add my personal experience to the story. As a second-year philosophy student, I attended one of Lukács's seminars on Kant's *Critique of Judgment*. This was one of the best philosophy seminars of my life, and Lukács's critical comments on the book have remained clearly engraved on my mind. In reading the *Heidelberg Aesthetics*, I reencountered that original kind of analysis and criticism, and not the type of Kant critique that became familiar in Lukács's work from the 1930s onward. Thus, it turns out that, at a deeper level or temporality, I actually participated in a 1917 seminar rather than one in 1948.

2. According to György Márkus, it is not impossible, though not very likely, that a chapter is missing.

3. Georg Lukács, *Soul and Form*, trans. Anna Bostock (London: Merlin Press, 1979), 11–12.

4. In his late aesthetics, Lukács combined both solutions. The "everyday" became a primary sphere, not as everyday life but as everyday thinking, in its capacity as the as-yet-undifferentiated sphere of two separate and pure modes of understanding (*Erkenntnis*).

5. The discovery of the fragments lends some credence to Michael Holzman's idiosyncratic reading of the first chapter of *The Theory of the Novel* (in *Lukács's Road to God: The Early Criticism against Its Pre-Marxist Background* [Lanham, Md.: University Press of America, 1985]). If Holzman is right, this seminal book, too, is characterized by the above-described oscillation between the two visions.

6. This interpretation will reappear in the more Hegelian *Theory of the Novel.*

7. *Intellektuelle Anschauung* was rather appreciated in the hints of Kant, in his "Critique of Teleological Judgment."

8.   This journey away from phenomenology is not carried out without inconsistencies in the work. Lukács sometimes picks up already-discussed matters on exactly the same level as the one on which they had been discussed in the first two chapters. One should not forget, however, that this work, although not a fragment, is a first draft.

9.   Lukács made an explicit reference to Kierkegaard's obvious influence on him, at that period of his life, in the preface to the 1962 German edition of *The Theory of the Novel.* See Georg Lukács, *Die Theorie des Romans* (Darmstadt: Neuwied, 1979), 12.

10.   Georg Lukács, "Heidelberger Philosophie de Kunst (1912–1914)," in *Georg Lukács Werke,* vol. 16 (Darmstadt: Luchterhand Verlag, 1974), 200; my translation. Hereafter abbreviated *GLW* and cited parenthetically in the text.

11.   See his autobiographical sketch, *Gelebtes Denken: eine Autobiographie im Dialog,* ed. Istvan Eörski (Frankfurt am Main: Suhrkamp, 1984).

12.   The common features between Lukács's conception and Kant's *Religion within the Limits of Reason Alone* are visible.

> The starting-point of critical elaboration is the consciousness of what one really is, and is "knowing thyself" as a product of the historical process to date which has deposited in you an infinity of traces, without leaving an inventory.
> —Antonio Gramsci, "The Study of Philosophy," in *The Prison Notebooks*

"Prediction and Perspective"

Textuality and Counterhegemonic Culture in Antonio Gramsci and Julia Kristeva

Thomas Foster

Gayatri Spivak sets out to show how "Marx uncovered the economic *text*" which underlies the "seemingly unified concept-phenomenon" of money or exchange-value.[1] She argues that, like Freud and Nietzsche as "the crucial Western thinkers of discontinuity," Marx was "betrayed or obliged" by his method "to unbridgeable gaps and shifts in planes." Her deconstructive reading finds his text "to be a battleground between the intimations of discontinuity and the strong pull toward constructing a continuous argument with a secure beginning (arché), middle (historical enjambement), and end (telos)."[2] The textuality and epistemological complications of political economy become apparent in James O'Connor's essay "Productive and Unproductive Labor": "The fact that workers may resist value production makes the whole notion of value as a quantity of labor or a number of labor hours problematic. . . . Necessary labor and surplus labor are not distinguishable *empirically* in terms of actual hours worked."[3] The definition of a historical agency specific to a worker, "the fact that workers may resist," is crucial here. The discontinuity or undecidability O'Connor points to is an effect of the conflict between two antagonistic subject positions within the productive process.[4]

I will argue here that Antonio Gramsci's writings theorize this "battleground" of textuality; they offer a way to define the place of textual practices in the elaboration of counterhegemonic value systems opposed to dominant interest groups in control of the state apparatus. The chapter "Prediction and Perspective" from "The Modern Prince" both theoretically thematizes and stylistically enacts what we now call textuality, while an earlier essay on the Italian Futurists demonstrates how Gramsci situates textual practice within a materialist theory of social change. A comparison to Julia Kristeva's work, especially her comments on Russian Futurism in an essay called "The Ethics of Linguistics,"[5] clarifies how Gramsci prefigures French post-structuralist critiques of language and representation and offers a materialist perspective on these contemporary critical theories.

Gramsci echoes post-structuralism before the letter with the notion that critical self-consciousness dissolves subjectivity into "a product of the historical process to date which has deposited in you an infinity of traces, without leaving an inventory."[6] This statement appears in a section of the English translation of *The Prison Notebooks* entitled "The Study of Philosophy," and this translation omits a sentence. The original continues, "Therefore it is imperative at the outset to compile such an inventory."[7] These two sentences define a double necessity for Gramsci. It is imperative both to recognize the diversity of historical process and to delineate a revolutionary agent or historical bloc. Counterhegemony respects both of these necessities, while capitalist hegemony involves only the constitution of a dominant historical agent. Defined in this way, counterhegemony would presuppose and preserve what Stanley Aronowitz has called an "antihegemonic" moment recognizing "the *permanence* of difference."[8] I will argue both that Gramsci understands this antihegemonic imperative and that the moment of antihegemony corresponds to textual disruptions which remain in excess of all structural unities. His awareness of the problematics of this double necessity brings Gramsci closer to Kristeva's position (at least in her earlier work) than to Derrida's.

The chapter "Prediction and Perspective" comes at a crucial point in the argument of "The Modern Prince," immediately after a long critique of economic determinism ("economism") that ends with Gramsci's very suggestive remarks on the necessity of "compromise" in the formation of a nonhierarchically organized oppositional group.[9] In the first paragraph, Gramsci introduces his basic distinction between hegemony and the repressive state apparatus, between consent and force, as a "'dual perspective' in political action and in national life" (*SPN,* 169). The first perspective corresponds both to coercive force and to the localized resistance that such oppressive conditions produce. Gramsci leads into the issue of prediction by arguing that the more this "first 'perspective' is 'immediate' and elementary, the more the second has to be 'distant' (not in time, but as a dialectical relation), complex and ambitious" (*SPN,* 170). The second level of hegemony represents the elaboration of the immediate interests of, for example, the trade union movement in Italy into an alternative system of cultural values and governance, aesthetics and ethics, potentially viable on at least a national level. Gramsci's point is that such a system is immanent in the immediate activities of mass oppositional tactics and "agitation." Collective action can prefigure the development of a new culture projected into the future as a goal dialectically inseparable from and latent in the present action which it channels and organizes.

So far, the argument closely follows Lenin in *What Is to Be Done?*[10] on the need for a political and ideological struggle conducted by Party professionals as the means of transcending the immediate level of trade-union activism and thereby transforming a movement aimed at specific local reforms (in wages and working conditions) into a broad-based revolutionary program. But Gramsci's discussion of prediction begins to raise new possibilities for defining the social and political value of cultural and specifically *textual* practices. For Gramsci, prediction expresses an implicit or explicit worldview and value system: "Anybody who makes a prediction has in fact a 'programme' for whose victory he [*sic*] is working, and his prediction is precisely an element contributing to that victory" (*SPN,* 171).[11] Sheila Rowbotham has opposed the "prefigurative forms"[12] of feminist organizations to the Leninist vanguard, which separates means and ends by establishing party hierarchies as the means for creating a nonhierarchic socialist state. Like Rowbotham, Gramsci asserts that "prediction" can avoid utopian futility only if it can also "consolidate existing practice" (*BF,* 147):[13] "only to the extent to which the objective aspect of prediction is linked to a programme does it acquire its objectivity" (*BF,* 171).

The objective aspect of prediction is its performative status, helping to formulate and thus advance knowledge and self-awareness of an oppositional "programme," which must therefore already exist in some form. But prediction also posits or clears a space for a new subjectivity, a position of agency in language and history, which need not have existed prior to the act of prediction itself. Gramsci writes, "[W]hen a particular programme has to be realised, it is only the existence of somebody to 'predict' it which will ensure that it deals with what is essential—with those elements [of historical process] which, being 'organisable' and susceptible of being directed or deflected, are in reality alone predictable" (*SPN*, 171), because they can be affected by the intervention of a historical subject, "somebody to 'predict.'"[14] The specification of possibilities for active change implicit in any "prediction" also necessarily specifies a location in the social structure where the action could be exerted, *whether or not* that position is already occupied by an organized collectivity capable of performing the action. Gramsci places quotation marks around the word "predict" in the sentence just quoted to call attention to the pun on pre-diction (Ital., *predire*), or speaking beforehand. This operation of speaking *as if* from a position of (for Gramsci) proletarian hegemony—that is, engaging in cultural production and political activity—prevents proletarian consciousness from remaining simply a negation of the bourgeois social order and so remaining bound up with the existing economic mode of production, a limitation which "economism" encouraged, as Lenin had already argued.[15]

As a form of discourse, pre-diction here designates the functioning of and is offered as the model for counterhegemonic cultural productions in general. To the extent that they accommodate new forms of subjectivity, such productions necessarily function as textual moments of discontinuity within things as they are. But before we examine the theoretical necessity for such a discourse and the form it might take in practice, a moment of textuality in this passage from Gramsci must be addressed, textuality in Spivak's sense of not merely "a moment of ambiguity or irony ultimately incorporated into the text's system of unified meaning but rather a moment that genuinely threatens to collapse that system."[16]

Gramsci seems to perform a textual somersault in the passages cited above. First he asserts that prediction is always interested, always implicated in an already existing political program. He then turns around and writes that prediction can precede such a program and in fact help to create it by defining the "elements" which are "susceptible" to change and thus "alone predictable" (meaning unpredictable under the terms of the existing hegemony, since the operation of prediction designates precisely that which is not decided or determined in advance but instead can be produced through intervention and struggle). The determination of discourse by the material existence of dominant or oppositional groups reverses itself. This contradiction between discourse as determined or determining corresponds, on the one hand, to a reading of Gramsci which stresses the "organic" relation between culture or intellectual activity and specific collective bodies and, on the other hand, to a reading which finds in the distinction between hegemony and brute force a privileging of the cultural struggle to obtain consent and ultimately determine (or continue to justify) control of the state apparatus. On this cultural level, conflicts of interest must at least be given lip service to preserve the appearance of consensus, so that possibilities for resistance are more readily available but are also more susceptible to appropriation and containment than they would be on a basic, material level.[17] The first reading sees Gramsci giving priority to the material level, while the second sees Gramsci defining cultural struggle as a means for opening the question of basic social change. Neither reading is wrong.

The presence of these two contradictory moments in Gramsci's text corresponds to a double necessity. First, on the level of cultural hegemony, he attempts to define a diversity of interests which cannot be reduced to or identified with those of the dominant paradigm for subjectivity, the bourgeois individual or masculine entrepreneur. But, equally, the proletariat as "identical subject-object of history" cannot be assumed to encompass this historical multiplicity, as Lukács had assumed it could.[18] Second, Gramsci remains committed to a program for radical social change which requires the positing of an agent, a clearly delimited subject position from which to act. The negotiation of this bind has emerged in this century as a crucial problem in social theory and the practice of social movements. As Stanley Aronowitz puts it, "[T]he crisis in historical materialism" means "it remains for us to find the bearers of a non-identical dialectic."[19]

Gramsci's linking of these two moments without apparent resolution or a reconciliation which would subordinate one to the other implies a redefinition of the revolutionary subject.[20] To posit the subject as historical repository of "an infinity of traces . . . *without an inventory*" is to reject the totalized proletarian consciousness of Lukács's teleological dialectic. Julia Kristeva has dealt at length with the double necessity for social movements to both define a limited subject position and acknowledge that the historical process cannot be reduced to the narrative of a single collective subject; her work clarifies Gramsci's comments on the value of textual pre-dictions for social movements.

In *Revolution in Poetic Language,* Kristeva defines the "text" as consisting of "two opposing terms that alternate in an endless rhythm," in which the negative terms "pass through all the theses capable of giving them meaning, go beyond them, and in so doing convey positivity in their path."[21] The "theses" are both intentional statements and the subject position implied by such an intentionality. The text then both establishes and exceeds the limit of the subject position which underwrites the meaningfulness of its discourse; by doing so, it enacts the historical dynamic of late capitalism which "ensures that human experience will be *broadened* beyond the narrow boundaries assigned to it by old relations of production and yet still be *connected* to those relations, which will consequently be threatened by it" (*RPL,* 105). Kristeva here describes the production of oppositional consciousness, which then rejects the limitations producing it by asserting its status as a subject and not merely the object of historical forces. She formulates the same double bind that Gramsci's text points to when she discusses how moments of textual heterogeneity represent "the diversity and multiplicity of social practices which disregard that moment in their own realization" (*RPL,* 213) and thus disregard the historical process as an "infinity of traces."

Kristeva explicitly defines the temporal structure of the text as proleptic or anticipatory. She designates this structure by the term "future anterior," a literal translation of the French for the verb tense of the future perfect (*futur anterieur*). What Gramsci calls pre-diction, Kristeva defines as the possibility of what will have been. For Kristeva, textual practice during moments of social instability "responds to its historical present . . . with a future then impossible, but which takes the appearance of an anteriority,"[22] a turn toward archaic material and a use of language preceding the communicative structures that insure sociability. In Kristeva's examples, particularly the avant-garde literary texts of Mallarmé and Lautréamont, such discourse is a "utopian" anticipation because it "ignores the concrete economic conditions necessary for its realization" (*RLP,* 389) and is "unrealizable at the moment of its enunciation" (*RLP,* 398). But it is precisely through its utopianism that "this practice rejoins the 'final goal' of dialectical materialism"; that is, it poses "to the worker's movement a problem that it will only be able to approach belatedly" (*RLP,* 389), since "such intellectual practices signal . . . what will become a program of the 'left' in the future" (*RLP,* 398). Kristeva is aware that the literary avant-garde's "utopianism" is also an elitism. She warns that "to abandon the notion" of class consciousness and a material subject position "carries the risk of placing negativity outside of the relations of production, in the transcendence of religion and art" (*RLP,* 389). But Kristeva also points out that Lukács's concept of class consciousness makes "Hegelian negativity incarnate itself in the proletariat as productive class" and thus causes "this negativity to act in the sense of perfecting the system of production" (*RLP,* 384).

In her essay "The Ethics of Linguistics," Kristeva uses the Russian Futurists Mayakovsky and Khlebnikov as exemplary of how poetry raises the linguistic code to a point where it "becomes receptive to the rhythmic body and . . . forms, in opposition to present meaning, another meaning, but a future impossible meaning," a "future anterior" ("EL," 33). But the apparent elitism of such texts results precisely from the Futurists' "strong attention to the explosion of the October Revolution." The historicity of experimental texts appears when "[a]nteriority and future join together to open that historical axis in relation to which concrete history will always be wrong: murderous, limiting, subject to regional imperatives (economic, tactical, political, familial . . .)" ("EL," 33). While Kristeva argues that poetic language is a "dramatic notion of language as a risky practice, allowing the speaking animal to sense the rhythm of the body as well as the upheavals of history,"[23] she also asserts that "[l]inguistic ethics . . . consists in following the resurgence of an 'I' coming back to rebuild an ephemeral structure in which the constituting struggle of language and society would be spelled out" ("EL," 34). It is this appropriation and joining of textual practice with an "I," the subject position or class consciousness produced by a social movement, which Gramsci stresses in an article called "Marinetti the Revolutionary," published in 1921.

Gramsci describes the attraction of workers to Futurism before World War I (when Marinetti in particular came out strongly for the war). Gramsci then uses Futurism to break with Lenin, arguing that the workers' support for this avant-garde movement stands as an "intuition . . . of an unsatisfied need in the proletarian field."[24] During the struggle to "found a new state" by seizing the "existing organization . . . constructed by the bourgeoisie," Gramsci agrees with Lenin's statement that "[f]or a certain time the workers ' state cannot be other than a bourgeois state without the bourgeoisie" (*SCW,* 50). But Gramsci goes on to write that "the creation of a new civilization," as opposed to the seizure of state power, "is, on the other hand, absolutely mysterious, absolutely characterized by the unforeseeable and the unexpected" (*SCW,* 50). Nothing can be certain except that "there will be a proletarian culture (a civilization) totally different from the bourgeois one and in this field too class distinctions will be shattered. Bourgeois careerism will be shattered and there will be a poetry, a novel, a theatre, a moral code, a language, a painting and a music peculiar to proletarian civilization" (*SCW,* 50).

Gramsci echoes Lenin, asking, "What remains to be done?" and answering, "Nothing other than to destroy the present form of civilization." Gramsci insists, however, that in the cultural field the phrase "'to destroy'" signifies a radically different task than in the struggle for a new state; it means "to destroy spiritual hierarchies, prejudices, idols, and ossified traditions" and "not to be afraid of innovations and audacities, not to be afraid of monsters" (*SCW,* 51). Kristeva argues that it was the Futurists' return to the pure signifier, anterior to the social determination of language as communicative vehicle, which prefigures this rejection of existing social and cultural structures ("EL," 32ff.). Gramsci ends by stating that in the cultural field

> it is likely to be a long time before the working classes will manage to do anything more creative than the Futurists have done. When they supported the Futurists, the workers' groups showed that they were not afraid of destruction, certain as they were of being able to create poetry, paintings and plays, like the Futurists; these workers were supporting historicity, the possibility of a proletarian culture created by the workers themselves. (*SCW,* 51)[25]

The Futurist text then was a pre-diction implying an empty space where there should be "somebody to predict it," a space the already existing proletarian subject could appropriate, redefining itself in terms external to the capitalist system in the process, or at least beginning that task.[26] Like Kristeva, Gramsci suggests that the only possible pre-diction of a society free from exploitation is an "impossible meaning," an absolute textual negativity represented by the Futurists' refusal to treat language as a communicative vehicle. But Gramsci also emphasizes the need to situate such moments of negativity and to posit concrete alternatives, that is, proletarian culture and not just its "possibility." In a later work from the 1930s, "Problems of Criticism," Gramsci would assert that "[t]he most common prejudice is this: that the new literature has to identify itself with an artistic school of intellectual origins, as was the case with Futurism. The premise of the new literature cannot but be historical, political, and popular. It must aim at elaborating *that which already is*" (*SCW,* 102).

But in the same essay, Gramsci warns that "[i]t is a serious error to adopt a 'single' progressive strategy according to which each new gain accumulates and becomes the premise of further gains," since "there are many [literary and ideological] 'conformisms,' many struggles for new 'conformisms' and various combinations of that which already exists (variously expressed) and that which one is working to bring about (and there are many people who are working in this direction)" (*SCW,* 101). The struggle for a new culture is overdetermined.[27] And following Kristeva we can suggest that Gramsci was aware how this heterogeneity can only express itself through the "empty space" provided by textuality. His awareness of this problematic would then be the reason why "every new civilization, as such . . . has always expressed itself in literary form *before* expressing itself in the life of the state" (*SCW,* 117; my emphasis).

In Louis Althusser's view, the "interpellation" of the subject into discourse is structured proleptically, his example being the act of "expecting" a child. The subject is always predicted or spoken for in the very act of trying to claim for him/herself the power of discourse and a place in language.[28] That reifying operation of anticipation, treating the future as if it must inevitably conform to already existing conditions, corresponds to the capacity of the existing hegemony to appropriate resistance movements and attempts to empower exploited groups. Through his distinction between hegemony and direct coercive force, Gramsci was one of the first Marxist theorists to emphasize this capacity. The problem then becomes where to locate what Lukács calls "the abstract negativity in the life of the worker,"[29] given that activities directed against the conditions which reduce the worker to a state of negativity tend to be appropriated through reforms on the material level of the base, while ideological and political activities are even more vulnerable due to the operations of the hegemonic, superstructural level in producing consensus.[30]

Gramsci's essay on Marinetti indicates that he, like Kristeva, finds a model for this fundamental, uncompromising negativity (as opposed to the necessary positivity of a social movement and the subjectivity it defines) in experimental cultural productions demonstrating the discontinuities, especially in language, which we have come to designate as moments of textuality. As a material practice, these texts seem to permit the recognition of irreducible multiplicity in the historical process which tends to be effaced for strategic reasons in the practice of specific social movements. Gramsci indicates his awareness of this problematic when he discusses the necessity of compromise in the formation of a counter-hegemony that would not sacrifice the interests of one social group to another or use hegemonic consent to perpetuate the imposition of a dominant group's interests on society as a whole (*SPN,* 168).[31] The implied redefinition of subjectivity emerging out of the practice of revolutionary movements begins with "the starting- point of critical elaboration," in a consciousness of oneself as "a product of the historical process to date which has deposited in you an infinity of traces, without leaving an inventory" (*SPN,* 324).

Gramsci's work emphasizes that the textual activity of prediction is linked with but not reducible to a definite perspective, a point of view in a narrative of resistance and social change. Today he provides a model for negotiating between the localized, microstructural analysis of discursive power and the macrostructural level where unities of gender, race, and class operate with an often brutal efficiency that must be contested on that level.[32] We must know ourselves marked by an infinity of traces as we move through plural and often contradictory positions, where the white male intellectual may also be constituted as a social subject by one of the discourses on the American citizen, the homeowner, children of working mothers, or distressed Southern farming communities.[33] But we must also compile an inventory, know how we are positioned, and make use of the opportunities for intervention opened up by the contradictions we live. Gramsci participates in postmodern critiques of the subject, but he also situates those critiques in a materialist theory of culture and social change. His theoretical writing in the 1920s and 1930s had already begun to answer Kristeva's question, "Is it possible to keep open the heterogeneous and contradictory moment, which is unbearable for the subject, within a text that represents, through this moment, the diversity and multiplicity of social practices which disregard that moment in their own realization?" (*RPL,* 213).

Notes

1. See Gayatri Chakravorty Spivak, "Scattered Speculations on the Question of Value," in *In Other Worlds: Essays in Cultural Politics* (New York: Methuen, 1987), 155.

2. Ibid., 292 n. 4.

3. James O'Connor, "Productive and Unproductive Labor," *Politics and Society* 5 (1975): 321–22; my emphasis.

4. Michael Ryan makes a similar argument for the priority of productive relations over productive forces, a priority foregrounded in his view by a rereading of Marx "in light of the deconstructive critique of classical dialectics." See his *Marxism and Deconstruction: A Critical Articulation* (Baltimore: Johns Hopkins University Press, 1982), 82.

5. See Julia Kristeva, "The Ethics of Linguistics," in *Desire in Language: A Semiotic Approach to Literature and Art,* trans. Thomas Gora, Alice Jardine, and Leon S. Roudiez, ed. Leon S. Roudiez (New York: Columbia University Press, 1980), 23-35; hereafter abbreviated "EL" and cited parenthetically in the text.

6. See Antonio Gramsci, *Selections from the Prison Notebooks,* trans. and ed. Quintin Hoare and Geoffrey Nowell Smith (New York: International Publishers, 1971), 324; hereafter abbreviated *SPN* and cited parenthetically in the text.

7. See Gramsci's *Quaderni del Carcere: Edizione critica dell' Instituto Gramsci,* 4 vols. (Torino: Giulio Einaudi, 1975), vol. 2, quaderno 11, § 12, p. 1376. The passage reads: "L'inizio dell'elaborazione critica è la coscienza di quello che è realmente, cioè un 'conosci te stesso' come prodotto del processo storico finora svoltosi che ha lasciato in te stesso un'infinità di tracce accolte senza beneficio d'inventario. Occorre fare inizialmente un tale inventario." Edward Said comments briefly on this passage in his "Zionism from the Standpoint of Its Victims," *Social Text* 1 (Winter 1979): 7-58.

8. See Stanley Aronowitz, *The Crisis in Historical Materialism: Class, Politics, and Culture in Marxist Theory* (New York: Praeger, 1982), 128.

9. In the same passage, Gramsci describes this oppositional group as being "without internal contradictions." It seems to me that it is not contradiction or difference itself but antagonistic contradictions that would be eliminated. As Aronowitz puts it, the desire for self-management among autonomous resistance movements "would not constitute the basis for antagonism; [the desires of these various groups] would no longer be the mask for privilege, only different modes of adaptation to society and nature based upon traditions that logically help form communities. A self-managed socialism would imply different visions of the world and different ways to negotiate our relations within the framework of the logics of non-domination" (*Crisis in Historical Materialism,* 135). Aronowitz is here drawing on Mao's essays on contradiction. See Mao Tsetung, *Five Essays on Philosophy* (Peking: Foreign Languages Press, 1977).

10. V. I. Lenin, *What Is to Be Done?: Burning Questions of Our Movement* (New York: International Publishers, 1969).

11. Sue Golding discusses Gramsci's redefinition of prediction as practical activity rather than the expression of scientific laws or a mechanical, deterministic causality. See her "The Concept of Philosophy of Praxis in the *Quaderni* of Antonio Gramsci," in *Marxism and the Interpretation of Culture,* ed. Cary Nelson and Lawrence Grossberg (Urbana: University of Illinois Press, 1988), 548-49, 552-23. See also Gramsci's essay "Problems of Marxism" (*SPN,* 437-38: "The Concept of 'Science'"). Gramsci here defines prediction "not as a scientific act of knowledge, but as the abstract expression of the effort made, the practical way of creating a collective will" (438).

12.   See Sheila Rowbotham, Lynne Segal, and Hilary Wainwright, *Beyond the Fragments: Feminism and the Making of Socialism* (London: Merlin Press, 1979); hereafter abbreviated *BF* and cited parenthetically in the text.

13.   Rowbotham also argues that the feminist movement promotes individual empowerment politically and culturally in ways that socialist organizations influenced by Lenin's concept of the vanguard party do not. This point seems to me very similar to Gramsci's insistence that both movements of the "dual perspective" are present simultaneously, both the struggle to seize the state apparatus and the struggle to create a new civilization and culture, but the latter are more distant dialectically, not temporally (*SPN,* 170). I therefore disagree with Rowbotham's extension of her critique of Lenin to Gramsci (*BF,* 119). At points in her argument, however, Rowbotham does indicate that Gramsci departs from the practices she is critiquing (*BF,* 146).

14.   Compare this statement of Gramsci's to the passage on production of new forms of subjectivity in Marx's *German Ideology,* which Gramsci seems to echo here: "Production not only provides the material to satisfy a need, but it also provides the need for the material. . . . Production accordingly produces not only an object for the subject, but also a subject for the object" (Karl Marx and Friedrich Engels, *The German Ideology,* ed. C. J. Arthur [New York: International Publishers, 1970], 132–33).

15.   This reading of Gramsci on prediction should be compared to Martin Jay's discussion of "a prefigurative counter-hegemony" in Gramsci, which would involve the "achievement of a linguistically unified community with shared meanings" as "the basis for socialism." See Jay's *Marxism and Totality: The Adventures of a Concept from Lukács to Habermas* (Berkeley: University of California Press, 1984), 165, 159. Jay directly compares Gramsci and Habermas in this respect.

16.   See Gayatri Chakravorty Spivak's translator's preface to Jacques Derrida's *Of Grammatology,* trans. Gayatri Chakravorty Spivak (Baltimore: Johns Hopkins University Press, 1987), lxxv.

17.   These two interpretive stances can be exemplified by R. Radhakrishnan and Joseph Buttigieg on the one hand, who stress Gramsci's concept of the organic intellectual, and by Louis Althusser on the other, who, as Fredric Jameson has pointed out, proposes a redefinition of the relationship among the various levels, including the cultural, of the capitalist mode of production through the concepts of "structural causality" and "relative autonomy." See Althusser's chapter "Marx's Immense Theoretical Revolution," in his and Etienne Balibar's *Reading Capital,* trans. Ben Brewster (London: Verso, 1979), and his essay on "Ideology," in ibid., pp. 135–36; R. Radhakrishnan's "Ethnic Identity and Post-Structuralist Difference," *Cultural Critique* 2 (Spring 1987): 199–220; and Joseph Buttigieg's "The Exemplary Worldliness of Antonio Gramsci's Literary Criticism," *Boundary2* 11 (Fall–Winter 1982–

83): 21–39. Radhakrishnan sets up an opposition between Gramsci's position on the organic relation of counterhegemonic intellectuals (in contrast to traditional intellectuals) and the post-structuralist critique of the subject as represented by Michel Foucault's essay "The Death of the Author." Also see Fredric Jameson, *The Political Unconscious: Narrative as a Socially Symbolic Act* (Ithaca, N.Y.: Cornell University Press, 1981), 32–39. One might add that Ernesto Laclau's and Chantal Mouffe's rejection of "the distinction between discursive and non-discursive practices" stands as one of the strongest developments of a "culturalist" position based in part on Althusser. See their *Hegemony and Socialist Strategy: Towards a Radical Democratic Politics,* trans. Winston Moore and Paul Cammack (London: Verso, 1985), 107. (They do not, however, attempt to redefine and generalize discourse as a model for a differential and "relational totality" [110].) Aronowitz also writes about "Gramsci's claim of the primacy of cultural contradictions" (*Crisis in Historical Materialism,* 132).

18. See Georg Lukács, *History and Class Consciousness: Studies in Marxist Dialectics,* trans. Rodney Livingstone (Cambridge, Mass.: MIT Press, 1971), 199. Gramsci's seeming refusal to accept Lukács's dialectical paradigm, where capitalism represents the single totalizing oppressive force in modern society and in which the industrial proletariat then becomes the motor of history as the only genuine revolutionary subject of history, might be a function of Gramsci's historical position and his direct encounter with fascism as a movement appealing to such marginalized groups as peasants and young unemployed persons. Faced with such a situation in Germany, Ernst Bloch proclaimed the theoretical and eminently practical necessity of developing a "polyphonous dialectics" which could accommodate coalition politics and enable the worker's movement to appeal to the groups from which the fascists were drawing support. See Bloch, "Nonsynchronism and the Obligation to Its Dialectics," *New German Critique* 11 (Spring 1977): 22–38.

19. Aronowitz, *Crisis in Historical Materialism,* 31. Paul Smith's *Discerning the Subject* (Minneapolis: University of Minnesota Press, 1988) is a full-length study of this problem in both Marxist and post-structuralist theories.

20. Spivak's version of this redefinition argues that a "materialist predication" or determination of the subject places certain groups in a textual position within the economic structure of capitalism. She specifies women and their traditional role in producing use-value as a deconstructive "lever" in the exchange system, and the concept of "affectively necessary" rather than socially necessary labor as the positive elaboration of a counterhegemonic value system from that potentially critical subject position ("Scattered Speculations," 162).

21. See Julia Kristeva, *Revolution in Poetic Language,* trans. Margaret

Waller (New York: Columbia University Press, 1984), 99; hereafter abbreviated *RPL* and cited parenthetically in the text. Kristeva refers to these opposing terms as "*instinctual dyads* (positive/negative, affirmation/negation, life drive/death drive)" (*RPL,* 90). Compare Paul de Man's definition: "We call *text* any entity that can be considered from such a double perspective: as a generative, open-ended, non-referential grammatical system and as a figural system closed off by a transcendental signification that subverts the grammatical code to which the text owes its existence" (*Allegories of Reading: Figural Language in Rousseau, Nietzsche, Rilke, and Proust* [New Haven, Conn.: Yale University Press, 1969], 270).

22.   The English translation of *Revolution in Poetic Language* contains only the first, primarily theoretical section of the much longer original, *La Revolution du langage poetique* (Paris: Edition du Seuil, 1974), 413; hereafter abbreviated *RLP* and cited parenthetically in the text. I am quoting from the third major section of the book, "L'etat and le mystere," which contains the chapter "Le futur anterieur" and involves a sustained engagement with Marxist theories of history and class consciousness. All translations from this section are my own.

23.   Kristeva's reference to the rhythms of the body should be read in relation to Gramsci's insistence on the intellectual activity latent in the worker's "muscular-nervous effort," in Gramsci's essay on "The Formation of Intellectuals" (*SPN,* 9).

24.   Antonio Gramsci, "Marinetti the Revolutionary," in *Selections from Cultural Writings,* trans. William Boelhower, ed. David Forgacs and Geoffrey Nowell Smith (Cambridge, Mass.: Harvard University Press, 1985), 50. This volume hereafter abbreviated *SCW* and cited parenthetically in the text.

25.   Gramsci's comments on the value of Futurism for the worker's movement imply that such avant-garde cultural productions can empower the immediate creation of alternative cultural institutions without deferring to existing standards. This empowerment would proceed on an individual as well as a collective basis. The reference to Lenin's notion of the dictatorship of the proletariat in the essay on Marinetti suggests a different narrative of the transition to socialism. The creation of alternative institutions, in a prefigurative counterhegemony, begins a process which makes the bourgeois state other to itself. When state power is seized, the conditions have thus been prepared which will allow a movement beyond "the bourgeois state without the bourgeoisie," to the "withering away of the state," the radical transformation of the state apparatus.

26.   Kristeva argues that the "social function of texts" is "the production of a different kind of subject, one capable of bringing about new social relations and thus joining in the process of capitalism's subversion" (*RPL,* 105–6). She cites Marx's statement that "the realm of freedom actually begins only where labour which is determined by necessity and mundane considerations

ceases; thus in the very nature of things it lies beyond the sphere of actual material production" (Karl Marx, *Capital*, 3 vols. [New York: International Publishers, 1974], 3:820). Kristeva draws on psychoanalytic theory, specifically the transference process, to define this production of a new subject position. She points out that through the transference "*discourse* establishes the subject within language precisely because transference permits the analysand to take over the (power of) language the analyst is presumed to hold" (*RPL*, 208). Louis Althusser's discussion of the "interpellation" or "hailing" of the subject by the ideological formations corresponds to this appropriation of the individual to preexisting social relations, as a process of "becoming locked into an identification that can do no more than adapt the subject to social and family structures," in Kristeva's words (*RPL*, 209). See Althusser, "Ideology and Ideological State Apparatuses," in *Lenin and Philosophy and Other Essays*, trans. Ben Brewster (New York: Monthly Review Press, 1971), 170–75. Since for Kristeva the text exceeds and rejects the theses of individual intentionality and identity, it offers no stable "represented focal point of transference" (*RPL*, 209); by eliciting the reader's identification with that lack of stable identity, the text opens an "empty space" (*RPL*, 210) where counter-hegemonic forms of agency can be elaborated.

27. See Althusser's essay "Contradiction and Overdetermination," in his *For Marx*, trans. Ben Brewster (New York: Vintage, 1969), and Laclau and Mouffe, *Hegemony and Socialist Strategy*, 111–14, for elaborations of this concept.

28. Althusser, "Ideology and Ideological State Apparatuses," 173–77.

29. Lukács, *History and Class Consciousness*, 172.

30. Gramsci leads into his critique of scientific causality and its criterion of predictability by making a similar point: "How can one derive from this way of seeing things the overcoming, the 'overthrow' of praxis?" (*SPN*, 437). Prediction as practical activity can then function as a form of negativity that does not necessarily remain bound up with the object it negates but can sublate the relationship itself. See Golding, "The Concept of Philosophy of Praxis," 548–49, on this passage.

31. See Chantal Mouffe's "Hegemony and New Political Subjects: Toward a New Concept of Democracy," in *Marxism and the Interpretation of Culture*, 98–99, 102–3. Mouffe distinguishes between a hegemony that functions by neutralization of difference and an "expansive hegemony" like the one I describe here.

32. Ryan describes the need for a "politicized version of deconstruction" that would supplement "Derrida's fine micrological critique of the structural principles and operations of the institutions of power and domination in philosophy with a more macrological and social mode of analysis" (*Marxism and Deconstruction*, 46). Cornel West argues for a neo-Gramscian viewpoint, combining "a microinstitutional (or localized)" level of analysis

with the macrostructural level of "class exploitation and political repression" ("Marxist Theory and the Specificity of Afro-American Oppression," in *Marxism and the Interpretation of Culture,* 21–22). West's point is that the move from a micro- to a macrostructural level prevents taking a class subject like the proletariat as the a priori revolutionary subject. Aronowitz suggests that Gramsci's notion of the "historical bloc" or counterhegemonic coalition can mediate between "a micropolitics of autonomous oppositional movements" and "the task of general emancipation" (*Crisis in Historical Materialism,* 127). The link between discursive formations and autonomous, local resistance movements in these analyses derives from Foucault's account of the "microphysics of power" as being dispersed throughout the social body rather than centralized. See Michel Foucault, *Discipline and Punish: The Birth of the Prison,* trans. Alan Sheridan (New York: Pantheon, 1977). Laclau and Mouffe offer one example of the need to retain both the micro- and the macrostructural levels of analysis. They critique the priority given to what they call a narrative of class identity over a secondary narrative of hegemony, in which a class takes over the social tasks of another class (as the Russian proletariat was seen by Lenin and others as taking over the tasks of the underdeveloped Russian bourgeoisie) (*Hegemony and Socialist Strategy,* 50–51). But Laclau and Mouffe seem to want to replace the second narrative with the first and replace political economy with discursive formations. On the other hand, Jameson argues that localized struggles like feminism and civil rights can be rewritten in terms of the larger narrative of Marxist class struggle (*Political Unconscious,* 19–20, 54 n. 31). Gramsci seems to me to offer a way of avoiding either of these extremes.

 33. There are, of course, competing discourses attempting to constitute different subjects with different possibilities for social action under the same sign of "American citizen." For example, a subject who can say, "I am an American citizen, I pay taxes, and I want my government to keep communists out of Central America" may be very different from the subject who says, "I am an American citizen, I pay taxes, and I don't want my money used to finance Ronald Reagan's defense buildup."

Part 4

Movements

The final four essays in this volume continue the explorations of the space between the political and the aesthetic, traveling paths toward the political implications of the aesthetic critique. In part 4, three domains come together: (1) the discursive space of inarticulability between form and content, enactment and statement; (2) the political interface between critique and the contemporary world; and (3) the dialogic interface between the future anterior and the historically given.

   Beyond an ideological politics of art, and having traversed the space between politics and art (aesthetic critique), there is a point at which the "political" and aesthetic critique can themselves engage in dialogue, an arena where they can understand, interpret, and interact with one another. To enter such a dialogic moment is to move toward a renewal of what constitutes "the political," at the point of incommensurability between text and metatext—that point at which dialogue seems fraught with a certain violence (see the introduction). At this point of confluence of three critical interstices, the three thematics of this volume—semiotics, the critique of ideology and ideologization, and the historicity of discourse—coalesce. In this dialogic moment, we engage with how the political movements of the last few decades sought to remake the political, to reconfigure and resignify social structures.

Yet the political will remain undefined. But that now means preserving its critical transformativity and resisting its reduction to the plane of ideological structure. If discourse and dialogue are understood as the generation as well as the apprehension of meaning, then definition must constitute the last step of political thinking—indeed, a step that closes (or slams) the door on the semiotic and on all that questions what it means to be definitive. In the absence of definitude, "the meaning of the political" becomes a space in which to move rather than a question to be answered. It is in order to return to that space of dialogue that aesthetic critique seeks to deconstruct ideology, universalization, and the universalizing force of definition. As such, deconstruction should not be seen as a procedure but as itself a way of entering and moving in that space, of giving meaning to its forms. In this part, four approaches to movement against the strictures of ideologization are presented. Don Bialostosky deconstructs Paul de Man's universalization of the "presence" of undecidability. Donald Marshall dialogically recontextualizes a dual ideologization of art and politics. Drucilla Cornell deconstructs the ideologization of the judicial interpretive process across the abyss between law's self-grounding and its reliance as a sign on what is incommensurable to it. And R. Radhakrishnan reaffirms the necessity and necessary historicity of all critiques of ideology by revealing the unremitting tendency toward universalization that enters even critiques of the universal.

A noteworthy subtheme that seems to have coalesced on its own in this volume emerges with a certain force here, namely, the existence and role of the third. It has two avatars, one who sees the act of seeing and one whose viewing of an object concretizes a connection between art and political form. That is, the third is not simply the Other who is outside each dialogue, for whom dialogue exists as an objective collective enactment. In part 1 the third played the role of viewer of the rhetorical object (aesthetics) and in part 3 the role of viewer of the political object (critique). Thus, the third is already interior to the space opened by form and to the dialogue between the political and aesthetic critique. It is between the third as internal and the third as Other that the problem of truth-content arises, which links the articulation of discerned objects with collective enactment. If the question of truth-content is shown to be irresolvable in particular realms, such as rhetoric, politics, law, and art, because these realms are too rich to be constrained within the dimensions of truth, what emerges in its stead is the double truth located in the two avatars of the third. Against the destruction of the third by conceptual definitude, the double dialogue of these two avatars remains the sign of the inarticulable enacted collectively.

In the opening essay, Bialostosky addresses Paul de Man's use of the concept and function of rhetoric. De Man seizes upon the sign of rhetoric and deploys it as the mark of a destructuring of grammatical structure. For Bialostosky, this move does two things. First, in its use of "rhetoric" as a sign rather than as a name for a category or discipline, it constitutes a particular figure (not unlike the notion of the figural McBride discusses in part 1). Second, its separation from traditional philosophical domains bestows upon it a new signification, one that attaches to the structure of separation between use (function) and philosophy (concept). If this separation reflects that between grammar and rhetoric, the sign of rhetoric finds itself in a dialectic between them.

Bialostosky deconstructs that dialectic by showing rhetoric to be an art that subverts the definitude of grammatical structure. If rhetoric reveals how grammatical construction produces conflicting meanings against itself, which it cannot resolve, then rhetoric itself becomes what separates into form and function, or trope and persuasion. That is, within de Man's deconstructed rhetorical structure, Bialostosky discerns a conflict or dialogue between persuasion and trope that goes beyond the sign. For instance, the ambiguity of a trope would frustrate the purpose of persuasion. If de Man constructs this conflict or space through the necessary undecidability that always accompanies the sign, Bialostosky argues, then he actually ends by universalizing the "presence" of undecidability. (And this recalls Geoffrey Hartmann's article in the *New Republic* [7 March 1988] in response to the discovery of de Man's Nazi collaboration in 1943, in which Hartmann argues that de Man's subsequent theorization of rhetoric was a long "repudiation in its very methodology" of the uselessness of mourning, revisiting, or excusing the past in order to escape or transcend it.)

Ironically, as an example of the dialectic of rhetoric, de Man makes reference to law courts. For him, the law court is paradigmatic of a paralogical arena. The rhetoric of legal argument leads judge and jury alike to know and to act without knowledge. To the extent that their knowledge is based upon testimony and argument that is never nonconflictual, it never ceases to evince or even flaunt its undecidability. The judicial decision becomes the injustice of decisiveness—in effect, a projection onto the pragmatics of law of the Lyotardian *différend* (see Steele's discussion in part 3). For Bialostosky, the implication that the structure of knowledge remains out of reach is that knowledge itself must be replaced by an attitude toward knowledge.

Donald Marshall's essay also invokes questions that were asked in part 3—for instance, what does a politics look like as a (cultural) sign when understood through an aesthetic critique? Marshall addresses that Manichaean attitude toward art under which either all art is political (as an adjunct to politics) or no art is (by definition). He gives an extended meditation on the problematic that art and politics present each other in their incommensurability. And he argues that any ideologized approach to art, because it must define art first, must be to that extent totalitarian. If dialogue is the arena of detotalization, then the problematic of art and politics is how to set them in dialogue.

Marshall pursues both the logic of such a dialogue and its conditions of possibility, not in terms of categories of meaning or mutual derivation but as aspects of discursive and social form. As an instance of form, he introduces the third, the indispensable spectator or observer, who plays a parallel role in both art and politics. The third is called upon to be the one who hears both sides as a site of conjunction or mutuality. But it is a conjunction that is also incommensurable in the sense that, for instance, the public gathered through a work of art remains indescribable in political economy, while, similarly, the temporality and unfolding of political economy are not representable in art. Hence, the third becomes the concretization of the incommensurability between the political and art. As a condition for social communication, beyond discursive content, the third makes that incommensurability real in the world.

From a somewhat similar perspective, Drucilla Cornell addresses the social text of law, not as an arena of discursive rhetoric (as de Man refers to it) but as a social enactment and interaction that must continually justify, reinterpret, and ground itself in what is incommensurable to it, namely, ethics and Right. In a sustained philosophical argument, she delineates the arena in which the disparate social categories of the Good, the Right, and legal principles or rules can be set into dialogue with each other and reconciled.

From Kant and Hegel to contemporary thinkers (she focuses on the legal positivists and Levinas), different responses to the question of grounding or justification of the Good, the Right, and law have been offered. Some hold that one or another is self-grounding (Kant and the positivists); others that the entire system is (Hegel); still others that the notion of grounding itself is empty (various postmodern views). What is at stake for Cornell is the possibility of legal interpretation as such. What would constitute a foundation for interpretation if the Good is indispensable to legal principles which can nevertheless function without it? Her project is to understand the form that the Good can take after the closure that legal principles define for themselves has been deconstructed and opened to ethical alterity. Only a deconstructive approach would draw out of such a hiatus a recontextualizing arena in which a dialogue between law and the Good could proceed.

For Cornell, the Good is already divided between the necessity of its universal applicability and the contingency of its operation in the concrete (a specific person and specific situations). It would be inadequate to treat this as a negation for the purposes of dialectical synthesis; the hiatus itself must be incorporated into the structure of legal meaning. That is, the deconstructive critique itself emerges as a formal structure of meaning that is also self-defining. And since it is a critique, it must be supplemented by a philosophical language that can assimilate the aporias and incommensurabilities that the critique discloses. This philosophical language would have to be appropriable in the critique's structure of semiosis while resisting ideologization or closure.

Cornell turns to Levinas, who argues that in both the Hegelian (ontological) account in which all subjects approach the law as the same and the positivist account of law in which the structure actually engenders the (pragmatic) individual through its bestowal of equality, violence is done to the Other. In both, the Other is reduced to the same. The same, whether ontological or pragmatic, is a metaphysical abstraction, a totality; as such, it can only participate as a cog in the functioning of metaphysical machinery, whether legal or political.

Cornell argues that a return to the Good from law and the legal machine must first obviate that violence. In the Levinasian structure, responsibility to the Other, for which dialogue is one of the forms, is essential to rather than derivative of the subject. It is this sense of responsibility and dialogue that informs the core of Cornell's discussion. For her, deconstruction is not ethical skepticism or conceptual nihilism but a call to responsibility, a positive political relation to the Other. The central issue becomes how to approach and articulate that responsibility. Yet the nonsameness of persons already resides in an inarticulability, the space of absence and nonimposition of sameness. Thus, this space provides the possibility of ethical or prescriptive choices that are just without the imposition of prior ideological or metaphysical principles.

In the final essay, R. Radhakrishnan brings together several themes of this volume: the opening of multiple meanings against the co-optative closures of metaphysics, a critique of ideologization through the (political) recognition of the hiatus between text and metatext, and a recontextualization of the incommensurability between the politics of art and the art of politics. He addresses Heidegger, to whom he gives credit for being one of the wellsprings of the post-structuralist critique itself, arguing that Heidegger also gets caught in metaphysics by focusing too centrally on the primordial to the point of giving it a certain presence.

Radhakrishnan discusses Heidegger's essay "The Origin of the Work of Art." And in particular, he revisits Heidegger's discussion and narrativization of one of Van Gogh's paintings of peasant shoes. Crucial to Heidegger's approach to art is his notion that the truth of art is an opening to the truth of Being. Radhakrishnan points out that if this opening invokes a sense of an origin, it involves, at the same time, a self-decentering of any origin. For him, an aporia is generated that homologically reflects itself throughout Heidegger's essay. In particular, where Heidegger uses the notion of *Gelassenheit* (letting-be) to contest ideological notions of art, he gives an ideological content to *Gelassenheit* itself.

Central to Heidegger's discussion of Van Gogh's painting is his narrativization of the peasant woman, whom Heidegger "sees" wearing the shoes. Heidegger sets out criteria under which the shoes are authentic for her. Radhakrishnan suggests that Heidegger is thereby speaking for the woman, thus obviating her speaking for herself or participating in dialogue. This is not only a position of power but a Eurocentric exoticization of her alterity (class, gender, and even historicity), which Heidegger has appropriated and allegorized through the shoes. Not only does Heidegger dehumanize her by dehistoricizing her; he also reveals that he has not historicized his own critique. He has not seen the Eurocentrism in it. And this failure to historicize reveals the ideological dimension of letting-be, namely, a certain participation in a stasis or in a status quo. That is, where Heidegger had set out to critique the anthropologism of metaphysics, he ends up establishing a different anthropologism.

In a manner reminiscent of de Man's analogical deployments of the sign of rhetoric (in Bialostosky's essay), Radhakrishnan discloses a number of analogous aporias, which function to reontologize what Heidegger deconstructs. For instance, Heidegger discusses the frame of the painting as mediated by the representation of the shoes, while that representation itself shifts the frame to an ontological elsewhere. Similarly, there is a utopianism in Van Gogh, who brings beauty out of peasant misery (Jameson), that is repeated in Heidegger's utopic return to a dehistoricized narrative of the peasant woman. For Radhakrishnan, the political weight of this dehistoricization reflects on an earth-world distinction that Heidegger makes in his call for ecological wisdom. Yet this distinction gets undermined by his not understanding that earth and world are marked by different temporalities. Their rehistoricization returns them to a binary entityhood that Heidegger had sought to escape.

We might end by noting that one no longer needs to point out the impossibility of discussing Heidegger without the ghost of his Nazi involvement lurking in the background. But it is insufficient to simply point a finger at the issue. As Derrida has said, to do so imposes a politics rather than reads Heidegger. As a final remark on what this volume is doing, however, we might point out that this insufficiency can be supplemented by the critique of ideologization offered in many forms on these pages. That is, the critique of ideologization has an as yet incompletely realized relevance to what it would mean to "read" Heidegger—and not only Heidegger. If alternatives to ideologization (of philosophy, art, and in particular political philosophy) reside in the political import of textual form and how that form structures the political, then it perhaps offers an avenue of escape from ideology's tragic trajectory. It is Heidegger, more so than others, who points to the criminal and tragic political moment when ideology and the machine gun end up in extreme service to each other—a moment which itself has become part of the "issue" of Heidegger.

Paul de Man and the Rhetorical Tradition

Don Bialostosky

Paul de Man places his literary theory and practice within what Joseph Schwartz and John A. Rycenga have called "the province of rhetoric,"[1] but he does not do much to mark the boundaries of his claims there. Though he repeatedly flies the banner of rhetoric over his work, beginning with the 1969 essay "The Rhetoric of Temporality," he does not carry out extensive engagements with any of the familiar writers, classic or modern, who have identified themselves with rhetoric and elaborated its tradition. Aristotle figures for de Man only as a definer of the trope of metaphor; Quintillian appears among the textbook writers who have considered rhetoric as "the humble and not-quite-respectable hand-maiden of the fraudulent grammar used in oratory."[2] Wayne Booth, who anticipated de Man's repeated use of the "Rhetoric of" title paradigm, gets a footnote for the idea of the unreliable narrator. Gérard Genette appears not as a rhetorical theorist but as a reader of Proust. Kenneth Burke gets credit for maintaining the distinction between rhetoric and grammar, but de Man, when he died in 1983, had not yet written his planned essay on Burke.[3] Nietzsche, who until recently was not recognized as a contributor to the rhetorical tradition,[4] is the only precedent rhetorical theorist on whose authority de Man selectively depends.

De Man's neglect of familiar rhetorical theorists increases the difficulty of understanding his terms and assessing his contribution to or departure from the rhetorical tradition his choice of terms invokes. Rather than distinguishing his usages from those of others, he uses familiar terms in unfamiliar ways without comment. Instead of defending his selection of some categories of rhetorical inquiry at the expense of others, he simply presents his selection as all there is to it. Without acknowledging the diversity of previous rhetorical theories and the controversy among them, de Man projects a single "rhetoric" as a dialectical counterpart to a single "grammar" whose limitations it exposes (see *RT,* passim, and *AR,* 3–19).

De Man's placement of rhetoric in relation to grammar does at least invoke a commonplace (if forgotten) context of the rhetorical tradition, however—the trivium of grammar, rhetoric, and logic of the classical verbal liberal arts. In lieu of a pure theoretical model of language, de Man recalls the trivium "not as a concept, but as a didactic assignment" of language from the "pragmatic history of 'language'" (*RT,* 13). He recognizes, furthermore, that contemporary literary theory is "one more chapter" in the discourse generated by the tensions among those three "sciences of language." But his argument first reduces the trivium to an opposition of grammar and rhetoric and then sets them against one another in a dialectical history that issues in the self-destruction of the trivium (*RT,* 12–17).

While de Man's placement of contemporary literary theory within the history of the trivium is suggestive, his schematic reductions and manipulations of the verbal liberal arts in contempt for their "merely historical" (*RT,* 11) manifestations does little to place his rhetoric in relation to the pragmatic, didactic tradition of the trivium. He does not explain how the verbal liberal *arts* of that tradition become his *sciences* of language, nor does he show how distinctions and concepts characteristic of each art have been redistributed, reclaimed, or forgotten from age to age. Though these contingent matters might appear to be of "limited theoretical interest" (*RT,* 11), they also might offer a healthy empirical or pragmatic resistance to de Man's seemingly arbitrary theoretical reductions. De Man himself acknowledges a "pragmatic moment" (*RT,* 8) in literary theory and an unavoidable fall into the pragmatic in speaking of it (*RT,* 5), but his argument repeatedly moves past that moment and rises from that fall to present theoretically necessary claims about interpretive and historical contingencies.

The contingencies of de Man's own intellectual allegiances flesh out his dialectical opposition of grammar and rhetoric. His repeated accounts of rhetorical reading as an undoing of grammatical interpretation bring together his investments in the grammatical project of European structural linguistics and in the rhetorical close reading of American New Criticism. The two projects share his major premise that literary theory is concerned with language, the one developing it as a theoretical claim and the other elaborating it as a practical and didactic experience of "bafflement" at "singular turns of tone, phrase, and figure" (*RT,* 23). De Man recognizes that grammar has sometimes claimed tropes and figures within its domain of inquiry and that contemporary structural linguistics attempts to expand its domain to replace "rhetorical figures by grammatical codes" (*RT,* 15), but he identifies theory, rhetoric, and reading all with the discovery of "the determining figural dimensions of a text" (*RT,* 15) that are not reducible to grammatical decoding. As New Critical poetic language resists "statement," rhetoric, the science of the figural dimensions of language, regularly baffles grammar, the systematization of linguistic universals.

De Man, then, treats rhetoric from the point of view of structuralist grammar as an anomalous residual category of linguistic figures that resist grammatical rationalization. He does not start with rhetoric as a field of positively rationalized ends and means but repeatedly *arrives* at rhetoric as a negative moment in reading at which grammatical hypotheses produce conflicting interpretations that grammatical investigation cannot resolve in its own terms.[5] Rhetoric for de Man is not an articulated intellectual discipline that offers him other terms for reformulating or resolving those conflicts but only the domain in which he regularly encounters them. From the point of view of the classical rhetorical tradition, "rhetoric" is the name for the limit of de Man's inquiry, not for its object, its discipline, or its tradition. De Man repeatedly crosses the disputed borders of the province of rhetoric, but he never moves in.[6]

De Man is not alone in identifying rhetoric with the study of "figures of speech or tropes, a component of language that straddles the disputed borderlines between" rhetoric and grammar (*RT,* 14).[7] Gérard Genette

has shown how he himself and a significant modern tradition have restricted the concept of rhetoric to the domain of what he calls "figuratics,"[8] a domain that corresponds to what de Man sometimes calls "tropology" and other times calls "rhetoric" in general. Genette, rehearsing what
Gerald Bruns calls the "pattern of decline from Aristotle (rhetoric at its
most philosophical) into tropology (rhetoric at its most rhetorical)" (*I*,
97), recounts the series of disappearing categories and collapsing distinctions by which the domain of classical rhetoric was thus diminished. Beginning with Aristotle's and Quintillian's balanced and comprehensive
rhetorics, Genette notes the loss of the distinction of deliberative, epideictic, and forensic genres; the restriction of the parts of invention, disposition, and elocution to matters of elocution only; the collapse within
elocution of the distinction between tropes and figures; the exclusion
from the figures of the figures of thought; and the reduction of the remaining figures to a grammar of schematically opposing kinds like metaphor and metonymy. He fails to note the loss of Aristotle's account of
properly rhetorical problems, those matters that "appear to admit of two
possibilities" (*FLD*, 11), and his distinction of means of persuasion—logical, ethical, and emotional—though these may all have gone out the door
with the large category of invention. Genette acknowledges, in any case,
the difference between a figuratics or tropology and a truly general rhetoric, and he argues, as early as 1970, for a revival of classical rhetoric
and an inquiry into general rhetoric for the sake of both understanding
and action.

De Man does not undertake such a revival, in part because rhetoric
for him has only "the appearance of a history" (*AR*, 131). The closest he
gets to Genette's distinction between tropology and general rhetoric is
to write of "two functions" or "two modes" of rhetoric, which he attributes to Nietzsche's rhetorical theory, trope and persuasion. De Man,
however, imagines an "eternally recurrent" question, gap, or aporia between these two functions or modes—of rhetoric as trope and rhetoric
as persuasion (*AR*, 130–31). Like rhetoric and grammar in his vision of
the trivium, these two modes of rhetoric become neither moments in a
history nor parts in a structure but equally weighted principles between
which it is impossible to decide.

For the classical tradition, however, trope and persuasion are not alternative functions or modes. Persuasion is a function; tropes are one category of stylistic devices subordinated to that function. Although in some
modern rhetorical theories, as Genette has shown, tropes come to be the
whole focus of interest, a rhetoric of tropes does not thereby offer an

account of the *function* of rhetoric distinct from a rhetoric of persuasion. Instead, in a rhetoric of tropes, attention turns from function to form; the category of function disappears or is taken for granted. But a rhetoric of tropes is no more an alternative to a rhetoric of persuasion than an architecture of ornaments is an alternative to an architecture of construction. Whole ages may be more interested in decoration than in construction and may elaborate their theories of decoration at the expense of cultivating important principles of construction, and others might cultivate construction in austere neglect of the rich interests of ornament, but it would still not make much sense to speak of architecture as an eternally recurrent and undecidable opposition between decoration and construction.

The analogy I have just proposed revives the classical treatment of tropes and figures of speech as verbal ornaments applied to a rhetorical structure designed for a persuasive function, but this analogy may be flawed, and de Man dismisses it (*RT,* 14). If language is not merely the dress of thought but its body, then the opposition between persuasion and trope would be between a design and the materials in which it is realized, not between a materialized functional whole and its surface ornaments. Even on this premise, however, tropes do not function independently of the designs in which they are mobilized, even if they do offer characteristic opportunities and resistances to the functions they are called on to serve.

From the point of view of rhetorical practice, language, both ordinary and ornamental, "is not," as Richard Weaver puts it, "a purely passive instrument, but . . . owing to [its] public acceptance, while you are doing something with it, it is doing something with you, or with your intention. It does not exactly fight back; rather it has a set of postures and balances which somehow modify your thrusts and holds."[9] One would not discover what Weaver calls the "rhetorical aspects of grammatical categories" or the rhetorical implications of tropes and figures except in the context of given persuasive ends. In relation to those ends, certain verbal choices would reveal themselves as cooperative or counterproductive. From this rhetorical point of view, tropes (and other verbal materials) both facilitate and frustrate persuasion, not in an eternally undecidable aporia but in determinate and determinable ways governed by the purposes and circumstances of persuasion. Grammatical norms and the tropes that violate them get their rhetorical character only in the context of persuasive purposes; apart from those purposes they remain rhetorically indeterminate. Insofar as de Man opposes tropes to persuasion instead of judging tropes in the light of persuasive purposes, he indeed always finds tropes to be rhetorically indeterminate, because he isolates tropes from the persuasive contexts that determine them.

But de Man also takes for granted a persuasive purpose in his account of the function of tropes that allows him to argue that tropes inevitably frustrate that purpose. He opposes tropes to persuasion not as ornament to structure or as material to design but as constative to performative or epistemological to practical. In terms of traditional rhetorical purposes, he opposes forensic to deliberative functions, arguments about what is the case to arguments about what is to be done. He does not, however, distinguish the contexts of these functions as two different sorts of occasions demanding two different kinds of judgment but juxtaposes them as two inseparable and incompatible aspects of all rhetoric. The "epistemological thrust" (*RT,* 14) or "epistemological impact" (*RT,* 18) of tropes is to produce undecidably different versions of what is the case that persuasion nevertheless compels us to decide. The "exhortative performatives" of persuasion, de Man writes, "require the passage from sheer enunciation to action. They compel us to choose while destroying the foundations of any choice. They tell the allegory of a judicial decision that can be neither judicious nor just" (*AR,* 245).

In this passage de Man clearly evokes the traditional context of forensic rhetoric, the law court. In a later passage from *Allegories of Reading,* he recognizes the traditional task of that rhetoric: to render just the decisions that bring individual cases under general laws (*AR,* 269). But de Man emphasizes that the action of deciding the case is always unwarranted by the rhetorical enunciation of it. "The incompatibility between the elaboration of the law and its application (or justice)," he writes, "can only be bridged by an act of deceit" (*AR,* 269). De Man thus insists not on rhetoric's power to provide probable grounds for deciding such cases but on its inability to provide necessary knowledge of them. While Aristotle declares that the absence of such necessary knowledge is precisely the condition that calls rhetoric into action to inform our decisions "about such things as appear to admit of two possibilities,"[10] de Man emphasizes that rhetoric always persuades us to decide between two possibilities of which it gives us no necessary knowledge. It persuades us to act where we have no knowledge, to issue a performative "guilty" or "not guilty" in the absence of cognitive warrant. The forensic judgment of the case reduces to a deliberative choice to act: "Justice is unjust" (*AR,* 269) and rhetoric is deceit.

By making the forensic rhetorical situation paradigmatic of all rhetoric, de Man emphasizes the scandalous discrepancy between a given case and the rhetorical figuration of that case. We easily presume in thinking about forensic argument that the guilt or innocence of the accused is somewhere already known or knowable independent of argument, even that the rhetorician already knows it but makes an argument that makes the case appear other than it is. Justice can only be unjust if a true state of affairs is misrepresented and made to prevail by persuasive devices, especially devices knowingly used to conceal or distort that true state of affairs. De Man's claim, as I understand it, is that rhetoric or figural language cannot represent any state of affairs truly, but this claim gets its force only by presupposing what Brian Caraher calls a positivist paradigm of true representation,[11] or what Bruns calls "an enlightened and systematic view of language" (*I,* 106).[12]

De Man does not pretend to occupy a positivist philosophical or scientific standpoint that could transcend this rhetorical scandal, but he does repeatedly enact the scandal as if such a standpoint, though unattainable, were nevertheless conceivable. His loyalty to the idea of that standpoint prevents him from entering the pragmatic province of rhetoric, even as his lack of belief in such a standpoint brings him repeatedly to the borders of that province. The celebrated rigor of de Man's position is to be found, I think, in his refusal to abandon a positivist standard of truth even as he insists upon rhetoric as the only and inadequate means of establishing such truth. He does not, like Aristotle, distinguish a pragmatic domain of rhetorical choice from an apodictic domain of scientific knowledge; nor does he, like Richard Rorty, cheerfully extend pragmatic standards of knowledge as the only ones we have to all domains of knowledge and action. Rather, he posits the ideal of scientific knowledge as the impossible goal to which, lacking a "model language" (*RT,* 19)—or what Bruns calls "a *Lingua Philosophica* whose operations are unencumbered by such natural contingencies as living or dying" (*I,* 106)—we can only bring our ever unreliable rhetorical means. Unmoved by Aristotle's liberal injunction to look for precision in each class of things just so far as the nature of the subject admits, he knowingly looks in vain for necessary truth in all cases.

But even forensic cases do not necessarily presuppose a truth known or knowable by anyone. The accused may not remember doing anything or know what was done or know how to characterize a deed as involuntary manslaughter or first-degree murder, and no one else may have witnessed the deed. The case may be indeterminate for everyone involved at the outset and reach a determination only through the arguments of the advocates and the evidence they adduce. The arguments may produce a conviction that existed nowhere prior to their making, a conviction that is the only knowledge of the case.

Forensic cases may also sometimes concern acts that knowingly and willfully conform to legal definitions, but deliberative cases concern matters which are always as yet unknown. Arguments about the expediency or inexpediency of future courses of action do not bring an epistemological question into play at all, and rhetoric directed to such cases escapes even the appearance of paradoxical tension between constative and performative modes. What will happen depends in part on what the deliberator chooses to do, and the rhetorician claims only to inform that choice but not to represent a knowable state of affairs.

De Man ignores this practical and political rhetorical domain as he ignores the ceremonial and aesthetic domain of epideictic rhetoric. There, too, the epistemological paradox de Man dwells on does not bear much weight, for the epideictic issue again does not raise a question of knowing but rather a question of attitude toward what is presumed to be known. The oration of praise evaluates the acknowledged facts of the hero's career rather than arguing, as forensic oratory might, that the accused did not do what he is accused of doing. And epideictic argument traditionally permits the orator to display his art beyond the limits required by the praise or blame of his subject. Here the figural productivity of rhetoric (and its inventive capacity as well) are free to show themselves without making the issue their adequacy or inevitable inadequacy to their subject.

De Man, in effect, holds that this issue is the only rhetorical issue, but the old rhetoric escapes his reduction. Indeed, the issue about de Man's rhetorical theory may itself be joined on forensic, deliberative, and epideictic grounds. Forensically, we could ask in conclusion, is rhetoric guilty of deceit, as de Man charges, and we might answer that de Man has mistakenly identified "rhetoric" with an arbitrarily limited part of rhetoric seen from an outsider's point of view. Deliberatively, we could ask if it is expedient for literary studies to carry out the rhetorical program of deconstruction de Man proposes, and we might reply that the program unnecessarily and inexpediently limits our interests and restricts our inquiries compared to the traditional rhetoric. Epideictically, we could ask if the rigor of de Man's rhetorical stance deserves our praise and perhaps emulation, and here we would encounter his strongest claim. For I believe that de Man's greatest power is his ethos of the uncompromising scholar, committed to producing "irrefutable" rhetorical readings even if they are, as he says, "boring, monotonous, predictable, and unpleasant" (*RT,* 19). We know how to admire the scientist who can subordinate his pleasures to truth, and we students of literature are even ashamed to confess our pleasures in our readings before one so dedicated to truth as to inflict boredom and pain upon himself and others in its name. But, to return to forensic grounds, de Man does not tell the whole truth about rhetoric, and to return to deliberative grounds, there is much still to do to discover that truth. De Man bears powerful witness to what Genette calls a "rhetoric restrained" (*FLD,* 101), but we need not rest in admiration or repetition of his rigorous and revealing blindness.

Notes

1. See Joseph Schwartz and John A. Rycenga, *The Province of Rhetoric* (New York: Ronald Press, 1965).

2. Paul de Man, *Allegories of Reading: Figural Language in Rousseau, Nietzsche, Rilke, and Proust* (New Haven, Conn.: Yale University Press, 1979), 130; hereafter abbreviated *AR* and cited parenthetically in the text.

3. Paul de Man, *The Resistance to Theory* (Minneapolis: University of Minnesota Press, 1986), xi; hereafter abbreviated *RT* and cited parenthetically in the text.

4. See Philippe Lacoue-Labarthe, "Le detour (Nietzsche et la rhetorique)," *Poetique* 5 (1971): 53–76.

5. For a contrast between de Man's and William Empson's negotiation of the border of rhetoric and grammar, see Christopher Norris, "Reason, Rhetoric, Theory: Empson and de Man," *Raritan* 5 (1985–86): 89–106.

6. From two other starting points, Robert Scholes and Tobin Siebers both arrive at a point where they deny that what de Man calls "rhetoric" is what we recognize as rhetoric. Scholes writes that "de Man . . . insists that all texts are rhetorical, but what he means by rhetoric is what has traditionally been meant by poetry" (*Textual Power* [New Haven, Conn.: Yale University Press, 1985], 77). Siebers concludes that, "in the end, de Man's theory is not a theory of rhetoric at all, but a theory of mourning" ("Paul de Man and the Rhetoric of Selfhood," *New Orleans Review* 13 [Spring 1986]: 9). Gerald Bruns notes the irony that de Man's unrhetorical program "sometimes disguises itself as, of all things, rhetoric" (*Inventions: Writing, Textuality, and Understanding in Literary History* [New Haven, Conn.: Yale University Press, 1982], 88; hereafter abbreviated *I* and cited parenthetically in the text).

7. Bruns notes that in de Man's thought the difference between rhetoric and grammar is "not, it turns out, a very forceful distinction, for rhetoric

in this connection amounts to no more than the taxonomy of figures and the analysis of figurative writing (or the figuration of writing). That is, rhetoric in this case is identified with that most systematic and textual portion of itself" (*I*, 97).

8.   Gérard Genette, *Figures of Literary Discourse,* trans. Alan Sheridan (New York: Columbia University Press, 1982), 122; hereafter abbreviated *FLD* and cited parenthetically in the text.

9.   Richard Weaver, "Some Rhetorical Aspects of Grammatical Categories," in *The Ethics of Rhetoric* (Chicago: Regnery Press, 1953), 116.

10.   Aristotle, *Rhetoric,* trans. Lane Cooper (Englewood Cliffs, N.J.: Prentice-Hall, 1932), 11.

11.   Brian Carraher, "Allegories of Reading: Positing a Rhetoric of Romanticism; or, Paul de Man's Critique of Pure Figural Interiority," *Pre/Text* 4 (Spring 1983): 41–42.

12.   Jonathan Arac observes in the same vein that "even to raise the question of 'truth and error' and thus challenge the aesthetic, [de Man] appealed to a sense of 'epistemology' that would offer a philosophic 'foundation' . . . for our beliefs" (*Critical Genealogies: Historical Situations for Postmodern Literary Studies* [New York: Columbia University Press, 1987], 252). See also Arac's critique of de Man's reinterpretation of classic rhetorical figures (239–59).

"Death Is the Mother of Beauty"

Aesthetics, Politics, and History in Gadamer

Donald Marshall

Ever since Plato's *Republic,* whenever the themes of aesthetics and politics are linked, the tone is one of reproach. The defense of art always comes too late against the self-evident legitimacy and supremacy of the political.[1] This reality is summed up for our era in Adorno's aphorism: to write poetry after Auschwitz is barbaric.[2] But the term "politics" is invoked frequently at the end of the analysis, as either a conclusive condemnation or a call to some unspecified action, as though everyone already understands what "politics" is.[3] When art is in question, the call for "politics" comes when the thinking is ended and nothing more need be said.

It is by now commonplace to remark that Alexander Baumgarten coined the term "aesthetica" in the process of inserting art into the

Cartesian framework he inherited from Leibniz via his teacher Christian Wolff.[4] He was responding to the modern grouping of the "fine arts," which emerged out of informal talk among connoisseurs at the end of the seventeenth century.[5] Against French theorists like Charles Batteux, who tried to link the new grouping to the traditional concept of "imitation," Baumgarten shifted to epistemology or rational psychology, paving the way for Kant's definitive formulation of the "aesthetic" in the *Critique of Judgment* (1790). What is at stake in this development is more disputed. Ernst Cassirer's *Philosophy of the Enlightenment* concludes with a convincing appreciation of the new understanding of human being that emerges here. A more suspicious reading of the theorists' political motives or ideology, whether seen as hegemonic or escapist, has been given by Terry Eagleton and especially Martha Woodmansee.[6]

Political critics might claim that they are simply rescuing art from its misrepresentation by "aesthetics." But in practice, the critique of aesthetic theory gets confused with a critique of art and of particular artworks. As a result, it is not easy to see exactly what is claimed. The assertion that every artwork's meaning and use are in fact political is evidently paradoxical, for it has to be demonstrated contrary to appearances by resorting to elaborate methods for extracting and formulating political contents and implications that are ex hypothesi necessarily covert.[7] That the particular results and the analytic methods are hotly debated shows plainly that the approach cannot self-evidently exhibit its legitimacy. To assert that artworks *should* be political concedes that they may not be; to say we *ought* always to use them for political purposes concedes that we could do otherwise. Both make the totalitarian assumption that the political is not simply a good, nor even the highest good, but the only good, so that every other sphere of life must be subordinated to and measured by it.[8] They further presuppose that the relation between a particular artwork and political purposes can be unambiguously specified as means to ends. Worst of all, they burke precisely the question at issue in politics, namely, what should be our political aims in any given situation? Even where the critique is targeted on "aesthetics" as a theory, merely pointing to the fact that "aesthetics" emerges within a particular historical situation and has been appropriated to specific social or political purposes evades the question of whether the theory nevertheless contains a valid insight. Certainly, the political approach has notorious difficulties dealing with the obvious claim at the heart of "aesthetic" theory, namely, that artworks in some sense transcend any political-historical dimension. Marx himself conceded that while it was easy to show how

Greek literature is connected to its milieu, the puzzle remains as to why this literature should remain for us a standard of artistic achievement. His explanation—that the Greeks exhibited the "normal childhood" of the race—is plainly unsatisfactory: there is nothing "childlike" about Athenian culture, nor can history be modeled on individual human development.[9] Recent attempts to link this evaluative standard with a work's historical "tendency" or a "utopian" element are more sophisticated, but still questionable.[10] Even Marx saw that a utopian future inevitably lacked the concrete content that would legitimate its invocation as a standard available for present-day judgment and practice.

The deeper and more interesting point is that the modern sense of politics presupposed in such debates may be no older than the modern notion of aesthetics. Martin Buber remarks that "political decision is generally understood to-day to mean joining . . . a group," a group which claims to know what benefits the community, a group which asserts its own exclusive authenticity and demands your unreserved complicity.[11] Its members seek the authentication of their own identity through the group's jargons and rituals, imagistic self-affirmations that short-circuit debate over concrete interests.[12] The question the political group poses to the work of art is whether it is for us or against us. This question absolutizes "the given political order by remaining within a horizon which is defined by . . . [that] order and its opposite."[13] The artwork is formal ornament plus an overt or covert "ideological" content, which can be extracted and measured by its support for or resistance to a party platform that is not open to question. The demand for complicity from the artwork is so absolute that no submission could be sufficiently abject and unreserved to satisfy it. Art belongs to the realm of "propaganda and information," that is, the realm of "public opinion," which a regime either nervously assesses by scientific polling or "intelligence gathering" or else shapes and controls by manipulating mass media. The content of politics is "power" or "power relations," seen strictly in terms of domination and submission.[14] The goal of those who seek or resist "power" is "liberation," which oscillates between contradictory specifications in terms now of economic autonomy, now of personal fulfillment. That is, the legitimating aim of politics is the care of the body and its life—the promise of "happiness" seen as the present satisfaction of human needs.[15] When this aim is achieved, the state will wither away and politics will become unnecessary. The *polis* will become an *oikos,* a huge household, where the ideal of *fraternité* is made real as "the family of man."

For a quite different tradition that runs from Plato to the Enlightenment, the core issue of politics is the power of collective life to shape the moral character of the individual by holding out opportunities for that character's highest exercise.[16] The political is founded on a mutual agreement about what is good and bad. But this agreement has the character of shared insight, not of deliberate or negotiated decision, so that it is always the hidden or tacit medium of collective and individual life.[17] Political life consists of collective actions which are decided by means of a discourse that aims to discern and actualize in particular situations the founding insight into the collective good; this sort of deliberation is something quite different from "planning." Political wisdom aims to achieve stability against external dangers and against the inevitable wearing away to which all human institutions are subject.

I would have to insist on a number of qualifications at this point. The account I have given of the modern sense of politics is by no means the only one possible. Likewise, there are other ancient conceptions of politics,[18] nor do I mean to imply that we could or should return to the conception I have so briefly sketched.[19] My point here is simply that in the conjunction of "aesthetics" and "politics," each term may be questioned. That questioning may reduce the one-sidedness in their current relation and make possible the sort of dialogue between them that characterizes genuine thinking. What then is the nature of a work of art and in what relation does it stand to political life? Following the reflections of Hans-Georg Gadamer, and particularly the collection under the title *The Relevance of the Beautiful*,[20] I want to focus this dialogue between art and politics on a few central issues.

Let us begin with the sense in which a work of art is a "work." In classical culture, the artwork is a "'work" in the sense of something deliberately made by somebody in accordance with a model and within a reliable social contract that relates artistic means to affective ends. "Classical" culture "presupposes the continuing existence of a binding tradition that is intelligible to all" (*RB*, 100). Here the artwork is seen immediately in its relation to religious and civic life as "ornament"—not a "decoration" but "the expression of an order."[21] That is, the artwork situates its content within a political and ultimately cosmic order. (This is equally the function of "eloquence" or "ornate style" in oratory.) The Enlightenment critique of tradition dissolved this conception and evoked a counter-definition of the artwork as "symbolic," that is, as a highly particularized fragment that generates an indeterminate anticipation of sense, ultimately of life as a significant whole. Here the work exists only in its active reception. "The identity of the work," Gadamer says, "is secured by the way in which we take [its] construction . . . upon ourselves as a task" (*RB*, 28). Even with this change in the nature of a "work," it remains the case that with the work of art "there is open recognition that some things are worth seeing or are made to be seen" (*RB*, 14). Gadamer proposes to call this perceived thing a *Gebilde,* a shaped structure that presents itself poised on itself in its own look and appearance (my translation; cf. *RB,* 126). The ontological function of the artwork is to assure us "that the truth does not lie far off and inaccessible to us, but can be encountered in the disorder of reality with all its imperfections, evils, errors, extremes, and fateful confusions" (*RB*, 15). "Truth" here does not mean a conceptual content that can be formulated in a proposition, but the presentation of something (*Sache*) that "shows itself as what it is" (*RB*, 108). It is a "pledge of order" (*RB*, 109), which brings near and holds what it shows us (*RB*, 113–15), and thus effects an increase in being.

In both classical and modern culture, we can thus distinguish the productive activity through which a work of art comes to stand from the work itself. But we have no obvious term for what comes to stand through political action. The question art here poses to politics is, does anything come to stand through political activity? Let us follow Hannah Arendt, who divides the active life into the spheres of labor, work, and action.[22] Labor involves the ceaselessly repeated production of means of life which disappear in their consumption. Work builds up the human world of durable, usable artifacts. In the realm of action, human beings achieve distinctness revealed and preserved in speech, particularly in stories. But such a story does not express personality or intent. No one "is the author or producer of his own life story" (*HC*, 184). History is not "made" by men (*HC*, 185). Like the artwork as *Gebilde,* a story is a self-supporting interplay of elements irreplaceable in its distinct particularity and released from the agent and processes that produced it.[23] Its ontological function is to generate irreplaceably particular symbols which manifest a shared insight into political order. To the modern mass production of disposable functional objects there corresponds the bureaucratic organization of smoothly functioning social processes. Politics as administration means managing human affairs by fitting human beings and their interactions within rules and regulations whose rational generality does not acknowledge distinctness. In contrast to mass-produced objects, the artwork resembles a "thing," as Heidegger characterizes it: something "essentially irreplaceable," whose "existence illuminates and testifies to order as a whole." Such an object is not a "real" product: it has no "use" and is therefore withdrawn from the sphere modern politics exists to organize. But only such an object has something historical or what we may call life. The artwork plays an exemplary role in "the never-ending [human] process of building a world" (*RB,* 103–4). In a parallel way, political action as Arendt characterizes it contrasts with the rational construction and administration of institutions. Political action is fashioned on and fashions myths, legends, and symbols, which express an insight into a possible order. Gadamer concludes, in terms I would apply equally to the artwork and political action, "Perhaps our capacity to preserve and maintain, the capacity that supports human culture, rests in turn upon the fact that we must always order anew what threatens to dissolve before us" (*RB,* 104).

The artwork and political action as classically understood thus possess an inescapable monumentality. Contemporary thought resists all talk of "greatness." "Great" literature is seen as a canon imposed by an elite, which exercises illegitimate power over the means of cultural reproduction to repress alternate voices. Receptiveness to the "greatness" of art is seen as unconscious victimization that must be therapeutically purged by a demystification of the "politics" of such dangerously enthusiastic passivity. It is true that artists themselves initiated this attack on the "aura" of great art when they absorbed the Enlightenment's critique of traditional authority. But, Gadamer protests, "[i]t is a profound mistake to think that our art is simply that of the ruling class" (*RB,* 51). The suspicion of "elitism" in politics has equally paradoxical ramifications. Is the totalitarian reduction of citizens to interchangeable and dispensable parts only accidentally connected with the "cult of personality"? The collapse of "leadership" into a personal rapport with the citizenry dissolves the requirement that the leader should articulate a distinctive insight into the demands of the current situation.[24]

"Anti-elitism" manifests itself in the renewed stress on the artwork's historical occasion. Occasionality is here understood as "the trace of the particular circumstances that are, as it were, hidden behind the work and are to be revealed by interpretation" (*TM,* 453). In fact, the work is seen as "an instrument of masked goals that only have to be unmasked for it to be unambiguously understood" (*TM,* 454). In a similar way, by unmasking hidden motives and interests, the "greatness" of political action, that is, its claim to our recognition and acknowledgment, is dissolved. Such a procedure extracts a meaning which can be judged according to a predetermined program. It universalizes its own prejudices by projecting them as categories of understanding which it refuses to put at risk.[25] But in fact the artwork and political action—or the story which manifests its enduring shape—reveal or shelter sense and also shroud or conceal it; they are essentially ambiguous. Herein lies their power to call into question one's own norms, that is, to generate a self-recognition and thus become the occasion of genuine thinking.

The suspicion of greatness and monumentality belongs to a transition already noted. The artwork retains its character as work only where traditional culture retains its self-evidence. When Enlightenment critique dissolved that self-evidence, the monumentality of the artwork lost its self-positing nature and was attributed negatively to an elitist conspiracy or positively to the creator's "genius." Modern art oscillates between these two poles, but seeks an exit from both by emphasizing instead the constructive role of the perceiver. Gadamer brings this out through an analogy to play. What comes to presentation in play is a specific movement, and the players must enter into the demands of supporting that movement's emergence.[26] For that movement to come to stand, a spectator is indispensable. Likewise, the story that conveys political action is perceptible only to a spectator prepared to assume the task of constructing it. In the modern notion, political power is defined by domination and submission or resistance. For the contrasting classical view, political action takes place "between men," in the realm of "interests" which lies between and binds men (*HC*, 182–83) rather than separating them into "interest groups" vying for power.

This transition to the spectator must not be taken as putting the spectator in the controlling position, as in certain versions of reader-response theory. A work of art or an action comes to stand only through "style," that is, "a unity of expression." In art as in politics, style makes the artist or actor "visible to others, so that they know with whom they have to deal" (*TM*, 452). But the expressiveness of this manifestation is limited by a normative reference "to something fixed and objective that is binding on individual forms of expression" (*TM*, 450). Ultimately, the spectator is called to dwell on the manifestation itself and to yield assent to it in an act of recognition (*RB*, 36). We may recall the role of ritual spectatorship, or *theoria*, in Greek cultic life. Gadamer observes, "Great art shakes us because we are always unprepared and defenseless when exposed to the overpowering impact of a compelling work" (*RB*, 37). The "blow" (*Stoss*) great art gives us reveals that "we are always other and much more than we know ourselves to be, and what exceeds our knowledge is precisely our real being," our "substance" as Hegel calls it (*RB*, 78). What we are is no more at our disposal than is the artwork. We do not judge it; it brings us to judgment, as when Rilke's poem on the torso of an antique Apollo concludes, "You must change your life." Political action that emerges into story similarly attains "great style" and reproaches or exhorts us with its exemplary eminence. It thus achieves something monumental which compels our recognition. This means acknowledgement of its power to repeat itself, that is, to retain its initiative of action on us by "continually becoming a new event" (*TM*, 454). As with the artwork, the "great leader's" capacity to draw from a people supreme political efforts is related to this activation of our real, substantial being.

According to Kant, the judgment of taste commands universal assent without negotiation, neither mediated by concepts nor settled by argument (*RB*, 18). The political risk of this claim is recognized in modern efforts to show the "class basis" of taste. No sphere of human life can be permitted to escape the realm of the political as it is conceived through this economic category. What commands universal assent without negotiation would be utopian or totalitarian—if it is possible to distinguish between the two; that is, it would require a harmony either preestablished or imposed by violence.[27] But, as Gadamer notes, Kant says we do not simply *possess* taste but must also develop it. Taste is communicative (*RB*, 19), not purely idiosyncratic and private. Communication in this case is completely removed from the exchange of information oriented toward a purpose, that is, toward a meaning which lies at our disposal. That one's freedom of action and judgment might presuppose responsiveness to a compelling insight—to "truth" as something that manifests itself, not as something we "establish" by a method of testing—founds authority not on the power of the one who exercises authority but on the recognition and acknowledgment of the one who submits to it. This again approaches the classical conception that politics rests on a mutual insight into the good, an insight that is compelling without being compulsory. Hence, for the Greeks, tragedy could belong to the sphere of public life. This did not mean that it contained sound political opinions nor that it obliquely intervened in current political debates.[28]

Conceived from the perspective of the audience, the function of art is not to express a preexistent harmony but to adumbrate the possibility of order by initiating an intensification of the life of the recipient, insofar as he/she assumes the task of constructing the work. One might connect this with the modern state's care for our "welfare" or preservation, which is carried out under the slogan of "enhancing the quality of life" and which in practice consists of establishing "programs" to whose aid individuals are "entitled" on the basis of "need." But the intensification of life through art, Nietzsche observed, has nothing to do with our preservation, but rather puts us at the greatest possible risk.[29] Art might thus seem a way of intensifying life that competes with modern politics' care of the body. But the conception of politics as the elimination of or at least management of risk contrasts equally with the classical conception of politics centered around "virtue," a self-mastery whose extreme is reached in the sacrifice of one's life in war. In modern culture, it becomes difficult, if not impossible, to understand war as art in a poem like the *Iliad* or *Aeneid.* Where art is removed from war, war really does become bloody murder, a view expressed equally in the paradoxically correlative ideas that the supreme aim of politics is peace and order (where "order" is understood in a very constrictive sense) and that war and violence as such contrast favorably with the dull routines of bourgeois life and should therefore be plunged into with suicidal enthusiasm.[30]

The peculiar relation to the spectator I am pursuing can be brought out if we take up a final topic, the temporality of the artwork and of political action. Gadamer's repeated examination of art throughout his work is to be attributed not to an expectation that it will confirm his hermeneutic views in an obvious way, but quite the contrary, that it challenges those views more sharply than any other phenomenon.[31] It is by no means clear that what the work of art demands of us is anything like what we would ordinarily call "understanding." This is certainly true if we take "understanding" to mean the reduction of the work to a harmony which denies its essential ambiguity and permits its appropriation by concepts or "ideas."[32] But even in the broad sense that Gadamer, following Heidegger, gives to the word "understanding," the work of art seems to generate an irreducible tension against the finitude or historicity of our existence. The self-standing particularity of the work of art is withdrawn from and overcomes the flow of contingency.

Gadamer argues, however, that the experience of art does not eliminate time but brings us closer to time's essential nature. This happens in two ways. The first is the temporality of recognition. The constructive activity in which we bring the work of art to stand is "recognition," which does not mean just "cognizing again," but cognizing *as.* The work is acknowledged as manifesting an essence that endures and reappears in time. This repeatability of the work is not an inert indifference to time nor an exact reproduction in various moments. Rather, the work of art has the capacity to establish itself in successive moments as a new event in which its audience takes part. Second, this gathering of the audience in participation can be understood by an analogy to festival. It is essential to festival that it "does not dissolve into a series of separate moments" (*RB*, 41) but stands as the repetition of something already fully there. Gadamer thus distinguishes two forms of temporality: empty and fulfilled time (*RB*, 41ff.).[33] Empty time is divisible and at our disposal, measured by the extremes of boredom, that is, too much time, in contrast to bustle, that is, too little time. Fulfilled or "intrinsic time," "time proper" (*Eigenzeit*), is discontinuous, seasonal, capable of tarrying (*verweilen*). Fulfilled time belongs to the structure of that whose time it is. The right tempo for a piece of music, the right rhythm for reciting a poem, the rhythmic unfolding of pictures or buildings to our perceptual access—in all these, the artwork is not subordinated to the continuous temporal flow of the background life from which it emerges but stands out in a way that absorbs its occasions into and opens them out from within itself. The work of art plays "itself out by trying out possibilities," so that it constantly involves itself again in time, "continually becoming a new event" (*TM*, 454).

In its festive character, art gathers a public, in contrast to the separating specialties of work (on which Plato hoped to found the Republic) or the divisions of labor (which Marx modulated into conflicting classes). "The essence of the beautiful is to have a certain standing in the public eye. This in turn implies a whole form of life that embraces all those artistic forms with which we embellish our environment" (*RB*, 50). Art transcends the limitations of any cultural definition (*RB*, 50). This does not mean that art is an end in itself, but the reason is not because it subserves the political but because it is withdrawn from the sphere of ends. Likewise, art transcends any limitations "associated with its privileged cultural status." The audience the artwork gathers around itself is not analyzable in the terms of political economy. This is not to claim that everyone has equal access to art or that no correlations can be established between taste and what is called "class." It is to say that in both festive celebration and the gathering that participates in the event of the artwork, the event "is meaningful only for those actually taking part" (*RB*, 49), that is, for those who accord the work recognition. This recognition or acknowledgment is inaccessible to an analysis in terms of function.

Political actions in a similar way invite festive celebration. It belongs to the festive character of political action that it can repeat the past by imitation,[34] that is, it can resituate in the present the expression of a recognized order. This is the production of "tradition," which "means transmission [*Ubertragung*] rather than conservation" (*RB*, 49). This is to say that tradition cannot exist unless we participate in producing "this shared community of meaning, which can be neither simply presupposed nor gratefully accepted" (*RB*, 48). In political action, we all—leader and follower—must learn "how to grasp and express the past anew." Tradition is translation (*RB*, 49). To say this is to say that the artwork and political action have the character of thinking, as Heidegger understands it.[35]

The felt inauthenticity of celebration in modern political life—including its degradation into engineered mass demonstration—testifies to a peculiar attempt to guard the continuities of life against the intrusion of the political. The reduction of politics to the task of applying scientific methods to the administration of public affairs pursues the modern ideal of "making politics concrete and mundane," that is, banal and rational.[36] Once critique strips custom of legitimacy, modern legislation becomes the endless burden of negotiating rules for the totality of our existence. This burden inevitably comes to set the predictive rationality of the legislator in opposition to the evasive cunning of those who must live under the rules, generating a predictable "bad" infinity of self-consciousness instead of the solidary familiarity of tradition generated through the receptive processes that shape custom and myth.[37] I have already touched on parallel moves by which modern criticism draws the work of art back into the flow of empty, everyday time from which it arose. This resistance may be broadly characterized as an urge to reduce historicity to history.[38] In art, this resistance is manifest in the split between an "art for art's sake," which stands outside our existence, where it can do us no harm, and a naturalist realism, where art shows us merely what is "relevant" to our present life and concerns.[39] In politics, the routine functioning of the bureaucracy, desired by both the bureaucrat and those whose lives are administered, is protected against the disruptive unpredictability of narrative, with its demand for greatness of spirit and action, a demand whose legitimation comes only with the completion of the narrative, that is, retrospectively.[40] But in fact the resistance to historicity is not simply external to it. Its possibility belongs to the "worldly" character of everything that comes to stand in our existence. I am thinking here of the "rift" (*Riss*) which, Heidegger claims, joins world and earth, disclosure and concealment, truth and error in every "work"—and, I would add, joins order and disorder in political action—with indissoluble ambiguity. The interplay of self-assertion (*Selbstbehauptung*) and releasement (*Gelassenheit*) belongs irreducibly to our mortal existence.[41]

As a closing summary, let me add a comment on my title. Ordinarily the assertion that the "aesthetic" is what stands outside the contingencies of political life opposes the polemical counterassertion that the analysis of art must reduce it back into the contingencies of political life. I proceeded by trying to displace the conception of politics which seems to me dominant in the modern world and unreflectively adopted in this opposition. I hoped thus to find common ground for a renewed dialogue between art and politics in "history." But I encountered a distinction between the history that could belong to what Gadamer calls "empty" time and the history or "historicity" that belongs to "fulfilled" time. This distinction is opened by the finitude of our existence. Finitude does not mean simply that we are creatures who live for a while and then disappear. It means that we experience the uniqueness of our existence, our particularity, in relation to our mortality. The durability of the work of art may seem to belong to an effort to deny that mortality. Likewise, it seems almost no exaggeration to say that the glory sought in political action comes to stand in the funeral oration and its promise of lasting fame. Such a view would be too hasty. For the endurance of the work of art or the political agent's fame is not mere inertness. It is a power to compel continuing recognition. The endurance both art and political action exhibit to us is thus achieved from within our embodied mortality. If there is no philosophy among the gods, neither is there art nor politics.

Notes

1.   Consider the proliferation of titles that mention "ideology" or the "politics" or "political responsibility" of the poet or critic. To paraphrase Harold Bloom, it would not occur to anyone to write a book on the responsibilities of politicians for—or to—poetry. Why not?

2.   Theodor Adorno, "Culutural Critique and Society," in *Prisms,* trans. Samuel and Shierry Weber (Cambridge, Mass.: MIT Press, 1983), 34; originally published as *Kulturkritik und Gesellschaft* (Berlin, 1951). Some took the remark as aimed at Paul Celan's "Todesfuge" ("Death Fugue"), a harrowing evocation of the death camps, though Adorno "probably did not know Celan's poem," according to John Felstiner, *Paul Celan: Poet, Survivor, Jew* (New Haven, Conn.: Yale University Press, 1995), 139. When Hans Magnus Enzensberger asserted that the example of Nelly Sachs disproved the remark, Adorno reaffirmed and even elaborated it (ibid., 188). Adorno later reprinted the essay containing the sentence, and when the journal *Merkur* used it to denigrate "Todesfuge," Celan retorted with justified bitterness, "[W]e finally know where the barbarians are to be found" (ibid., 225). Adorno finally relented: "Perennial suffering has as much right to expression as the tortured have to scream; hence it may have been wrong to say that no

poem could be written after Auschwitz" (ibid., 232). This grudging concession is unsatisfactory. Celan was not screaming; he was writing a poem.

3.   Thus Walter Benjamin's famous dictum that fascism renders politics
aesthetic; communism responds by politicizing art ("The Work of Art in the
Age of Mechanical Reproduction," in *Illuminations,* trans. Harry Zohn [New
York: Schocken, 1968], 242). With this cryptic aphorism, Benjamin "signs
off" his celebrated essay on cinema. But the remark is, to use his own term,
"plump," crude: it substitutes a neat chiasmus for serious thinking. On the
one hand, it takes fascism too much at its own self-valuation. Hitler's
Wagnerian spectacles were not art but kitsch. "Politicized" art—socialist realism, Soviet monumental statuary, the tomb of Lenin (one would like to read
Roland Barthes on *that* "mythology")—is symmetrically kitsch. Both sides
are hostile to art, vengefully subordinating it to propaganda purposes. The
chiasmus presents no real alternative.

4.   See Alexander Baumgarten, *Aesthetica* (1750–58; Hildesheim:
G. Olms, 1961).

5.   See Paul Oskar Kristeller, "The Modern System of the Arts," in *Renaissance Thought II: Papers on Humanism and the Arts* (New York:
Harper and Row, 1961), 163–227.

6.   Ernst Cassirer, *Philosophy of the Enlightenment,* trans. Fritz Koelln
and James P. Pettegrove (Princeton, N.J.: Princeton University Press, 1951);
Terry Eagleton, *The Ideology of the Aesthetic* (Cambridge, Mass.: Blackwell,
1990); Martha Woodmansee, *The Author, Art, and the Market: Rereading the
History of Aesthetics* (New York: Columbia University Press, 1994).

7.   The same paradox is found in the work of ancient and medieval
theorists who defend poetry by claiming it has an allegorical meaning. If the
philosophical or religious meaning is evident, then no one would fail to see
it and mistakenly find poetry immoral. If it is hidden, then it can affect only
the initiated few who have learned how to extract it. The belief that "ideology" can work behind everyone's back is another "hidden hand" theory and
obviously moves politics out of the public realm of mutual deliberation, since
one side is mired in "false consciousness," so that its arguments on principle
must not be taken seriously. It follows that politics is the manipulation of
groups and masses by initiates—for example, the "party" as "avant-garde of the
working class"—who are "in the know" about where history is really going.

8.   Siegfried Kracauer, *History: The Last Things before the Last* (New
York: Oxford University Press, 1969), notes the parallel tendency to see the
whole of history as a rigidly integrated totality. He proposes instead that history is composed of autonomous and unintegrated lumps. The difficulties in
holding such a theory are nicely symmetrical with the unsolved problems of
integrating everything under, say, the "means of production" without falling
into crude scientisms. The brandishing of a talismanic formula like "in the

last analysis" or "in the last resort" to ward off obvious doubts is an instructively desperate gesture with suggestive resemblances to certain religious practices.

9. Karl Marx, *A Contribution to the Critique of Political Economy* (1859), trans. Maurice Dobb (New York: International Publishers, 1970). See the relevant excerpt in *Critical Theory since Plato,* ed. Hazard Adams (New York: Harcourt Brace Jovanovich, 1971), 633.

10. See Georg Lukács, "Marx and Engels on Aesthetics," in *Writer and Critic,* trans. and ed. Arthur Kahn (London: Merlin Press, 1970), 82ff., on "tendency" and the "tendentious" element in literature; but the idea is pervasive in Lukács's critical thinking. On the "utopian," see Fredric Jameson, *The Political Unconscious: Narrative as a Socially Symbolic Act* (Ithaca, N.Y.: Cornell University Press, 1981), especially chapter 6, "Conclusion: The Dialectic of Utopia and Ideology." Both thinkers have the virtue of seeing that without a principle of evaluation, Marxist criticism degenerates into positivist, determinist historicism on the model of Hippolyte Taine. But a Marxist evaluative principle cannot derive from a classicist or rationalist view of the fixed ideality of forms and rules, nor from a romantic conception of genius. To remain historical, it must be attached to something dynamic but not directionless in history itself. How it can do so and escape turning itself into a liberal humanism is not easy to see.

11. Martin Buber, *Between Man and Man,* trans. Ronald Gregor (New York: Collier Macmillan, 1965), 67.

12. See Richard Sennett, *The Fall of Public Man* (New York: Knopf, 1977), especially chapter 10.

13. Leo Strauss, "What Is Political Philosophy?" in *What Is Political Philosophy? and Other Studies* (Glencoe, Ill.: Free Press, 1959), 24.

14. Contrast Buber: "'History' is not the sequence of conquests of power and actions of power but the context of the responsibilities of power in time" (*Between Man and Man,* 73).

15. See Michael Ignatieff, *The Needs of Strangers* (New York: Viking, 1984). Ignatieff shows how modern politics comes to birth in Adam Smith's passage from reflections on moral sentiments through jurisprudence to the wealth of nations. Politics becomes "economic and human development." Human needs, freed from political supervision and restraint, were released into the infinity of their historical progress. Marx fantasized a "plenitude at the end of time" which would deliver human society from history (127). In *The Future of an Illusion* (1927), Freud treats it as a mere commonplace that civilization is the sum of the means for producing and distributing what meets biological needs. See Sigmund Freud, *The Standard Edition of the Complete Psychological Works of Sigmund Freud,* trans. and ed. James Strachey, 24 vols. (London: Hogarth Press, 1953–74), 21:6.

16. This is essentially the tradition traced with great penetration and

learning by Robert Denoon Cumming, *Human Nature and History,* 2 vols. (Chicago: University of Chicago Press, 1969).

17. That this shared insight is essentially hidden, which means that it is not simply at our disposal, sets a limit to any social contract theory. See Hans-Georg Gadamer, *Truth and Method,* trans. and ed. Garrett Barden and John Cumming (New York: Seabury Press, 1975), 286–87; hereafter abbreviated *TM* and cited parenthetically in the text.

18. One need only mention Augustine's *City of God.*

19. It will probably not forestall criticism if I say that I am fully aware that much has changed irrevocably in the modern world. In *Dominations and Powers: Reflections on Liberty, Society and Government* (New York: Scribners, 1951), George Santayana remarks that his earlier treatment of human society in *The Life of Reason* was based on Aristotle and Plato, but that he has come to realize "they hardly consider non-territorial powers, such as universal religions, nor the relation of the State to the non-political impulses of human nature" (vii). Many more phenomena could be mentioned: bureaucracy, professional specialization (including that of the military), mass media, technology and science, the governmental responsibility for economic development and welfare, parties, foreign policy based on the interaction of sovereign states, and so on.

20. Hans-Georg Gadamer, *The Relevance of the Beautiful,* trans. Nicholas Walker, ed. Robert Bernasconi (Cambridge: Cambridge University Press, 1986); hereafter abbreviated *RB* and cited parenthetically in the text. The earliest essay Bernasconi has chosen dates from 1954, the most recent from 1980, with the bulk from the 1970s.

21. Cumming, *Human Nature and History,* 2:55 n. 76.

22. Hannah Arendt, *The Human Condition* (Chicago: University of Chicago Press, 1958); hereafter abbreviated *HC* and cited parenthetically in the text.

23. The sense that political action is released from its agent contrasts with the modern insistence on locating with precision the agent of every political act and holding that agent (the "executive") accountable to a system of rules and ultimately to rule makers (the "legislative"), that is, an elected, and therefore "responsible" body (or the electorate itself). In the "Irangate" affair, the Congressional inquiry increasingly focused on who precisely was responsible for what act and under what rule. The proceedings thus took on the shape of a trial to determine guilt. That a judicial proceeding was conducted by an ineluctably partisan body guaranteed that the outcome would be generically mixed and politically ambiguous. Pushed entirely into the background was any deliberation on how the foreign policy of the United States should be decided and conducted. Even that procedural question obscures the most basic issue: what are the interests and therefore what should be the foreign policy of the United States?

24. Sobering is Freud's *Group Psychology and the Analysis of the Ego* (1921): members of the group attain equality and fraternal feeling only by uncritical submission to a shared ego ideal. To be sure, Freud is a disillusioned liberal seeking a self-exculpating explanation for the failure of Austrian liberalism, but Sennett, while critical of Freud, reaches similar conclusions by a more sociological route in *The Fall of Public Man.*

25. Compare the quotation from Strauss above. As Strauss argues, positivism, in order to found its interpretive categories, seeks universals by investigating other and earlier societies. It thus transforms itself into historicism. But to avoid missing the meaning of other societies by simply imposing its own categories, it must understand those cultures as they understood themselves ("What Is Political Philosophy?" 25). I do not agree with the phrasing and have thus restated the insight in Gadamer's terms: to understand, one does not simply replace one's own view with that of the other, but certainly one has to put one's own view at risk.

26. See the discussion of play in *TM,* 91–119.

27. See G. W. Leibniz, *Monadology,* § 78, on *harmonie préétablie.* I owe the reference to an unpublished paper by Frank R. Ankersmit, "Political Representation: On the Aesthetic State."

28. One should mention here Gerald Else, *The Origin and Early Form of Greek Tragedy* (Cambridge, Mass.: Harvard University Press for Oberlin College, 1965). Else argues persuasively that Greek tragedy originates in political rather than cultic life. Tragedy's central formal structure—a hero or protagonist whose self-presented action is held in dialectic with the view taken of it by the chorus as representative of the people—incarnates Solon's political compromise.

29. I am thinking not only of *The Birth of Tragedy* but of course of Heidegger's comment on Hölderlin's remark that language is the most dangerous of possessions. See Martin Heidegger, "Hölderlin and the Essence of Poetry," trans. Douglas Scott, in *Existence and Being* (Chicago: Regnery, 1949), 293–315, especially 296–99.

30. I mean to allude to "futurism" and similar attempts to connect the "dangerous" nature of art with the disruptiveness of modern technology and with a notion that political violence will be "redemptive." This applies equally to the "left-wing" politics of surrealism and the equation of artistic with political "revolution."

31. That is his starting point in "Aesthetics and Hermeneutics," in Hans-Georg Gadamer, *Philosophical Hermeneutics,* trans. David E. Linge (Berkeley: University of California Press, 1976), 95–96.

32. This point is made forcefully throughout the work of Gerald Bruns. See, for example, "Against Poetry: Heidegger, Ricoeur, and the Originary Scene of Hermeneutics," in *Meanings in Texts and Actions: Questioning Paul Ricoeur,* ed. David E. Klemm and William Schweiker (Charlottesville:

University Press of Virginia, 1993), 26–46, and my "Response to Gerald Bruns," in ibid., 318–25.

33. For a full and powerful development of this idea, see Hans-Georg Gadamer, "Concerning Empty and Fulfilled Time," trans. R. Phillip O'Hara, *Southern Journal of Philosophy* 8 (1970): 341–53, and the partially overlapping essay "The Western View of the Inner Experience of Time and the Limits of Thought," in *Time and the Philosophies* (Paris: UNESCO, 1977), 33–48.

34. See the contrast between modern historicism and the humanist sense of history as "imitation" in Cumming, *Human Nature and History,* vol. 1, chapter 6, "The Historical Origin of Historicism."

35. Heidegger's own political thinking shows, I would want to insist, that this is anything but reassuring. It is possible to think very badly indeed.

36. See Gadamer's "Notes on Planning for the Future," *Daedalus* 95 (1966): 572–89; the phrases here are from pp. 577 and 580.

37. I am adapting here Hans Blumenberg's emphasis on receptivity as the shaping power for myth, though my line of thought differs from his. See his *Work on Myth,* trans. Robert M. Wallace (Cambridge, Mass.: MIT Press, 1985), passim.

38. See Eric Voegelin, *In Search of Order,* vol. 5 of *Order and History* (Baton Rouge: Louisiana State University Press, 1987), 35–39.

39. A similar ambivalence governs the notion of the artist. On the one hand, where the artist is either genius or outcast, his/her life stands outside everyday rules. By thus excusing the artist, this separation protects not so much the artist from the rules but the rules from what exceeds their competence. The everyday historical world is guarded against the intrusion of what comes to appearance in art. At the opposite pole, the authenticity of a work is seen as bound to the author's membership in the social milieu the work depicts. Two recent examples illustrate the point. A highly praised novel about barrio life by a young Chicano was dropped with embarrassment when its pseudonymous author turned out to be an older Jewish man. The agreement to publish a Pakistani woman's story of Asian women immigrants in London was withdrawn when the pseudonymous author turned out to be a young English vicar. What this sudden drop in commercial value exemplifies is no ordinary case of fraudulent misrepresentation, since what was misrepresented was the author's identity, while the work itself was unchanged. One might argue that readers implicitly hold a theory of how a work of genuine art is created—for instance, that the artist transforms his/her actual experience; if it turns out the author has not had these experiences, it would follow that the artwork could not be "genuine." In line with Wittgenstein's critique in the *Philosophical Investigations* of the theory that meaning depends on the user's having a prior "intention," I am skeptical about attributing to readers either a theory or deductive thinking. The tone of the response suggests that readers feel not that some theory has been falsified but that

their trust has been betrayed. What is at stake is not the truth of what the novel says (in any sense of "true") but who has the right to say it. The reader thus refuses to accept responsibility for the work or for his/her own response to it, insisting instead that the author's "sincerity" underwrite in advance the authenticity of the reader's response to the work. Clearly, many, if not most, people read novels as though they were newspaper feature articles, that is, basically factual accounts by reliable eyewitnesses, presented under the guise of fiction. Artistic form and factual content neutralize each other, so that the reader is protected against responsibility for either, though in opposite directions.

40. Success, that is, greatness in political action, obviously cannot be guaranteed in advance by rules. As C. Northcote Parkinson noted in *The Law and the Profits* (Boston: Houghton Mifflin, 1960), the businessman acts so as to increase profits. The bureaucrat acts so as to build up a file in case there is an investigation. He can then prove that he followed the regular procedures. Government as action that follows rules not only dispenses with but positively excludes "greatness." As Gadamer observes ("Notes on Planning," 579–80), the fact that its rationality is not of a scientific-predictive kind does not make political or ethical action irrational but releases its own proper rationality. This rationality is essentially narrative and retrospective: it is legitimated by the story it will be possible to tell about it, should the action succeed. From the point of view of instrumental rationality, nothing could be more scandalously irresponsible.

41. I take "self-assertion" from Hans Blumenberg, *The Legitimacy of the Modern Age,* trans. Robert M. Wallace (Cambridge, Mass.: MIT Press, 1983). On *Gelassenheit,* see Martin Heidegger, *Discourse on Thinking,* trans. John M. Anderson and E. Hans Freund (New York: Harper and Row, 1969).

From the Lighthouse

The Promise of Redemption and the Possibility of Legal Interpretation

Drucilla Cornell

Blanchot says:

> Laws—prosaic laws—free us, perhaps, from the Law by substituting for the invisible majesty of time the various constraints of space. Similarly rules suppress, in the term law, what power—ever primary—evokes. Rules also suppress the rights which go along with the notion of law, and establish the reign of pure procedure which—a manifestation of technical competence of sheer knowledge—invests everything, controls everything, submits every gesture to its administration, so that there is no longer any possibility of liberation, for one can no longer speak of oppression. Kafka's trial can be interpreted as a tangle of three different realms (the Law, laws, rules).[1]

Drucilla Cornell

My purpose in this essay is to tell three different stories relevant to what the tangle of the three realms to which Blanchot refers means for the unfolding of a postmodern/modern jurisprudence. The three realms as I interpret them are (1) the Good, or the Law of Law; (2) the Right, or the moral Law of the self-legislating subject; and (3) the principles inherent in an existing legal system. There are two senses in which I refer to the Good. First, the Good should be understood in the strong sense of the universal, as an irremissible necessity for all subjects. Second, the Good should be anticipated as the immanent possibility of ethical reinterpretation of the concrete, universals within a given legal system conceptualized as an indeterminate *nomos*. These three realms—the Good, the Right, and legal principles—are not reducible to categories of the mind, because they describe types of human interaction. The first story I will tell is Hegelian, in which the three realms are shown to be a part of the system that ultimately gives each realm its meaning. Hegel, of course, recognizes the interplay between the three realms, but even so their true meaning is only given to us in Absolute Knowledge in which the Good is fully revealed. Hegelianism is, of course, only one attempt among others to ground an actual legal system in a conception of the Good. But I focus on Hegel for a specific reason.

Hegel rejects deontological theories of the right as the basis for a modern legal system. Hegel argues against the neo-Kantian that the normativity of the right cannot be self-grounding. Hegel, in other words, reminds us that even in modernity or in postmodernity we are still caught in the tangle of the three realms: the Law of Law, the Law of the self-legislating subject, and legal rules and principles. It is precisely the realm of the Good that the neo-Kantian morality argues is inconsistent with modernity. The Law of Law, or the Good, is replaced by the law of the self-legislating, free subject. In Hegel's view, we cannot escape the *Law* of law understood as a conception of the Good, because theories of right can only be normatively grounded through an implicit reference to the Good. It is precisely this insistence on the inevitable interplay of the three realms that also distinguishes the "postmodern" stories I will tell from neo-Kantianism. As we will see, what is rejected are not the ideals of modernity, and certainly not the "gains" of a modern legal system, but instead the illusion that a normative conception of modernity can be so self-grounding that the realm of the Good is at best irrelevant and at worst a regression to the premodern. Hegel always reminds us that the very idea of law as the *nomos* of a community implies a story of the good life. This fundamental insight is recast but not rejected in the "postmodern" stories I offer.

The "postmodern" story has at least two versions. Neither version is directly traceable to any particular author, although each borrows from a number of thinkers frequently labeled (by others if not by themselves) as postmodern—Derrida, Blanchot, and Levinas. Both versions of the postmodern story reveal the inevitable diremption of the Hegelian reconciliation of the three realms, once the Hegelian system has been unraveled. Both versions also agree that there can be no *foundationalist* grounding of any given system of legal rules and norms in the Law of Law. I might also add that both versions not only reject the illusion of the normative *self-grounding* of the right in transcendental subjectivity; they also reject the positivist solution to *Grundlosigkeit* which finds the Law of Law within the mechanism of validation internally generated by an existing legal system. For the legal positivist, the Law of Law of a modern legal system can only find its grounding in its own positivity. But in order for the Law of Law to be reduced to the mechanism of the perpetuation of legal rules, the legal positivist must postulate a self-maintaining, even if evolving, cognitive system in which there is normative closure. Deconstruction, on the other hand, persistently exposes the fallacy of legal positivism by showing us the moment of ethical alternity inherent in any purportedly self-enclosed cognitive system, legal or otherwise.

But how is the moment of ethical alternity "presented" in deconstruction and in other strands of "postmodern" discourse? In the first version of the story, the Law of Law is only "present" in its absolute absence. The "never has been" of an unrecoverable past is understood as the lack of origin "presentable" only as allegory. The Law of Law, in other words, is the figure of an initial fragmentation, the loss of the Good. But this allegory is inescapable because the lack of origin is the fundamental truth. There is no horizon of reconciliation, no matter how projected into the future as the ethical promise of the *not yet* of the *never has been*. This version of the postmodern story has often been received as the "truth" of deconstruction in both American literary and legal circles. As we will see, I will reject this version of the story. In the second version, the Good remains as the disruption of ontology that continually reopens the way beyond what "is." As the call to responsibility for the Other, the Law of Law is irreducible to negative theology or to the allegory of an "initial" fragmentation. The Law of Law echoes as the call of the Good.

But does the call to witness to the Other involve the projection of a horizon of reconciliation as the promise of the never has been, which is the promise of redemption? Redemption, as I use the word, means that we will be saved from the fallen world as it "is" in the name of a world that would try to be worthy of the beyond. But redemption, as I will suggest, cannot be envisioned as purely negative, as the endless rejection of the "is." As I hope to show, it is precisely the projection of a horizon of reconciliation that is essential to the possibility of legal interpretation. It is only once we grasp the complex relationship between the delimitation of ontology and the recognition of its inevitable reinstatement through linguistic stabilization of systems of representation that we can understand why the promise of redemption, even within a modern/postmodern legal system, remains crucial for the possibility of legal interpretation. Of course, we should not forget that deconstruction has been vigilant in its reminder that when we project the future as the promise of the past that can never be made fully present to the mind, we are inevitably unfaithful to that promise. The promise commits us to the not yet of what has never been present, cannot be fully recalled, and therefore cannot be adequately projected. Yet, as we will see, this reminder both calls us to the commitment to the impossible, the full realization of the Good, and to the need to defy the impossible by projecting a horizon of reconciliation. The significance for legal interpretation of the Derridean double gesture can only be understood once we understand the double gesture not as cynical duplicity but as a response to the call of the Good.

At stake in the recent debates in American jurisprudence over the possibility of legal interpretation is the answer to the most fundamental question: can we escape from the Penal Colony in a modern/postmodern legal system?[2] If law is reduced to the positive legitimation of institutional power through established legal procedure, we only will know the meaning of a legal proposition as it is engraved in our backs. Robert Cover has rightfully insisted that we must remember that the legal sentence takes on meaning "in a field of pain and death."[3] Law has only too much power to enforce its meaning. It is for this reason that the central error of the "irrationalists" in the Conference of Critical Legal Studies has tragic potential. The central error is to confuse *Grundlosigkeit* with *Unsinnlosigkeit*, a confusion that is repeatedly made in the tirades against deconstruction as well as by its friends in the conference.[4] If legal sentences can have no ethical meaning, not even institutionalized meaning, then the machine is free to make us feel its meaning nevertheless. The machine needs no justification to keep on running. The hope for salvation, however, is precisely in the impossibility of such a machine. The machine of Kafka's parable literally runs amuck once it is no longer seen by the one who runs it as an instrument of the Good. The central message of this essay is that we cannot escape the appeal to the Good as we interpret legal sentences. Therefore, the possibility of escape from the Penal Col-

language or in law, because for Levinas all language, and therefore the very possibility of meaning, presupposes the words, the command of the Other: "You shall not murder me." The Other is first on the scene. The subject endures a latent birth from his contact with Her.

> Signification as proximity is thus the Latent birth of the subject. Latent birth for prior to an origin, an initiative, a present designatable and assumable, even if by memory. It is an anachronous birth, prior to its own present, a non-beginning, an anarchy. As a Latent birth, it is never a presence, excluding the present of coinciding with oneself, for it is *in contact,* in sensibility, in vulnerability, in exposure to the outrages of the Other.[7]

He is not born in an act of self-conscious assertion; he instead comes to himself in his proximity to Her. This proximity "is" "there" as the contact with the Other to whom we are fated to be exposed and who in turn is fated to be exposed to us. But the trace also points us toward the future as a prescriptive command. In that sense, the trace of the Other is also anterior. The prescriptive command "Be just" calls us not only in the particular case before us; it calls us to judge again and to live up to the command in each new case.

The birth of the subject out of this *anarchy* is constitutive of the order of signification generally and more specifically of the proximity to the Other, which is the "law" of responsibility to which we are called. But, in Levinas, the trace of the Other that remains in proximity cannot be understood, as in Hegel, as the establishment of a fully present relationship between the three realms: the Law of Law, the law of the self-legislating subject, and legal rules and principles that can be comprehended as the Good of the relations of reciprocal symmetry. As Levinas explains of our proximity which constitutes me through the face of the Other: "It is the significance of signs. It is the humanity of man not understood on the basis of transcendental subjectivity. It is the passivity of exposure, a passivity itself exposed. Saying does not occur in consciousness nor in a commitment understood in terms of consciousness or memory; it does not form a conjuncture and a synchrony" (*OB,* 139).

Hegelian reconciliation, which reduces the Other to a relation with me, even if that relationship is rooted in the stance of reciprocal symmetry, is still violence. There is always a trace of otherness that cannot be captured by my identifying with the Other in relations of mutual recognition. She is before me; I cannot grasp the essence of the Other in "the we that is I and the I that is we." The basis of the ethical relationship, then, is not identification with those whom we recognize as like our-selves. Instead, the ethical relation inheres in the encounter with the Other, the stranger whose face beckons us to heed the call to responsibil-ity. The precedence of the Other means that my relationship to Her is nonreciprocal and asymmetrical—at least if we think about reciprocal symmetry as I suggested Hegel did, as temporally rooted in a shared pres-ent and spatially based on a horizontal plane. For Levinas, proximity is not a "we" in a common present. Through the encounter with the Other who calls me, the subject first experiences the resistance to encapsula-tion of the Beyond. We encounter God as the transcendence of the face-to-face. In Levinas, transcendence is temporal, not spatial, although he himself frequently relies on the image of the vertical plane which rein-states the Other as master. In the face-to-face of the ethical relation we confront the infinity that disrupts totality, as a meeting with the Other who cannot be captured by me. The Law of Law, or the Good, is precisely the echo of the Call of the Other as a prescriptive command directed toward the future that disrupts the Hegelian system and the pretense of any system to have adequately represented the totality of what "is" Good. The Law of Law "is" a rupture of the status quo. This is why Blanchot postulates the Law as disaster: "Would law be the disaster? The supreme or extreme Law, that is: the excessiveness of uncodifiable law—that to which we are destined without being party to it. The disaster is not our affair and has no regard for us; it is the heedless unlimited; it cannot be measured in terms of failure or as pure and simple loss."[8]

The Good as the Law of Law is also not to be understood as simply the limit of signification. Such an understanding would again establish Saying in a common frontier with what is. The Saying, in other words, would once again be reduced to a relationship synchronized with the said, and therefore, no longer disruptive of its claim to full presence.

But the call to responsibility by the Other does disrupt the Kantian notion of the free subject of morality. The Kantian subject is enthralled by duty, but duty is still self-imposed. The Kantian subject of morality is self-legislating. It is only by rising above contamination by the *heteros* that the self achieves moral freedom. For Levinas, on the other hand, the subject is bound to the Other, and it is this very tie to the *heteros* that marks the ethical relation. Indeed, we can never truly be free from the Other, even when we try desperately to stifle Her call. If Kant gives us a morality of duty, Levinas gives us an ethic of responsibility in which the subject recognizes autonomy as illusion, and the attempt at freedom from the heteronomous as a form of denial that is profoundly unethical. For

Levinas, then, the ethical cannot be self-grounding in the law of the transcendental subject.

We now turn to the realm of the system of existing legal rules. How does Levinas understand the significance of the rebellion against the Hegelian system for the interpretation of legal rules? As we have seen in Hegel, legal rules are given ethical meaning by reference to the realized Good of relations of reciprocal symmetry. When I use the word "meaning," I am not referring to institutionalized linguistic meaning in the sense of the intelligibility of sentences but instead to ethical meaning. As we have seen, Hegel understood that the dilemma of legal interpretation does not turn on whether we can cement linguistic meaning. Legal rules are justified in Hegel through the appeal to the realized relations of reciprocal symmetry, which give them ethical justification. In Hegel, the Good, in the strong sense of the ultimate universal, is immanent in social institutions and therefore capable of being grasped by the human mind. But as we have also seen in Levinas, the Good is precisely what eludes our full knowledge. We cannot grasp the Good but only follow it. The Good, as the Other beyond us, is a star that beckons us to follow (I am aware that by portraying the Good as a star that beckons us to follow I am lingering within desire, and that Blanchot, although perhaps not Levinas, would have the Law of Law eclipse even the symbolization of the Good as a star). It is precisely the Good, the Law of Law, as responsibility to the Other that calls us to justice. In Levinas, although there is an inevitable diremption between the Law of Law, the Good, and the actual, we also cannot escape our responsibility — particularly if we are law professors, judges, and lawyers — to elaborate principles of justice which can guide us in the effort to synchronize the competing claims of individuals and to adjudicate between divergent interpretations of doctrine.

Within the Conference of Critical Legal Studies, there is a well-developed story that, contrary to my reading of Levinas, has represented the deconstruction of antifoundationalist philosophy as the complete loss of the Good — as if such a loss could ever be represented. Although the "irrationalists" in the Conference of Critical Legal Studies rarely cite Levinas, they have been deeply influenced by Derrida, and it is to Derrida that they often attribute their own proposition that the absence of a fully cognizable good leaves us with the irrationality of all legal and ethical choice. Ethical responsibility is reduced to a choice among other choices the individual can make. But, as we have seen in Levinas, responsibility is not a choice at all but an irremissible necessity.

In a more in-depth exploration of the relationship between Derrida and Levinas, the identification of deconstruction with ethical skepticism is a serious misinterpretation. (Indeed, as I have argued elsewhere, the very practice of deconstruction should be understood as a response to the Law of Law as the call to responsibility.)[9] Such a misappropriation of Derrida, however, has serious consequences for the way in which the postmodern story of the tangle of the three realms of the Law of Law, the law of self-legislating subjectivity, and legal rules and legal principles has been understood, at least by the irrationalists in the Conference of Critical Legal Studies.[10]

This misappropriation, in other words, has served as the basis of the first version of the postmodern story as it has been translated into law. The irrationalist story tells us that if there is no "real" Good that can guide us in our day-to-day activities as lawyers and judges, there can be no rational limiting principle by which to judge competing interpretations of legal doctrine. As there is no Good, present or immanent, in social life to guide us, there is also no transcendental ego that can legislate its own law. Instead, we have presented to us a self torn apart by conflicting impulses. The self longs both for community and for individuality, connection and freedom. There can be no hope for a rational reconciliation or synchronization between the competing impulses. Such selves can create only a legal and social order torn apart at the center. As a result of the account of the phenomenology of the self, the Law of Law, or the Good, cannot be replaced by the second realm, the law of the self-legislating subject, because the self cannot overcome the contradictory impulses that rend it apart and therefore become truly self-legislating.[11]

This means that the deconstruction of legal positivism carried forward by the Conference of Critical Legal Studies leaves a vacuum which cannot be filled by an ethical vision. Legal positivism argues that legal systems are self-enclosed hierarchies that generate their own elements and procedures as part of the mechanism of the self-perpetuation of the system. In Anglo-American jurisprudence, legal positivism has traditionally been based on the writing of H. L. A. Hart.[12] Hart proposed that all legal systems are based on a master rule of recognition, which establishes the initial hierarchies of the elements of the legal system. From this master rule of recognition, Hart argued that it would be possible to directly derive two categories of secondary rules: the rules of process by which the law is applied and the rules of prescription we think of as a doctrine in a common law system. The early critique of Hart initiated by Ronald Dworkin[13] showed that interpretation is fundamentally an ethical enterprise, because the derivation of secondary rules cannot escape an appeal to their justification that is based only in the mechanism for the self-generation of the hierarchy of rules. I will not repeat Dworkin's argument here, but I do want to add that the "irrationalists" in the conference have not only shown that rules of procedure cannot escape an appeal to an *outside* ethical justification. They have also shown us that the very idea of a rule as a force that pulls us down the track through each new fact situation, determining the outcome of a particular case, is false. Therefore, no line of precedent can fully determine a particular outcome in a particular case, because the rule itself is always in the process of reinterpretation as it is applied. It is interpretation that gives us the rule and not the other way around. This insight is what has come to be known as the "indeterminacy thesis," which has been mistakenly identified (at times by the proponents of the thesis themselves) with the proposition that there is no institutionalized meaning, no "real" intelligibility of the legal sentence. The "proposition" should instead be understood to be that law cannot be reduced to a set of technical rules, a self-sufficient mechanism that pulls us down the track though each new fact situation. Law, in other words, cannot be reduced to a self-generated and self-validating set of cognitive norms. Interpretation always takes us beyond a mere appeal to the status quo. I will return to the significance of this insistence on the appeal to the beyond as inherent in legal interpretation when I discuss why deconstruction is helpful in rethinking the current debates in American legal circles. It should be noted here, however, that, according to the "irrationalists" in the conference, we cannot replace legal positivism with a rational, ethical vision. Such a vision could only be found through an appeal to the Good, the Law of Law, or to the Right, the law of Kant's self-legislating subject.

As a result, ethical responsibility is reduced to an existential choice. In spite of themselves, the "irrationalists" in the Conference of Critical Legal Studies reinstate the subject-centered approach to the ethical that Levinas and, I would add, Derrida reject. It would be a serious mistake, however, to interpret the "irrationalists" in the Conference of Critical Legal Studies as rejecting the need to make ethical commitments because they are inevitably subjective. Indeed, their insistence on the "irrationality" of personal ethical commitments can itself be understood to have an ethical dimension. In this view, no one can proclaim his/her moral position as the truth of the real. Each one of us is free to make his/her choice. The "irrationalists," in other words, although they have not put it in this way, want to join with Levinas to deny the ultimate hubris of ontology. The "irrationalists" want to interrupt the Logos as "the last dominating all meaning, the word of the end, the very possibility of the ultimate and the result" (*OB*, 19). If one interprets the "irrationalists" to expose—with Derrida and with Levinas—the ethical delimitation of ontology, then it is possible to rethink the ethical significance of their message. Unfortunately, the "irrationalists" in the conference have not adopted this interpretation, reverting instead to a recast existentialism. As a result, they have tended to confuse the deconstruction of the hubris of ontology with radical skepticism and with *Unsinnlosigkeit.*

The central error of the first version of the "postmodern" story, which has made itself felt in the work of the "irrationalists," is to replace the truth of reconciliation with the truth of castration. The Good is forever beyond us. It has no constituting force. The Good is only as absolute absence, as lack. The Good, in other words, does not leave its mark on us. On this reading the "postmodern" conception of the Good resembles one understanding of negative theology. Levinas, on the other hand, is very careful to distinguish the Good, as otherwise than being, from negative theology. The Good does leave its mark. Indeed, the Good constitutes the subject as responsible to the Other.

> The limits of the present in which infinity betrays itself break up. Infinity is beyond the scope of the unity of transcendental apperception, cannot be assembled into a present, and refuses being recollected. This negation of the present and of representation finds its positive form in proximity, responsibility, and substitution. This makes it different from the propositions of negative theology. The refusal of presence is converted into my presence as present, that is, as a hostage delivered over as a gift to the Other. (*OB*, 15)

Derrida has also carefully distinguished himself from the ethical skepticism that proclaims the "truth" of the absent Good as lack: "The difference which interests me here is that—a formula to be understood as one will—the lack does not have its place in dissemination."[14]

There is another version of the significance of the postmodern deconstruction of foundationalist philosophy. This second version has been defended by writers in feminist jurisprudence. Unlike the "irrationalists" in the Conference of Critical Legal Studies, the feminist position does not defend ethical skepticism. The Good is not represented as absent. Instead, the Good is the recognition and acceptance of difference beyond any attempt to categorize others from a universal vantage point.[15] Rather than try to replace legal positivism with explicit ethical principles, we should instead simply accept the fallibility of judicial discretion as a better way to respect difference. Difference, it is argued, belies the attempt to identify universal conditions of equal personhood. It certainly belies the legitimacy of an appeal to the Good in the strong sense as an irremissable necessity for all subjects. But it also rejects the move to achieve universality even within a particular culture. The adoption of legal principles which "universalize" within a particular culture would still, so the argument goes, lead to a formal approach that is reductionist. The good judge is one who recognizes that there is no universal perspective in either of the two above senses of the good from which she speaks. Nor can the law of the transcendental ego replace the appeal to the Good. There are only perspectives that represent different viewpoints. The best the judge can do is to try to sensitively weigh each competing perspective, taking each seriously and refusing to condemn any of the competing perspectives as unworthy of attention ("SC," 90–95). There is an important truth in the insistence that the judge must recognize her own perspective and not pretend to speak as the law of transcendental subjectivity. But the problem, of course, is that we cannot escape the condemning power of law. Law is exclusionary. When the judge vindicates one normative interpretation over another, she necessarily delegitimates, at least for a period of time, one of the competing perspectives. Robert Cover has identified the silencing of competing normative perspectives through legal decision-making as the "jurispathic" aspect of law. In a complex modern state, Cover does not believe we can escape this "imperial" function of the law.

> It is the problem of multiplicity of meaning—the fact that never only one but always many worlds are created by the too fertile forces of jurigenesis—that leads to the imperial virtues and the imperial mode of world maintenance. . . . The sober imperial mode of world maintenance holds the mirror of critical objectivity to meaning, imposes the discipline of institutional justice upon norms, and places the constraint of peace on the void at which strong bonds cease.[16]

As Cover points out, the "jurispathic" aspect of law is necessary for the creation of a legal system that can operate effectively as a state-organized mechanism of social control. It is also, however, part of the development of law as a *nomos,* which creates a normative legal world and which helps to reengender a sense of belonging to a "community." The power of law to establish "universal" principles within a community both represents imperial power and its ability to regenerate the paideic pattern of law-making as world of shared percepts.

> The paideic is an etude on the theme of unity. Its primary psychological motif is attachment. The unity of every paideia is being shattered—shattered, in fact, with its very creation. The imperial is an etude on the theme of diversity. Its primary psychological motif is separation. The diversity of every such world is being consumed from its onset by domination. Thus, as the meaning in a *nomos* disintegrates, we seek to rescue it—to maintain some coherence in the awesome proliferation of meaning lost as it is created—by unleashing upon the fertile but weakly organized jurisgenerative cells an organizing principle itself incapable of producing the normative meaning that is life and growth. ("NN," 109–10)

It is precisely the "jurisgenerative" power of law to create normative meaning that makes law other than a mere mechanism of social control. Since the "jurispathic" aspect of law inheres in its "jurisgenerative" power to create unified meaning through the establishment of generalizable or universalizable standards, we cannot escape the comparison of competing normative visions through the appeal to ethical principles. Nor do we want all differences to be recognized by the law. To do so carries within it the very real danger of legally freezing hierarchies already in place. We do, indeed, need principles developed through the appeal to contextual universals by which we can distinguish between differences we want to be recognized by the law from those we condemn in the name of justice. But, of course, the question remains: do we need an appeal to the Good which is the universal?

Before returning to that question, we can still insist that the mistake made in this version of feminist jurisprudence is to try to *directly* translate the postmodern insight that the Good is not, as Hegel tried to show in his *Logic,* fully actual in the real into the practice of legal decision-making. But it is precisely because the Good can never be simply identified with a state of affairs that we need not fear its oppressive power to obliterate difference. The attempt at direct translation of the ethical relation into the sphere of law misunderstands the central insight of Levinas's philosophy of alternity. The ethical relation, even as it is an irremissible necessity, cannot be fully enacted in the actual. The ethical relation can only be conceived within time as a diachronic "power." As a result, the Good can never be fully enacted in space. That is why, as a prescriptive command, it points us toward the future. The Good can only be translated differently because there is no state of affairs that the command "Be just" mandates as its exact fulfillment. Yet, this being said, the command "Be just" does turn us to the situation at hand. It is only within a specific situation that we can meet the command, and the specific situation in the legal context is what gives us the contextual universals. Of course, it is true that legal principles inevitably categorize, identify, and in that sense violate difference by creating analogies between the like and the unlike. If we cannot escape this violation of difference in a legal system, however, we can still develop principles that minimize it. Even so, law is inevitably unfaithful to the ethical relationship. But if law inevitably violates difference through the establishment of shared meaning and generalized standards, should we not then attempt to escape from legality altogether? Levinas clearly thinks not.

As Levinas reminds us, we are inevitably fated to fall into law, understood now as a system of legal principles, because I am never just alone with the Other. The entry of the third is inevitable, and with the entry of the third comes the need to make comparisons and to synchronize the competing demands of individuals within the space of a given legal system.

The third party interrupts the face-to-face. It is with the third party that justice begins. But the call to justice should not be understood as an unfortunate empirical necessity given that we are never just alone with the Other.

> It is not that the entry of a third party would be an empirical fact, and that my responsibility for the other finds itself constrained to a calculus by the "force of things." In the proximity of the other, all the others than the other obsess me, and already this obsession cries out for justice, demands measure and knowing, is consciousness. (*OB*, 158)

The aspiration to a just and egalitarian state proceeds from the irreducible responsibility of the subject to the Others. Each other has her claim, and her claim must be heeded. All claims, however, cannot be vindicated even if they must be heard. We need legal principles that guide us through the maze of competing legal interpretations, precisely because all claims cannot be vindicated. "The extraordinary commitment of the other to the third party calls for control, a search for justice, society, and the State, comparison and possession, thought and science, commerce and philosophy, and outside of anarchy, the search for a principle" (*OB*, 161).

As I use the term here, a principle is not a rule, at least not in the sense of a force that literally pulls us down the tracks and fully determines the act of interpretation. A principle is instead only a guiding light. It involves the appeal to and enrichment of the "universal" within a particular *nomos*. We can think of a principle as the light that comes from the lighthouse, a light that guides us and prevents us from going in the wrong direction. A principle, however, cannot determine the exact route we must take in any particular case. A principle, in other words, does not pretend that there is only one right answer. It can, however, serve to guide us by indicating when we are going in the wrong direction. If a principle cannot give us one right answer, it can help us define what answers are wrong in the sense of being incompatible with its realization. For example, we might not all agree what the principle of reciprocal symmetry means, but given its historical significance as the expression of the breakdown of the vertical relations of law, we can rule out certain legal outcomes as incompatible with its realization. An example that Hegel himself often used is the legal rejection in modernity of all forms of indentured servitude. Of course, this mode of interpretation is circular, but the very structure of legal argumentation is that we argue from within the *nomos* of law. In this specific sense, the form of legal interpretation is that of discovery. As for which principles we ultimately adopt within the *nomos,* we are left with the process of pragmatic justification based on the ability of a principle to *synchronize* the competing universals embodied in the *nomos.* A jurisprudence of principle, then, can survive the indeterminacy thesis, which reminds us that a rule cannot be fully determinative of the outcome of a particular case. A legal principle, of course, even as I have just described, would not necessarily involve the appeal to the Good in the sense of an irreversible necessity for all subjects. But, as I will suggest, in the end, it does.

This process of elaborating principles of justice involves what Levinas calls "thematization" in the said, the world of established representational systems. Thematization in postmodern philosophy is a term of art meaning the synchronization of the Good with Being in such a way as to purportedly deny the diachronic force of time. But we can also explain thematization more prosaically. Thematization can be understood to be the need to sound the common themes within the *nomos,* so that it is possible to appeal to contextual principles. This attempt to sound the common themes still has the effect of synchronizing the good with being as a given state of legal affairs, because it appeals to the Good as it has manifested itself, even if only as unrealized potential. An essential aspect of thematization is the practical use of *reason* to synchronize the competing demands and perspectives of individuals through the appeal to legal principle. Reason, in other words, is essential to thematization, and thematization inheres in the narratives we develop to justify a particular state of legal affairs. As Robert Cover has explained:

> No set of legal institutions or prescriptions exists apart from the narratives that locate it and give it meaning. For every constitution there is an epic, for each decalogue a scripture. Once understood in the context of the narratives that give it meaning, law becomes not merely a system of rules to be observed, but a world in which we live. ("NN," 95)

In this sense, law is embedded in ontology, in a shared social reality. But as the *nomos,* it is also a "critical" point within ontology. This critical point is what allows us to engage in the struggle within our *nomos* to meet the command "Be just." Thematization, then, is never just descriptive. It is precisely the critical, normative dimension of law that demands reasonable assessment of competing legal principles. "Reason consists in ensuring the co-existence of these terms, the coherence of the one and the other despite their difference, in the unity of a theme; it ensures the agreement of the different terms without breaking up the present in which the theme is held," says Levinas (*OB,* 165). Reason is not understood to ground legal principles in the traditional neo-Kantian sense. But it is a serious mistake to confuse *Grundlosigkeit* with irrationalism.

In law, reason is a "practical faith" we are called upon to exercise as an essential aspect of the task of elaborating principles of justice. But, of course, if reason cannot ground legal principle in the foundationalist sense through the appeal to the law of the self-legislating subject, we must be ready to concede to the force of the better interpretation. The exercise of practical reason, in other words, demands that we continually engage in dialogue with one another. It demands that we make a Derridean double gesture. We need to recognize both that thematization in law is necessary and that no thematization into a system of justice can pretend to have the last word as the truth of a "reconstructive science." We must encourage the process of interruption of any current state of legal affairs, not in the name of the irrationality of competing narratives, but in the name of the exercise of reason itself which demands that we participate in the acts of judgment to which the command "Be just" calls us. The Derridean double gesture invites us to new worlds as part of the very commitment to reason. The commitment to reason is essential to the exercise of ethical responsibility to the Other.

On the other hand, both Levinas and Derrida remind us that without a foundationalist conception of reason in either the neo-Kantian or the Hegelian sense, the "secularization" of the modern world will remain incomplete. I am defining secularization as the process "where ideas and knowledge are detached from their original source, and become accessible to human reason under its own power." [17] It is the reminder of the inevitability of incomplete secularization that has led to the accusation that "postmodernism" is "premodernism" in disguise and therefore an inherently conservative intellectual movement. It is, of course, true that both Derrida and Levinas reject the organization of time determined *teleologically* by an idea of emancipation. If one identifies modernity with a teleological organization of time guided by an idea of emancipation, then and only then can Derrida and Levinas be understood to reject modernity. Ironically, the very disjuncture between the modern and the postmodern implies the very linear, narrative organization of time that both thinkers reject. Both thinkers recognize the necessity of thematization as the projection of ideals and principles of justice. It would, then, be more correct to envision the relationship between, on the one hand, the modern call to realize universal principles of justice within the *nomos,* and, on the other, the postmodern insight that we can never escape the interplay of the three realms, as a "laying beside" essential to the practice of dialogic fallibilism. First of all, it reminds us of the status of the narratives we tell in order to "ground" our system of justice. The narratives we tell to justify one state of legal affairs over another are just that, narratives. They can only be judged practically.

But the crucial message inherent in the recognition of incomplete secularization is even more explicitly ethical. Derrida in particular always wants to remind us, with Cover, of the "jurispathic" aspect of any claim to normative closure, particularly in a legal system. Derrida is only too aware of the power of law to enforce institutionalized legal meaning. Once we correctly interpret the ethical concern of the "double gesture," we can hear the message in the deconstruction of Rousseau's "delusion of presence mastered" other than as a defense of ethical skepticism, because all ethical systems are inevitably opened in violence. As Derrida says, "There is no ethics without the presence *of the other* but also, and consequently, without absence, dissimulation, detour and difference, writing. The arche-writing is the origin of morality as of immorality. The non-ethical opening of ethics. A violent opening." [18]

It is, of course, possible to interpret the above quotation to indicate that we can never "ethically" choose between competing normative thematizations, since they all originate in a "non-ethical opening." It is this interpretation of deconstruction that has led thoughtful commentators of Levinas to argue that Derrida is deaf to the ethical voice of Saying. Certainly, Levinas would disagree with the position that holds that ethical thematizations inevitably have a violent opening, insisting instead that the "opening" of the ethical in the face-to-face is not violent. I would defend Levinas's interpretation of the nonoriginal but also nonviolent opening of the ethical. But I want to give a different emphasis to the above quotation. If all ethical thematizations are "equal" in the sense that they cannot claim to be grounded in first principles, then we must always recognize the *"equal claim"* of competing interpretations to be heard. If all interpretations are "ungrounded," then no interpretation can *theoretically* win out, shutting off from the very beginning the need for practical debate and assessment. Deconstruction has certainly shown us that the claim to inherent *theoretical* superiority of one ethical system over another is unfounded. But on the interpretation I am offering here, it would also be unethical to theoretically reduce to an inferior position the standing of competing normative perspectives. The real challenge we are left with as law professors, lawyers, and judges in the wake of deconstruction has been eloquently summarized by Cover: "The challenge presented by the absence of a single, 'objective' interpretation is, instead, the need to maintain a sense of legal meaning despite the destruction of any pretense of superiority of one *nomos* over another" ("NN," 143). The truth of *Grundlosigkeit* is that we are to be forever left with that challenge. We are called to remain open to the invitation to create new worlds.

I have so far emphasized the close relationship between Derrida and Levinas that is evident once deconstruction is read ethically. On an ethical reading, deconstruction does not mark the inevitable delimitation of ontology in order to drop us into the abyss of skepticism and irrationalism. Instead, deconstruction exposes ethical "transcendence" within the very iteration of the same. Derrida continuously shows us that the same is not a totality closed in upon itself. As we have seen, it is also a mistake to read Levinas as if the Good was absolutely Other. In *Otherwise than Being,* Levinas seeks to indicate just how the unsayable echoes in the Saying of the said. The Good "is" in the day-to-day confrontation with the Other. (In his most recent essay on Levinas, Derrida clearly echoes the cry of ethical revolt of Saying.[19] Derrida, too, then, is concerned to heed the echo of the call in the Saying of the said.)

But there is a subtle difference between the two thinkers that makes a difference and that is rarely brought to light because the ethical message of deconstruction has been obscured by the interpretation of Derrida as our latest "irrationalist." Derrida's first essay on Levinas is often interpreted to show that the very necessities of the language in which Levinas must speak of the breakup of the domination of the logos inevitably reinscribes his testament in the language of ontology.[20] Of course, Derrida does make this point. But Derrida's emphasis in this essay is not on the inevitable fall back into ontology. He is not just concerned to show us that Levinas's project is dragged back into the "is." Instead, Derrida emphasizes the "self-transcendence" of the Same. The iteration of the same "is" as transformation. Even if Levinas is read to displace the rigid dichotomy of transcendence and immanence—and I believe this is how he should be read—he does not, like Derrida, focus our attention on the self-transcendence of the Same. Derrida always seeks to protect the radical difference of the not yet of the Saying, but he also exposes the iteration of the Same as an infinite spiral of possibility. I am aware that Derrida is rarely read as a thinker of transformative possibility. Certainly, what I am offering is an interpretation of deconstruction. But I believe that the interpretation I offer is "true" to Derrida's deconstruction of Levinas. Deconstruction, then, is not the witness to the paralysis of "repetition." To come around again is to reevolve; in this specific sense it involves a reevaluation. Derrida does not focus on "the deadly work of paralysis" because he thinks we are helpless. Instead, he makes us think differently about the beyond. Iteration "is" as possibility, because a system of representation given to us in language cannot be self-identical with itself and therefore truly a totality. This possibility is an "opening" to the beyond as a threshold we are invited to cross. As "a science of the threshold," deconstruction dares us to make the commitment to "crossover" and perhaps, by so doing, to avoid the horror of having the door of the Law of Law finally shut in our faces. Derrida, in other words, can be understood to more successfully displace the dichotomy of transcendence and immanence through the exposure of the "immanence" of ethical alternity in the iteration.

This displacement is important in the legal interpretation of a system of norms. The Good, as it is interpreted to be manifested in the *nomos,* is never simply the mere repetition of conventional norms, because there can be no mere repetition. In this sense, the Good, or the Law of Law, cannot be conceived as the truth of a self-enclosed system that perpetuates itself. The dissemination of convention as a self-enclosed legal system does not leave us with a fundamental lack but with an opening. What I am suggesting is that the dissemination of convention through *différance* "as the non-full, non-simple, and differentiating" origin of "differences"[21] disrupts the claims of ontology to fill the universe, and more specifically the legal universe. This means that there cannot be the normative closure upon which the positivist insists. The Good is beyond any of its current justifications. As a result, when we appeal "back" to what has been established, we must *look* forward to what "might be." As we do so, we represent what "might be." Without a simple origin, the very process of discovery of legal principles from within the *nomos* will also involve invention. It is this specific appeal to the "ought to be" that demands a vision of redemption that goes beyond the appeal to convention. The "origin" we evoke in our thematizations is ultimately a representation of the future. Legal interpretation demands that we remember the future.

Thus, the deconstructive emphasis on the opening of the ethical self-transcendence of a system which exposes the threshold of the "beyond" of the not yet is crucial to any conception of legal interpretation that argues that the "is" of Law can never be completely separated from the elaboration of the "should be" dependent on an appeal to the Good. Ethical alternity is not just the command of the Other; it is also the Other within the *nomos* that invites us to new worlds and reminds us that transformation is not only possible but inevitable.

There cannot be the radical immanence insisted upon by legal positivism, because the "is" of the so-called legal system is never a totality that generates its own evolution. However, even if we agreed that law as a system of norms demanded an appeal to the Good, we would still be within legal positivism if the norms could be mandated as a self-enclosed system. Derrida, then, is extremely helpful to us in the development of an understanding of Law as the *nomos* which is not reducible to the objective meaning of established legal convention—because the Good of the *nomos* is itself always undergoing transformation—and which at the same time is not just a utopian projection from the outside. Again to quote Robert Cover:

> Law may be viewed as a system of tension or a bridge linking a concept of reality to an imagined alternative—that is, as a connection between two states of affairs, both of which can be represented in their normative significance only through the devices of narrative. Thus, one constitutive element of a *nomos* is the phenomenon George Stevens has labeled "alternity," the "Other than the case," the counter-factual propositions, images, shapes of will and evasion with which we charge

> our mental being and by means of which we build the chang-
> ing, largely fictive milieu for our somatic and our social exis-
> tence. ("NN," 101)

This link between the Other, the more of a given state of legal affairs, is also the threshold we are constantly invited to cross through the de-limitation of ontology, which in turn creates the opening for "new" inter-pretations. This link, the "threshold," is both the invitation to cross over, the call to interpretation, and yet a barrier to full accessibility. As both a bar-rier and an invitation, it is also the Derridean hymen. This call to interpre-tation is continually echoed in deconstruction. "As in *La folie du jour* by Maurice Blanchot, the law does not command without demanding to be read, deciphered, translated. It demands transference (Ubertragung and Ubersetzung and Uberleben). The *double bind* is in the Law." [22]

As we have seen for Cover, the double bind in the law includes the "jurispathic" aspect of law in the very search for and assertion of "paideic" unity within the community. Law creates a normative world by imposing itself in the name of the reconciled whole. But if the "recon-ciled whole" is no longer thought to be the truth of the actual as in Hegel, then it is always a myth. It is made true through the very power of the state to assert its meaning and vision against that of other communities. "There is, however, danger in forgetting the limits which are intrinsic to this activity of legal interpretation; in exaggerating the extent to which any interpretation rendered as part of the act of state violence can ever constitute a common and coherent meaning" ("VW," 236).

The "jurispathic" power of legal decision-making concerned Cover in his "Supreme Court Foreword," but there he saw not just the necessity but the inevitability of interpretation. But, in his essay "Violence and the Word," written shortly before his death, the mythic status of any narrative of a reconciled whole led Cover to conclude that the very act of interpre-tation masked the violence of the imposition of the legal sentence. Cover used the example of the criminal defendant to graphically make his point that the "community interest" with which the criminal himself was sup-posed to identify was clearly a myth. The criminal "goes along" with the sentence not because he recognizes the validity of what is happening to him in the name of a shared communal standard, the Good, but because of the enforcement power of the state.

> Revolutionary constitutional understandings are commonly
> staked in blood. In them, the violence of the Law takes its most
> blatant form. But the relationship between legal interpretation

and the infliction of pain remains operative even in the most routine of legal acts. The act of sentencing a convicted defendant is among the most routine of acts performed by judges. Yet it is immensely revealing of the way in which interpretation is shaped by violence. First, examine the event from the perspective of the defendant. The defendant's world is threatened. But he sits, usually quietly, as if engaged in civil discourse. If convicted, the defendant customarily walks—escorted—to prolonged confinement, usually without significant disturbance to the civil appearance of the event. It is, of course, grotesque to assume that the civil facade is "voluntary" except in the sense that it represents the defendant's autonomous recognition of the overwhelming array of violence ranged against him, and of the hopelessness of resistance and outcry. ("VW," 210)

The "Good" of the community is not the Good of the criminal. Yet, of course, if the Law of Law had been fully actualized, there would only be the one shared Good, which is why Hegel insisted that the criminal could be "reconciled" to his sentence. Both the victim and the criminal experience the rift in community caused by the criminal act. This rift unleashes "the causality of fate" in which the community seeks to overcome the rift through the punishment of the victim, who is respected as an ethical being, precisely in and through his punishment. The criminal is an ethical being since he, too, is inserted in the reign of the realized Good. Legal interpretation is fidelity to the Law of Law as the realized Good enacted even in the criminal sentence. The Hegelian system pretends to heal the rift that Cover wants to remind us cannot be healed. Thus, the danger of legal interpretation for Cover is that since it purports to heal the rift, it blinds us to the wound or the fragmentation of our so-called community as we violate the perspective of the other in the criminal sentence. "'Law' is never just a mental or spiritual act. A legal world is built only to the extent that there are commitments that place bodies on the line. The torture of the martyr is an extreme and repulsive forum of the organized violence of institutions. It reminds us that the interpretive commitments are realized, indeed, in the flesh" ("VW," 208).

The legal system as a mechanism of social control operates through the inscription of the sentence on the backs of its victims. And yet what Cover at least recognized in his "Supreme Court Foreword" was that the appeal to universality in the name of a shared good embodied in the narratives of legal opinions is not only inevitable; it is also essential to the creation of the Law as *nomos.* Therefore, we cannot escape the task of interpretation. Cover's suspicion of the power of the state led him to conclude that we can now only find shared meaning without violence in smaller communities that cannot impose their *nomos* against others through force. But this belies his own insight that the very search for "paideic" unity is exclusionary and, indeed, "jurispathic."

This is the profound sense in which Derrida, on the other hand, recognizes that we cannot escape the "double bind" of the Law of Law. The Law of Law calls us to interpretation, and this process of interpretation appeals to the promise of a reconciled whole, or the Good, which is itself only an interpretation and not the last word on what the Good of the community actually could be. Indeed, it cannot be the last word, once we understand that even the appeal "back" to established principle cannot avoid the projection forward of the "might be," since the origin is simply not there. Even so, the Law of Law is that we justify our interpretation through an appeal to the Good. What Derrida says of translation could equally well be said of legal interpretation.

> Translation, as holy growth of languages, announces the messianic end, surely, but the sign of that end and of that growth is "present" (*gegenwärtig*) only in the "knowledge of the distance," in the Entfurnung, *the remoteness* that relates us to it. Yet it puts us in contact with that "language of the truth" which is the "true language" ("so ist diese Sprache der Wahrheit—die Wahre Sprache"). This contact takes place in the mode of "presentiment," in the "intensive" mode that renders present what is absent, that allows remoteness to approach as remoteness, *fort:da.*[23]

But the "contact" is still there; at the same time, we cannot know its full meaning. Yet, when one legal interpretation is vindicated as to what constitutes the Good, it is imposed upon the other as if the Good had been achieved. Indeed, as Cover reminds us, this seeking to impose or universalize one's vision is the central characteristic of redemptive legal movements. Cover defines redemptive legal movements as follows:

> I shall use "redemptive constitutionalism" as a label for the positions of associations whose sharply different visions of the social order require a transformational politics that cannot be contained within the autonomous insularity of the association itself. . . . Redemption takes place within an eschatological schema that postulates: (1) the unredeemed character of real-

ity as we know it, (2) the fundamentally different reality that should take its place, and (3) the replacement of the one with the other. ("NN," 132)

The "projection" of a redeemed world and the commitment to realize it in this one should be understood as an essential part of thematization. But this entails the opposition to the current state of legal affairs. The most obvious example of a "redemptive legal movement" is the struggle to overthrow and outlaw apartheid in South Africa. This movement does not, it should be noted, just plead that apartheid is immoral in South Africa. It insists that apartheid is wrong at any time and in any place. The resistance movement does not then appeal to the cultural good of a specific context but to the universal Good. If apartheid was outlawed,[24] the normative view of the whites who had enforced their legal sentence on the flesh of blacks would indeed be silenced. And this would be violence to their "difference." But as Derrida, among others, has reminded us, it is a deserved and necessary "violence" we are called to by any version of the Good worthy of its name. As I have already suggested, the reminder about the violent opening of ethics is not made to paralyze us. The double bind that inheres in the call to legal interpretation means that we must make a double gesture as part of the very commitment to the ethical responsibility to which we are called. We must both accept the challenge of thematization, including the projection of a redeemed world, and acknowledge the status of any interpretation we offer. The "double gesture" does, however, express the humility and, indeed, the humor that must be kept if we are to avoid the abuses of an apocalyptic rhetoric.

It would be a serious mistake, then, to read the testament of the "postmodern" story of the three realms—the Law of Law, the law of self-legislating subjectivity, and the principles of a legal system—as the witness to the inevitability of nihilism. Of course, to tell a story is to side with diachronic allegory, which "pretends to know how to tell stories," rather than the other figure of memory, the synchronic allegory "that feigns amnesia."[25] But then we must risk the story in order to counter the mistaken account that identifies deconstruction with nihilism. Deconstruction reminds us that the meaning of the "ethical" is necessarily displaced into the future because the Good is not fully present to the mind, as it is in Hegel's system. Interpretation is transformation, and as we interpret we are responsible for the direction of that transformation. We cannot escape the responsibility implicit in every act of interpretation. The delimitation of ontology reminds us of the positivist fallacy that the legal world is just given to us as a self-perpetuating mechanism. We are left with a reminder of the inescapability of our responsibility for the *nomos* as it is perpetuated and thus transformed.

Notes

1. Maurice Blanchot, *The Writing of the Disaster,* trans. Ann Smock (Lincoln: University of Nebraska Press, 1986), 144.

2. Franz Kafka, *The Penal Colony, Stories, and Short Pieces,* trans. Willa and Edwin Muir (New York: Schocken, 1948), 191–227.

3. Robert Cover, "Violence and the Word," in *Narrative, Violence, and the Law: The Essays of Robert Cover,* ed. Martha Minow, Michael Ryan, and Austin Sarat (Ann Arbor: University of Michigan Press, 1992), 203; hereafter abbreviated "VW" and cited parenthetically in the text.

4. For an excellent discussion of why *Grundlosigkeit* should not be identified with *Unsinnlosigkeit,* see Richard J. Bernstein, *Beyond Objectivism and Relativism* (Philadelphia: University of Pennsylvania Press, 1983).

5. D. Cornell, "Institutionalization of Meaning, Recollective Imagination, and the Potential for Transformation in Legal Interpretation," *Penn. Law Review* 136, no. 2 (1988): 1135–1229.

6. Emmanuel Levinas, *Totality and Infinity,* trans. Alphonso Lingis (Pittsburgh: Duquesne University Press, 1969), 7–8; hereafter abbreviated *TI* and cited parenthetically in the text.

7. Emmanuel Levinas, *Otherwise than Being: or, Beyond Essence,* trans. Alphonso Lingis (The Hague: Martinus Nijhoff, 1981), 139; hereafter abbreviated *OB* and cited parenthetically in the text.

8. Blanchot, *The Writing of the Disaster,* 2.

9. D. Cornell, "Post-Structuralism: The Ethical Relation, and the Law," *Cardozo Law Review* 9, no. 6 (August 1988): 1587.

10. See G. Peller, "The Metaphysics of American Law," *Calif. Law Review,* 73, no. 4 (1985): 1160–70.

11. See Duncan Kennedy, "Form and Substance in Private Adjudication," 89 *Harvard Law Review* 89, no. 8 (1976):1685.

12. See H. L. A. Hart, *The Concept of Law* (Oxford: Clarendon Press, 1961).

13. Ronald Dworkin, *Taking Rights Seriously* (Cambridge, Mass.: Harvard University Press, 1978).

14. Jacques Derrida, *The Post Card: From Socrates to Freud and Beyond,* trans. Alan Bass (Chicago: University of Chicago Press, 1987), 441.

15. M. Minow, "The Supreme Court, 1986 Term—Foreword: Justice En-

gendered," *Harvard Law Review* 101, no. 1 (1987): 10; hereafter abbreviated "SC" and cited parenthetically in the text.

16. Robert Cover, "Nomos and Narrative," in *Narrative, Violence, and the Law,* 109; hereafter abbreviated "NN" and cited parenthetically in the text. Cover's essay was originally published as "The Supreme Court, 1982 Term—Foreword: Nomos and Narrative," *Harvard Law Review* 97, no. 1 (1983): 4–68.

17. M. Stallmann, *Was ist Sakularisierung* (Tübingen: J. C. B. Mohr, 1960), 33; my translation.

18. Jacques Derrida, *Of Grammatology,* trans. Gayatri Chakravorty Spivak (Baltimore: Johns Hopkins University Press, 1976), 140.

19. Jacques Derrida, "At This Very Moment in This Work Here I Am," trans. Robin Berezdivin, in *Re-reading Levinas,* ed. Robert Bernasconi and Simon Critchley (London: Routledge, 1990), 11–48.

20. Jacques Derrida, "Violence and Metaphysics," in *Writing and Difference,* trans. Alan Bass (Chicago: University of Chicago Press, 1978), 79–153.

21. Jacques Derrida, "Différance," in *Margins of Philosophy,* trans. Alan Bass (Chicago: University of Chicago Press, 1982), 11.

22. Jacques Derrida, "Des Tours de Babel," in *Difference in Translation,* trans. and ed. Joseph F. Graham (Ithaca, N.Y.: Cornell University Press, 1985), 184.

23. Ibid., 203.

24. This essay was written in 1988, before the abolition of apartheid.

25. Jacques Derrida, *Memories for Paul de Man,* trans. Cecile Lindsay et al., ed. Avital Ronell and Eduardo Cadava (New York: Columbia University Press, 1986).

Aesthetic Truth

Production or "Letting Be"

R. Radhakrishnan

The relationship of Martin Heidegger to post-structuralist thought is profoundly problematic and ambivalent. On the one hand, it is clearly demonstrable that the works of Michel Foucault and Jacques Derrida would not have been possible but for the prior intervention of Heidegger;[1] post-structuralist readings of philosophy repeatedly receive and reconstruct Heideggerian thought as a point of departure for their own "break" with the tradition. On the other hand, though Heidegger's thinking makes it possible for succeeding thinkers to call into question and "de-struct" the entire metaphysical onto-theological tradition, it does not succeed in achieving such an epistemological "break" on its own behalf. In the final analysis, Heideggerian thought remains complicit with what it critiques. To put it in Derrida's terms, the same Heidegger who taught us "to turn the pages of philosophy in a certain way," alas, himself gets caught in that "turn." The chief reason why Heidegger's thought folds back into metaphysical closure, according to Derrida, is Heidegger's obsession with a certain primordial, originary, and preconstituted Being or Presence.[2] It is not that such an investment in itself is conservative and recuperative, but rather that there is something in Heidegger's rhetoric that thematizes Being as Presence rather than as radical absence. And this to me is the important question: is Heidegger's thinking recuperative and conservative and, if so, to what purpose and to what end? My focus in this essay will be on Heidegger's treatment of the "work of art" and the kind of hermeneutic commitment that it exacts from him. It seems to me that it is in the context of the work of art that Heidegger's thinking is called upon to enact and thematize some of its basic and constitutive contradictions.

It is significant that the two concepts that govern and direct the essay "The Origin of the Work of Art"[3] are "origin" and "Truth"; the third subterranean concept is that of "nature." What is the origin of a work of art and how does this origin express the nature of the work of art? How is such a nature coincident with its own truth? How can such a truth be disclosed as "speaking naturally" and speaking on behalf of itself, that is, how does the artwork set truth into work without any ontological loss? And finally, how should the critical-hermeneutic act or intervention conduct itself in a way that is both a historical intervention in the nature and the origin of the work of art and at the same time a way of "letting the artwork be"? How does the artwork enable us to understand, historically and allegorically, the nature of the horizonal relationship between the anteriority of Being as Truth and the secondarity of Method?[4] Is the anteriority of Being as Truth itself a product of the hermeneutic will or is it of the order of an absolute "always already" that is transcendent of the positivity of the human will to knowledge? How does the figurality of the truth set in work in the work of art interpellate and constitute the human subject? And finally, when Heidegger responds to the call of the work of art, to what exactly is he responding: to an originary historicity, to his own determinate historicity, or to the conflictual tension between a perennial primordiality and the finite contingency of an anthropocentric historicity?

Heidegger begins his essay with a definition of "origin": "Origin here means that from and by which something is what it is and as it is" ("OWA," 17). The question then arises: can anything be understood except in terms of its origin? Is it possible to produce a theory of knowledge without also meditating reverentially on the origin of the object of study? The origin, to Heidegger, protects the object of study from the deracinating violence of the epistemological enterprise. But how is it possible for thought to understand something without at the same time denaturalizing, decontextualizing, and transforming it? Are we then back to the canonical opposition between knowledge as adequate representation and knowledge as production? What is in question here is the ontological/ historical and cognitive status of the origin.

First, the origin could be construed as something transcendent and authoritative. What we would be left with in that case is some form of foundationalism that in mandating the split between the originary and the secondary, the transcendent and the historical, would seek to contain the diachronic dispersions of history within the synchrony of a primordial presence. Such an epistemology would also contain the historicity of method within the transcendent nomology of Truth. Second, we could deconstruct the notion of an absolute origin and propose a transformative epistemology that would insist that origins are themselves the products of retroactive historical operations. We could then develop a notion of progressive historicity that is incommensurable with notions of truth as origin and abiding Presence. Such an epistemology would have no hesitation in equating the historicity of progressive thought with the momentum of denaturalization and deregionalization. Indeed, the production of truth would be coextensive with the destruction of the protective aura of origin.[5] This model would be based on neither an *arche* nor a *telos* but would respond to the very immanence of the thinking process as it constitutes both itself and the object of its cognition. A third alternative is an epistemology or a thinking style that perennially raises and erases the question of origin, that is, given the ontology of the origin, critical-hermeneutic thinking finds itself committed to a "double session"[6] whereby it can neither entirely do away with (that is, prehistoricize) the origin nor be entirely determined by it. The origin is represented in its very unrepresentability, and systems of thought are condemned to fetishize the absence of "the origin" within their own contemporaneous materiality. I do not have the opportunity here to go into some of the distinctions between Heideggerian destruction and Derridean deconstruction, but suffice it to say that, in general, Derrida's protocols of reading seek to put the very origin in question, whereas Heidegger attempts to shore up a certain authority as well as authenticity on behalf of a timelessly autochthonous notion of the origin.

In the name of what is this shoring up undertaken? The very first paragraphs of Heidegger's essay make it clear that Heidegger is interested in "letting the art work be." But it also turns out that the principle of *Gelassenheit* to which Heidegger resorts to protect the artwork from epistemological violence is itself an ideologically loaded polemic. As Derrida and others have pointed out, Heidegger's polemic seeks to revitalize the centrality of the aesthetic mode and the ability of this mode to engender a sense of authentic contemporaneity.[7] How is art to be validated and in the name of what is it to be celebrated?

With the locution "in the name of," we have touched a central nerve in the problematic. In the name of what does Heidegger address the work of art and in the name of what does he legitimate and valorize the work of art? One could say, "in the name of Art itself." To quote from Heidegger's text: "In themselves and in their interrelations artist and work *are* each of them by virtue of a third thing which is prior to both, namely that which also gives artist and work of art their names—art" ("OWA," 17). Heidegger is careful to isolate and capitalize the third element, art itself, within whose aprioristic and given authority the artist, the artwork, and, we could add, the philosopher-interpreter assume an equiprimordial valence. What is important to notice is the necessary priority or the absolute antecedence of *art-as-such*, which needs to be both posited and left alone, that is, protected. *Art-as-such*, in whose name the artist and the artwork receive their baptism, is (1) a name; (2) a name under erasure; and (3) the allegorical name of a name that is not to be entirely instantiated in and exhausted by the revelatory process that is at work in the artwork. The name, then, in whose name Heidegger shores up the truth is nothing other than the reality of the frame, the *parergon* that resists totalization and plenary semanticization. As Derrida suggests, as soon as the *parergon* takes place, it dismantles the most reassuring conceptual oppositions;[8] and here we must keep in mind the thoroughgoing rigor with which Heidegger plays out and displaces such overdetermined oppositions as "in" and "out" and "form" and "content." But the question that we need to ask here is: can the "truth" of the *parergon* be thought of as a truth at all? In many ways what we are talking about here is the process of "framing." When the "supplemental" logic of the frame secedes from the truth of that which is to be framed, it sets in motion an infinite regress that cannot be finally accommodated; and so, why does Heidegger, in spite of his method, seek to accommodate Being?

I would like to digress a little at this point just to be able to show how momentous this dispute over the nature of "framing" is particularly in a post-structuralist context. I would like to recall the controversy between

Lacan and Derrida regarding the nature of meaning in "The Purloined Letter." Derrida's critique of an otherwise radical Lacanian reading is that in the final analysis Lacan triangulates the story in the name of psychoanalytic truth or certitude. What Derrida points to is the violence of "naming" the truth and the ideological foreclosure we all participate in when we finally arrive at the truth of the text. The Lacanian thesis, though it is radical vis-à-vis a metaphysical and phenomenological thesis of meaning as interiority, perpetrates a violence of its own when it names truth as the truth of psychoanalysis. In other words, the open-ended frame, which denominationally cannot be anybody's frame, is made to ossify into a terminal frame. And psychoanalytic truth takes on a magisterial and axiological name that refuses to problematize its own authority and will to meaning. What Derrida then does by way of undoing this sclerosis is to detriangulate the Lacanian reading by opening up a fourth frame within the Poe story: the frame of literature or the frame of rhetoricity that had been silenced by the Lacanian thesis. By doing this, Derrida attempts to open up the textual field to free play all over again.[9] But here again the question crops up: in the name of what authority is this deconstructive operation being performed? If the answer is "literature," then we are faced with the same problem: the authority of psychoanalysis has been replaced by the authority of literature; in other words, what has changed is the "content" or the valence that occupies the structure called "in the name of," but not that structure itself. In attempting to make available what Heidegger would call "the Open," both Lacan and Derrida could be deemed guilty of naming and thus losing the Open altogether, unless we understand "literature" and "psychoanalysis" as allegorical non-names that are simultaneous with the decapitated or subjectless process of reading itself. Heidegger, Lacan, and Derrida are troubled by the way "man transposes his propositional way of understanding things into the structure of the thing itself" ("OWA," 24).

In Heidegger's hermeneutic encounter with the work of art we can witness three agonistic or conflictual tensions. First, there is the tension between the self-presencing of Truth and the representational model through and in spite of which such a presencing takes place or is disclosed. Second, there is the circular hermeneutic tension between the ontological status of truth and the historical-phenomenological foregrounding of the act of understanding. Once the questioner is included within the question, it becomes virtually impossible to exorcize the historicity of the questioner. And third, there is the tension between the anthropocentric positivity of the mode and form of understanding and the nature of that which is to be known in all its self-seclusion. Here, decidedly, Heidegger's concern is with the ecology of knowledge production: the concern not to hurt Being with our conative, appetitive, and purposive knowledge of it.

It is in this triple context that I wish to situate Heidegger's discussion of Van Gogh's peasant shoes. The shoes are involved in a multiple relationship: (1) insofar as they pertain to the peasant woman and her quotidian rhythms; (2) insofar as they have been reconstituted by the artistic vision; and (3) insofar as they speak to the philosopher-interpreter of Truth. Heidegger is careful to make a distinction between the shoes in their natural and occupational habitat and their presence in the painting. He goes on to claim that it is in the field that the shoes are most authentically what they are. "They are all the more genuinely so, the less the peasant woman thinks about the shoes while she is at work, or looks at them at all, or is even aware of them" ("OWA," 33). Here begins my criticism of Heidegger's reading. The question that Heidegger does not ask is whether there might not be some brutal and non-negotiable contradiction between his aesthetic consciousness of the shoes and the peasant woman's quotidian consciousness of them. The genuineness or authenticity of the shoes, in Heidegger's reading, is in inverse relationship to the peasant woman's awareness of the shoes qua shoes. Consequently, our aesthetic idealization of the shoes becomes possible only when we make the following chain of connections: (1) the peasant woman inheres in the shoes; (2) the shoes inhere in the earth; and (3) the shoes and the peasant woman are part of a world that is and ought to be totally unreflexive of itself.

What would indeed fracture the univocal and monothetic harmony of this picture is the emergence of the peasant woman's consciousness in transgression of the universal nostalgia with which Heidegger cathects it. Heidegger cannot celebrate the peasant woman's state of being except as an outsider who exoticizes it and constructs it in the image of a beautiful, romantic, and unsullied alterity. It becomes necessary for Heidegger to legislate, for the sake of aesthetic harmony, that whatever alienation the peasant woman may be experiencing in her working condition be dehistoricized and renamed as a oneness with nature. What is desirable, from Heidegger's point of view, is a paradisal and prelapsarian picture wherein the labor of the peasant woman is reduced to a proportionate spectacle within the undifferentiated panorama of a primordial Being. In integrating the peasant woman with the rhythms of Nature, he deprives her of her very specific class- and gender-based historicity. In other words, the worldview that Heidegger reads off the shoes in their real-life, equipmental context is deeply antisecular and antihistorical. It is a worldview that disallows the rift between nature and culture, between natural and elemental time and cultural memory: a worldview that has very little use for self-reflexivity or for the politics or ideology of interpretation (not that it is devoid of its own tacit politics and ideological investment). What is ironic about this scenario is that the philosopher who is so concerned by the violence of representational thinking should submit the peasant woman to processes of dehumanization in the name of a superior acquiescence in a timelessly benign Being.

There are two criticisms that need to be made of Heidegger's position. First, Heidegger seems unaware that the peasant woman is being "spoken for" here and thus preempted, first by Van Gogh and then by himself. (I believe that Heidegger does not problematize this oppressive representational model because his essential categories are ontological and not historical.) Second, although the project to critique and step beyond the hubristic narcissism of the anthropocentric measure is quite laudable, such a critique cannot (1) bypass the historicity as well as the unavoidable anthropocentrism of the negative critique, and (2) get away with such an indeterminate and undifferentiated notion of the human as the anthropological—a notion that refuses to take into account the specificity of such determinations as race, color, class, gender, sexuality, colonialism, imperialism, and ethnocentrism. Even at the level of formal hermeneutic complexity and sophistication, the Heidegger who discourses on language and art, unlike the Heidegger of *Being and Time,* tends to monitor and preordain the self-reflexive energies of *Dasein.* What we find in Heidegger is a readiness to lapse into the felicitous quietism of a descriptive phenomenology, a mode of thinking that celebrates and justifies the status quo. What is elided in all this is the historical reality that a critique of anthropocentrism can only be yet another anthropocentric move ad infinitum. In his passion to witness the dis-closure of the be-ing of Being within the representational model, Heidegger opts to terminate the infinite regress of self-reflexive thought.[10] The questioner does not get questioned within the question; for now, the questioner is Being itself. In terms of Van Gogh's painting, we are left with a generalized sense of Being that speaks for and on behalf of the peasant, the painter, and the philosopher-interpreter without a trace of internal contradiction or ideological false consciousness. The different chronotopes occupied and instantiated by these different and nonsynchronous subject positions are sublated in the name of a sacral and authentic Being that unifies recalcitrant diachronies. Adorno's critique of "the jargon of authenticity" comes to mind here, but, more pointedly, I wish to introduce Fredric Jameson's critical perspective on the peasant shoes.

In his essay "Postmodernism, or the Cultural Logic of Late Capitalism," Jameson first of all periodizes the Van Gogh painting as "high modernist" (whereas, from a Heideggerian point of view, Being is not periodizable at all; little wonder then that Heidegger does not raise questions concerning the historicity of modernism, of Van Gogh's determinate historicity, as well as the historicity of European art at a specific conjuncture) and then goes on to offer a diagnostic (as against Heidegger's epiphanic) account of the painting: "In Van Gogh, that content, those initial raw materials, are, I will suggest, to be grasped simply as the whole object world of agricultural misery, of stark rural poverty, and the whole rudimentary human world of backbreaking peasant toil, a world reduced to its most brutal and menaced, primitive and marginalized state."[11] This does not mean that Jameson is insensitive to the sensuous fullness of Van Gogh's world; but what he offers us is the diagnosis of a contradiction, the phenomenon of an unreal and utopian overcompensation in the realm of art. Jameson argues "that the willed and violent transformation of a drab peasant object world into the most glorious materialization of pure color in oil paint is to be seen as a Utopian gesture" ("P," 58–59). Jameson's criticism correctly points out that Heidegger's utopian gesture toward Van Gogh's utopian gesture toward the condition of the peasant woman denies historicity and what Johannes Fabian would call "coevalness" to that very condition.[12] In seeking to redress the violence of one sort of representation, Heidegger's rhetoric perpetrates a more fundamental representational violence in the name of a transhistorical Being. What we are witnessing here is the molestation of the peasant woman by the indifference of Being. What Heidegger produces here is an apologistic and apostolic reading on behalf of Being, and the peasant woman is a mere detail that carries the burden of an ontological allegory. Heidegger's reading says "so be it" to the status quo.

Heidegger's representation of the truth of the state of being instantiated by the peasant woman is much like William Wordsworth's impassioned address to "the solitary reaper" in his poem of that title.[13] The solitary reaper sings in a dialect the poet does not understand. Sure enough, the romantic poet makes a gestural commitment: "Will no one tell me what she sings?" But "what she sings" is not really the poet's theme: it is rather his imaginative ability to produce an allegorical meaning out of a history he does not understand, much less share. "Whatever the theme the maiden sang," it really does not matter, the philosophic message of the poet will still stand. What the romantic poet needs is a peg to hang his inspired subjectivity on, and the more alterior and the more ineffable the peg, the better for the performance of his editorial-allegorical intention. The poet's lyric derives its eloquence from the "un-knowability" of the peasant woman's own narrative.[14] In much the same way, Heidegger, too, makes the silence of the peasant woman an absolute precondition for his own hermeneutic persuasiveness.

It is predictable that the aesthetic principle underlying Heidegger's reading is none other than the Kantian "purposive purposelessness." The materiality as well as the equipmentality of the shoes are bracketed and thus thematized by the painting. The coordinates within the painting are the coordinates of a no-place; but strangely, it is within the transcendent plenitude of this no-place, where the historical density of the shoes is nihilated, that the truth of the shoes begins to speak out. And this is significant, not to the peasant but to the philosopher-interpreter. The aesthetic mode is thus made the only mode for understanding history, but unfortunately, since this mode does away with history, we are left with a form of knowledge that explains away that which is to be explained. This model also ensures that peasant reality, for its emergence into philosophic respectability, will be eternally dependent on a philosophic consciousness that is not organic to it.[15] Could this be an example of a traditional intellectual misrepresenting an organic reality and, correspondingly, an example of the allegorical method begging the question of history with impunity?

The allegorical oversight in Heidegger of historical density or specificity is but a variation of the preemption of history by ontology. Even the radicality of a work like *Being and Time* addresses Time in an ontological mode, thus subsuming questions of history under the general and "natural" problematic of Time. For Heidegger, the notion of Time and its natural equiprimordiality with Being is the radical principle in the name of which *Dasein* is to claim its historicity. In other words, there is a univocal "nature" that underwrites the de-structive project. Unlike Foucault or Fabian, for instance, Heidegger will not raise the question of the ideological constitution of Time for purposes of the anthropological, colonialist, and imperialist subjugation of the Other. He will not identify his "time" as the naturalized time of Eurocentric thought. Of course, Heidegger, like Nietzsche, inveighs against the metaphysical nominalization of time, but unlike Nietzsche he will not make the connection between a general ontology and its very specific historico-political effects of empire building and perspectival dominance. In Heidegger's thought, ontological time does not get unpacked or narrativized into history. The allegorical decoding of history (as with the principle of the ontico-ontological difference) is of a second-order intelligibility that does not connect with the first order. The allegorical reading either eviscerates the contents of history to make history intelligible or it takes on the mastery of a grand algebra whose relationship to the variables of history is one of a distant and panoptic control. In Heidegger's thought on language and art, this allegory also celebrates and justifies the "natural order" of what is; it all becomes just a matter of how well tuned we are to Being. A particularly good example of this tendency is the later work of Gadamer with its insistence on "the eminent text" and the importance of locating contemporary historicity within the mastery of the tradition. To sum up, the allegorical song on behalf of Being is in fact the justification and endorsement of a particular Western Eurocentric tradition. Heidegger's own handling of non-Western thought and his belief in the superiority of Western/ Germanic thought is indeed part of the same problem.

I now turn, less critically and more appreciatively, to the second half of "The Origin of the Work of Art," with its famous formulation of the Earth-World conjuncture. In this section of the essay, Heideggerian *Gelassenheit* receives a more general and, for that reason, a more persuasive treatment. And yet, this formulation, too, in spite of its generosity, fails to make the historical connection. Heidegger is concerned here in rectifying the arrogant positivity of the anthropocentric will to knowledge that maims, colonizes, ravages, and technologizes nature, reducing it to a "standing reserve" for human utilization. As counter to this tendency, Heidegger offers us a sensitive ecology of knowledge that in taking up responsibility for its own misdeeds commits itself to the task of conserving nature and protecting it against human rapacity. It is a highly charged and relevant theme, all the more so today. And Heidegger is right on target. The Heidegger who speaks out here is continuous with the Heidegger who made the trenchant diagnosis that it is science that makes nothing of "nothingness" — the Heidegger who made thinking sensitive to a creative and affirmative nothingness or concealment that underlies and nourishes the positive finitude of all knowledge. Jameson I think oversimplifies this aspect of Heidegger's agenda when he translates the Earth-World gap "as the meaningless materiality of the body and nature and the meaning-endowment of history and the social" ("P," 59). Jameson's interpretation is too formulaic in its application of the mode-of-production logic in Marxist thought to what is at hand, and thus it misses altogether the very different trajectory of Heidegger's thought. Even from a Marxist point of view, this reading is too wooden in its invocation of the mode-of-production principle. A number of recent feminist-Marxist essays, in particular the collection *Feminism as Critique*,[16] have problematized the axiology of the mode of production from the point of view of nature, sexuality, and reproduction.

The crucial distinction that Heidegger makes is between two kinds of "worlding": one that is brash and self-serving and disavows a commitment to the dark concealedness or unknowability of the Earth, invoking nemesis upon itself (one could call it the furious return of the repressed); and another that, in the context of a penumbral symbiosis with the abiding Earth principle, groundlessly grounds the world and thus protects it from violent self-immolation. There are two imperatives contained in this. The first is to realize the finite closure of form as an invitation to an opening, that is, "to keep it Open." Heidegger's thinking would like to avoid at all costs the reification or the fetishization of form. We cannot but recall here Heidegger's analysis of the "jug," where he locates the ethic of the jug's morphology not in its ostensible materiality but in the holding void that is both finitely brought into being by the form of the jug and, at the same time, as void, is transcendent of the form of the jug.[17] The second imperative is to consider the world as authentic only when such a production points beyond itself to the mystery of the unknowable. To quote from Heidegger: "The work moves the earth into the Open of a world and keeps it there. *The work lets the earth be an earth*" ("OWA," 46). And again: "The earth is essentially self-secluding. To set forth the earth means to bring it into the Open as the self-secluding" ("OWA," 47).

In other words, the knowledge of the world is double coded. On the one hand, the world is thematized as knowable, with the cognitive appropriation that goes with it; on the other, the negative knowledge that brings the earth into the open lets its unknowability be. To know the earth is to know it as the self-secluding and the unknowable. What Heidegger is striving toward is a kind of Lacanian psychoanalysis and a Keatsian negative capability. The earth principle endlessly revitalizes our worldly projects, and Heidegger's exhortation is that the way we conduct our world should empower such a recycling. Heidegger also visualizes the earth-world relationship as an endless strife that brings out the best in each toward higher and higher planes of realization. Perhaps there are some tacit connections between this thesis and the Marxian thesis of wresting Freedom from the world of Necessity. But here again, unlike Marx, Heidegger's emphasis is on something beyond history.

So far, so good. What is lacking, however, in Heidegger is an active sense of history and the awareness of ideological productions of meaning. The artwork never gets situated or periodized. Its particular systems of inclusions and exclusions, presences and absences, "saids" and "not-saids," never get identified, evaluated, or accounted for.[18] Heidegger's thought takes the form of a rhapsody that is "always already" on the far side of ideology. But how and by what critical method was such transcendence achieved? If in some sense the objective of the artwork is utopian, how does it articulate this vision through the specificity of its actual history? As I have mentioned already, Heidegger shuns history in favor of ontology; consequently, even the potentially liberating earth-world nexus falls prey to the ideology of a prelapsarian innocence.

I say "ideology" for two reasons. First, Heidegger's notion of a common world does not problematize its Eurocentric bias. Given the dominance of the Eurocentric world that is naturalized as "the world," the notion of the earth remains specific to the Eurocentric world. In other words, such an earth remains the possession of the dominant world. In geopolitical terms, the ineffable earth in Heidegger is not all that different from Conrad's "heart of darkness," that is, a colonialist-imperialist conception that is incapable of visualizing "other" worlds and earths.[19] The confrontation of the world with *its* earth becomes an ideal occasion for the dominant discourse to contemplate itself in reverse narcissism and erect, in Hélène Cixous's terms, "monuments to lack."[20] Also, when we substitute for the world the notion of "hegemonic history" and for the earth the notion of "denial of history," the innocence of this model is instantly impugned. Europe is the luminous world, and "the dark continents" are out there.

Second, Heidegger's enabling and benevolent references to self-seclusion within the artwork make it impossible for us to ask questions such as: given the period and the historicity of the artwork, what type of contents were proscribed and privileged within the aesthetic format? What possibilities were dehistoricized and repressed by the "freedom" of the work? What dominant ideology rewards, confirms, and reproduces itself through the artwork, and why? What are the discursive constraints that mediate and govern the connections between voice, genre, and ideology? In short, Heidegger is not interested in the symptomatology of art. Instead, he romanticizes silences, gaps, and repressions in the name of an ontological gestalt. His reading of art places it on a pedestal, where it is virtually unassailable by historically determinate readings. The artwork is purified of the taint of historically contaminated origin and freed of all problems of reception. Within aesthetic space, all that is possible is adoration and celebration.

However, the earth-world conjuncture, when politicized and historicized, would raise the following questions. At any point in world history, which constituencies are "worlding" and which are marked for "self-seclusion"? Are not the constituencies that are "worlding" doing so at the expense of those other areas that have had the "condition of being earth" thrust upon them? One need only think of the culture of imperialism to realize how exploitative and brutalizing this scenario is. Earth and world are marked by multiple and unequal temporalities, and by asymmetries and imbalances of power. We need to ask: whose world, and whose earth? Who determines how the world and the earth are to be historicized? Why this binary obsession with lack and plenitude? Given the geopolitical volatility and contestability of these terms, that is, "world" and "earth," it would seem naive and dangerous to formulate an ontology on behalf of an earth-world figurality. It seems to me that Heidegger fails to make a distinction between a historically implicated "negative capability" and a laissez-faire ontology. What is most troubling in Heidegger's formulation is the lingering faith in a Universal Subject that can and should speak for all. I would conclude then by saying that the modality that Heidegger proposes for art is deeply nostalgic; the "letting be" pertains to the past and not to the future and seeks to maintain an "innocent present."

Notes

1.   Heidegger's influence on Derrida is more easily demonstrable than his influence on Foucault. As for Foucault, it is interesting that in one of his last interviews he acknowledged that the two philosophers who had affected his own development most were Heidegger and Nietzsche.

2.   For a brilliant analysis of the status of "presence" in Heidegger's philosophy, see Jacques Derrida, "Ousia and Gramme: Note on a Note from *Being and Time*," in *Margins of Philosophy*, trans. Alan Bass (Chicago: University of Chicago Press, 1982), 29–67.

3.   Martin Heidegger, "The Origin of the Work of Art," in *Poetry, Language, Thought*, trans. Albert Hofstadter (New York: Harper and Row, 1971), 15–87; hereafter abbreviated "OWA" and cited parenthetically in the text.

4.   The interaction between "Truth" and "Method" has been the focus of all of Hans-Georg Gadamer's hermeneutic philosophy. But I would submit

that, in spite of its radical promise, Gadamer's work eventually capitulates to the Great Tradition and the Eminent Text.

5.   See Walter Benjamin, "The Work of Art in the Age of Mechanical Reproduction," in *Illuminations,* trans. Harry Zohn (New York: Schocken, 1969), 217–51, for a "postmodern" account of the "aura" of art.

6.   I refer here to the deconstructive strategy proposed by Derrida, particularly in *Dissemination, Positions,* and *Of Grammatology,* that forges a complex relationship between "memory" and "promise" by way of the "orphaned" present.

7.   See Jacques Derrida, *The Truth in Painting,* trans. Geoff Bennington and Ian McLeod (Chicago: University of Chicago Press, 1987). A significant part of this work is devoted to a discussion of Heidegger's notions of art and artistic truth.

8.   Ibid., 56ff.

9.   See Jacques Derrida, "Le facteur de la vérité," in *The Post Card: From Socrates to Freud and Beyond,* trans. Alan Bass (Chicago: University of Chicago Press, 1987), 411–96.

10.   In contrast to Heidegger's controlled use of self-reflexivity, we have Derrida, who is interested in mobilizing self-reflexivity as a form of "play" that will imperil any pregiven center or signified. We see a similar trajectory at work in Foucault's notion of "the analytic of finitude" in *The Order of Things* (New York: Vintage, 1970).

11.   Fredric Jameson, "Postmodernism, or the Cultural Logic of Late Capitalism," *New Left Review* 146 (July–August 1984): 58; hereafter abbreviated "P" and cited parenthetically in the text.

12.   I refer here to Johannes Fabian's sensitive work *Time and the Other: How Anthropology Makes Its Object* (New York: Columbia University Press, 1983).

13.   In my reading, both Wordsworth and Heidegger are romantics insofar as they are both invested in the idea of a common, simple, and natural alterity waiting to be narrativized into existence by the "self" of the dominant culture.

14.   A similar ideological mystification constitutes the psychoanalytic account of femininity and "the truth of woman." It is only by positing unilaterally and violently that "woman is unknowable" that psychoanalytic discourse produces its phallocentric authority.

15.   My reference here is to the powerful distinction that Antonio Gramsci makes between "organic" intellectuals and "traditional" intellectuals ("The Intellectuals," in *Selections from the Prison Notebooks,* trans. and ed. Quintin Hoare and Geoffrey Nowell Smith [New York: International Publishers, 1971], 5–23). Insofar as Heidegger's ontology seeks to be originary and allegorical, I would classify Heidegger as "traditional."

16.   *Feminism as Critique,* ed. Seyla Benhabib and Drucilla Cornell (Minneapolis: University of Minnesota Press, 1987).

17.   See Martin Heidegger, "The Thing," in *Poetry, Language, Thought,* 163–86. He analyzes the "jugness" of the jug in terms that demonstrate the poverty of the putative form-content dichotomy.

18.   Pierre Macherey, an Althusserian Marxist critic, in *A Theory of Literary Production,* trans. Geoffrey Wall (Boston: Routledge and Kegan Paul, 1978), 154, proposes the thesis that every text is a system of "determinate absences" or "not-saids." Macherey thus reads the text symptomatologically and not acquiescently.

19.   A vibrant attempt at articulating "other worlds" is Gayatri Chakravorty Spivak's book *In Other Worlds: Essays in Cultural Politics* (London: Methuen, 1987).

20.   In *The Newly Born Woman,* trans. Betsy Wing (Minneapolis: University of Minnesota Press), Catherine Clément and Hélène Cixous discuss the dangers of locating feminism within the logic of "male adversarial theory" that all too easily succumbs to the romantic temptation of building "monuments to lack." Also see Alice Jardine's *Gynesis* (Ithaca: Cornell University Press, 1985).

Bibliography

Adams, Hazard, ed. *Critical Theory since Plato.* New York: Harcourt Brace Jovanovich, 1971.

Adorno, Theodor. *Aesthetic Theory.* Trans. C. Lenhardt. New York: Routledge and Kegan Paul, 1984.

———. "Commitment." Trans. Francis McDonagh. In *The Essential Frankfurt School Reader,* ed. Andrew Arato and Eike Gebhardt, 300–18. New York: Urizen Books, 1978.

———. *Negative Dialectics.* Trans. E. B. Ashton. New York: Seabury Press, 1973.

———. *Prisms.* Trans. Samuel and Shierry Weber. Cambridge: MIT Press, 1983.

———. "Reconciliation under Duress." Trans. Rodney Livingstone. In *Aesthetics and Politics,* ed. Ronald Taylor, 151–76. London: Verso, 1977.

Agamben, Giorgio. *Language and Death: The Place of Negativity.* Trans. Karen E. Pinkus with Michael Hardt. Minneapolis: University of Minnesota Press, 1991.

Ahern, Daniel R. *Nietzsche as Cultural Physician.* University Park: Pennsylvania State University Press, 1995.

Althusser, Louis. "Contradiction and Overdetermination." In *For Marx,* trans. Ben Brewster, 87–128. New York: Vintage, 1969.

———. "Ideology and Ideological State Apparatuses." In *Lenin and Philosophy and Other Essays,* trans. Ben Brewster, 127–86. New York: Monthly Review Press, 1971.

Altman, Andrew. *Critical Legal Studies: A Liberal Critique.* Princeton, N.J.: Princeton University Press, 1990.

Alway, Joan. *Critical Theory and Political Possibilities: Conceptions of Emancipatory Politics in the Works of Horkheimer, Adorno, Marcuse, and Habermas.* Westport, Conn.: Greenwood Press, 1995.

Anderson, Pamela Sue. *Ricoeur and Kant: Philosophy of the Will.* Atlanta: Scholars Press, 1993.

Arac, Jonathan. *Critical Genealogies: Historical Situations for Postmodern Literary Studies.* New York: Columbia University Press, 1987.

Arendt, Hannah. *The Human Condition.* Chicago: University of Chicago Press, 1958.

Aristotle. *Rhetoric.* Trans. Lane Cooper. Englewood Cliffs, N.J.: Prentice-Hall, 1932.

Aronowitz, Stanley. *The Crisis in Historical Materialism: Class, Politics, and Culture in Marxist Theory.* New York: Praeger, 1982.

Auerbach, Erich. "Figura." In *Scenes from the Drama of European Litera-*

ture, trans. Ralph Manheim, 11-76. 1959; Minneapolis: University of Minnesota Press, 1984.

Aufderheide, Patricia, ed. *Beyond PC.* St. Paul: Graywolf Press, 1992.

Augustine. *The City of God.* Trans. Marcus Dods. Edinburgh: T. and T. Clark, 1871-72.

——. *Confessions.* Trans. R. S. Pine-Coffin. New York: Penguin, 1961.

——. *De Doctrina Christiana.* Turnholti: Brepols, 1962.

Bambach, Charles R. *Heidegger, Dilthey, and the Crisis of Historicism.* Ithaca, N.Y.: Cornell University Press, 1995.

Bann, Stephen. "The Truth in Mapping." *Word and Image* 4 (1988): 498-509.

Barker, Stephen. *Autoaesthetics: Strategies of the Self after Nietzsche.* Atlantic Highlands, N.J.: Humanities Press, 1992.

Barthes, Roland. *Elements of Semiology.* Trans. Annette Lavers and Colin Smith. New York: Hill and Wang, 1964.

——. *Image, Music, Text.* Trans. Stephen Heath. New York: Hill and Wang, 1977.

——. *S/Z.* Trans. Richard Miller. New York: Hill and Wang, 1974.

Baudrillard, Jean. *The Mirror of Production.* Trans. Mark Poster. St. Louis: Telos Press, 1975.

Baumgarten, Alexander. *Aesthetica.* 2 vols. 1750-58; Hildesheim: G. Olms, 1961.

Beardsworth, Richard. *Derrida and the Political.* New York: Routledge, 1996.

Beckett, Samuel. "An Imaginative Work!" Review of *The Amaranthers* by Jack B. Yeats, in *Dublin Magazine* (July-September 1936). Reprinted in *Disjecta: Miscellaneous Writings and a Dramatic Fragment by Samuel Beckett,* ed Ruby Cohn, 89-90. New York: Grove, 1984.

Behler, Ernst. *Confrontations: Derrida/Heidegger/Nietzsche.* Trans. Steven Taubeneck. Stanford, Calif.: Stanford University Press, 1991.

Beiner, Ronald, and William James Booth, eds. *Kant and Political Philosophy: The Contemporary Legacy.* New Haven, Conn.: Yale University Press, 1993.

Benhabib, Seyla. "Epistemologies of Postmodernism: A Rejoinder to Jean-François Lyotard." *New German Critique* 33 (1984): 103-26.

——. *The Reluctant Modernism of Hannah Arendt.* Thousand Oaks, Calif.: Sage Publications, 1996.

Benhabib, Seyla, and Drucilla Cornell, eds. *Feminism as Critique.* Minneapolis: University of Minnesota Press, 1987.

Benjamin, Walter. *Illuminations.* Trans. Harry Zohn. New York: Schocken, 1969.

Bennington, Geoff. *Lyotard: Writing the Event.* Manchester: University of Manchester Press, 1988.

Berman, Paul, ed. *Debating PC.* New York: Laurel Press, 1992.

Bernasconi, Robert. *The Question of Language in Heidegger's History of Being.* Atlantic Highlands, N.J.: Humanities Press, 1985.

Bernstein, Richard J. *Beyond Objectivism and Relativism.* Philadelphia: University of Pennsylvania Press, 1983.

Bialostosky, Don H. *Making Tales: The Poetics of Wordsworth's Narrative Experiments.* Chicago: University of Chicago Press, 1984.

———. *Wordsworth, Dialogics, and the Practice of Criticism.* New York: Cambridge University Press, 1992.

Bigger, Charles P. *Kant's Methodology: An Essay in Philosophical Archeology.* Athens: Ohio University Press, 1996.

Blanchot, Maurice. *The Space of Literature.* Trans. Ann Smock. Lincoln: University of Nebraska Press, 1982.

———. *The Writing of the Disaster.* Trans. Ann Smock. Lincoln: University of Nebraska Press, 1986.

Bloch, Ernst. "Nonsynchronism and the Obligation to Its Dialectics." *New German Critique* 11 (Spring 1977): 22–38.

Blondel, Eric. *Nietzsche: The Body and Culture.* Trans. Seán Hand. Stanford, Calif.: Stanford University Press, 1991.

Bloom, Allan. *The Closing of the American Mind.* New York: Simon and Schuster, 1987.

Blumenberg, Hans. *The Legitimacy of the Modern Age.* Trans. Robert M. Wallace. Cambridge, Mass.: MIT Press, 1983.

———. *Work on Myth.* Trans. Robert M. Wallace. Cambridge, Mass.: MIT Press, 1985.

Boileau-Despréaux, Nicolas. *Ouevres de Boileau: L'art poétique.* Strasbourg: J. H. E. Heitz (Heitz and Mundel), 1909.

Bourdieu, Pierre. *The Political Ontology of Martin Heidegger.* Trans. Peter Collier. Stanford, Calif.: Stanford University Press, 1991.

Breazeale, Daniel. Introduction to "On Truth and Lies in a Nonmoral Sense." In *Philosophy and Truth: Selections from Nietzsche's Notebooks of the Early 1870s,* trans. Daniel Breazeale, xiii–xlix. Atlantic Highlands, N. J.: Humanities Press, 1979.

Bruns, Gerald L. "Figuration in Antiquity." In *Hermeneutics: Questions and Prospects,* ed. Gary Shapiro and Alan Sica, 147–64. Amherst: University of Massachusetts Press, 1984.

———. *Heidegger's Estrangements: Language, Truth, and Poetry in the Later Writings.* New Haven, Conn.: Yale University Press, 1989.

———. *Inventions: Writing Textuality, and Understanding in Literary History.* New Haven, Conn.: Yale University Press, 1982.

Buber, Martin. *Between Man and Man.* Trans. Ronald Gregor. New York: Collier Macmillan, 1965.

Burke, Edmund. *Philosophical Enquiry into the Origin of Our Ideas of the*

Sublime and the Beautiful. Ed. J. T. Boulton. 1759; Notre Dame: University of Notre Dame Press, 1968.

————. *Reflections on the Revolution in France.* Ed. Thomas Mahoney. New York: Bobbs-Merrill, 1955.

Buttigieg, Joseph. "The Exemplary Worldliness of Antonio Gramsci's Literary Criticism." *Boundary2* 11 (Fall–Winter 1982-83): 21-39.

Butts, Robert E. *Historical Pragmatics: Philosophical Essays.* Boston: Kluwer Academic, 1993.

Bynum, Caroline Walker. *Docere Verbo et Exemplo: An Aspect of Twelfth-Century Spirituality.* Missoula, Mont.: Scholars Press, 1979.

Calinescu, Matei. "The Silence of the Avant-Garde." In *Five Faces of Modernity,* 275-79. Durham, N.C.: Duke University Press, 1987.

Calvino, Italo. *Invisible Cities.* Trans. by William Weaver. New York: Harcourt Brace Jovanovich, 1978.

————. *Six Memos for the Next Millennium.* Cambridge, Mass.: Harvard University Press, 1988.

Caputo, John D. *The Mystical Element in Heidegger's Thought.* Athens: Ohio University Press, 1978.

————. "The Poverty of Thought: Reflections on Heidegger and Eckhart." In *Heidegger: The Man and the Thinker,* ed. Thomas Sheehan, 209-16. Chicago: Precedent, 1981.

Caraher, Brian. "Allegories of Reading: Positing a Rhetoric of Romanticism; or, Paul de Man's Critique of Pure Figural Interiority." *Pre/Text* 4 (Spring 1983).

Carroll, David. *Paraesthetics.* New York: Methuen, 1987.

Cassirer, Ernst. *Kant's Life and Thought.* New Haven, Conn.: Yale University Press, 1980.

————. *Philosophy of the Enlightenment.* Trans. Fritz Koelln and James P. Pettegrove. Princeton, N.J.: Princeton University Press, 1951.

Caudill, David Stanley. *Disclosing Tilt: Law, Belief, and Criticism.* Amsterdam: Free University Press, 1989.

Cavell, Stanley. "The Avoidance of Love: A Reading of *King Lear.*" In *Must We Mean What We Say?* 267-353. Cambridge: Cambridge University Press, 1976.

————. *In Quest of the Ordinary: Lines of Skepticism and Romanticism.* Chicago: University of Chicago Press, 1988.

Cave, Terence. *Recognitions: A Study in Poetics.* Oxford: Clarendon Press, 1988.

Celan, Paul. *Collected Prose.* Trans. Rosmarie Waldrop. Riverdale-on-Hudson, N.Y.: Sheep Meadow Press, 1986.

————. *Gesammelte Werke in Funf Banden.* Ed. Beda Allemann and Stefan Reichert in collaboration with Rudolf Bucher. Frankfurt am Main: Suhrkamp, 1983.

Charbonnier, Georges. *Le Monologue du peintre.* Paris: Julliard, 1959.

Clark, Carol. *The Web of Metaphor: Studies in the Imagery of Montaigne: Essais.* Lexington, Ky.: French Forum, 1978.

Cixous, Hélène, and Catherine Clément. *The Newly Born Woman.* Trans. Betsy Wing. Minneapolis: University of Minnesota Press, 1986.

Cockburn, Alexander. "Beat the Devil." *Nation,* 27 May 1991, 685ff.

Cornell, Drucilla. *Beyond Accommodation: Ethical Feminism, Deconstruction, and the Law.* New York: Routledge, 1991.

———. "Institutionalization of Meaning, Recollective Imagination, and the Potential for Transformation in Legal Interpretation." *Penn. Law Review* 136, no. 2 (1988): 1135–1229.

———. *The Philosophy of the Limit.* New York: Routledge, 1992.

———. "Post-Structuralism: The Ethical Relation, and the Law." *Cardozo Law Review* 9, no. 6 (August 1988): 1587–1628.

———. *Transformations: Recollective Imagination and Sexual Difference.* New York: Routledge, 1993.

Cornell, Drucilla, Michel Rosenfeld, and David Gray Carlson, eds. *Deconstruction and the Possibility of Justice.* New York: Routledge, 1992.

Cottrell, Robert D. *Sexuality/Textuality: A Study of the Fabric of Montaigne's* Essais. Columbus: Ohio State University Press, 1981.

Cover, Robert. *Narrative, Violence, and the Law: The Essays of Robert Cover.* Ed. Martha Minow, Michael Ryan, and Austin Sarat. Ann Arbor: University of Michigan Press, 1992.

Crane, T. F., ed. *The Exempla or Illustrative Stories from the Sermones Vulgares of Jacques de Vitry.* Publications of the Folk-Lore Society, no. 26. London: D. Nutt.

Crawford, Donald W. *Kant's Aesthetic Theory.* Madison: University of Wisconsin Press, 1974.

Cumming, Robert Denoon. *Human Nature and History.* 2 vols. Chicago: University of Chicago Press, 1969.

Curtius, Ernst Robert. *European Literature and the Latin Middle Ages.* Trans. Willard R. Trask. Princeton, N.J.: Princeton University Press, 1953.

Dallmayr, Fred R. *Life-World, Modernity, and Critique: Paths between Heidegger and the Frankfurt School.* Cambridge: Polity Press, 1991.

Davidson, Arnold I. "Archaeology, Genealogy, Ethics." In *Foucault: A Critical Reader,* ed. David Couzens Hoy, 221–33. Oxford: Basil Blackwell, 1986.

Davidson, Donald. "On the Very Idea of a Conceptual Scheme." *Proceedings of the American Philosophical Association* 47 (1973–74): 5–20.

Deleuze, Gilles. *Kant's Critical Philosophy: The Doctrine of the Faculties.* Trans. Hugh Tomlinson and Barbara Habberjam. Minneapolis: University of Minnesota Press, 1984.

————. *Nietzsche and Philosophy.* Trans. Hugh Tomlinson. London: Athlone Press, 1983.

Deleuze, Gilles, and Félix Guattari. *Anti-Oedipus: Capitalism and Schizophrenia.* Trans. Robert Hurley, Mark Seem, and Helen R. Lane. New York: Viking Press, 1977.

————. *A Thousand Plateaus.* Trans. Brian Massumi. Minneapolis: University of Minnesota Press, 1987.

Delgado, Richard, ed. *Critical Race Theory: The Cutting Edge.* Philadelphia: Temple University Press, 1995.

De Man, Paul. *Allegories of Reading: Figural Language in Rousseau, Nietzsche, Rilke, and Proust.* New Haven, Conn.: Yale University Press, 1979.

————. "Hegel on the Sublime." In *Displacement: Derrida and After,* ed. Mark Krupnick, 139–53. Bloomington: Indiana University Press, 1983.

————. "Phenomenality and Materiality in Kant." In *Textual Sublime: Deconstruction and Its Differences,* ed. H. Silverman and G. Aylesworth, 87–105. Albany: State University of New York Press, 1990.

————. *The Resistance to Theory.* Minneapolis: University of Minnesota Press, 1986.

Derrida, Jacques. "At This Very Moment in This Work Here I Am." Trans. Robin Berezdivin. In *Re-reading Levinas,* ed. Robert Bernasconi and Simon Critchley, 11–48. London: Routledge, 1990.

————. "Declarations of Independence." *New Political Science* 15 (Summer 1986): 7–15.

————. "Des Tours de Babel." In *Difference in Translation,* trans. and ed. Joseph F. Graham, 165–248. Ithaca, N.Y.: Cornell University Press, 1985.

————. *Dissemination.* Trans. Barbara Johnson. Chicago: University of Chicago Press, 1981.

————. *The Gift of Death.* Trans. David Wills. Chicago: University of Chicago Press, 1995.

————. *Limited Inc.* Ed. Gerald Graff. Evanston, Ill.: Northwestern University Press, 1988.

————. "Living On/Border Lines." In *Deconstruction and Criticism,* trans. James Hulbert, 75–175. New York: Seabury Press, 1979.

————. *Margins of Philosophy.* Trans. Alan Bass. Chicago: University of Chicago Press, 1982.

————. *Memories for Paul de Man.* Trans. Cecile Lindsay et al. Ed. Avital Ronell and Eduardo Cadava. New York: Columbia University Press, 1986.

————. "My Chances/*Mes Chances:* A Rendezvous with Some Epicurean Stereophonies." In *Taking Chances: Derrida, Psychoanalysis, and Literature,* ed. Joseph H. Smith and William Kerrigan, 1–32. Baltimore: Johns Hopkins University Press, 1984.

————. *Of Grammatology.* Trans. Gayatri Chakravorty Spivak. Baltimore: Johns Hopkins University Press, 1976.

Art. Trans. Thomas Gora, Alice Jardine, and Leon S. Roudiez. Ed. Leon S. Roudiez. New York: Columbia University Press, 1980.

———. *La Revolution du langage poetique.* Paris: Editions du Seuil, 1974.

———. *Revolution in Poetic Language.* Trans. Margaret Waller. New York: Columbia University Press, 1984.

Kroker, Arthur, and Susan Cook. *The Postmodern Scene.* New York: St. Martin's Press, 1986.

Laclau, Ernesto, and Chantal Mouffe. *Hegemony and Socialist Strategy: Towards a Radical Democratic Politics.* Trans. Winston Moore and Paul Cammack. London: Verso, 1985.

Lacoue-Labarthe, Philippe. "Le Detour: Nietzsche et la rhetorique." *Poetique* 5 (1971): 53–76.

Lacqueur, Thomas. "Orgasm, Generation, and the Politics of Reproductive Biology." *Representations* 14 (Spring 1986): 1–41.

Lang, Berel. *Heidegger's Silence.* Ithaca, N.Y.: Cornell University Press, 1996.

———. "Postmodernism in Philosophy: Nostalgia for the Future, Waiting for the Past." In *Literature and the Question of Philosophy,* ed. Anthony J. Cascardi, 314–32. Baltimore: Johns Hopkins University Press, 1987.

Leibniz, Gottfried Wilhelm. *The Monadology and Other Philosophical Writings.* Trans. Robert Latta. London: Oxford University Press, 1951.

Lenin, V. I. *What Is to Be Done?: Burning Questions of Our Movement.* New York: International Publishers, 1969.

Leonard, Jerry, ed. *Legal Studies as Cultural Studies: A Reader in (Post) Modern Critical Theory.* Albany: State University of New York Press, 1995.

Levinas, Emmanuel. "Being and the Other: On Paul Celan." Trans. Stephen Melville. *Chicago Review* 29, no. 3 (Winter 1978): 16–21.

———. *Otherwise than Being; or, Beyond Essence.* Trans. Alphonso Lingis. The Hague: Martinus Nijhoff, 1981.

———. *Totality and Infinity.* Trans. Alphonso Lingis. Pittsburgh: Duquesne University Press, 1969.

Llewelyn, John. *The Middle Voice of Ecological Conscience: A Chiasmic Reading of Responsibility in the Neighborhood of Levinas, Heidegger, and Others.* New York: St. Martin's Press, 1991.

Löwith, Karl. *Martin Heidegger and European Nihilism.* Trans. Gary Steiner. Ed. Richard Wolin. New York: Columbia University Press, 1995.

Lukács, Georg. *Gelebtes Denken: eine Autobiographie im Dialog.* Ed. Istvan Eörski. Frankfurt am Main: Suhrkamp, 1984. Translated by Rodney Livingstone as *Record of a Life: An Autobiographical Sketch.* London: Verso, 1983.

Bibliography

————. *Heidelberger Asthetik (1916–1918)*. Ed. and abridged Gyorgy Markus and Frank Benseler. Darmstadt: Luchterhand, 1975.

————. "Heidelberger Philosophie de Kunst (1912–1914)," in *Georg Lukács Werke,* vol. 16. Darmstadt: Luchterhand Verlag, 1974.

————. *History and Class Consciousness: Studies in Marxist Dialectics.* Trans. Rodney Livingstone. Cambridge, Mass.: MIT Press, 1971.

————. "Marx and Engels on Aesthetics." In *Writer and Critic,* trans. and ed. Arthur Kahn, 61–88. London: Merlin Press, 1970.

————. *Die Theorie des Romans.* Darmstadt: Neuwied, 1979.

Lyon, James K. "Paul Celan and Martin Buber: Poetry as Dialogue" *PMLA* 86 (January 1971): 110–20.

Lyotard, Jean-François. *The Différend: Phrases in Dispute.* Trans. Georges Van Den Abbeele. Minneapolis: University of Minnesota Press, 1988.

————. *L'Enthousiasme: La critique kantienne de l'histoire.* Paris: Galilée, 1986.

————. "Histoire universelle et differences culturelles." *Critique* 456 (1985): 559–68.

————. "Interview." *Diacritics* 14 (1984): 16–23.

————. "Judiciousness in Dispute, or Kant after Marx." Trans. Cecile Lindsay. In *The Aims of Representation: Subject/Text/History,* ed. Murray Krieger, 23–67. New York: Columbia University Press, 1987.

————. *Political Writings.* Trans. Bill Readings and Kevin Paul. Minneapolis: University of Minnesota Press, 1993.

————. *The Postmodern Condition.* Trans. Geoff Bennington and Brian Massumi. Minneapolis: University of Minnesota Press, 1984.

————. *Le Postmoderne expliqué aux enfants.* Paris: Galilée, 1986.

————. *Toward the Postmodern.* Ed. Robert Harvey and Mark S. Roberts. Atlantic Highlands, N.J.: Humanities Press, 1993.

Lyotard, Jean-François, with Jean-Loup Thebaud. *Just Gaming.* Trans. Brian Massumi. Minneapolis: University of Minnesota Press, 1985.

Macherey, Pierre. *A Theory of Literary Production.* Boston: Routledge and Kegan Paul, 1978.

Makkreel, Rudolf. *Dilthey: Philosopher of the Human Studies.* Princeton, N.J.: Princeton University Press, 1992.

————. *Imagination and Interpretation in Kant: The Hermeneutical Import of the* Critique of Judgment. Chicago: University of Chicago Press, 1990.

————. "Tradition and Orientation in Hermeneutics." *Research in Phenomenology* 16 (1986): 73–85.

Manuel, Frank. *Shapes of Philosophical History.* Stanford, Calif.: Stanford University Press, 1965.

Mao Tsetung. *Five Essays on Philosophy.* Peking: Foreign Languages Press, 1977.

Marshall, Donald G. *Contemporary Critical Theory: A Selective Bibliography.* New York: Modern Language Association of America, 1993.

Marx, Karl. *Capital.* 3 vols. New York: International Publishers, 1974.

——. *A Contribution to the Critique of Political Economy.* Trans. Maurice Dobb, 1859; New York: International Publishers, 1970.

——. *The German Ideology.* Ed. C. J. Arthur. New York: International Publishers, 1970.

May, Todd. *The Moral Theory of Poststructuralism.* University Park: Pennsylvania State University Press, 1995.

Minow, Martha. *Making All the Difference: Inclusion, Exclusion, and American Law.* Ithaca, N.Y.: Cornell University Press, 1990.

Montaigne, Michel de. *Oeuvres complètes.* Ed. Albert Thibaudet and Maurice Rat. Paris: Gallimard, 1962.

——. *The Complete Essays of Montaigne.* Trans. Donald M. Frame. Stanford, Calif.: Stanford University Press, 1965.

Mouffe, Chantal. "Hegemony and New Political Subjects: Toward a New Concept of Democracy." In *Marxism and the Interpretation of Culture,* ed. Cary Nelson and Lawrence Grossberg, 89–104. Urbana: University of Illinios Press, 1988.

Murphy, Jeffrie G. *Kant: The Philosophy of Right.* Macon, Ga.: Mercer University Press, 1994.

Nehamas, Alexander. *Nietzsche: Life as Literature.* Cambridge, Mass.: Harvard University Press, 1985.

Nietzsche, Friedrich. *Basic Writings of Nietzsche.* Trans. and ed. Walter Kaufmann. New York: Modern Library, 1992.

——. *Beyond Good and Evil.* Trans. Walter Kaufmann. New York: Vintage, 1966.

——. *The Birth of Tragedy and Genealogy of Morals.* Trans. Francis Golffing. New York: Doubleday, 1956.

——. *The Gay Science.* Trans. Walter Kaufmann. New York: Vintage, 1974.

——. *On the Genealogy of Morals and Ecce Homo.* Trans. Walter Kaurmann. New York: Vintage, 1969.

——. *Thus Spoke Zarathustra.* Trans. Walter Kaufmann. New York: Viking, 1974.

——. *Twilight of the Idols and The Anti-Christ.* Trans. R. J. Hollingdale. Harmondsworth, Middlesex: Penguin, 1978.

——. *The Use and Abuse of History.* Trans. A. Collins. Indianapolis: Bobbs-Merrill, 1949.

——. *The Will to Power.* Trans. Walter Kaufmann. New York: Vintage, 1968.

Norris, Christopher. *The Contest of Faculties.* New York: Methuen, 1984.

——. "Reason, Rhetoric, Theory: Empson and de Man." *Raritan* 5 (1985–86): 89–106.

Bibliography

————. *What's Wrong with Postmodernism: Critical Theory and the Ends of Philosophy.* Baltimore: Johns Hopkins University Press, 1990.

O'Connor, James. "Productive and Unproductive Labor." *Politics and Society* 5 (1975): 297–336.

O'Neill, John. "The Essay as a Moral Exercise: Montaigne." *Renaissance and Reformation* 21, no. 3 (1985): 210–18.

————. *Essaying Montaigne: A Study of the Renaissance Institution of Writing and Reading.* London: Routledge and Kegan Paul, 1982.

————. *Five Bodies: The Human Shape of Modern Society.* Ithaca, N.Y.: Cornell University Press, 1985.

————. "The Literary Production of Natural and Social Science Inquiry." *Canadian Journal of Sociology* 6, no. 2 (Spring 1981): 105–20.

————. "A Realist Model of Knowledge: With a Phenomenological Deconstruction of Its Model of Man." *Philosophy of the Social Sciences* 16, no. 1 (March 1986): 1–19.

Owen, David. *Nietzsche, Politics, and Modernity: A Critique of Liberal Reason.* Thousand Oaks, Calif.: Sage, 1995.

Paglia, Camille. "Junk Bonds and Corporate Raiders: Academe in the Hour of the Wolf." In *Sex, Art, and American Culture,* 170–248. New York: Vintage Press, 1992.

Parkinson, C. Northcote. *The Law and the Profits.* Boston: Houghton Mifflin, 1960.

Peller, G. "The Metaphysics of American Law." *Calif. Law Review* 73, no. 1 (1985): 1160–70.

Peperzak, Adriaan T., ed. *Ethics as First Philosophy: The Significance of Emmanuel Levinas for Philosophy, Literature, and Religion.* New York: Routledge, 1995.

Plato. *The Republic.* Trans. Richard W. Sterling and William C. Scott. New York: Norton, 1985.

Plutarch. *Conjugalia praecepta.* In *Plutarch Moralia,* 16 vols., with an English translation by Frank Cole Babbitt. London: Heinemann, 1928.

Pöggeler, Otto. *Spur des Worts: Zur Lyrik Paul Celans.* Freiburg and Munich: Karl Alber, 1986.

Putnam, Hilary. *Reason, Truth, and History.* Cambridge: Cambridge University Press, 1981.

Radhakrishnan, R. *Diasporic Mediations: Between Home and Location.* Minneapolis: University of Minnesota Press, 1996.

————. "Ethnic Identity and Post-Structuralist Difference." *Cultural Critique* 2 (Spring 1987): 199–220.

Rajchman, John. *Michel Foucault: The Freedom of Philosophy.* New York: Columbia University Press, 1985.

Rockmore, Tom. *Heidegger and French Philosophy: Humanism, Antihumanism, and Being.* New York: Routledge, 1995.

Rorty, Richard. "Habermas and Lyotard on Postmodernity." In *Habermas and Modernity,* ed. Richard Bernstein, 161–75. Cambridge, Mass.: MIT Press, 1985.

———. "Habermas, Lyotard et la post-modernité." *Critique* 244 (March 1984): 181–97.

———. "The Historiography of Philosophy: Four Genres." In *Philosophy in History,* ed. Richard Rorty et al., 49–75. Cambridge: Cambridge University Press, 1984.

———. "Is Derrida a Transcendental Philosopher?" *Yale Journal of Criticism* 2, no. 2 (1989): 207–17.

———. "Solidarity or Objectivity." In *Post-Analytic Philosophy,* ed. John Rajchman and Cornel West, 3–19. New York: Columbia University Press, 1985.

Rosen, Allen D. *Kant's Theory of Justice.* Ithaca, N.Y.: Cornell University Press, 1993.

Rosenstein, Leon. "Mysticism as Preontology: A Note on the Heideggerian Connection." *Philosophy and Phenomenological Research* 39, no. 1 (September 1978): 57–73.

Rowbotham, Sheila, Lynne Segal, and Hilary Wainwright. *Beyond the Fragments: Feminism and the Making of Socialism.* London: Merlin Press, 1979.

Ryan, Michael. *Marxism and Deconstruction: A Critical Articulation.* Baltimore: Johns Hopkins University Press, 1982.

Said, Edward. "Zionism from the Standpoint of Its Victims." *Social Text* 1 (Winter 1979): 7–58.

Sallis, John. *The Gathering of Reason.* Athens: Ohio University Press, 1980.

———. *Spacings.* Chicago: University of Chicago Press, 1987.

Santayana, George. *Dominations and Powers: Reflections on Liberty, Society and Government.* New York: Scribners, 1951.

———. *The Life of Reason; or, The Phases of Human Progress.* New York: Collier, 1962.

Sartre, Jean-Paul. *Being and Nothingness: An Essay on Phenomenological Ontology.* Trans. Hazel E. Barnes. New York: Philosophical Library, 1956.

———. *No Exit and Three Other Plays.* New York: Vintage, 1960.

———. *What Is Literature?* Trans. Bernard Frechtman. New York: Harper and Row, 1965.

Schacht, Richard. "Nietzsche's Second Thoughts about Art." *Monist* 64 (1981): 241–47.

Scheman, Naomi. *Engenderings: Constructions of Knowledge, Authority, and Privilege.* New York: Routledge, 1993.

Scherer, Irmgard. *The Crisis of Judgment in Kant's Three Critiques: In Search of a Science of Aesthetics.* New York: P. Lang, 1995.

Bibliography

Schiller, Friedrich. *On the Aesthetic Education of Man: In a Series of Letters.* Trans. and ed. Elizabeth M. Wilkinson and L. A. Willoughby. Oxford: Clarendon Press, 1982.

Scholes, Robert. *Protocols of Reading.* New Haven, Conn.: Yale University Press, 1989.

———. *Textual Power.* New Haven, Conn.: Yale University Press, 1985.

Schrag, Calvin. *Communicative Praxis and the Space of Subjectivity.* Bloomington: Indiana University Press, 1986.

Schrift, Alan D. *Nietzsche's French Legacy: A Genealogy of Poststructuralism.* New York: Routledge, 1995.

Schroeder, Brian. *Altared Ground: Levinas, History, and Violence.* New York: Routledge, 1996.

Schultz, William R. *Genetic Codes of Culture?: The Deconstruction of Tradition by Kuhn, Bloom, and Derrida.* New York: Garland, 1994.

Sedgwick, Eve. *Between Men: English Literature and Male Homosocial Desire.* New York: Columbia University Press, 1985.

Sennett, Richard. *The Fall of Public Man.* New York: Knopf, 1977.

Shapiro, Gary. "Nietzschean Aphorism as Art and Act." *Man and World* 17 (1984): 399–429.

———. *Nietzschean Narratives.* Bloomington: Indiana University Press, 1989.

Siebers, Tobin. "Paul de Man and the Rhetoric of Selfhood." *New Orleans Review* 13 (Spring 1986).

Silverman, Hugh J. *Inscriptions: After Phenomenology and Structuralism.* Evanston, Ill.: Northwestern University Press, 1997.

———. *Textualites: Between Hermeneutics and Deconstruction.* New York: Routledge, 1994.

Smith, Gregory B. *Nietzsche, Heidegger, and the Transition to Postmodernity.* Chicago: University of Chicago Press, 1996.

Smith, Paul. *Discerning the Subject.* Minneapolis: University of Minnesota Press, 1988.

Spivak, Gayatri Chakravorty. "Scattered Speculations on the Question of Value." In *In Other Worlds: Essays in Cultural Politics,* 154–75. New York: Methuen, 1987.

———. *The Post-Colonial Critic.* New York: Routledge, 1990.

———. "Translator's Preface." In Jacques Derrida, *Of Grammatology,* trans. Gayatri Chakravorty Spivak, ix–lxxxvii. Baltimore: Johns Hopkins University Press, 1987.

Stallmann, M. *Was ist Sakularisierung.* Tübingen: J. C. B. Mohr, 1960.

Steele, H. Meili. *Realism and the Drama of Reference.* University Park: Pennsylvania State University Press, 1988.

———. "Value and Subjectivity: The Dynamics of the Sentence in James' *The Ambassadors." Comparative Literature* 43 (Spring 1991): 113–33.

Steinmetz, Rudy. *Les Styles de Derrida.* Brussels: De Boeck-Wesmael, 1994.

Stevenson, Robert Louis. *Dr. Jekyll and Mr. Hyde and Other Stories.* Harmondsworth, Middlesex: Penguin, 1979.

Strauss, Leo. "What Is Political Philosophy?" In *What Is Political Philosophy? and Other Studies,* 9–55. Glencoe, Ill.: Free Press, 1959.

Suleiman, Susan. "Le Récit exemplaire: Parabole, fable, roman et thèse." *Poetique,* no. 32 (November 1977): 468–89.

Swartz, Joseph, and John A. Rycenga. *The Province of Rhetoric.* New York: Ronald Press, 1965.

Taminiaux, Jacques. *Heidegger and the Project of Fundamental Ontology.* Trans. and ed. Michael Gendre. Albany: State University of New York Press, 1991.

Thiele, Leslie Paul. *Timely Meditations: Martin Heidegger and Postmodern Politics.* Princeton, N.J.: Princeton University Press, 1995.

Todorov, Tzvetan. *La Notion de littérature et autre essais.* Paris: Editions du Seuil, 1987.

Tubach, Frederic L. "Exempla in the Decline." *Traditio* 18 (1962): 407–17.

Tynan, Stephen. "Mysticism and Gnosticism in Heidegger." *Philosophy Today* 28 (Winter 1984): 358–77.

Ulmer, Gregory. *Applied Grammatology: Post(e)-Pedagogy from Jacques Derrida to Joseph Beuys.* Baltimore: Johns Hopkins University Press, 1985.

Valéry, Paul. "Au sujet du 'Cimetière Marin.'" In *Variétés III,* 57–74. Paris: Gallimard, 1936.

Vattimo, Gianni. *The End of Modernity: Nihilism and Hermeneutics in Postmodern Culture.* Trans. Jon R. Snyder. Baltimore: Johns Hopkins University Press, 1988.

Veyne, Paul. "Foucault Revolutionizes History." In *Comment on écrit l'histoire.* Paris: Editions du Seuil, 1978.

Voegelin, Eric. *In Search of Order.* Vol. 5 of *Order and History.* Baton Rouge: Louisiana State University Press, 1987.

Vycinas, Vincent. *Earth and Gods.* The Hague: Martinus Nijhoff, 1961.

Ward, James F. *Heidegger's Political Thinking.* Amherst: University of Massachusetts Press, 1995.

Weaver, Richard. "Some Rhetorical Aspects of Grammatical Categories." In *The Ethics of Rhetoric,* 115–42. Chicago: Regnery Press, 1953.

Weber, Samuel. "Afterword: Literature—Just Making It." In Jean-François Lyotard with Jean-Loup Thébaud, *Just Gaming,* trans. Wlad Godzich. Minneapolis: University of Minnesota Press, 1985.

Welter, J. Th. *L'Exemplum dans la littérature religieuse et didactique du moyen âge.* Paris: E. H. Guittard, 1927.

Welte, Bernhard. "God in Heidegger's Thought." *Philosophy Today* 26 (Spring 1982): 85–100.

Bibliography

West, Cornel. "Marxist Theory and the Specificity of Afro-American Oppression." In *Marxism and the Interpretation of Culture,* ed. Cary Nelson and Lawrence Grossberg, 17–33. Urbana: University of Illinois Press, 1988.

Williams, Patricia J. *The Alchemy of Race and Rights.* Cambridge, Mass.: Harvard University Press, 1991.

Wittgenstein, Ludwig. *Philosophical Investigations.* Trans. G. E. M. Anscombe. New York: Macmillan, 1958.

Wolosky, Shira. *Language Mysticism: The Negative Way of Language in Eliot, Beckett, and Celan.* Stanford, Calif.: Stanford University Press, 1995.

Woodmansee, Martha. *The Author, Art, and the Market: Rereading the History of Aesthetics.* New York: Columbia University Press, 1994.

Yovel, Yirmiahu. *Kant and the Philosophy of History.* Princeton, N.J.: Princeton University Press, 1980.

Ziarek, Krzysztof. *Inflected Language: Toward a Hermeneutics of Nearness: Heidegger, Levinas, Stevens, Celan.* Albany: State University of New York Press, 1994.

Žižek, Slavoj. *Tarrying with the Negative: Kant, Hegel, and the Critique of Ideology.* Durham, N.C.: Duke University Press, 1993.

Notes on Contributors

Stephen Barker is the chair of drama, the director of interdisciplinary studies in fine arts, and a member of the Emphasis of Critical Theory Group at the University of California, Irvine. His books include *Autoaesthetics: Strategies of the Self after Nietzsche* (1992), *Excavations and Their Objects: Freud's Collection of Antiquity* (1996), and *Signs of Change: Premodern, Modern, Postmodern* (1996). He has nearly finished a book on Beckett and has published articles on Beckett, Joyce, Jarry, Cocteau, Faulkner, Nietzsche, Derrida, and others.

Don Bialostosky is a professor in the rhetoric and composition program and the head of the English department at Pennsylvania State University. His recent books are *Wordsworth, Dialogics, and the Practice of Criticism* (1992), which contains a chapter on de Man's readings of Wordsworth and reflections on an expanded modern rhetoric, and *Rhetorical Traditions and British Romantic Literature* (1995), edited with Lawrence D. Needham.

Drucilla Cornell is a professor of law at Rutgers University, Newark. She has written extensively on feminism, deconstruction, and the law and was one of the organizers of the seminal 1989 conference on deconstruction and the law, "Deconstruction and the Possibility of Justice," at Cardozo Law School. Together with Michel Rosenfeld and David Gray Carlson, she edited a volume of the same name, collecting papers from that conference. Her published works include *Feminism as Critique: On the Politics of Gender,* edited with Seyla Benhabib (1987), *Beyond Accommodation: Ethical Feminism, Deconstruction, and the Law* (1991), *The Philosophy of the Limit* (1992), *Transformations: Recollective Imagination and Sexual Difference* (1993), and *The Imaginary Domain: Abortion, Pornography, and Sexual Harassment* (1995).

Thomas Foster is an assistant professor of English at Indiana University. He is currently completing two books: *Homelessness at Home: The Transformation of Spatial Metaphors in Modern Women's Writing* and a book on postmodern science fiction tentatively titled *Incurably Informed: Postmodern Narratives and the Rescripting of Postmodern Theory.* He has published many articles on pop culture, cyber-culture, gender studies, and contemporary philosophy.

Timothy Gould is the chair and a professor of philosophy at Metropolitan State College in Denver. His book *Hearing Things: Voice and Method in the*

Writing of Stanley Cavell was published in 1998. He is completing a book
entitled *Traces of Freedom: An Archeology of Kant's Aesthetics.* He has published a number of articles on feminism and the neoclassical philosophical
tradition.

Agnes Heller is Hannah Arendt Professor of Philosophy and Political Science at the New School for Social Research in New York City. She has written
extensively on political philosophy and the possibility of alternate or oppositional politics, often in conjunction with Ferenc Feher. Her recent titles include *Beyond Justice* (1987), *The Postmodern Political Condition* (1988),
Can Modernity Survive? (1990), *A Philosophy of Morals* (1990), *From Yalta
to Glasnost: The Dismantling of Stalin's Empire* (1991; with Feher), *The
Grandeur and Twilight of Radical Universalism* (1991; with Feher), *A Philosophy of History in Fragments* (1993), *Biopolitics* (1994; with Feher), and
The Ethics of Personality (1996).

Bruce Krajewski is a professor of English at Laurentian University in On-
tario, Canada. He has published several articles on art and aesthetics. His
book *Traveling with Hermes: Hermeneutics and Rhetoric* was published in
1992. He recently translated and edited a volume of essays by Hans-Georg
Gadamer entitled *Gadamer on Celan: "Who Am I and Who Are You" and
Other Essays* (1997).

Rudolf A. Makkreel is a professor of philosophy at Emory University in
Atlanta. He is the editor of the *Journal of the History of Philosophy* and has
written extensively on Kant, contemporary German philosophy, and the philosophy of history. He has edited several volumes on Dilthey and of Dilthey's
works. His many published works include *Dilthey, Philosopher of the Human Studies* (1975) and *Imagination and Interpretation in Kant: The Hermeneutical Import of the* Critique of Judgment (1990). He recently edited a
volume of essays entitled *Hermeneutics and the Study of History* with
Frithjof Rodi (1997).

Donald Marshall is a professor of English at the University of Illinois, Chicago. He is the translator (together with Joel Weinsheimer) of Hans-Georg
Gadamer's *Truth and Method.* He published *Literature as Philosophy, Philosophy as Literature* in 1987 and *Contemporary Critical Theory: A Selective Bibliography* in 1993.

Steve Martinot is an independent scholar in Berkeley, California. He has
published several articles on Sartre and his relation to various post-

structuralist thinkers, and he is completing a book entitled *Forms in the Abyss* in which a philosophical bridge between Sartre and Derrida is constructed. His translation from the French of Albert Memmi's latest work, entitled *Racism,* was published in 1999.

William Thomas McBride is an assistant professor of English at Illinois State University in Normal. He has written on film theory, literary theory, and Marxism.

John O'Neill is Distinguished Research Professor of Sociology at York University, Toronto, an affiliate of the Centre for Comparative Literature at the University of Toronto, and a fellow of the Royal Society of Canada. From 1993 to 1994, he served as a senior scholar at the Laidlaw Foundation, working on the Children at Risk Program. He is the author of *Sociology as a Skin Trade* (1972), *Making Sense Together* (1974), *Essaying Montaigne: A Study of the Renaissance Institution of Writing and Reading* (1982), and *Five Bodies: The Human Shape of Modern Society* (1985). His more recent books are *The Communicative Body: Studies in Communicative Philosophy, Politics, and Psychology* (1989), *Plato's Cave: Desire, Power, and the Specular Functions of the Media* (1991), *Critical Conventions: Interpretation in the Literary Arts and Sciences* (1992), *The Missing Child in Liberal Theory* (1994), and *The Poverty of Postmodernism* (1995). He is a coeditor of the international quarterly *Philosophy of the Social Sciences.* He is currently working on the political economy of child suffering, welfare-state theory, and civic practice.

Bernard Picard is a professor of French emeritus at Manhattan Community College, City University of New York. He has written articles on eighteenth- and twentieth-century literature and philosophy.

R. Radhakrishnan is a professor of English at the University of Massachusetts, Amherst. He is the author of *Diasporic Meditations: Between Home and Location* (1996) and *Theory in an Uneven World.*

Charles Shepherdson teaches European studies at the Graduate Institute for the Liberal Arts and is on the faculty of the Psychoanalytic Studies Program at Emory University. He is an affiliated scholar at the Pembroke Center for Teaching and Research on Women at Brown University; in 1998 he received an appointment to the Institute for Advanced Study in Princeton. His publications include *Vital Signs: Nature and Culture in Psychoanalysis* (1999) and *The Epoch of the Body.*

Meili Steele is an associate professor of comparative literature at the University of South Carolina. He is a poet who has written several articles on the critique of language. He has published three books: *Realism and the Drama of Reference: Strategies of Representation in Balzac, Flaubert, and James* (1988), *Critical Confrontations: Literary Theories in Dialogue* (1997), and *Theorizing Textual Subjects: Agency and Oppression* (1997).